1975 **FILMS OF THE** 2000

AMERICAN INDIAN FILM FESTIVAL®

FILMS OF THE
AMERICAN INDIAN FILM FESTIVAL®
1975 - 2000

Presented by the

American Indian Film Institute

Films of the American Indian Film Festival® 1975 - 2000
Copyright©2001 by the American Indian Film Institute

Published by the American Indian Film Institute, 333 Valencia Street, Suite 322, San Francisco, California 94103

Book design by Verne Balagot

Films of the American Indian Film Festival® was funded by Grant No. 90NA7212, Administration for Native Americans, U.S. Department of Health & Human Services, Washington, DC.

ISBN 0-9713794-0-8

First Edition

Dedication

We dedicate *Films of the American Indian Film Festival*® to the memories of Chief Dan George and Will Sampson — and to all the Native actors who came before — and all those to follow.

Credits

Project Director
Michael Smith

Archivist / Lead Research
Jennifer F. Shinall

Archivist / Preliminary Research
Jennifer Vest, Ph.D.

Research Team
J. Paulette Sawyers
Mytia Rose Smith

Text Editing
Anna-Marie Shinall

Design and Layout
Verne Balagot

CD-ROM Design
Sheldon Brahms
Josh Brahms

Project Accountant
Sheri Flying Hawk

Forward: A Gathering
Reid Gómez, Ph.D.

San Francisco State University Interns
Chandra Johnson
Chris Arrujo
Ai Kurokawa
Sarah K. Hellström
Steven Morales

FILMS OF THE
AMERICAN INDIAN FILM FESTIVAL®
1975 - 2000

The cornerstone of the American Indian Film Institute is our Annual Film Festival. Over the course of 25 years we have screened 626 films and videos from American Indian and Canada First Nation communities. Film's greatest power lies in its innate ability to affect mass public perception. Without AIFI, many of these films would not have been seen. Our annual Film Festival is North America's oldest and most respected venue dedicated to Native Cinema. There is nothing like it anywhere. Integrity and dignity are our boundary. Every year we are making history and building community.

During the American Indian Film Festival, over 5,000 participants witness Native stories and visual documents to contemporary lives and issues. The films we screen raise awareness about the issues currently at the heart of Indian Country, through honest and truthful artistry and testimony. Our greatest power continues to lie in our ability to tell out own stories in our own words and images. The festival plays an indispensable role in that truth. Our venue continues to raise the bar and set the standard for American Indian filmmaking today.

Michael Smith
Founder/President
American Indian Film Institute

A Gathering

This catalogue marks a quarter century celebration, and is elemental in the American Indian Film Institute's mission to create positive change. The films detailed here make living testimony to the lives of Indian people across North America. AIFI has witnessed a tremendous amount of history and creative work over a very short period of time, 25 years. Through our programming, we intend to keep this history alive by passing on the wonder and information, transforming the film industry and ourselves in the process. Over the last 25 years our film festival has served as a place to meet and share our experience and creative process. **Films of the American Indian Film Festival 1975-2000** takes its place in our larger project to establish a film library and archive. This is for the generations.

Between these pages are motion picture recordings, not dead documents or archival tapes of lost or decimated peoples. Motion, light, and vibration, the primordial elements recording us to the earth through our flesh, philosophy, and spirit. Recording is the daily task that strengthens us. Our morning and evening prayers, stretch across time just as powerfully as they stretch through each vertebra. Animating us, via thought, via electricity, via the ancestors and their prayers and memories which account for our survivals, each and every one of us.

We are as rich as the stories we remember and actively retell. A person without stories is poor and alone. The stories come before us, and follow behind us, creating our place in the world, providing us direction and relations. The stories are alive. They make the way. There is no story without imagination, the people and the dream are one.

While the focal point of the film institute has always been the Annual American Indian Film Festival - we have grown and this book illustrates our growth. It goes with the festival, the individual filmmaker and the tribes from which the stories spring from. The films reflect relationships across tribal Nations, inside city limits and on our respective reservations. The institute continues to do its best to always acknowledge and appreciate community and to give back to the tribes by reaching out to the youth. Films need to be seen. To see them you must know they exist.

The expansion of the AIFI library to over 600 titles is a significant step towards building a place where artists and audiences can come together to locate each other, learn about each other and simply be inspired to create their own work and become a part of our intertribal circle. Along with the hope of acquiring other collections and spreading word and image is the dream of establishing a National Indian Media Arts Center where people can view films, participate in workshops, and acquire skills they can bring back to their own communities. We begin here.

Over the years we have always understood the importance of influencing and creating positive change in programming. Here are 626 titles to choose from. Our own programming commitments emphasize relationship building, community based outreach and inclusive events where grandmother and grandchild are equally welcome and necessary. We have been fortunate to receive the support of many tribal governments, private foundations, municipal, federal, and state governments as well as private individuals, financially and spiritually. Their generosity has contributed to the success and longevity of the institute. Films make money and films cost money. Together we are realizing new opportunities to support each other across Nations and across psychological and public health models for activism and social service. We are returning to our centers.

Commitment is necessary. As artists have come together to make something they can be proud of, so has the institute. You must care for something to grow, whether it is our children, our tribal Nations or the continued development of the institute itself.

Film takes cooperation, commitment, vision, technical skill and economic development based on imagination, not resource extraction. The filmmakers catalogued here give back, fertilizing and supplying riches in terms of image, dream, narrative, memory and responsible use of technology and electricity.

This catalogue is part of our mission to spread the word, to testify, to shape and document. If offers a glimpse into the possibilities for each of our Nations, in part because of where we've come from and our responses to the changes we've actively been, and continue to be, a part of. Sovereignty requires that all decisions exists within the philosophy of the tribe. As Indians we can come together and witness each of our unique victories, here in these films and in the conversations that are born from them.

A Give Away

Beyond providing education and accessibility, this collection of films honors our unique perspectives with special attention to the integrity and vision of the tribe, not America's Indian. The specific detail, experience, language and philosophy of the tribe are our point of origin. Individual artists stand in the center of their world, not outside it, translating it, or mistaking it for individualized fame and fortune. These artists come from different traditions, and offer more meaningful expressions. We see here, artists firmly rooted in their own histories. They make film and video to stand true to those understandings. Their stories and images stand in service to the tribes, articulating who we are in the world, where we come from and how we are meant to carry ourselves in motion.

These films are what we think of ourselves, as Kumeyaay, Yurok, Sioux, Ojibwe, Seminole, Onondaga, and Diné. For that alone they are monumental. In this way we insure our survival. It's an old idea really, to carry forward that which makes you who you are, to make babies and teach them to be elders. Each tribe has its own origin and must remain true to those teachings. The generations depend on us to imagine ourselves strong and whole, head in place. These films testify to our ability to think right in light of the constant assault on our memory and imagination. What we share, together across Nations, is our heritage of survival. These statements are our own.

A Keeper Of The Fire: Integrity, Strength And Vision

The camera may not capture your soul, but it could capture your imagination. For years Hollywood has bought and sold its idea of the Indian. As children and as elders we have been raised along side that idea. We are keepers of the fire that destroy as well as create. We each come from communities intimate with the power of transformation. Bring an elder some coffee and some tobacco, show yourself and your intention. Sit. Ask for a story and it may come. Come back, tomorrow, laughing. Tell your children so they can tell theirs. As technologies have changed so have we. Through everything we remain, strong. Tradition is the process by which we confront the changing world.

Over the years each tribe has endured and adapted to the changing politics of the hemisphere, retaining their language and cultural integrity. Part of these adaptations was the masterful use of the media during the 1970's. The camera and the reporter were recruited in our physical resistance to the continued occupation of our homelands. The fish-in of the northwest coast and California, along side the occupation of Alcatraz, Wounded Knee and the BIA offices in Washington marked a moment when tribal leaders firmly rooted in their own spiritual traditions, oral histories and languages came together with young leaders able to articulate, for the mass media, the precise nature of our struggle. From these struggles came many victories, both personal and communal. In changing our perceptions of ourselves we stand proud of who we are today, as contemporary Indians in a contemporary reality.

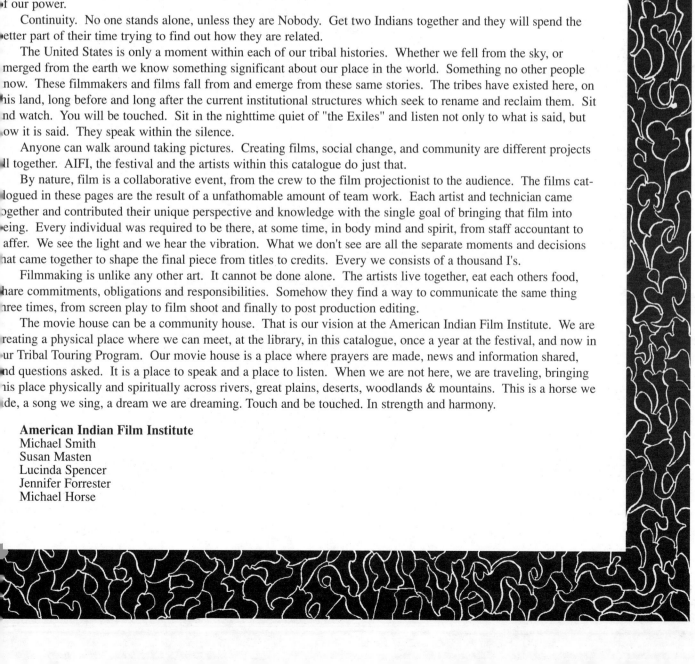

Continuity. No one stands alone

We continue to survive the lies that have been told about us.

These films reveal our integrity as Peoples, artists and political activists. At the core of tribal expression and organization lies the belief that the creative process brings about social change. Some aspect of the process is restorative and medicinal. Regardless of the genre, we are supporting ourselves in the ways we represent ourselves. We keep whole, and realize our capacity for meaning in this way. We share ourselves and our idea of ourselves, pre and post production. We laugh. We make joy. We create space for ourselves and our tribes, today, as thriving peoples with very special knowledge and talent. In thinking good about who we are we make medicine. This is a plan for the survival of our languages, our memories and our imaginations. The elders have done this since the beginning. This is our beginning also.

Art has always been an integrated part of the tribe. We make things to have power and meaning. These films are made with the intention of preventing the further destruction of our bodies and our homelands. They remind us of our power.

Continuity. No one stands alone, unless they are Nobody. Get two Indians together and they will spend the better part of their time trying to find out how they are related.

The United States is only a moment within each of our tribal histories. Whether we fell from the sky, or merged from the earth we know something significant about our place in the world. Something no other people know. These filmmakers and films fall from and emerge from these same stories. The tribes have existed here, on this land, long before and long after the current institutional structures which seek to rename and reclaim them. Sit and watch. You will be touched. Sit in the nighttime quiet of "the Exiles" and listen not only to what is said, but how it is said. They speak within the silence.

Anyone can walk around taking pictures. Creating films, social change, and community are different projects all together. AIFI, the festival and the artists within this catalogue do just that.

By nature, film is a collaborative event, from the crew to the film projectionist to the audience. The films catalogued in these pages are the result of a unfathomable amount of team work. Each artist and technician came together and contributed their unique perspective and knowledge with the single goal of bringing that film into being. Every individual was required to be there, at some time, in body mind and spirit, from staff accountant to gaffer. We see the light and we hear the vibration. What we don't see are all the separate moments and decisions that came together to shape the final piece from titles to credits. Every we consists of a thousand I's.

Filmmaking is unlike any other art. It cannot be done alone. The artists live together, eat each others food, share commitments, obligations and responsibilities. Somehow they find a way to communicate the same thing three times, from screen play to film shoot and finally to post production editing.

The movie house can be a community house. That is our vision at the American Indian Film Institute. We are creating a physical place where we can meet, at the library, in this catalogue, once a year at the festival, and now in our Tribal Touring Program. Our movie house is a place where prayers are made, news and information shared, and questions asked. It is a place to speak and a place to listen. When we are not here, we are traveling, bringing this place physically and spiritually across rivers, great plains, deserts, woodlands & mountains. This is a horse we ride, a song we sing, a dream we are dreaming. Touch and be touched. In strength and harmony.

American Indian Film Institute
Michael Smith
Susan Masten
Lucinda Spencer
Jennifer Forrester
Michael Horse

Title	Director	Country	Genre	Time
ABANDONED HOUSES ON THE RESERVATION	Darlene Naponse	Canada	LS	3
ABNAKI	Jay Kent	USA	DS	29
ACTS OF DEFIANCE	Alec G. MacLeod	USA	DF	105
AGAIN A WHOLE PERSON I HAVE BECOME	Matt Tortes	USA	DS	20
AIDS EDUCATION:				
Prevention for the American Indian Community	April Skinas	USA	PS	15
AKWESASNE: Another Point of View	Bob Stiles	USA	DS	28
ALCATRAZ IS NOT AN ISLAND	Jim Fortier	USA	DF	85
ALIEN THUNDER (a.k.a. Dan Candy's Law)	Claude Fournier	Canada	FF	90
ALLAN HOUSER HAOZOUS:				
The Lifetime Work of an American Maaster	Phil Lucas	USA	DF	58
AMAROK'S SONG - THE JOURNEY TO NUNAVUT	Ole Gjerstad, Martin Kreelak	Canada	DF	75
AMERICA'S GREAT INDIAN LEADERS	Bob Hercules, Bruce Lixey	USA	DF	60
AMERICA'S GREAT INDIAN NATIONS	Bob Hercules, Bruce Lixey	USA	DF	55
AMERICAN COWBOYS	Cedric and Tania Wildbill	USA	DS	27
AMERICAN HOLOCAUST:				
When It's All Over I'll Still Be Indian	Joanelle Romero	USA	DS	29
AMERICAN INDIAN ARTIST II-Jaune Quick-To-See Smith	Tony Schmitz	USA	DS	15
AMERICAN INDIAN ARTIST II-Larry Golsh	Don Cirillo	USA	DS	14
AMERICAN INDIAN DANCE THEATRE:				
Dances for the New Generations	Hanay Geiogamah, Phil Lucas	USA	DF	56
AMERICAN INDIAN EXPOSITION	Shawnee Brittan	USA	DS	24
AMERICAN INDIAN WOMEN'S TALKING CIRCLE				
CERVICAL CANCER PROJECT	Felicia Schanche Hodge	USA	PS	20
AMERICAN INDIANS - Yesterday and Today	Don Klugman	USA	DS	18
AMERICAN SCENE	Dan Jones	USA	IND	12
AMIOTTE	Richard Muller	USA	DS	30
AMISK	Alanis Obomsawin	Canada	DS	40
AN ACT OF RENEWAL - A Museum to the American Indian	Heather Giugni	USA	DS	26
AN ANCIENT GIFT	Patricia Barey	USA	DS	18
ANCESTORS OF THOSE YET UNBORN	Anthony Brown	USA	DS	28
ANCESTRAL SONGS: Kwa-Kwa-Ka' Wakw Family	Peter von Puttkamer	Canada	PS	6
... AND WOMAN WOVE IT IN A BASKET...	Bushra Azzouz, Marlene Farnum	USA	DF	70
ANISHINAABE NIIJII (Friends of the Chippewa)	Al Gedicks	USA	DS	49
ANNIE MAE - Brave Hearted Woman	Lan Brookes Ritz	USA	DF	86
ANNUAL WORLD ESKIMO - Indian Olympics (21ST)	Skip Blumberg	USA	DS	27
APACHE MOUNTAIN SPIRITS	B. Graham	USA	FF	60
ARROW CREEK		USA	DS	
ARROWS		USA	LS	
ARTISTRY, SPIRIT AND BEAUTY: Great Basin Weavers	Creel Snider	USA	DS	29
AVENGING WARRIORS	Robert Bouvier	Canada	FF	85
BACK TO TURTLE ISLAND	Byron McKim	Canada	LS	25
BACKBONE OF THE WORLD: The Blackfeet	George Burdeau	USA	DF	57
BACKROAD, THE	Ramona Emerson	USA	LS	10
BAD MONEY	John Hazlett	Canada	FF	89
BALANCE - Healing Through Helping	Melanie Goodchild	Canada	PS	44
BALLAD OF CROWFOOT, THE	Willie Dunn	Canada	DS	10
BAND-AID	Daniel Prouty	Canada	DS	42
BEARWALKER (formerly: BACKROADS)	Shirley Cheechoo	Canada	FF	83
BEAUTY OF A WOVEN ROAD	Shawna Shandin Sunrise	USA	DS	8
BEAUTY OF MY PEOPLE, THE	Alan Collins	Canada	DS	29
BEFORE THE OWL CALLS MY NAME artist: Tom Jackson	Grant Harvey	Canada	MV	4
BETWEEN TWO WORLDS	Barry Greenwald	Canada	DF	58
BETWEEN TWO WORLDS (Part 1 &II)	Sheera and Peter von Puttkamer	Canada	PS	60
BEYOND RESERVATION ROAD	George Burdeau	USA	DS	26
BIG BEAR	Gil Cardinal	Canada	FF	183
BITTER EARTH: Child Sexual Abuse in Indian Country	Charles Dixson, Jane Stubbs	USA	IND	54
BLACK INDIANS: An American Story	Chip Richie	USA	DF	60
BLACK ROBE	Bruce Beresford	Canada	FF	105
BLESS ME WITH A GOOD LIFE	Jillian Spitzmiller, Hank Rogerson	USA	DS	30
BLOCKADE	Nettie Wild	Canada	DF	90
BLOOD MEMORY	Deborah Dennison	USA	FF	70
BLOOD RIVER	Kent Monkman	Canada	LS	23
BLUE: A Tlingit Odyssey	Robert Ascher	USA	ANS	6
BONDING CIRCLE OF BREAST-FEEDING	Kem Murch	Canada	DS	15
BONNIE LOOKSAWAY'S IRON ART WAGON	Wes Studi	USA	LS	36
BORN TO THE WIND	Laszlo Pal	USA	DF	240
BOWL OF BONE - Tale of the Syuwe	Jan-Marie Martell	Canada	DF	118
BOX OF DAYLIGHT, THE	Dave Hunsaker, Lisle Hebert, Janet Fries	USA	LS	8
BRAVE NEW WORLD	Robin Crichton	Scotland	DS	49
BREAKING THE ICE	Jonathan Nordlicht	USA	ANS	23
BREATH OF LIFE	John Grabowska	USA	DS	27
BRINGING IT ALL BACK HOME	Chris Eyre	USA	DF	55
BROKEN RAINBOW	Maria Florio and Victoria Mudd	USA	DF	70

Key   DS: Documentary Short; DF: Documentary Feature; FF: Feature Film; LS: Live Short; IND: Industrial; MV: Music Video; PS: Public Service; ANS: Animated Short; DD: Docu-Drama

I

Title	Director	Country	Genre	Time
BROKEN TREATY AT BATTLE MOUNTAIN	Joel L. Freedman	USA	DF	60
BROTHERS BEHIND THE WALLS	Spencer E. Ante	USA	DS	8
BUFFALO BILL AND THE INDIANS	Robert Altman	USA	FF	120
BUFFALO HUNT, THE	Chet Kincaid	USA	LS	20
BY WORD OF MOUTH	Chris Landry	USA	DS	30
CAMP NY-MU-MAH	Jane Stubbs	USA	DS	19
CARVED FROM THE HEART- A PORTRAIT OF GRIEF, HEALING AND COMMUNITY	Ellen Frankenstein	USA	DS	30
CELEBRATION	R. Kennedy Tuesday	Canada	DS	9
CHANGING THE IMAGE	Dave Wheelock	USA	DS	9
CHARLIE SQUASH GOES TO TOWN	Duke Redbird	Canada	ANS	5
CHETAN, THE INDIAN BOY	Hark Bohm	Germany	FF	93
CHILDREN OF WIND RIVER	Victress Hitchcock	USA	DS	28
CIRCLE MOVING, THE	Gary Nichol	Canada	DS	28
CIRCLE OF LIFE	Will Hommeyer	USA	LS	43
CIRCLE OF THE SUN	Colin Low	Canada	LS	30
CIRCLE OF VOICES	Doug Cuthand and Tasha Hubbard	Canada	DS	45
CIRCLE OF WARRIORS	Phil Lucas	USA	DS	27
CIRCLES	Shanti Thakur	Canada	DF	58
CLEARCUT	Richard Bugajski	Canada	FF	98
COLA UND KANU (COLA & CANOE)	Ralf Marschallek	Germany	DS	44
COLD JOURNEY	Martin Defalco	Canada	FF	75
COLLIDING WORLDS	Orie Sherman	USA	DS	33
COLVILLE TRIBAL FORESTRY	Jim Desautel	USA	IND	7
COMING TO LIGHT: Edward S. Cutrtis and the North American Indian	Anne Makepeace	USA	DF	85
COMPUTER GRAPHICS AT IAIA	Dana Dupris	USA	DS	4
CONTRARY WARRIORS: A Story of the Crow Tribe	Pamela Roberts, Constance Poten	USA	DF	60
COPPERMINE	Ray Harper	Canada	DF	56
CORN IS LIFE	Patricia Barey	USA	DS	16
COYOTE SPEAKS	Vladan Mijailovic	USA	LS	18
CRAZY HORSE RETURNS	Paul Aguilar	USA	DS	4
CRAZY HORSE: Spirit Behind the Name	David R. Anderson and Nick Guroff	USA	DS	27
CREE WAY	Tony Ianzelo	Canada	DS	26
CROSSING THE RAINBOW BRIDGE	Kat High	USA	DS	28
CROW-MAPUCHE CONNECTION, THE	Arvo Iho	USA	DS	15
DANCE ME OUTSIDE	Bruce McDonald	Canada	FF	87
DANCES WITH WOLVES	Kevin Costner	USA	FF	180
DANCING BOY	Pat Matt, Jr.	USA	DS	12
DANCING WITH PHOTONS	Beverly Morris	USA	DS	27
DAWN RIDERS		USA	DS	
DEAD MAN	Jim Jarmusch	USA	FF	120
DEBBY AND SHARON: The Recovery Series	Moira Simpson	Canada	DS	15
DEEP INSIDE CLINT STAR	Clint Alberta	Canada	DF	89
DENE FAMILY	John & Joan Goldi	Canada	DS	20
DENE FAMILY from The Everywhere Spirit	Don Marks	Canada	DS	30
DENE NATION	Rene Fumoleau	Canada	DS	30
DETOUR: or How I Spent My Weekend	Deron Twohatchet	USA	LS	28
DIABETES: Lifetime Solutions	Peter von Puttkamer	Canada	PS	30
DINEH NATION	Russell Richards	USA	DS	30
DINEH: The People	Stephen Hornick	USA	DF	28
DISCOVER INDIAN AMERICA	Dan Jones and George Burdeau	USA	DS	12
DIVIDED LOYALTIES	Mario Azzopardi	Canada	FF	102
DIVIDED TRAIL, THE	Jerry Aronson	USA	DF	83
DO:GE: GAGWE:GO O'JAGWADA' (We Stood Together)	Allan Jamieson	USA	DS	31
DONALD MARSHALL YOUTH CULTURAL CAMP	Rod Carleton	Canada	DS	26
DOORS FACING EAST	Margot Dubin	USA	DS	13
DREAMER	Raymond E. Spiess, Jr.	USA	LS	10
DRUM MAKING	Gilles Tasse-La Fountaine	USA/Canada	DS	29
DRUM SONG	Ron Braun, Brian Stethem	Canada	FF	52
DRUMBEAT FOR MOTHER EARTH	Joseph DiGangi, Amon Giebel	USA	DF	54
DUNCAN CAMPBELL SCOTT: The Poet and the Indians	James Cullingham	Canada	DF	56
EAGLE AND THE RAVEN, THE: Purification by Banishment	Vladan Mijailovic	USA	DF	60
ECHOES OF OUR PAST	Vern Korb	USA	DS	24
ECHOES OF THE SISTERS - First Nations Women: Breast Cancer	Richard Hersley	Canada	PS	24
EDUCATION OF LITTLE TREE, THE	Richard Friedenberg	USA	FF	117
ERNIE PEPION AND THE ART OF HEALING	Terry Macy	USA	DS	28
ESTHER SHEA: The Bear Stands Up	Ward Serrill	USA	DS	29
FACES YET TO COME	David W. Stamps	USA	PS	10
FACING THE WIND - A Song for Yellow Thunder Camp	Chuck Banner, David Hopper	USA	DF	60
FAMILY OF THE GREAT MYSTERY	Na Bahe Keedinihii	USA	DS	28
FARTHER WE RUN, THE CLOSER WE GET, THE		USA	DS	28

Key   DS: Documentary Short; DF: Documentary Feature; FF: Feature Film; LS: Live Short; IND: Industrial; MV: Music Video; PS: Public Service; ANS: Animated Short; DD: Docu-Drama

Title	Director	Country	Genre	Time
FEATHER OF HOPE	Gil Cardinal	Canada	DS	30
FEATHERS IN THE SUN	Ray Baldwin Louis	USA	DS	28
FEDERAL INDIAN LAW	Joel L. Freedman	USA	DS	19
FIRST NATION BLUE	Daniel Prouty	Canada	DS	48
FIRST NATIONS: Breast Self Examination	Jacqueline Davis	Canada	PS	18
FISH: A SPECIAL RELATIONSHIP	Peter von Puttkamer	Canada	PS	6
FISH HAWK	Donald Shebib	USA	FF	93
FISHING PEOPLE: The Tulalip Tribe	Heather Oakson	USA	DS	17
FIVE O'CLOCK WORLD artist: Hal Ketchum	Glen DiVencenzo	USA	MV	3
FOLLOW ME HOME	Peter Bratt	USA	FF	99
FOLLOW THE CHILDREN / ONE BRIGHT DAY	Carlos Reynosa	USA	MV	8
FOLLOW YOUR HEART'S DESIRE artist: Ulali	Ramin Ninmi	USA	MV	4
FONSECA: In Search of Coyote	Mary Louise King	USA	DS	30
FOR ANGELA	Daniel Prouty, Nancy Trites Botkin	Canada	LS	21
FORGOTTEN WARRIORS	Loretta Todd	Canada	DF	51
FORT GOOD HOPE	Ron Orieux	Canada	DS	47
FOSTER CHILD	Gil Cardinal	Canada	DS	43
FOUR		Canada	DS	30
FOUR CORNERS: A National Sacrifice Area?	Christopher McLeod	USA	DF	59
FOUR DIRECTIONS: A Canoe for the Making	George Bloomfield	Canada	LS	22
FOUR DIRECTIONS: Borders	Gil Cardinal	Canada	LS	22
FOUR DIRECTIONS: Flat Mountain Taxtales	Kit Hood	Canada	LS	22
FOUR DIRECTIONS: THhe Hero	Gary Farmer	Canada	LS	22
FRENCH MAN, NATIVE SON	Monika Ille	Canada	DS	27
FRITZ SCHOLDER: A Film Profile		USA	DS	28
FROG MONSTER, THE	Joshua M. Vermette, Indian Island students	USA	ANS	10
FROM FOUR DIRECTIONS: A Call to Consciousness	Mark Halfmoon	USA	DF	52
FROM THE ROOTS: Califonia Indian Basketweavers	Sara Greensfelder	USA	DS	28
FROZEN CAUTION	Elizabeth C. Moes	Canada	DS	12
FRY BREAD- JUST SAY NO	Pam Belgarde	USA	DS	9
GABRIEL WOMEN: Passamaquoddy Basketmakers	Michael Sacca & Robert Atkinson	USA	DS	28
GERONIMO: An American Legend	Walter Hill	USA	FF	110
GERONIMO JONES		USA	DS	21
GHOST DANCE	Tim Scwab, Christina Craton	USA	DS	9
GIFT OF CHOICE - YOU CHOOSE	Vern Korb	USA	PS	18
GIFT OF THE GRANDFATHERS, THE	Doug Cuthand	USA	DS	44
GIFT, THE	Gary Farmer	Canada	DS	49
GIFT TO ONE, A GIFT TO MANY -				
James Jackson Sr., Ojibwe Medicine Man	Phillip Norrgard, Lorraine Slabbaert-Norrgard	USA	DF	58
GOING BACK TO THE BLANKET	Michael Doxtater	Canada	DS	28
GOLDEN SEAL, THE	Frank Zuniga	USA	FF	94
GOOD MEDICINE	Tamsin Orion Seidler	USA	DS	21
GOOD MEDICINE	Christopher Gaul	USA	DS	48
GRAND AVENUE	Dan Sackheim	USA	FF	165
GRAND CIRCLE, THE	Pierre Lobstein, Richard Whitman	USA / France	LS	12
GRANDFATHER SKY	Victress Hitchcock	USA	LS	50
GREAT SPIRIT WITHIN THE HOLE, THE	Chris Spotted Eagle	USA	DF	60
GREAT WOLF AND LITTLE MOUSE SISTER	Phil Lucas	USA	DS	26
GREY OWL	Richard Attenbourough	USA	FF	117
GRIZZLY ADAMS AND THE TREASURE OF THE BEAR	John Huneck	USA	FF	101
GROUND ZERO / SACRED GROUND	Karen Aqua	USA	ANS	9
GROWING UP NAVAJO - Teens on the Rez	Heather Spaulding	USA	DF	52
HAIRCUTS HURT	Randy Redroad	USA	LS	10
HAND GAME	Lawrence Johnson	USA	DF	66
HANDS OF HISTORY	Loretta Todd	Canada	DF	52
HANTAVIRUS: Reducing the Risk	Judy Preston	USA	IND	10
HAROLD OF ORANGE	Richard Weise	USA	LS	30
HAUDENOSAUNEE: Way of the Longhouse	Bob Stiles	Canada	DS	13
HE WHO DREAMS:				
MICHAEL GREYEYES ON THE POWWOW TRAIL	Alan Burke	Canada	DF	53
HEALING JOURNEY	Greg Coyes	Canada	DS	25
HEALING OF NATIONS	George Amiotte & Peter von Puttkamer	Canada	DS	48
HEAR ME	Larry Carey	Canada	MV	5
HEART OF THE PEOPLE:				
LIFE, DEATH AND REBIRTH OF A GREAT RIVER	Peter von Puttkamer	Canada	DF	59
HEART OF THE SPIRIT	Robert Ybanez	USA	LS	36
HIDDEN MEDICINE	Robby Romero	USA	LS	15
HIGH HORSE	Randy Redroad	USA	LS	40
HISTORY OF THE LUISENO PEOPLE:				
LA JOLLA INDIAN RESERVATION - Christmas 1990	Isaac Artenstien	USA	LS	27
HIV/AIDS NATIVE FOCUS	Frank Tyro	USA	PS	2
HOCAK YOUTH LEADERSHIP CAMP AND NIKJAGI'U	Daryl Lonetree, Marlon White Eagle	USA	DS	9
HOLLOW WATER	Bonnie Dickie and Tina Mason	Canada	DS	48
HOME	Elizabeth Downer	USA	LS	15

Key   DS: Documentary Short; DF: Documentary Feature; FF: Feature Film; LS: Live Short; IND: Industrial; MV: Music Video;
PS: Public Service; ANS: Animated Short; DD: Docu-Drama

Title	Director	Country	Genre	Time
HOMELAND	Hank Rogerson and Jilann Spitzmiller	USA	DF	58
HONEY MOCCASIN	Shelley Niro	Canada	LS	49
HONORABLE NATIONS	Chana Gazit & David Steward	USA	DF	54
HONORING KUMAT	Daniel Golding	USA	DS	13
HONORING THE PAST, SHAPING THE FUTURE	Jim Browder	USA	IND	6
HOPI PROPHECY	Kiyoshi Miyata	Japan	DF	75
HOPI: Songs Fromthe Fourth World	Pat Ferrero	USA	DF	58
HOPILAVAYI	T. Bart Hawkins	USA	DS	18
HORSE SONG	Norman Patrick Brown	USA	FF	56
HOUSE MADE OF DAWN	Richardson Morse	USA	FF	88
HOUSE OF PEACE	Cathleen Ashworth	USA	DS	30
HOW PANTHER GOT HIS TEARMARKS	Vern Korb	USA	ANS	12
HUCHOOSEDAH: Traditions of the Heart	Katie Jennings	USA	DF	57
HUNT, THE	Tamara Bell	Canada	LS	10
I AM ALCOHOL	Don Burnstick	Canada	LS	33
I AM DIFFERENT FROM MY BROTHER	Tony Charles	USA	LS	20
I HEARD THE OWL CALL MY NAME	Daryl Duke	USA	FF	78
I NEVER GAVE UP HOPE	Darryl Kesslar	Canada	MV	5
I' TUSTO: To Rise Again	Barb Cranmer	Canada	DF	54
I WILL FIGHT NO MORE FOREVER	David L. Wolper	USA	FF	106
I'LL TAKE MANHATTAN	Robin M. Craig	USA	LS	30
IF IT CAN HAPPEN TO ME, IT CAN HAPPEN TO YOU	Harlan McKosato	USA	DS	27
IKWE	Norma Bailey	Canada	FF	57
IMAGES OF INDIANS: The Great Movie Massacre	Phil Lucas	USA	DS	30
IN MACARTHUR PARK	Bruce Schwartz	USA	FF	90
IN OUR OWN IMAGE:				
Alaska Native Doll-Makers and Their Creations	Leonard Kamerling	USA	DS	28
IN THE BEST INTEREST OF THE CHILD	Carol & Vern Korb	USA	DS	20
IN THE BLUE GROUND: A North of 60 Movie	Alan Simmonds	Canada	FF	94
IN THE LAND OF THE WAR CANOES (1914)	Edward S. Curtis	USA	DS	47
IN THE LIGHT OF REVERENCE	Christopher McLeod	USA	DF	72
IN THE SPIRIT OF OUR FOREFATHERS		Canada	DS	32
IN THE WHITE MAN'S IMAGE	Christine Lesiak	USA	DF	59
IN WHOSE HONOR? American Indian Mascots in Sports	Jay Rosenstein	USA	DS	46
IN-BREAKER	Bob Elliot, James Margellos	Canada	FF	91
INCIDENT AT OGLALA	Michael Apted	USA	DF	90
INDIAN	Kieth Merrill	USA	FF	86
INDIAN ACT: The Facts, the Fears and the Future	Kem Murch	Canada	DS	26
INDIAN BLOOD	Milton L. Brown	USA	DS	35
INDIAN COUNTRY	Michael Kirk	USA	DF	60
INDIAN POSSE: Life in Aboriginal Gang Territory	Katerina Cizek, Catherine Bainbridge	Canada	DS	39
INDIAN RIGHTS-INDIAN LAW	Joe Consentino	USA	DS	28
INDIAN TIME I	David Devine	Canada	PS	48
INDIAN TIME II - Fly With Eagles	Don Marks	Canada	PS	48
INDIAN TRIBAL GOVERNMENT	Joel L. Freedman	USA	DS	16
INNU TOWN	Michel Brault	Canada	MV	4
INSTITUTE FOR THE DEVELOPMENT OF INDIAN LAW	Joel L. Freedman	USA	DS	35
INUIT	Bo Boudart	Canada	DS	30
INUIT KIDS	Paulle Clark	USA	DS	15
INUPIATUN	Peter Haynes, Harold Tichenor	Canada	DF	55
INVISIBLE PEOPLE-				
Genocide of the Tradtional Navajo People	Marrissa Kelley	USA	DS	12
ISAAC LITTLEFEATHERS	Les Rose	Canada	FF	95
ISHI: The Last of His Tribe	Robert Ellis Miller	USA	FF	130
ISHI, The Last Yahi	Jed Riffe, Pamela Roberts	USA	DF	60
IT CAN'T RAIN ALL THE TIME	Lance Richmond	USA	LS	35
IT STARTS WITH A WHISPER	Shelley Niro & Anna Gronau	Canada	LS	27
ITAM HAKIM HOPIIT	Victor Masayesva, Jr.	USA	DF	58
JAY SILVERHEELS: The Man Beside the Mask	David Finch and Maureen Marovitch	Canada	DS	44
JENNY	Ray Ramayya	Canada	LS	48
JOE PANTHER	Paul Krasny	USA	FF	110
JOHNNY GREYEYES	Jorge Manzano	Canada	FF	80
JOURNEY HOME	Peter von Puttkamer	Canada	PS	39
JOURNEY TO MEDICINE WHEEL	Raymond Chavez	USA	DF	52
JOURNEY TO SPIRIT ISLAND	Laszlo Pal	USA	FF	93
JUSTICE OR JUST US	Don Marks	Canada	DF	55
KABLOONAK	Claude Massot	Canada	FF	105
KAINAI	Raoul Fox	Canada	DS	27
KAMIK	Elsie Swerhone	Canada	DS	15
KANATA: Legacy of the Children of Aataentsic	Rene Sioui LaBelle	Canada	DF	52
KANEHSATAKE: 270 Years of Resistance	Alanis Obomsawin	Canada	DF	119
KASHTIN ETERNAL DRUM	Jean-Jacques Sheitoyan	Canada	DS	47
KEEP THE CIRCLE STRONG	Joel Bertomeu, Luc Cote, Robbie Hart	Canada	DS	28
KEEPERS OF THE FIRE	Christine Welsh	Canada	DF	55

Key   DS: Documentary Short; DF: Documentary Feature; FF: Feature Film; LS: Live Short; IND: Industrial; MV: Music Video; PS: Public Service; ANS: Animated Short; DD: Docu-Drama

Title	Director	Country	Genre	Time
KEEPERS OF THE WATER	Al Gedicks	USA	DS	38
KEETOOWAHS COME HOME, THE	Larry Foley	USA	DS	26
KINAALDA, NAVAJO RITE OF PASSAGE	Lena Carr	USA	DF	57
KING OF THE GRIZZLIES	Ron Kelly	USA	FF	93
KOLUSKAP AND HIS PEOPLE	Joshua M. Vermette	USA	ANS	7
KUPER ISLAND: Return to the Healing Circle	Peter C. Campbell, Christine Welsh	Canada	DS	45
KUSAH HAKWAAN	Sean Morris	USA	DF	75
KWA'NU'TE': Micmac and Maliseet Artists	Catherine Martin, Kimberlee McTaggart	Canada	DS	41
KWEKANAMAND: The Wind is Changing	Carlos Ferrand	Canada	DF	54
LA GUAJIRA (special invitation)	Calogero Salvo	Venezuela	DF	58
LACROSSE: The Creator's Game	Kem Murch	Canada	DS	25
LADIES OF THE INLET	Annie Frazier Henry	Canada	DS	27
LAKOTA QUILLWORK: Art & Legend	H. Jane Nauman	USA	DS	27
LAKOTA STRAIN	Richard L. Rohrer, Jr.	USA	LS	5
LAKOTA WOMAN: Siege at Wounded Knee	Frank Pierson	USA	FF	110
LAND IS OURS, THE	Laurence Goldin	USA	DF	57
LAND OF THE WANNABE FREE	Tom Bee	USA	MV	5
LAND RIGHTS from Storytellers of the Pacific	Phil Lucas, Lurline McGregor	USA	DF	58
LANDS OF OUR ANCESTORS	Allan Forbes, Jr.	USA	DS	42
LAST DAYS OF OKAK, THE	Anne Budgell, Nigel Markham	Canada	DS	24
LAST OF THE DOGMEN	Tab Murphy	USA	FF	118
LAXWESA WA - Strength of the River	Barb Cranmer	Canada	DF	54
LAY YOUR BURDEN DOWN	Lee Tiger and Tom Bea	USA	MV	4
LEARNING PATH, THE	Loretta Todd	Canada	DF	56
LEARNING PLACE, THE	Bill N. Baker	USA	IND	15
LEGEND OF THE LONE RANGER, THE	William A. Fraker	USA	FF	98
LEONARD PELTIER	Hart Perry	USA	MV	4
LIFE SPIRIT	Fidel Moreno	USA	DS	24
LIGHTING THE 7TH FIRE	Sandra Sunrising Osawa	USA	DS	41
LIKE THE TREES	Kathleen Shannon	Canada	DS	14
LISTEN TO THE DRUM	Victor Romero	USA	IND	14
LITTLE BIG MAN	Arthur Penn	USA	FF	150
LITTLE ROCK'S RUN	James LuJan	USA	DF	59
LITTLE TRAPPER, THE	Dorothy Schreiber	Canada	DS	25
LIVE AND REMEMBER	Henry Smith	USA	DS	30
LIVING WITH TRADITION	Anthony Brown	USA	DS	28
LONG WAY FROM HOME, A	Bernice Dahl	USA	DS	9
LONGBOAT	David Storey	Canada	DS	23
LOOKS INTO THE NIGHT	Lorraine Norrgard	USA	LS	37
LOYALTIES	Anne Wheeler	USA	FF	98
MAHEO'S RACE	Sharon Altman	USA	ANS	9
MAHK JCHI	Victor Ginzburg	USA	MV	4
MAKAH: The Whale Harvesters	Ralf Marshalleck	USA/Germany	DF	117
MAKE MY PEOPLE LIVE: THE CRISIS IN INDIAN HEALTH	Linda Harrar	USA	DF	60
MAKING A DIFFERENCE	Barbara Alexander	USA	DS	30
MAKING A NOISE	Dana Heinz Perry	USA	DF	57
MAN, THE SNAKE AND THE FOX, THE	Tony Snowsill	Canada	LS	12
MATTER OF RESPECT, A	Ellen Frankenstein	USA	DS	29
MATTER OF TRUST, A	Rod Carleton	Canada	DS	35
MAZERUNNER: The Life and Art of T.C. Cannon	Phillip Albert	USA	DS	7
MEDICINE FIDDLE	Michael Loukinen	USA	DF	81
MEDICINE MEN	Gary Maynard	USA	LS	18
MEDICINE RIVER	Stuart Margolin	Canada	FF	94
MEDICINE WHEEL, THE	Richard Hersley	Canada	DS	25
MENOMINEE NATION POWWOW, THE	Martha Gilespie	USA	DS	44
MESA VERDE: LEGACY OF STONE AND SPIRIT	Gray Warriner	USA	DS	23
MI'KMAQ FAMILY: Migmaeio Otjiosog	Catherine Anne Martin	Canada	DS	32
MIND OF A CHILD, THE	Gary Marcuse	Canada	DF	60
MINO-BIMADIZIWIN: The Good Life	Deb Wallwork	USA	DF	59
MISTRESS MADELEINE	Aaron Kim Johnston	Canada	FF	57
MOON'S PRAYER: The Wisdom of the Ages	John deGraf	USA	DS	50
MORE THAN BOWS AND ARROWS	Gray Warriner	USA	DF	56
MOTHER OF MANY CHILDREN	Alanis Obomsawin	Canada	PS	58
MOTHER'S CHOICE, A	Peter von Puttkamer	Canada	PS	26
MOVIN' UP	Shawnee Brittan	USA	PS	22
MUCKLESHOOT: A People and their Language	Scott Ross	USA	DS	50
MY LAND IS MY LIFE	Joan Goldi	Canada	DS	55
MY NAME IS KAHENTIIOSTA	Alanis Obomsawin	Canada	DS	30
MY NATIVE SELF	Marco Mascarin	Canada	DF	54
MY VILLAGE IN NUNAVIK	Bobby Kenuajuak	Canada	DS	46
MYSTERY OF THE LOST RED PAINT PEOPLE, THE	T.W. Timreck & William Goetzman	USA	DF	60
NANIBAA'	David Grotell	USA	LS	18
NANOOK TAXI	Edward Folger	Canada	FF	90
NATION IS COMING, A	Kent Monkman	Canada	LS	24

Key   DS: Documentary Short; DF: Documentary Feature; FF: Feature Film; LS: Live Short; IND: Industrial; MV: Music Video; PS: Public Service; ANS: Animated Short; DD: Docu-Drama

Title	Director	Country	Genre	Time
NATIONAL MUSEUM OF THE AMERICAN INDIAN	Lisa Donner	USA	IND	10
NATIVE AMERICAN RIGHTS: Plundered or Preserved	Bill Fogarty, Judy Uphouse	USA	DF	58
NATIVE ENCOUNTER, THE	Veronica Smith, Pamela Hurley	USA	LS	6
NATIVE FOODS DAY	Shamino Taylor	USA	DS	7
NATIVE VETERANS: A Warrior's Story	Joe Beardy	Canada	DS	40
NATURALLY NATIVE	Jennifer Wynne Farmer and Valerie Red-Horse	USA	FF	108
NAVAJO CODE TALKERS	Tom McCarthy	USA	DS	28
NAVAJO MEDICINE: We Do the Work		USA	DF	29
NAVAJO NATION: Meeting the Challenge to Develop	Ken Kauffman	USA	DS	16
NAVIGATE	Andrew Unangst	USA	MV	4
NEGUAGUON - LAC LA CROIX: What We're Asking	Judith Doyle	Canada	DF	60
NEW INDIANS, THE	Terry Sanders	USA	DF	60
NEW PATH OF HOPE, A				
NATIONAL AMERICAN INDIAN LISTENING CONFERENCE	Nedra Darling	USA	DS	17
NEW TRAILS		USA	DS	25
NEWE SOGOBIA IS NOT FOR SALE! -				
The Struggle for Western Shoshone lands	Jesse Drew	USA	DS	28
NEZ PERCE: Portrait of a People	Phil Lucas	USA	DS	23
NIKJAGI'U (DOLLS)	Daryl Lonetree, Marlon White Eagle	USA	DS	15
NO ADDRESS	Alanis Obomsawin	Canada	DF	56
NO MORE SECRETS	Loretta Todd	Canada	PS	23
NO SURRENDER	Shelia Jordan	Canada	DF	52
NO TURNING BACK	Gregory Coyes	Canada	DS	47
O'SIEM	Gilliam Darling Kovanic	Canada	DF	54
OCTOBER STRANGER	Alan Collins	Canada	LS	26
OH CANADA	Rebeca Wolfchild	USA	DS	7
OJIGWANONG: Encounter With an Algonquin Sage	Andre Gladu	Canada	DS	26
OKIMAH	Paul M. Rickard	Canada	DF	51
ON AND OFF THE RES' WITH CHARLIE HILL	Sandra Osawa	USA	DF	58
ON THE WINGS OF TOMORROW	Bill Baker	USA	IND	13
ONE FLEW OVER THE CUCKOO'S NEST (1975)	Milos Forman	USA	FF	129
ONE HEART, ONE SONG	Kelly Parker	Canada	DS	23
OTHER SIDE OF THE LEDGER, THE:				
AN INDIAN VIEW OF THE HUDSON'S BAY COMPANY	Martin Defalco, Willie Dunn	Canada	DS	42
OUR CHILDREN ARE OUR FUTURE	Tony Snowsill	Canada	DF	51
OUR DANCES	Tiana M. Vermette	USA	DS	27
OUR DEAR SISTERS	Kathleen Shannon	Canada	DS	15
OUR LIVES IN OUR HANDS	Harald Prins	USA	DS	49
OUR PAST IS OUR FUTURE	Daniel Jumper, Robert Frank, Jeannette Cypress	USA	DS	17
OUR SACRED LAND	Chris Spotted Eagle	USA	DS	28
OUR TOTEM IS THE RAVEN		Canada	LS	21
OUTLAW JOSEY WALES, THE	Clint Eastwood	USA	FF	135
OVERWEIGHT WITH CROOKED TEETH	Shelley Niro	Canada	LS	5
PAHA SAPA: The Struggle for the Black Hills	Mel Lawrence	USA	DF	60
PAINTER'S SONG artist: Tiger Tiger	Stephen Tiger	USA	MV	5
PASSAGEWAY TO THE INFINITE SELF	Vladan Mijailovic	USA	DS	23
PATRICK'S STORY	Doug Cuthand	Canada	DS	24
PAULINE	Scott Calbeck, Morgan Earl	Canada	DS	49
PENOBSCOT: The People & Their River	David Westphal	USA	DS	28
PEOPLE ARE DANCING AGAIN, THE		USA	DS	
PEOPLE OF THE KLAMATH: PRESERVING A WAY OF LIFE	James Culp	USA	DS	28
PEPPER'S POWWOW	Sandra Osawa	USA	DF	58
PETROGLYPHS, THE	Pamela Hurley	USA	PS	1
PEYOTE ROAD, THE	Fidel Moreno, Gary Rhine, Phil Cousineau	USA	DF	59
PICTURING A PEOPLE:				
George Johnston, Tlingit Photographer	Carol Geddes	Canada	DS	50
PINTO FOR THE PRINCE, A	Colin Low, John Spotton	Canada	DS	17
PLACE OF THE FALLING WATERS, THE	Roy Bigcrane, Thompson Smith	USA	DF	90
PLACES NOT OUR OWN	Derek Mazur	Canada	FF	57
POCAHONTAS	Mike Gabriel, Eric Goldberg	USA	FF	87
POINT, THE - THE LEGACY OF THE RIVER PEOPLE	Peter Monahan	USA	DF	60
POISONING PARADISE	Barb Allard, Kelly Reinhardt	USA	DS	42
POLTERGEIST II: THE OTHER SIDE	Brian Gibson	USA	FF	91
POMO BASKETWEAVERS: A Tribute to Three Elders	David Ludwig	USA	DF	59
POPOL VUH - Cosmogenesis Maya (special invitation)	Patricia Amlin	USA	ANS	12
PORTRAITS OF LEADERSHIP	Daniel Housberg	USA	DS	28
POUNDMAKER'S LODGE - A Healing Place	Alanis Obomasawin	Canada	DS	29
POW WOW	K.C. Chaimberlain	USA	DS	30
POWER	Magnus Isacsson	Canada	DF	77
POWWOW	Elaine Middletown	USA	DS	22
POWWOW HIGHWAY	Jonathan Wacks	USA	FF	90
POWWOW MOSH	Eli Funaro	USA	DS	9
PRAYER OF PASSAGE	Chris Zeller	USA	LS	11
PRESERVING OUR PAST	Ben W. Baker	USA	DF	60

Key   DS: Documentary Short; DF: Documentary Feature; FF: Feature Film; LS: Live Short; IND: Industrial; MV: Music Video; PS: Public Service; ANS: Animated Short; DD: Docu-Drama

Title	Director	Country	Genre	Time
PRICE WE PAID, THE	Business Council, Colville Confederated Tribes	USA	DS	
PRIDE AND THE POWER TO WIN	Dave and Cyndee Wing	USA	DS	28
PRIMAL MIND	Don Lenzer	USA	DF	58
PROBABLE PASSING OF ELK CREEK	Rob Wilson	USA	DF	60
PROTEIN FROM THE SEA	Gray Warriner	USA	DS	25
QATUWAS - People Gathering Together	Barb Cranmer	Canada	DF	58
RABBIT BOSS	Mark Gandolfo, JoAnne Peden, Tom King	USA	DS	27
RADIOACTIVE RESERVATIONS	Ed Harrisman	USA / UK	DF	52
RANCHERIA	Timothy Ramos	USA	LS	12
REAL INDIAN	Malinda Maynor	USA	LS	7
REASON TO FEAR: The Cultural Defense of Hooty Croy	Steve Patapoff	USA	DF	56
REBURIAL, THE	Eric Mathes	USA	DS	40
RED MAN	Will Geiger	USA	LS	7
RED ROAD TO SOBRIETY, THE	Chante Pierce, Gary Rhine	USA	DF	90
REDSKINS, TRICKSTERS AND PUPPY STEW	Drew Hayden Taylor	Canada	DF	55
RETURN OF NAVAJO BOY, THE	Jeff Spitz	USA	DF	56
RETURN OF THE COUNTRY	Bob Hicks	USA	LS	30
RETURN OF THE NATIVE - THE STORY OF THE INTER TRIBAL BISON COOPERATIVE	Sam Hurst	USA	IND	21
RETURN TO THE CIRCLE	Emily Chavez Haack	USA	DS	10
RETURN TO THE CIRCLE: GEWI TAH BI WIN	Richard Reeder	USA	DS	35
RETURNINGS	Shivon Robinsong	Canada	DS	27
REZ, THE (Canadian TV series) 4 Episodes:				
Strange Bedfellows	Graeme Lynch	Canada		
Poster Girl	E. Jane Thompson	Canada		
Like Father, Like Son	TW Peacock	Canada		
Lust	John L'Ecuyey	Canada	LS	116
RICHARD CARDINAL: Cry From a Diary of a Metis Child	Alanis Obomsawin	Canada	DS	29
RIDE TO WOUNDED KNEE, THE	Robert Clapsaddle	USA	DF	86
RIVER PEOPLE: Behind the Case of David Sohappy	Michal Conford & Michele Zaccheo	USA	DF	51
ROCK ART TREASURES OF ANCIENT AMERICA	Dave Caldwell	USA	DS	25
ROCKIN' WARRIORS	Andy Bausch	USA	DF	56
RUN, APPALOOSA, RUN	Larry Lansburgh	USA	FF	48
RUN OF THE SACRED HOOP	Aggie Lukaszewski	USA	DS	33
RUN TO SAVE SINKYONE, THE	Jonathan L. Rosales	USA	DS	46
RUNNING AWAY		Canada	MV	4
RUNNING BRAVE	D.S. Everett	USA	FF	105
SACRED BUFFALO PEOPLE	Deb Wallwork	USA	DF	58
SACRED GROUND	Geroge McCowan	USA	DF	52
SACRED GROUND	Charles B. Peirce	USA	FF	100
SACRIFICE AREA	Otto Schuurman, Ernie Damen	Netherlands	DF	60
SALT WATER PEOPLE	Maurice Bulbulian	USa	DF	122
SCHOOL IN THE BUSH	Ian Rankin	Canada	DS	15
SEA IS OUR LIFE, THE	Bo Boudart	USA	DS	16
SEASON OF GRANDMOTHERS, A		USA	DS	30
SEASONS OF A NAVAJO	John Borden	USA	DF	57
SELF DETERMINATION from Storytellers of the Pacific	Phil Lucas	USA	DF	58
SEVENTH GENERATION, THE	Laura Milliken	Canada	DS	28
SHINGEBISS	Sharon A. Altman	USA	ANS	2
SILENCING THE GUNS	Rock Demers	Canada	FF	86
SILENT ENEMY, THE (1930)	H.P. Carver	USA	FF	84
SILENT TEARS	Shirley Cheechoo	Canada	LS	28
SILENT TONGUE	Sam Shepard	USA	FF	96
SINGING OUR STORIES	Annie Frazier Henry	Canada	DS	49
SLA-HAL: The Bone Game	P.J. Chvany	USA	DS	26
SLEEPING CHILDREN AWAKE	Rhonda Kara Hanah	Canada	DS	50
SMOKE SIGNALS	Chris Eyre	USA	FF	89
SOMEDAY, I'LL BE AN ELDER	Vern Korb, Richard Johnson	USA	DS	25
SOMEPLACE YOU DON'T WANT TO GO	Matt Tortes	USA	DS	22
SOMETHING LEFT TO DO	Cordell Wynne	Canada	DS	23
SONG OF HIAWATHA	John Danylkiw	Canada	FF	114
SONGKEEPERS	Bob Jackson, Bob Hercules	USA	DS	48
SOOP ON WHEELS	Sandy Greer	Canada	DF	52
SOUNDS OF FAITH	Malinda M. Maynor	USA	DS	14
SOVERIGNTY TOUR	Monique Sonoquie	USA	DS	10
SPIDER'S WEB — A Washoe History, Legend and Modern Story for Youth	Jane Van Camp, Bill Thorpe	USA	DS	30
SPIRIT LIVES, THE	Terri Li	USA	DS	42
SPIRIT OF CRAZY HORSE, THE	James Locker	USA	DF	55
SPIRIT OF THE DAWN	Heidi Schmidt Emberling	USA	DS	29
SPIRIT OF THE HUNT	Deborah Peaker	USA	DS	28
SPIRIT OF THE LAND: ALASKA: The Yup'ik Eskimos	Gail K. Evenari	USA	DS	28
SPIRIT OF THE WIND	Ralph Liddle	USA	FF	98
SPIRIT OF TURTLE ISLAND, THE	Lenore Keeshig Tobias, Alan Collins	Canada	DF	53

Key   DS: Documentary Short; DF: Documentary Feature; FF: Feature Film; LS: Live Short; IND: Industrial; MV: Music Video; PS: Public Service; ANS: Animated Short; DD: Docu-Drama

Title	Director	Country	Genre	Time
SPIRIT RIDER	Michael Scott	Canada	FF	120
SPIRIT WITHIN, THE	Wil Cambell, Gil Cardinal	Canada	DF	51
SPUDWRENCH - Kahnawake Man	Alanis Obomsawin	Canada	DF	58
STAND AND BE COUNTED		USA	PS	10
STARING AT A FEARFUL OCEAN	Norm Fassbender	Canada	LS	6
STEWART INDIAN SCHOOL: Uncommon Ground	Creel Snider	USA	DS	30
STORIES FROM THE SEVENTH FIRE	Gregory Coyes, Tantoo Cardinal	Canada	ANS	24
STORY OF LIGHT	Ivica Bilich	USA	LS	20
STORY OF THE COAST SALISH KNITTERS, THE	Christine Welsh	Canada	DF	52
STORYTELLER	Richard S. Dargan	USA	LS	12
STRAND IN THE WEB, A	Madeline Muir	USA	DS	28
STRANGE CASE OF BUNNY WEEQUOD, THE	Steve Van Denzen	Canada	LS	24
STUMBLINGBEAR: The video	Dan Bigbee, Jr.	USA	ANS	3
SUBSISTENCE: A Way of Life	Vern Korb	USA	DS	16
SUMMER LEGEND	Francoise Hartmann	Canada	ANS	8
SUMMER OF THE LOUCHEUX: Portrait of a Northern Indian	Graydon McCrea	Canada	DS	28
SUN, MOON, & FEATHER	Jane Zipp, Bob Rosen	USA	DS	30
SUPER CHIEF	Nick Kurzon	USA	DF	75
SURVIVING COLUMBUS	Diane Reyna	USA	DF	120
SWEAT	Valentina Lopez-Firewalks	USA	LS	27
SXWEXWXIY'AM: The Story of Siwash Rock	Annie Frazier Henry	Canada	LS	24
T'LINA: The Rendering of Wealth	Barb Cranmer	Canada	DS	50
TAOS PUEBLO, THE	Paulle Clark	USA	DS	9
TEACHING ROCKS, THE	Lloyd Walton	Canada	DS	19
TEARS OF THE RAVEN	Bill Baker	USA	DS	49
TECUMSEH AND THE DREAM OF CONFEDERACY	Gary Foreman	USA	DS	43
TEMAGAMI: A Living Title to the land	James Cullingham	Canada	DS	30
:: TENACITY	Chris Eyre	USA	LS	10
THAT WAS HAPPY LIFE	Mark Gandolfo, JoAnne Penden	USA	DS	28
THINGS WE DO	Chris Eyre	USA	MV	5
THIRD VERSE, 500 YEARS, THE LAND OF THE CHILDREN	Joanelle Romero	USA	DS	9
THIS WORLD IS NOT OUR HOME	Kim Johnson	USA	DS	13
THOUSAND YEARS OF CEREMONY, A	Christopher McLeod	USA	DS	37
THREE WARRIORS	Kieth Merrill	USA	FF	98
THROUGH THE EYES OF A BASKETMAKER	Kathy Wallace	USA	DS	26
THUNDER AND LIGHTNING	Jonathon Nordlicht	USA	ANS	12
THUNDER IN THEIR HEARTS	Robert Yuhas	USA	DS	24
THUNDERHEART	Michael Apted	USA	FF	127
TIKINAGAN from As Long as the Rivers Flow	Gil Cardinal	Canada	DF	57
TIME IMMEMORIAL	Hugh Brody	Canada	DF	60
TO BE CALLED A NATION	Tom Zapiecki	USA	DS	28
TO FIND OUR WAY and FIRST STEPS	Tim Farrow	USA	DS	31
TO RETURN: The John Walkus Story	Annie Frazier Henry	Canada	DS	45
TOBACCO: Keep It Sacred	Don Thompson	USA	PS	10
TODAY IS A GOOD DAY: Remembering chief Dan George	Loretta Todd	Canada	DS	44
TOKA	Dave & Cyndee Wing	USA	DS	24
TONKA	Lewis R. Foster	USA	ANS	97
TOTEM TALK	Annie Frazier Henry	Canada	ANS	22
TRACKS IN THE SNOW	Shirley Cheechoo	Canada	DS	28
TRADITIONAL KIND OF WOMAN, A: Too Much, Not 'Nuff	Lance Richmond	USA	DS	45
TRADITIONAL USE OF PEYOTE	Gary Rhine, Fidel Moreno	USA	DS	17
TRANSITIONS: Destruction of a Mother Tongue	Darrell Kipp, Joe Fisher	USA	DS	28
TRAUMA OF YOUTH SUICIDE: Voices of Hope	Sue Hutch	Canada	DS	19
TRAVELING THE DISTANCE	Ziggy Attis, Ofer Cohen	USA	DF	54
TRIAL OF BILLY JACK	TC Frank	USA	FF	171
TRIAL OF STANDING BEAR, THE	Marshall Jamison	USA	DD	117
TRIBAL BUSINESS IN THE GLOBAL MARKETPLACE	Thomas Hudson	USA	IND	11
TRIBAL TOBACCO POLICIES - Protecting Communities	Carole Nee-Takey Marie	USA	PS	15
TROUBLE IN PARADISE: Crisis on the Chemehuevi Reservation	Larry Cano, Rusty Two Crows Sandate (assoc.)	USA	DF	58
TRUE WHISPERS	Valerie Red-Horse	USA	DS	15
TULALIP TRIBES & ADMINISTRATION FOR NATIVE AMERICANS	Bev Hauptli	USA	IND	20
TULALIP TRIBES: Yesterday and Today	Bev Hauptli	USA	IND	11
TUSHKA	Ian Skorodin	USA	FF	90
TWO DECADES OF INUPIAT SELF-DETERMINATION	Beth Rose	USA	IND	40
TWO TRIBES, ONE LAND	Mary Fitzpatrick	USA	DS	25
UNBOWED	Nancy Rosov	USA	FF	120
UNCLE SAM'S MEN	Mike Martz	USA	DS	26
UNDERSTANDING THE AMERICAN INDIAN RELIGIOUS FREEDOM ACT	Gary Rhine	USA	DS	15
UNSETTLED	Charlotte Hill	USA	DS	43
URANIUM	Magnus Isacsson	Canada	DS	48
URBAN ELDER	Robert S. Adams	USA	DS	29

Key DS: Documentary Short; DF: Documentary Feature; FF: Feature Film; LS: Live Short; IND: Industrial; MV: Music Video; PS: Public Service; ANS: Animated Short; DD: Docu-Drama

Title	Director	Country	Genre	Time
URBAN FRONTIER	Gray Warriner	USA	IND	29
UTE MOUNTAIN TRIBAL PARK	Doug Bowman	USA	IND	15
VIDEO BOOK	Beverly R. Singer	USA	LS	10
VISION OF SEEKS-TO-HUNT-GREAT, THE	John Reynolds	USA	LS	25
VISIONS: A Poetry Film	Annie Frazier Henry	Canada	LS	9
VOICES FROM THE TALKING STICK	Todd Tyarm	Canada	DS	20
VOICES IN THE WIND	Gary Moss	USA	DD	57
VOYAGE OF REDISCOVERY	Phil Lucas	Canada	DS	47
WABANAKI: A New Dawn	Dennis Kostyk, David Westphal	USA	DS	28
WAKE, THE	Norma Bailey	Canada	FF	58
WALKING IN PAIN: Warriors of the Plains	Harvey Crossland	Canada	DF	50
WAR AGAINST THE INDIANS, THE	Harry Rasky	Canada	DF	145
WAR PARTY	Franc Roddam	USA	FF	97
WARRIOR CHIEFS IN A NEW AGE	Dean Curtis Bear Claw	USA	DS	28
WARRIOR IN TWO WORLDS	Ann Spurling	USA	DF	56
WARRIOR: The Life of Leonard Peltier	Suzie Baer	USA	DF	84
WARRIORS - Honoring Native American Veterans of the Vietnam War	Deb Wallwork	USA	DF	60
WARRIORS SONG	Vladan Mijailovic	USA	DS	40
WASHING OF TEARS, THE	Hugh Brody	Canada	DF	55
WAYS OF THE GLADES	Leslie M. Gaines	USA	MV	4
WE ARE THESE PEOPLE	Carol and Vern Korb	USA	LS	15
WE BELONG TO THE LAND	Shenandoah Film Productions	USA	DS	30
WE HAVE NO WORDS FOR THIS		Canada	DF	60
WE HAVE SUCH THINGS AT HOME	James Cullingham	Canada	DF	53
WE HOLD THE ROCK - The American Indian Occupation of Alcatraz 1969-1971	Jon Plutte	USA	DS	23
WE PRAY WITH TOBACCO	John and Ismana Carney	USA	DF	60
WE REMEMBER	Raymond Yakalaya	Canada	DF	60
WE'RE THE BOYZ	Magnet Films, Edward Nachieb	USA	MV	4
WEAVE OF TIME, A	Deborah Gordon	USA	DF	60
WELCOME HOME HERO	Nancy Trites Botkin	Canada	LS	22
WELCOME TO HEAD START	David W. Stamps	USA	DS	10
WEMAWE: Fetsh Carving of the Zuni Pueblo	Anistacia Barrak, Michelle Nunez	USA	DS	26
WHEN MY SHIP COMES IN	Larry Carey	Canada	MV	4
WHEN THE FIRE DIMS	Daniel Golding	USA	LS	17
WHERE THE RED ROAD MEETS THE INFORMATION SUPERHIGHWAY	Gary Robinson	USA	PS	14
WHERE THE RIVERS FLOW NORTH	Jay Craven	USA	FF	111
WHERE THE SPIRIT LIVES	Bruce Pittman	Canada	FF	108
WHISPERS: The Chumash	George Angelo, Jr.	USA	DS	29
WHITE DAWN, THE	Philip Kaufman	USA	DF	110
WHITE SHAMANS AND PLASTIC MEDICINE MEN	Terry Macy, Daniel Hart	USA	DS	26
WHO OWNS THE PAST?	Jed Riffe	USA	DF	56
WHO WE ARE: A Celebration of Native Youth	Bob Ellison, Kem Murch	Canada	PS	34
WHOSE LAND IS THIS?	Renae Morriseau	Canada	DF	60
WIIGWAASIJIIMAAN (The Birchbark Canoe)	Yvonne Hogg (project coordinator)	USA	DS	25
WINDWALKER	Kieth Merrill	USA	FF	105
WIPING THE TEARS OF SEVEN GENERATIONS	Fidel Moreno, Gary Rhine	USA	DF	52
WISDOM OF TWO WORLDS	James Mulryan	USA	DS	46
WITH CLEAN HANDS AND STRAIGHT EYES	Nicole Paradis Grindle	USA	DS	7
WITH HAND AND HEART	Bill Synder	USA	DS	28
WITHIN ALL WOMEN	Randy Croce	USA	DS	28
WITHOUT RESERVATIONS: Notes on Racism in Montana	Native Voices Collaborative Production	USA	LS	27
WOMEN AND MEN ARE GOOD DANCERS	Arlene Bowman	USA	LS	6
WOMEN IN THE SHADOWS	Norman Bailey	Canada	DF	56
WOODLANDS - The Story of the Mille Lacs Ojibwe	Tom Jenz	USA	DF	55
WOPILA TATANKA	Fidel Moreno	USA	IND	19
WORDS OF WISDOM	Annie Frazier Henry	Canada	LS	15
WORKING TOGETHER: Califonia Indians and Basketry Tradition	Rick Brazeau, Vern Korb	USA	DS	9
YAKOANA	Ahn Crutcher	USA/Brazil	DF	60
YEHA NOAH	Hitesh Teli	USA	MV	4
YELLOW WOODEN RING	Barrett Tripp	USA	LS	39
YOUR HUMBLE SERPENT: The Wisdom of Reuben Snake	Gary Rhine	USA	DF	60
YUXWELUPTUN: Man of Masks	Dana Claxton	Canada	DS	22

Key   DS: Documentary Short; DF: Documentary Feature; FF: Feature Film; LS: Live Short; IND: Industrial; MV: Music Video; PS: Public Service; ANS: Animated Short; DD: Docu-Drama

ABANDONED HOUSES ON THE RESERVATION

Country Canada   **Year** 2000   **Length** 3 m.   **Genre** LS
Director Darlene Naponse
Producer Darlene Naponse
Distributor
V-Tape Distributions
401 Richmond Street W., Suite 452
Toronto, Ontario
M5V 3A8 Canada
416 351-1317 [b] 416 351-1509 [f]
www.vtape.org
Please call for pricing.

A short narrative poem drives this film. A mosaic of images, words, texture
and music are blended together to tell a disturbing story of domestic violence.

Abandoned Houses on the Reservation is a poetic story dealing with the
realities of abuse. It was originally shot on Mini Digital by writer/director
Darlene Naponse in the essence and spirit of independence. The director's
vision was to tell a story of emotions and memory through words, textures,
and visuals.

ABNAKI

Country USA   **Year** 1984   **Length** 29 m.   **Genre** DS
Director Jay Kent
Producer Jay Kent
Distributor
Not in distribution.

A beautifully realized portrait of the four Indian tribes of Maine describing
the tribes' persistence within the dominant American society. Through personal reminiscence and narration, the film explores the historical, economic, cultural and spiritual factors that have aided in their survival.
Culminating with the consideration of the settlement of the huge and long-
standing land claim by two of Maine's tribes for two-thirds of the state, the
film is a moving portrait of a great people.

ACTS OF DEFIANCE

Country USA   **Year** 1992   **Length** 105 m.   **Genre** DF
Director Alec G. MacLeod
Producer Mark Zannis, Dennis Murphy
Distributor
National Film Board of Canada Library
22-D Hollywood Avenue
Ho-Ho-Kus, NJ 07423
1 800 542-2164 [b] 201 652-1973 [f]
US $440.00 VHS, call for rental information and prices.
For purchase within Canada visit the NFB website at www.nfb.ca
1 800 267-7710 toll free within Canada

In the spring of 1990, a small stand of pine trees in Oka, Quebec became the object of a struggle between Mohawks, who claimed the land belonged to them, and the municipality of Oka, who wanted to develop the land for a golf course extension. For months, Mohawks maintained a blockade across a seldom-used dirt road to block the bulldozers, while legal battles were being fought.

On July 11, 1990, the Quebec provincial police - the Surete de Quebec (SQ) - attempted to remove the barricades by force. Shots were exchanged and a policeman was killed.

Word of the police raid in Oka spread to the Mohawk reservation of Kahnawake on Montreal's South Shore. In a show of support, the Warrior Society of Kahnawake blocked off all roads leading into their territory, including the Mercier Bridge, a vital link for suburban communters who work in Montreal.

And suddenly, these two tiny Mohawk communities grabbed the world's attention.

Acts of Defiance leaves viewers with a powerful sense of the contradictions and confusion surrounding this painful chapter in Canadian history, including the tense political negotiations; the media's frantic attempts to keep abreast of the crisis; and the reactions of the soldiers who found themselves placed between the opposing parties, ordered to bear arms against their fellow Canadians.

AGAIN A WHOLE PERSON I HAVE BECOME

Country USA   **Year** 1983   **Length** 20 m. **Genre** DS
Director Matt Tortes
Producer Shenandoah Films
Distributor
Shenandoah Film Productions
538 "G" Street
Arcata, CA 95221
707 822-1030 tele 707 822-1035 fax
US $200.00 VHS, US $45.00 VHS rental

This film features a Wintu medicine woman, a Karuk spiritual leader (fatavena), and a Tolowa headman. These three tribal leaders from geographically distant areas symbolize Native American leaders across the country. They speak of the ultimate wisdom of the old ways. Dances and gatherings are featured. Their teachings set them upon a path that leads to wholeness.

AIDS EDUCATION / PREVENTION FOR THE AMERICAN INDIAN COMMUNITY

Country USA   **Year** 1994   **Length** 15 m.   **Genre** PS
Director April Skinas
Producer April Skinas
Distributor
Not in distribution.

AIDS is devastating to the American Indian community because our population is the smallest in numbers compared to other communities. The Indian community has the highest rate of teenage pregnancies, teenage suicide, sexually transmitted diseases, alcoholism, and AIDS. Our people are leaving reservations and rural areas, coming to big cities. Unfortunately, risky sexual behavior increases the percentages of contracting AIDS. Many Indians are unaware that they are infected with HIV and return "home" to their rural/reservation homes spreading the virus where they also might not get the necessary medical protocols. Some individuals are knowingly infected, and just go back "home" to die. The purpose of the video is to educate the American Indian community and demonstrate how to prevent the AIDS virus from spreading.

AKWESASNE: ANOTHER POINT OF VIEW

Country USA   **Year** 1982   **Length** 28 m.   **Genre** DS
Director Bob Stiles
Producer Don Klugman
Distributor
First Run / Icarus Films
32 Court Street, 21st Floor
Brooklyn, NY 11201
718 488-8900 tele   718 488-8642 fax
US $280.00 VHS, US $55.00 VHS rental

A portrait of an Indian community faced with two choices: survival or assimilation. This film explores the obstacles faced by traditional Mohawk people during two years of struggle to establish peace in their territory. *Akwesasne: Another Point of View* is a fast paced film, replete with clear and succinct descriptions of a contemporary Indian community fighting to retain traditional rights.

ALCATRAZ IS NOT AN ISLAND

Country USA   **Year** 1999   **Length** 85 m.   **Genre** DF
Director Jim Fortier
Producer Jon Plutte, Millie Ketcheshawno
Distributor
Currently unavailable.
Diamond Island Productions
1129 Mazanita Drive
Pacifica, CA 94044
650 738-9105 [b]

For thousands of Native Americans, the infamous Alcatraz is not an island, it is an inspiration. After generations of oppression, assimilation, and near genocide, a small group of Native American students and "Urban Indians" began the occupation of Alcatraz Island in November 1969. They were eventually joined by thousands of Native Americans, retaking "Indian land" for the first time since the 1880s.

Alcatraz Is Not An Island chronicles how this historic event altered U.S. Government Indian Policy and programs, and how it forever changed the way Native Americans viewed themselves, their culture, and their sovereign rights. The story of the occupation of Alcatraz is as complex and rich as the history of Native Americans. This documentary examines the personal sacrifices, tragedies, social battles, and political injustices many Native Americans experienced under the United States Governments policies of assimilation, termination, and relocation - all eventually leading to Alcatraz. Out of Alcatraz came the "Red Power" movement of the 1970s, which has been called the lost chapter of the Civil Rights era.

After 30 years, *Alcatraz Is Not An Island* provides the first in-depth look at the history, politics, personalities, and cultural reawakening behind this historic event, which sparked a new era of Native American political empowerment and cultural renaissance.

ALIEN THUNDER (A.K.A. DAN CANDY'S LAW)

Country Canada   **Year** 1975   **Length** 90   **Genre** FF
Director Claude Fournier
Producer Claude Fournier
Distributor
Available on Amazon.com
www.amazon.com
Also, contact your local Suncoast Video store to inquire on availablity.

Alien Thunder is based on the true story of Almighty Voice, a Cree Indian
fugitive who eluded the Royal Canadian Mounted Police for over a year.
According to the legends, Almighty Voice had the power to make himself
invisible and change into animal forms, which he used to evade his pur-
suers. The film is alternately sympathetic towards the Mounties and the
Native American characters. Two of the First Nations stars of the film are
Oscar-nominated actor Chief Dan George, in the role as Sounding Sky, and
Gordon Tootoosis, who plays Almighty Voice in his screen debut. Donald
Sutherland, in a scene-stealing performance, is Dan Candy, the tall tale-
telling, determined Mountie who is obsessed with "getting his man." *Alien
Thunder* is recommended for its vivid depiction of early Canadian life and
Northern Cree culture.

ALLAN HOUSER HAOZOUS: THE LIFETIME WORK OF AN AMERICAN MASTER

Country USA   **Year** 1998   **Length** 58 m.   **Genre** DF
Director Phil Lucas
Producer Phil Lucas
Distributor
Allan Houser, Inc.
P.O. Box 5217
Santa Fe, NM 87502
505 471-1528 [b] 505 471-1482 [f]
US $25.00 VHS

Allan Houser was a world-class, pioneering artist whose Warm Springs
Chiricahua Apache heritage was the source of his imagery: his father's stories, his own early memories of women's shawls and skirts around the
bonfire of the Apache Mountain Spirit Dance, the bitterly won taste of his
tribe's freedom after a generation of forced relocation and imprisonment.
With impeccable mastery of his medium, the sculptor condensed these elements, and the universal experiences of being human, into the graceful and
simple curve of a mother's arm around her child. A young warrior in
bronze lifts his sacred pipe to the four directions, and in the upward steep
of that gesture is captured the dignity, beauty, and ageless tradition of
Allan Houser's ancestors. Here, in this beautifully produced documentary,
is an introduction to the man and his art.

AMAROK'S SONG - THE JOURNEY TO NUNAVUT

Country Canada   **Year** 1999   **Length** 75 m.   **Genre** DF
Director Ole Gjerstad, Martin Kreelak
Producer Janice Epp, Ole Gjerstad, Malcolm Guy, Joe MacDonald,
Graydon McCrea, Lucie Pageau
Distributor
National Film Board of Canada Library
22-D Hollywood Avenue
Ho-Ho-Kus, NJ 07423
1 800 542-2164 [b] 201 652-1973 [f]
US $275.00 VHS, call for rental information and prices.
For purchase within Canada visit the NFB website at www.nfb.ca
1 800 267-7710 toll free within Canada

This is the story of the Caribou Inuit family who were Canada's last
nomads. With the voices of three generations, they tell of their journey
from an independent life hunting on the Keewatin tundra to the present,
when they take the reins of the new territory of Nunavut on April 1, 1999.
Amarok's Song: Journey to Nunavut is the result of the close collaboration
between Ole Gjerstad, a southern Canadian, and Martin Kreelak, an Inuk.
Martin is a member of the family in the film and one of its principal characters. *Amarok's Song* speaks through three distinct voices. Elders, led by
80-year-old Amarok and his wife, Elizabeth, take us back to a time marked
by incredible hardship, pride and a startling spiritual universe. Martin's
generation has a foot in each world: they have borne the brunt of cultural
clashes between southern and Inuit societies--and they are the ones who
will set the course for their new homeland. Teens and young adults who
were born in the settlements and grew up with satellite TV also speak
through their own short video stories, shot by students at Baker Lake High
School. A shorter video, *Journey to Nunavut: The Kreelak Story* (48 min),
is also available. It focuses on Martin Kreelak's generation and that of the
elders, represented by Amarok and Elizabeth.

AMERICA'S GREAT INDIAN LEADERS

GERONIMO   QUANAH PARKER   CRAZY HORSE   CHIEF JOSEPH

Country USA   **Year** 1994   **Length** 60 m.   **Genre** DF
Director Bob Hercules, Bruce Lixey
Producer Albert Nader
Distributor
Questar Video
P.O. Box 11345
Chicago, IL 60611-0345
1 800 544-8422 [b]
US $29.95 VHS

Leaders who came forward, willing to die to preserve a way of life…

As the 19th century moved toward a close, Native American nations saw
their rich heritage coming to an end. Advancing expansion, broken government promises, and hatred by the military establishment left them little
land or territory. Four Native American leaders emerged, not just to fight
for territory, but to protect their people and culture. Crazy Horse, "Sacred
Warrior of the Lakota," refused to bring his people into submission. Chief
Joseph, "Guardian of the Nez Perce," led his people on a 1,700 mile flight
from the U.S. Army. Geronimo, "Brilliant Medicine Man of the Apaches,"
used his powers to vanish and reappear, confounding pursuers. Quanah
Parker, "Last Chief of the Comanche" and son of a white woman, guided
his people between two worlds, white and Indian. It's all here, a poignant,
tragic episode in American History.

AMERICA'S GREAT INDIAN NATIONS

Country USA   **Year** 1995   **Length** 55 m.   **Genre** DS
Director Bob Hercules, Bruce Lixey
Producer Albert Nader
Distributor
Questar Video
P.O. Box 11345
Chicago, IL. 60611-0345
1 800 544-8422 [b]
US $29.95 VHS

This is the story of six mighty Indian nations and how their cultures and
struggle became an important part of American history: the Iroquois — the
most powerful of the eastern tribes; the Seminoles of Florida, who took
freed slaves into their own nation; the Shawnee, whose chief Tecumseh
formed a great confederacy of eastern Indian tribes to protect their land;
the Navajo of the Southwest, who were led by their Chief Manuelito in an
undeclared war against the U.S. Army; the Cheyenne of the Great Plains,
who were victims of the savage Sand Creek Massacre in 1864; and the
Lakota Sioux, whose leaders led the momentous Battle of Little Big Horn.
Rich landscapes, dramatic reenactments, historical photographs and haunting music combine to provide a compelling look inside six of the most
powerful, feared and honored tribes throughout American History.

AMERICAN COWBOYS

Country USA   **Year** 1999   **Length** 27 m.   **Genre** DS
Director Cedric and Tania Wildbill
Producer Wildbill Productions
Distributor
Lucerne Media
37 Ground Pine Road
Morris Plains, NJ 07950
1 800 341-2293 [b]   973 538-0855 [f]
www.lucernemedia.com   LM@lucernemedia.com
US $99.00 VHS educational

American Cowboys tell the stories of legendary rodeo cowboys George
Fletcher and Jackson Sundown, the first African American and the first
Native American to compete in the World Title at the Pendleton Round-
Up. This documentary reveals the glory of being the best, the frustration of
being ignored, and the rewards for not giving up on a dream. Jackson
Sundown, a Nez Perce name that has grown to mythical proportions, was
said to be the best horseman around, but it wasn't until he was 52 years
old that the Pendleton Round-Up judges let him compete for the world
title. Then in 1916, at age 53, Jackson won the championship at the
Pendleton Round-Up. He was the first Native American to win the honor.
George Fletcher, a black cowboy who lived most of his life on the
Umatilla Indian Reservation, was the best bronco rider, but the 1911
Pendleton Round-Up judges couldn't bring themselves to award a black
man the prize saddle and gave it to a white man instead. Fans were in such
an uproar that they cut Fletcher's hat up into pieces and sold the pieces to
raise money to buy him the saddle. Told through narratives from historians
and accounts from family and tribal members the story of Sundown and
Fletcher's journey to Pendleton ends with them winning a battle of their
own – recognition from their community. Both men came from humble
beginnings to become two of the greatest cowboys ever.

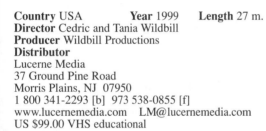

AMERICAN HOLOCAUST: WHEN IT'S ALL OVER I'LL STILL BE INDIAN

Country USA   **Year** 2000   **Length** 29 m.   **Genre** DS
Director Joanelle Romero
Producer Joanelle Romero, Teddy Parker, Larry Sellers
Distributor
Spirit World Productions
818 703-5084 [b] & [f]
Please call for pricing.

American Indians are a colonized people, and colonization has affected every fiber of American Indian existence: physically, mentally, culturally, and emotionally. Its impact is still visible within Indian communities today. American Indians have some of the highest rates of poverty, unemployment, death by accident, alcoholism and suicide of any group in America.

The indigenous population of North America dwindled from approximately 12 to 19 million at the time of European contact to around 250,000 in the early 1900s. This decimation of the Indian population was due to well-documented official and unofficial European and U.S. government programs of warfare, disease and murder.

This documentary short film explores the historical, social and religious roots of the American Indian Holocaust, examines the long term and current effects of this destructive process and explores the possible ramifications for the future of American Indian people in the 21st Century. *American Holocaust* is a true American story that will affect every citizen of this country. As a nation, America must face it and acknowledge this truth, so that we can move on and all heal from it together.

AMERICAN INDIAN ARTIST II - JAUNE QUICK TO-SEE SMITH

Country USA   **Year** 1983   **Length** 15 m.   **Genre** DS
Director Tony Schmitz
Producer Frank Blythe
Distributor
Lucerne Media
37 Ground Pine Road
Morris Plains, NJ 07950
1 800 341-2293 [b] 973 538-0855 [f]
www.lucernemedia.com   LM@lucernemedia.com
US $99.00 VHS educational

The abstractionist paintings and collages of Shoshone French Cree artist Smith reflect her deep concern for protecting the environment. Produced by Native American Public Telecommunications, the series documents the life and work of contemporary artists who are Native Americans. The film is narrated by noted author N. Scott Momaday.

AMERICAN INDIAN ARTIST II-LARRY GOLSH

Country USA   **Year** 1983   **Length** 14 m.   **Genre** DS
Director Don Cirillo
Producer Frank Blythe
Distributor
Lucerne Media
37 Ground Pine Road
Morris Plains, NJ 07950
1 800 341-2293 [b]   973 538-0855 [f]
www.lucernemedia.com   LM@lucernemedia.com
US $99.00 VHS educational

A Pala Mission Indian jeweler who works in gold and precious stones, Larry Golsh discusses the ways his Indian heritage and his family have influenced his work. Produced by Native American Public Telecommunications, the series documents the life and work of contemporary artists who are Native Americans. The film is narrated by noted author N. Scott Momaday.

AMERICAN INDIAN DANCE THEATRE: DANCES FOR THE NEW GENERATIONS

Country USA   **Year** 1993   **Length** 56   **Genre** DF
Director Hanay Geiogamah, Phil Lucas
Producer Phil Lucas
Distributor
Oyate
2702 Mathews Street
Berkeley, CA 94702
510 848-6700 [b]   510 848-4815 [f]
www.oyate.org
$35.00 VHS

"Song is the stronghold of who we are." This 1993 Emmy Award nominee explores the many ways dance has provided generations of American Indians with one of their most effective means of preserving, passing along and celebrating Native American heritage and culture in the face of assimilation and active suppression. From the Kwakiutl Potlatch Dances from the Pacific Northwest to the Pow Wow dancing of the Southwest and Central plains, the filmmakers have woven the past with the present to show how the dances have changed, but the reasons for dancing have remained. "It's a carrier of tradition. We get courage and strength from dancing."

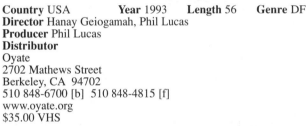

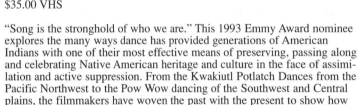

AMERICAN INDIAN EXPOSITION

Country USA   **Year** 1979   **Length** 24 m.   **Genre** DS
Director Shawnee Brittan
Producer Shawnee Brittan
Distributor
Not in distribution.

The American Indian Exposition is the only Indian owned and operated celebration of its kind in the United States.

It is produced by the fifteen western American Plains Indian Tribes, including the Comanche, Arapaho, Wichita, Delaware, Oloe-Missouria, Caddo, Ponca, Kiowa, Apache, and Iowa, and takes place each August in Anadarko, Oklahoma.

During the weeklong Indian celebration, activities consist of horse races, parades, dancing, visiting family and friends, and setting up camp on the exposition grounds. In the camping area are seen tipis, wigwams, travel trailers, and mobile homes—quite a mixture of the old and new.

In 1976, at the 45th annual show, the Exposition was named a National Bicentennial Event.

AMERICAN INDIAN WOMEN'S TALKING CIRCLE CERVICAL CANCER PROJECT

Country USA **Year** 1995 **Length** 20 m. **Genre** PS
Director Felicia Schanche Hodge
Producer Stu Sweetow
Distributor
Center for American Indian Research and Education
1918 University Avenue, Suite 2-A
Berkeley, CA 94704
510 843-8661 [b]
Purchase Price: Free to all Native Health, Cultural, Community, Educational Organizations

The American Indian Women's Talking Circle seeks to increase cervical cancer screenings and enhance the quality of life among American Indian women. Cervical cancer is a significant problem in Native populations; Indian women have one of the highest incidence rates and the poorest 5 year survival rates.

The project is unique in that it uses both health materials and traditional stories in a Talking Circle format. This is an important way to educate and motivate American Indian women to seek appropriate cancer screening. The video illustrates the concept of utilizing the tradition of storytelling in an educational program.

AMERICAN INDIANS — YESTERDAY AND TODAY

Country USA **Year** 1982 **Length** 18 m. **Genre** DS
Director Don Klugman
Producer Filmfair Communications
Distributor
AGC / United Learning
1560 Sherman Avenue, Suite 100
Evanston, IL 60201
1 800 323-9084 [b] 1 874 328-6706 [f]
www.agcunitedlearning.com
US $95.00 VHS, DVD, 3/4"
Please call for rental pricing

Native Americans inhabited the North American continent for thousands of years before the European people came. To show that various Indian tribes have different histories and ways of life, a young Shoshone-Paiute man from Owens Valley in California, an elderly Northern Cheyenne man from Lame Deer, Montana, and a young Seneca woman from New York State relate history and modern lifestyles of their tribes. The similarities and differences are discussed by actor/narrator Ned Romero.

AMERICAN SCENE

Country USA **Year** 1997 **Length** 12 m. **Genre** IND
Director Dan Jones
Producer Julia Brescia
Distributor
Not in distribution.
Dan Jones
2647 S. Barrington Avenue, #7
Los Angeles, CA 90064
310 477-3434

Although there have been Native American actors in the film industry from the beginning, they have struggled many years for the opportunity to portray themselves in featured roles. *American Scene* encourages the non-traditional casting of Indian performers. This video was produced so that Native American performers will no longer have to contend with the limited opportunities of playing period pieces or stereotypical roles. It seeks to reflect Native American performers as people in all walks of life.

AMIOTTE

Country USA   **Year** 1978   **Length** 30 m.   **Genre** DS
Director Richard Muller
Producer Bruce Baird
Distributor
Lucerne Media
37 Ground Pine Road
Morris Plains, NJ 07950
1 800 341-2293 [b] 973 538-0855 [f]
www.lucernemedia.com   LM@lucernemedia.com
US $99.00 VHS educational

This film explores talented Sioux painter Arthur Amiotte's art, his reasons
for returning to his Native culture and religion, his stylistic evolution, and
the influences of a traditional medicine man in transferring his childhood
memories to new media.

AMISK

Country Canada   **Year** 1977   **Length** 40 m.   **Genre** DS
Director Alanis Obomsawin
Producer Dorothy Courtios, Wolf Koenig, Alanis Obomsawin
Distributor
National Film Board of Canada Library
22-D Hollywood Avenue
Ho-Ho-Kus, NJ 07423
1 800 542-2164 [b] 201 652-1973 [f]
US $125.00 VHS, call for rental information and prices.
For purchase within Canada visit the NFB website at: www.nfb.ca
1 800 267-7710 toll free within Canada

A week-long festival was organized by a group of Montreal residents to
raise funds in support of the Cree Indians who stood to lose their land
because of the James Bay hydro-electric project. This film, made by
Native filmmaker Alanis Obomsawin, alternates between spectacular performances by Indian and Inuit peoples and the meeting halls of Mistassini,
where they talk of their past as a way of defending their future.

AN ACT OF RENEWAL –
A MUSEUM TO THE AMERICAN INDIAN

Country USA   **Year** 1988   **Length** 26 m.   **Genre** DS
Director Heather Giugni
Producer Heather Giugni, Lurline Mc Gregor, Esther Figueroa
Distributor
Juniroa Productions
928 Nu'uanu Avenue, Penthouse
Honolulu, Hawaii 96817
808 533-4788 [b] 808 533-4789 [f]
juniroa@aol.com
US $30.00 VHS

An Act of Renewal—A Museum to the American Indian describes a propos-
al introduced by Senator Daniel K. Inouye, Chairman of the Senate Select
Committee on Indian Affairs, to build a museum to the American Indian
on the last major site on the National Mall in Washington, D.C.

The program explains three issues in the legislation, which include the pro-
posal to build a museum on the National Mall in Washington D.C. dedicated to American Indians; the transfer of the collection of the Museum of the
American Indian, Heye Foundation, in New York to this new museum; and
the question of what should be done with the Indian and Eskimo skeletal
remains in the Smithsonian's National History Museum collection.

AN ANCIENT GIFT

Country USA   **Year** 1983   **Length** 18 m.   **Genre** DS
Director Patricia Barey
Producer Tellens Inc.
Distributor
UC Extension Center for Media and Independent Learning
2000 Center Street, Fourth Floor
Berkeley, CA 94704-1223
510 642-0460 [b] 510-643-9271 [f]
cmil@uclink.berkeley.edu
US $47.00 VHS rental

"To care for sheep like a mother is, for the Navajo, to care for the Navajo people." In *An Ancient Gift*, the english-speaking Navajo narrator who says this utters a simple truth that to him and to all Navajos stems from an equally simple fact of human experience: you care for, love and honor that which gives you life and nurtures you.

To Navajos, this includes the Navajo woman, Mother Earth, whom they call Changing Woman, and sheep, her gift to the Navajo people, all three linked biologically and spiritually as the source of Navajo survival and prosperity.

ANCESTORS OF THOSE YET UNBORN

Country USA   **Year** 1979   **Length** 28 m.   **Genre** DS
Director Anthony Brown
Producer Anthony Brown
Distributor
Lucerne Media
37 Ground Pine Road
Morris Plains, NJ 07950
1 800 341-2293 [b] 973 538-0855 [f]
www.lucernemedia.com LM@lucernemedia.com
US $99.00 VHS educational - part of the "Forest Spirit" series

Although the size of their nation is smaller now, the Menominee still live in the same basic region in northern Wisconsin that they have occupied for hundreds of years. This film is one of a seven part series entitled "Forest Spirits." It was filmed on location in Wisconsin.

ANCESTRAL SONGS: KWA-KWA-KA' WAKW FAMILY
FROM FIRST NATIONS PORTRAITS SERIES

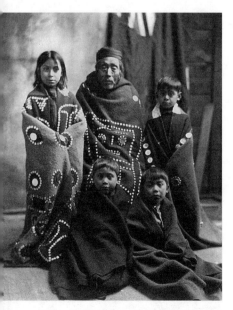

Country Canada   **Year** 1994   **Length** 6 m.   **Genre** PS
Director Peter von Puttkamer
Producer Peter von Puttkamer
Distributor
Gryphon Productions Ltd.
P.O. Box 93009, 5331 Headland Drive
West Vancouver, BC
V7W 3C0 Canada
604 921-7627 [b] 604 921-7626 [f] gryphon@telus.net
US $148.00 VHS series - US $35.00 VHS single segment
CAD $175.20 VHS series

Ancestral Songs was part of the "First Nations Portraits" series produced for the Provincial Government of British Columbia to commemorate 1993, Year of the World's Indigenous Peoples. The purpose of the series was to educate the general public about the richness and diversity of First Nations cultures in British Columbia.

Ancestral Songs examines the importance of "Family" to the Kwa-kwa-ka'wakw (Kwakiutl) people. Featuring rarely seen footage at a family pot-latch in Alert Bay, we hear from hereditary chiefs, clan mothers and Native historians about the importance of children and family lineage at the pot-latch. We see how the masked dances and songs are passed from genera-tion to generation. We also learn about ties which bind together the First Nations' extended family: for example, first cousins are called brothers and sisters amongst many Northwest Coast peoples.

The purpose of the video is to show how family unity and the passing of knowledge within the family has helped maintain the centuries-old tradi-tions of the Kwa-kwa-ka'wakw people.

... AND WOMAN WOVE IT IN A BASKET...

Country USA   **Year** 1990   **Length** 70 m.   **Genre** DF
Director Bushra Azzouz, Marlene Farnum, Nettie Kuneki
Producer Bushra Azzouz, Marlene Farnum
Distributor
Women Make Movies, Inc.
462 Broadway, Suite 500
New York, NY 10013
212 925-0606 [b] 212 925-2052 [f]
www.wmm.com   orders@wmm.com
US $250.00 VHS, US $75.00 VHS rental

... And Woman Wove it in a Basket... is an oral history of the Klickitat Indian basket, the story of Nettie Jackson Kuneki and an exploration of Klickitat river culture. It attempts to capture an often neglected history: Native life as it is experienced and articulated by a contemporary Native woman. At the core of the film is the problem of cultural preservation, loss and change — preservation not only in archives and museums but in the daily practice and memory of the people.

Imbricated basketry is a traditional craft of the Klickitat women that has waned over the last generations. The film documents the making of a basket from start to finish: the gathering and processing of materials, the choice of designs and the social interaction centered around the weaving.

In interweaving diverse voices and fragments, the film attempts to negate the omnipotent voice of documentary that neatly explains and dissects reality — an attempt not "to speak about or for" but to witness and evoke, question and interact." *... And Woman Wove it in a Basket...* unfolds on "Indian time" to respect the rhythm of the activity and the telling.

ANISHINAABE NIIJII (FRIENDS OF THE CHIPPEWA)

Country USA   **Year** 1994   **Length** 49 m.   **Genre** DS
Director Al Gedicks
Producer Al Gedicks
Distributor
Mining Center
210 Avon Street, #4
La Crosse, WI 54603
608 784-4399 [b] 608 784-8486 [f]
US $50.00 VHS, US $15.00 VHS rental

Anishinaabe Niijii examines how an Indian environmental coalition came together to resist a highly controversial open pit copper mine on the banks of the Flambeau River in the dairy country of northwestern Wisconsin. The film traces the conflict with archival film footage of the major events and with interviews among key participants in the community of Ladysmith, in the Chippewa community, and among environmental activists in the Flambeau Summer Coalition. The producer/director was a participant in the coalition and a founding member of Anishinaabe Niijii.

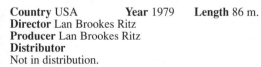

ANNIE MAE-BRAVE HEARTED WOMAN

Country USA   **Year** 1979   **Length** 86 m.   **Genre** DD
Director Lan Brookes Ritz
Producer Lan Brookes Ritz
Distributor
Not in distribution.

Annie Mae - Brave Hearted Woman chronicles the life and work of Annie Mae Aquash. Her life and death is a metaphor for the human rights struggle in the 1970s. The film covers significant American Indian Movement demonstrations and take overs, the Jumping Bull shootout on the Pine Ridge Indian Reservation in South Dokota and the aftermath when Annie Mae was killed.

ANNUAL (21st) WORLD ESKIMO INDIAN OLYMPICS

Country USA   **Year** 1983   **Length** 27 m.   **Genre** DS
Director Skip Blumberg
Producer Skip Blumberg
Distributor
In Motion Productions
373 Broadway, E3
New York, NY 10013
212 431-8480 [b] 212 431-8603 [f]
US $80.00 VHS
For rental please all E.A.I. at: 212 325-0680 [b]

Exciting and unique ancient sports such as the blanket toss, knuckle hop, high kicks, four man carry, whale blubber eating and seal skinning contests are highlighted in this fast-paced feature about modern Eskimos and Indians in Alaska.

For centuries Native people of the Arctic have gathered in small villages near the top of the world to compete in these fascinating games. The contests not only provide a reason to keep in shape, both mentally and physically, for survival in the extreme climate, but friendly competition and fun during the long summer days and winter nights.

Based on this tradition, the World Eskimo-Indian Olympics have been held as an organized event in Fairbanks, Alaska since 1961. The 21st Annual Games held in July, 1982 were the largest ever with several hundred competitors coming from all over Alaska. More than ten thousand fans filled the stands through the preliminaries and finals during the three day event.

APACHE MOUNTAIN SPIRITS

Country USA   **Year** 1988   **Length** 60 m.   **Genre** FF
Director B. Graham
Producer John & Jennie Crouch
Distributor
Silvercloud Video Productions, Inc.
5755 North Camino Escalante
Tucson, AZ 85718
520 615-0283 [b]
www.southwestseries.com
US $20.00 VHS purchase

Apache Mountain Spirits tells two stories. One is an ancient legend, shown for the first time. This story describes the meeting of the Apache with the Gaan, the Mountain Spirits.

The second story is a modern testimonial to the power of the Gaan today. The White Mountain Apache people were involved in all aspects of development of this project.

ARROW CREEK

Country USA   **Year** 1978   **Genre** DS
Producer College of Arts & Crafts
Distributor
College of Arts & Crafts
5212 Broadway
Oakland, CA 94618
510 653-8118 [b]

Arrow Creek is an independently produced film, made at the California College of Arts and Crafts. The footage for this film was all shot in the summer of 1977, on the Crow Indian Reservation in Southeastern Montana. The Crow Fair, a major source of the imagery in the film, is an annual event every third week in August. The All-Indian rodeo, the parade and the dance around the camp, along with scenes of preparing for the fair and daily life, show a contemporary view of the Crows. Optical printing was done to achieve slow and reverse motions.

ARTISTRY, SPIRIT AND BEAUTY: GREAT BASIN WEAVERS

Country USA   **Year** 1996   **Length** 29 m.   **Genre** DS
Director Creel Snider
Producer Creel Snider, Phil Kowalski
Distributor
Currently unavailable.
Truckee Meadows Community College
7000 Dandini Blvd. - M09
Reno, NV 89512
775 673-7000 [b]

Artistry, Spirit and Beauty: Great Basin Weavers discusses the beauty and utility of Washoe woven baskets. The film focuses on the famous basketweaver of the early part of the century, Datso Lalee. Her influence is still felt by today's generation of basket weavers who sell their handiwork to Nevada's tourists. Though some Washoe still practice the art of basket weaving, the lack of materials make the baskets a cherished craft.

AVENGING WARRIORS

Country Canada   **Year** 1990   **Length** 85 m.   **Genre** FF
Director Robert Bouvier
Producer Robert Bouvier, Andreas Schneider
Distributor
Currently unavailable.

Three modern-day Native Indians embark on a quest through the wilderness to be the first to lay claim to an ancient valuable spring with magical powers.

Aside from having to overcome hazardous natural obstacles, the three are caught in numerous life-threatening confrontations with Northern Hunt, a high-tech exploration company, also in pursuit of the spring for their own greedy exploitations.

In order to meet these challenges, the three Natives adopt the traditional ways of their ancestors.

BACK TO TURTLE ISLAND

Country USA   **Year** 1996   **Length** 25 m.   **Genre** LS
Director Byron McKim
Producer Byron McKim
Distributor
Turtle Island Productions, Inc.
P.O. Box 317, 125A-1030 Denman Street
Vancouver, BC
V6G 2M6 Canada
604 983-9879 [b]
turtle-island-prod@home.com
US $195.00 VHS

Back to Turtle Island is a mythical story of a man coming full circle with
his life: a lost soul's journey to find his personal and spiritual existence.
Back to Turtle Island tells the story of Elijah Brooks (Bryon Chief Moon),
who journeys back through his traumatic past filled with physical abuse,
racial humiliations, criminal activity, and alcohol. At a desperate and desti-
tute level, Elijah realizes his purpose in this world. However, to truly
accomplish his work, he must have a spiritual existence. Elijah must find a
balance through the spiritual healing of the sweat lodge. From this point of
spiritual renewal, Elijah can go forward reaching others.

BACKBONE OF THE WORLD: THE BLACKFEET

Country USA   **Year** 1998   **Length** 57 m.   **Genre** DF
Director George Burdeau
Producer Pamela Roberts
Distributor
Rattlesnake Productions
P.O. Box 266
Bozeman, MT 59771
406 586-1151 [b]
US $99.00 VHS, US $59.00 VHS rental

Set amidst the breathtaking splendor of the northern Rockies is a story of
one man's journey home and his tribe's crucial struggle to heal and forge a
new identity. Weaving together this story with the ancient tribal story of
"Scarface," whose healing journey gave the Blackfeet people their religious traditions, the film makes clear that today the Blackfeet live in two
worlds - modern America and the Blackfeet Nation. Within this odyssey
the tension between traditions and the encroaching Western culture are
examined.

BACKROAD, THE

Country USA   **Year** 2000   **Length** 10 m.   **Genre** LS
Director Ramona Emerson
Producer Kelly Byars
Distributor
Cracken Films
3539 Thaxton Avenue, Southeast
Albuquerque, NM 87106
US $20.00 VHS

This live short subject is based on a true story. Two sisters are sent on an
errand by their Grandmother. On the way to the store, the sisters are told
of a party later that evening, out on the backroad, a place their
Grandmother has warned them about: a place where their Grandfather saw
a *Skinwalker*.

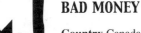

BAD MONEY

Country Canada   **Year** 1999   **Length** 89 m.   **Genre** FF
Director John Hazlett
Producer John Hazlett, James Gottseling
Distributor
Not in distribution.

Bad Money is a comedy that revolves around the humiliating lengths to which people resort just to cope with an unstable financial world. From applying for welfare, to the compromise of personal ideals, to armed robbery, the film follows four characters in their amusingly frantic struggle to hold on to their already tenuous grip on life. The deftly interwoven stories form a cautionary tale of how people deal with the search for quick cash. In desperate times even good people turn to bad money.

Starring Graham Greene, Stephen Spender, and Karen Sillas

BALANCE - HEALING THROUGH HELPING

Country Canada   **Year** 1997   **Length** 44 m.   **Genre** PS
Director Melanie Goodchild
Producer
Distributor
Currently unavailable.

Balance - Healing Through Helping is an upbeat look into the lives of many of our Aboriginal youth in Canada. The young people in this film believe a healthy lifestyle includes a well-balanced combination of physical, spiritual, mental, and emotional elements. They speak frankly about issues that affect their everyday lives such as peer pressure, family values, physical fitness, goals, personal health and other topics. Rather than focus on the negative or on preachy messages, the youth in this video choose to portray the positive and healthy lifestyle choices they have made. *Balance - Healing Through Helping* is a message for today's youth that features a holistic approach to living a healthy lifestyle.

BALLAD OF CROWFOOT, THE

Country Canada   **Year** 1977   **Length** 10 m.   **Genre** DS
Director Willie Dunn
Producer Barrie Howells
Distributor
National Film Board of Canada Library
22-D Hollywood Avenue
Ho-Ho-Kus, NJ 07423
1 800 542-2164 [b] 201 652-1973 [f]
US $99.00 VHS, call for rental information and pricing.
For purchase within Canada visit the NFB website at: www.nfb.ca
1 800 267-7710 toll free within Canada

"There's still the hypocrisy,
There's still the hate.
Was that in the treaties, is that our fate?
We're all unhappy pawns in
the Government's game,
and it's always the Indians
who get the blame....
Crowfoot, Crowfoot, why the tears?
You've been a brave man for many years.
Why the sadness? Why the sorrow?
Maybe there'll be a better tomorrow."

This graphic history of the Canadian West was created by a member of a film crew composed of Canadian Indians who wish to reflect the traditions, attitudes and problems of their people. An impressionistic, haunting, often bitter account of the opening of the Canadian West, presented through still photography and the words and music of Willie Dunn, a Micmac from Montreal.

BAND-AID

Country Canada   **Year** 1999   **Length** 42 m.   **Genre** DS
Director Daniel Prouty
Producer Joe MacDonald, Graydon McCrea
Distributor
National Film Board of Canada Library
22-D Hollywood Avenue
Ho-Ho-Kus, NJ 07423
1 800 542-2164 [b] 201 652-1973 [f]
US $225.00 VHS, call for rental information and prices.
For purchase within Canada visit the NFB website at: www.nfb.ca
1 800 267-7710 toll free within Canada

Audrey Mandamin and Cindy Cameron are making a difference in the rural First Nations community of Wabassemong in northwestern Ontario. And in the process of helping others, they're helping themselves.

Volunteer members of a locally based First Response Team, the two women provide emergency life-saving medical services to people in life and death situations. *Band Aid* affords a look into an Aboriginal community and a program that offers a critical support system that would not exist without the initiative of volunteers. Their efforts are a model for community action in rural areas and illustrate the benefits of shared responsibility.

BEARWALKER (FORMERLY: BACKROADS)

Country Canada   **Year** 2000   **Length** 83 m.   **Genre** FF
Director Shirley Cheechoo
Producer Shirley Cheechoo
Distributor
Currently unavailable.
Shirley Cheechoo
Box 59
West Bay, ON
Canada P0P 1G0

Bearwalker is a compelling contemporary Native American drama about a family dealing with murder and the complex relationships that develop within the reservation community. Writer/director Shirley Cheechoo presents a powerfully authentic portrayal based on the real-life experiences of Native women.

Set on Manitoulin Island, Canada, *Bearwalker* is a poignant journey into the lives of First Nation Canadian women living on the reserve in 1976 and the presence of spiritual phenomena that employs the dark side.

Ella Lee Thompson, the only married sister of four, is a wife and mother oppressed by her abusive husband Eric. She wants out. Ruby is a brash, strong advocate for Ella Lee who takes control and with their other sister, Tammy, seeks to find solutions to the impossibility of the situation Ella Lee is in. Grace, a lawyer who left the reserve seventeen years ago, returns to her home to help. She is the voice of reason - the one sister, who although caught between two worlds, returns to Wabtamook to face her past and the undeniable presence of the dark energy - the greatest villain of all, the Bearwalker.

Bearwalker is a strong story about family love and the courage to take control in a world where justice is truly skin-deep. Starring Renae Morriseau, Sheila Tousey, Greta Cheechoo and Shirley Cheechoo.

BEAUTY OF A WOVEN ROAD

Country USA **Year** 1995 **Length** 8 m. **Genre** DS
Director Shawna Shandin Sunrise
Producer Shawna Shandiin Sunrise & Institute of American Indian Arts
Distributor
Not in distribution - student film
IAIA
Avan Nu Po Road
Santa Fe, NM 87505
505 424-2300 [b]

This self-narrated documentary introduces us to Pearl Sunrise, an educator, artist, and a Navajo woman. In this video, we visually travel with her through past life experiences into the present. Throughout this reflection, she describes the things in her life that gave her the strength to pursue higher education and other goals, while maintaining the importance of family and the balance of creativity through cultural traditions.

BEAUTY OF MY PEOPLE, THE

Country Canada **Year** 1979 **Length** 29 m. **Genre** DS
Director Alan Collins
Producer Alan Collins
Distributor
Alfa Nova Productions
139 Booth Avenue
Toronto, Ontario
M4M 2M5 Canada
416 778-4307 [b] carabas@visinet.ca
Call for disribution information on this film.

Arthur Shilling, the sensitive and talented Ojibway artist, is the subject of this film. His closest friends describe his achievements and personal traumatic experiences. The influences of the seasons on his life and painting are also vividly depicted.

BEFORE THE OWL CALLS MY NAME
ARTIST: TOM JACKSON

Country Canada **Year** 1998 **Length** 4 m. **Genre** MV
Director Grant Harvey
Producer Sue Hutch
Distributor
Not in distribution.

In this music video, the singer describes a journey he is on and his desire to make it back home before "the owl calls his name," a traditional Native reference to death coming. The video depicts many different individuals who, for various reasons, are away from their home base and are also trying to make it back to their loved ones. We see a trucker who is on the road, a stripper who leaves her profession to return to her child, a car repairman who just wants to be with his wife, and street kids making a living washing windows. The "owl" is represented by a Native dancer, always there, always waiting.

BETWEEN TWO WORLDS

Country Canada   **Year** 1991   **Length** 58 m.   **Genre** DF
Director Barry Greenwald
Producer Peter Raymont & Barbara Sears
Distributor
National Film Board of Canada   1 800 267-7710 toll free within Canada
For purchase within Canada visit the NFB website at: www.nfb.ca

White Pine Pictures (US purchase)
822 Richmond Street, W Suite 200
Toronto, Ontario
M6J 1C9 Canada
416 703-5580 [b]   416 703-1619 [f]   www.whitepinepictures.com
US $26.00 VHS

In 1991, Native Canadians were in the headlines demanding recognition for their aboriginal rights. Many of Canada's aboriginal people say they live in a separate world. In the 1950s, Joseph Idlout, a Canadian Inuk (Eskimo), tried to bridge those two worlds. *Between Two Worlds* is his story.

The star of books and films, Idlout was the most famous Inuk of his time. And as the leader of the Inuit hunters pictured for many years on the back of the Canadian two dollar bill, Idlout's fortunes were crystallized in that idealized, out-of-time image. Like Robert Flaherty's "Nanook of the North," Joseph Idlout became a heroic, half-mythic symbol of his people. But instead of finding a hero, the filmmakers have found a victim. As the documentary *Between Two Worlds* makes clear, the reality of Idlout's tragic life symbolizes Canada's colonization of the Arctic and the radical, destructive changes it has wreaked on Inuit society.

BETWEEN TWO WORLDS (PART I &II)

Country Canada   **Year** 1995   **Length** 60 m.   **Genre** PS
Director Sheera and Peter von Puttkamer
Producer Peter von Puttkamer
Distributor
Gryphon Productions Ltd.
P.O. Box 93009, 5331 Headland Drive
West Vancouver, BC
V7W 3C0 Canada
604 921-7627 [b]   604 921-7626 [f]   gryphon@telus.net
US $155.00 VHS, CAD $197.60 VHS

Today, in Canada, many young Native Indian mothers are single, living off the reservation, trying to raise their children in the absence of their communities without support. Many of these mothers grow despondent, thinking they have no one to turn to for help.

These films were created to motivate and inspire young, single Moms into seeking out their extended family and culture as well as urban support programs to assist them in raising their children.

Between Two Worlds (part 1) looks into the lives of two Native women: Theresa, an Okanagan who lives in Vernon, B.C. who has been receiving support from the local Indian Friendship Center, and Rhonda, a Sto:lo Native from Sardis, B.C. who receives assistance from family and friends in raising her child.

Part 2 portrays two other young Native women: Kim, a Nisga'a from Prince Rupert, BC who relies upon the support and love of her mother to get through her everyday life, and Shelly, a Kwakiutl Native from Alert Bay, BC who is a member of a powerful family with a strong sense of their culture.

BEYOND RESERVATION ROAD

Country USA **Year** 1996 **Length** 26 m. **Genre** DS
Director George Burdeau
Producer George Burdeau & Liz Sykes Carp
Distributor
Lucerne Media
37 Ground Pine Road
Morris Plains, NJ 07950
1 800 341-2293 [b] 973 538-0855 [f]
www.lucernemedia.com   LM@lucernemedia.com
US $99.00 VHS educational

Beyond Reservation Road is an inspiring story of how a grassroots effort by a community can make a positive difference in people's lives. Plagued by high unemployment, school dropouts, vandalism and teenage pregnancy, the Cherokee community of Cherry Tree, Oklahoma determined to build a ballfield and provide constructive activities that would give their young people a sense of pride and purpose. How the combined efforts of youth and adults achieved their goal - and even surpassed it - provides a model for communities interested in developing similar projects.

BIG BEAR

Country Canada **Year** 1998 **Length** 183 m. **Genre** FF
Director Gil Cardinal
Producer Claudio Luca, Dorothy Schrieber, Colin Neale, Doug Cuthand
Distributor
Available on Amazon
www.amazon.com
$35.99US DVD

Big Bear is the epic story of visionary leader and Plains Cree Chief, Big Bear (Gordon Tootoosis), told from the point of view of the Cree. The drama begins in 1875 as the Canadian government is expanding westward and staking out new claims. The Cree have always hunted these plains freely. Now the buffalo have all but disappeared, and government officials promise reserves, annuities, and food rations in exchange for control of the plains. Big Bear refuses to acknowledge white ownership of the land or sign away his people's way of life. A spellbinding orator, he tries again and again to speak to the Canadian authorities without success. The law of the land has changed. Now everything is decided on paper, and the government treaties overrule ancestral rights.

Big Bear's band grows, as Cree in search of an alternative to the new system flock to him. In a relentless quest for land, food and justice for his people, Big Bear tries to unite all Indians to speak with one strong voice and fight the treaties with laws, not guns. Soon, however, the Cree warriors lose faith in Big Bear's peaceful tactics. Big Bear's son, Little Bad Man (Lorne Cardinal), and war chief Wandering Spirit (Michael Greyeyes) see armed resistance as the only way to preserve Cree freedom and dignity. As Big Bear holds out, famine rips apart his nation. Finally, he is forced to choose food over freedom. He signs Treaty Six in 1882, and joins the dismal poverty of reserve life.

By 1885, starvation continues to ravage Big Bear's band and resentment is rampant due to wretched living conditions and indifference on the part of the government. Big Bear refuses to be tied to a reserve and vows to renew his challenges to the government. His warriors, through years of hardship, starvation and mistreatment, have been pushed to the breaking point. They revolt, rejecting Big Bear's non-violent leadership once and for all. The violent actions of his warriors undermine Big Bear's long quest for justice. In a final confrontation with government troops, Big Bear surrenders in order to speak to the government on behalf of his people and their future. Instead of being heard, he is sentenced to three years in jail for treason. He falls ill, is released and dies on the reserve in 1888. Today, as the Aboriginal peoples of Canada continue to pursue change and fight the injustices of unfair treaties, Big Bear's struggle lives on.

BITTER EARTH:
CHILD SEXUAL ABUSE IN INDIAN COUNTRY

Country USA   **Year** 1993   **Length** 54 m.   **Genre** IND
Director Charles Dixson, Jane Stubbs
Producer National Indian Justice Center, Joseph Myers
Distributor
National Indian Justice Center
7 Fourth Street, Suite 46
Petaluma, CA 94952
707 762-8113 [b] 707 762-7681 [f]
nijc@aol.com
$49.00US VHS

Bitter Earth is an educational tool for increasing the awareness of sexual abuse in Indian Country among community members and non-Indian service providers. The video can be shown in groups, families or can be viewed privately by individuals. The content of the video may be disturbing to some viewers, as it may trigger memories of abuse. Prior to viewing the video, it will be helpful to inform people of the reactions that they may experience and to identify the local resources available to provide counseling or other assistance. While some may wish to view the video in private, it is important for everyone to know that emotional responses to part of the video are normal for people who have experienced or witnessed abuse.

BLACK INDIANS: AN AMERICAN STORY

Country USA   **Year** 2000   **Length** 60 m.   **Genre** DF
Director Chip Richie
Producer Steven R. Heape and Chip Richie
Distributor
Rich-Heape Films, Inc.
5952 Royal Lane #254-4
Dallas, Texas 75230
214 696-6916 [b] 212 696-6306 [f]
richheape@aol.com
US $24.95 VHS

Black Indians: An American Story brings to light a forgotten part of America's past — the cultural and racial fusion of Native and African Americans. A critical piece of our multi-cultural heritage, this subject is more often than not downplayed in the annals of American History and modern day classrooms. A multitude of themes emerge from interviews with Black Indians from the Narragansetts, Pequots, Seminoles, Cherokees and other tribes. Leading historians deem blood versus culture, de-tribalization, and the importance of personal identity as critical issues in our increasingly multi-cultural world. These issues bring to light the need for a historically accurate and objective examination of this topic.

Narrated by James Earl Jones with music from the Neville Brothers, this presentation explores what brought the two groups together, what drove them apart, and the challenges that they face today. From the Atlantic Seaboard to the Western Plains, family memories and historical highlights reveal the indelible mark of this unique ancestry, and its continuing influence throughout the generations.

BLACK ROBE

Country Canada **Year** 1991 **Length** 105 m. **Genre** FF
Director Bruce Beresford
Producer Robert Lantos, Stephane Reichel, Sue Miliken
Distributor
Available on Amazon
www.amazon.com
US $13.99 VHS, US $21.49 DVD
Also available on www.cdnow.com

The year is 1634 and Father Laforgue (Lothaire Bluteau) has arrived in northern Quebec from France. Ambitious and determined, the idealistic priest sets off on a perilous 1,500-mile journey upriver to reach a remote mission outpost. A fervent believer in the afterlife, Laforgue embarks on a quest to baptize or "save the souls" of the Indians.

Laforgue is unaccustomed to the brutal cold and depravations of his new surroundings and enlists the help of a group of Algonquin Indians who nickname him "Black Robe." He is aided by a young translator named Daniel (Aden Young), who falls in love with Annuka (Sandrine Holt), the beautiful daughter of the Algonquin chief, Chomina (August Schellenberg).

While Daniel easily adopts the ways of the Indians, Laforgue finds himself alienated by their traditional lifestyle and by his own spiritual crisis. He falls victim to the physical harshness of nature, and the emotional turmoil within his mind.

BLESS ME WITH A GOOD LIFE

Country USA **Year** 1994 **Length** 30 m. **Genre** DS
Director Jillian Spitzmiller, Hank Rogerson
Producer Jillian Spitzmiller, Hank Rogerson
Distributor
Philomath Films
454 1/2 N. Spaulding Avenue
Los Angeles, CA 90036
323 655-8490 [b] 323 655-6132 [f]
philomath@earthlink.net
US $35.00 VHS

Bless Me With a Good Life weaves a contemporary portrait of American Indian elders, through the voices of the elders themselves, and through vibrant images of their daily lives. The video reveals the elders' struggle with a legacy of poverty, left in the wake of more than 800 treaties that have been broken by the U.S. Government. Specifically, *Bless Me With a Good Life* focuses on the startling shortfalls of the Older Americans Act, which barely reaches Indian country. The video illustrates that despite the odds, these elders remain optimistic, and are a continual source of invaluable wit and wisdom.

BLOCKADE

Country Canada   **Year** 1994   **Length** 90 m.   **Genre** DF
Director Nettie Wild
Producer Christian Bruyere, Betsy Carson, Don Haig, Barbara Janes, Gary Marcuse, Nettie Wild
Distributor
Canada Wild Productions
1818 Grant Street
Vancouver, BC
V5L 2Y8 Canada
604 251-0770 [t]   604 251-9149 [f]   carson@smartt.com
US $50.00 VHS
National Film Board of Canada   1 800 267-7710 toll free within Canada
For purchase within Canada visit the NFB website at: www.nfb.ca

Blockade takes place in the mountains and valleys of British Columbia, at the heart of the boldest aboriginal land claims case to challenge the white history of Canada. The Gitksan and Wet'suwet'en hereditary chiefs claim that everything within 22,000 square miles, including the trees, is rightfully theirs. A lot of white people don't agree.

The Hobenshields are the sons of white settlers. After 60 years of logging and living in the valley, they figure they are about as native to this part of the country as you can get.

Art Loring is a Gitksan, a wing chief of the Eagle clan. For 17 years he was a logger. Now he's blockading the Hobenshield brother's logging crews from cutting trees on the Eagle Clan's hereditary lands.

Down river, a white couple are building their retirement home on the banks of the Skeena. Thirty members of the Frog Clan confront the family, evicting them from what the Gitksan consider to be their traditional fishing site.

In the final scene of *Blockade,* the Gitksan try to force the goverment to the negotiating table. They cripple the economy of northern British Columbia by blockading the Canadian National Railway, halting all shipments of coal, grain and lumber to the coast.

The environment is the final bargaining chip in this story, as *Blockade* follows Natives and whites fighting for the clearest manifestation of self-determination: control of the land. This hardball, northern style story is dramatically played out in the logging towns and Native villages across Canada, and in boardrooms and stock markets around the world.

BLOOD MEMORY

Country USA   **Year** 1994   **Length** 70 m.   **Genre** FF
Director Deborah Dennison
Producer Deborah Dennison
Distributor
Currently unavailable.

The eastern plains of Colorado saw a maelstrom of horror in November of 1864, when the power of the three great universal evils - greed, hatred, and ignorance was unleashed on an encampment of Cheyenne women, children and elders. The atrocities that followed the attack — the sexual mutilations of women and the torture of children — make the true story of the events at Sand Creek one that is virtually unknown in our popular culture.

A tragic event lost in history? Hardly. Emotions still run so high on the subject of this massacre that the rancher who currently owns the site called the film's director, Deborah Dennison, before shooting began and threatened her. And the racism which motivated these crimes against humanity is alive and well and living all over the United States.

BLOOD RIVER

Country Canada   **Year** 2000   **Length** 23 m.   **Genre** LS
Director Kent Monkman
Producer Gisele Gordon
Distributor
V-Tape
401 Richmond Street West, Suite 452
Toronto, ON
M5V 3A8 Canada
416 351-1317 [b] 416 351-1509 [f]   www.vtape.org
CAD $250.00, US $187.50 VHS educational
CAD $50.00, US $37.50 VHS home use

Feeling at odds with her white suburban environment, Rose, a hip Native law student (Jennifer Podemski), can barely tolerate her well-meaning but clueless adoptive mother, Claire (Tantoo Cardinal). Rose searches for her Native family in order to find something "real."

Through Rose's vivid hallucinatory nightmares, we see a Native youth (later revealed to be her brother) trying to survive on the streets of a big city. As he is pimped, bullied and bashed, Rose experiences his terror and isolation. When she finally stumbles onto the secret behind her brother Clayton, it's hard to bridge the gap behind the harsh reality of his life and her sugar coated existence. Maybe she has been too quick to dismiss what she does have.

Writer/Director Kent Monkman explains, "*Blood River* is a fictional story, but it is based on the true, and sometimes disturbing, stories of Native friends and relatives. The realities that we touch on in *Blood River* are well known in the Native community, hard hitting and at times disturbing to watch."

BLUE: A TLINGIT ODYSSEY

Country USA   **Year** 1991   **Length** 6 m.   **Genre** ANS
Director Robert Ascher
Producer Robert Ascher
Distributor
Canyon Cinema
2325 Third Street, #338
San Francisco, CA 94107
415 626-2255 [b]
films@canyoncinema.com
US $100.00 16mm, US $20.00 16mm rental

Blue is a visual rendering of the Tlingit hero myth. The Tlingit are Native Americans who live in Southeast Alaska. In their version of the myth, the heroes are four brothers who go in search of blue.

The film starts with a necessary preface. The world is dark. Rave, the trickster, releases the sun from its box, the world is illuminated, and the odyssey begins. One of the brothers dies in the storm; the others, with their gift of blue, complete the trip home. During the preface, a voice, speaking in Tlingit, accompanies the images and tells how raven brought daylight to the world. In part one, "The Search," the brothers set out on a sea journey encountering marvelous creatures along the way. Action in the second part "The Find," takes place mostly within a cave where the brothers find blue. Having found and taken something so valuable, the brothers are pursued and a storm develops.

BONDING CIRCLE OF BREAST-FEEDING

Country Canada　　　**Year** 1991　　**Length** 15 m.　　　**Genre** DS
Director Kem Murch
Producer Kem Murch
Distributor
Not in distribution.
Kem Murch Productions
330 Central Avenue
London, ON
Canada　N6B 1X4
519 673-3342 [b]

The Bonding Circle of Breast-Feeding was developed out of the concern for the nutrition of Native infants. As more families have chosen alternate, more "modern" infant feeding methods, there has also been an increase in infant health problems because alternate methods are not affordable or sustainable.

BONNIE LOOKSAWAY'S IRON ART WAGON

Country USA　　　　**Year** 1997　　**Length** 36 m.　　　**Genre** LS
Director Wes Studi
Producer Wes Studi, Bruce King (writer and producer)
Distributor
Contact Bruce King (writer/producer) for information
on VHS pricing at 505 438-7706 [b].

Bonnie Looksaway's Iron Art Wagon tells the story of a beautiful young Native American woman (Valentina Lopez-Firewalks) who takes off from art school on a weekend trip to sell her paintings. For extra credit, she films the adventure, which turns sour when her 1985 Pontiac, the "Iron Art Wagon" of the title, breaks down. After a handsome stranger shows up to help her, things take a turn for the worse as he drives away with Bonnie's possessions. But with the help of two older men, after several plot twists, Bonnie is back on the road with a lesson learned.

In his script, Bruce King, Oneida, has created a story that captures contemporary Indian life and debunks stereotypes. Director Wes Studi came to prominence acting in such box office hits as *Dances With Wolves*, *Last of the Mohicans*, and *Geronimo* and makes his directorial debut with this film.

BORN TO THE WIND

Country USA　　　　**Year** 1981　　**Length** 240 m.　　**Genre** FF
Producer Edgar Sherrick
Distributor
Currently unavailable.

Born to the Wind is a made for television mini-series about the culture, lives and ways of the Plains Indians during the latter half of the 18th century.
Starring A. Maritnez, Will Sampson, Dehl Berti, Emilio Delgado, and Rose Portillo.

BOWL OF BONE - TALE OF THE SYUWE

Country Canada   **Year** 1992   **Length** 118 m.   **Genre** DF
Director Jan-Marie Martell
Producer Jan-Marie Martell (Betsy Carson, Gillian Darling, Barbara Janes, Jack Silberman)
Distributor
Please call the National Film Board of Canada for distribution information:
212 629-8890 [b] within the US
1 800 267-7710 toll free within Canada

Filmed over a period of 15 years, *Bowl of Bone* is a quixotic, celluloid vision quest. The film emerges as an astonishing, moving encounter between two very different women in which nothing happens as expected. Combining magic realism, cinema verite and an evocative score, *Bowl of Bone* follows an expatriate American woman who retreats into British Columbia's spectacular Fraser Canyon to film a documentary about a Salish Native healer. She is disillusioned, naive, and spiritualy restless, encumbered by the Vietnam War, a dead high school sweetheart, and an abortion.

She meets, films, and is haphazardly guided by an unlikely trio: Annie, the elder and herbalist; Arthur, Annie's inscrutable "attache"; and Josephine. Annie, the healer, helps her by becoming ill herself; Auntie Josephine blesses her in absentia; Arthur sends her up a tree, and shows her his modest collection of pocket watches, in a film that challenges conventional narrative in a captivating way.

BOX OF DAYLIGHT, THE

Country USA   **Year** 1991   **Length** 8 m.   **Genre** LS
Director Dave Hunsaker, Lisle Hebert, Janet Fries
Producer Janet Fries, Eric Eckholm
Distributor
Sealaska Heritage Foundation
1 Sealaska Plaza, Suite 201
Juneau, Alaska 99801
907 463-4844 [b] 907 586-9293 [f]
www.shfonline.org
US $12.00 VHS

The film portrays a Tlingit myth in which Raven, the Trickster, transforms himself into a human child and is born the grandson of a wealthy nobleman. This nobleman owns three great treasures — the stars, the moon, and the sun — which he keeps in boxes in his house. One by one, Raven sneaks to the boxes and opens them up, bringing the stars, the moon and daylight to the world for the first time.

BRAVE NEW WORLD

Country Scotland   **Year** 2000   **Length** 49 m.   **Genre** DS
Director Robin Crichton
Producer Robin Crichton
Distributor
Interama
301 West 530 Street, Suite 19
New York, NY 10019
212 977-4830 [b] 212 581-6582 [f]
US $100.00 VHS

This film is the extraordinary rags to riches story of the Meskwakis, a tribe of Eastern Woodland Indians. For over 150 years, they have owned settler's rights to their old hunting grounds and have resisted all attempts by the American government to assimilate them. Filmed over a period of forty years, the film centers on a particular family and tells how the tribe gained control over their own affairs, having now become the largest employers in the state of Iowa.

BREAKING THE ICE

Country USA   **Year** 1991   **Length** 23 m.   **Genre** ANS
Director Jonathan Nordlicht
Producer Jonathan Nordlicht
Distributor
Currently unavailable.

Breaking the Ice is a comical tale in claymation, about a humorous series of events which occurred on the arctic tundra. The film is about the time not very long ago when a strange assortment of world leaders and Yupik Indian people worked together to achieve a common goal. The story begins as a Yupik Indian girl and her grandfather make a startling discovery near the top of the world.

BREATH OF LIFE

Country USA   **Year** 1998   **Length** 27 m.   **Genre** DS
Director John Grabowska
Producer John Grabowska
Distributor
Not in distribution
Can be seen at the Salinas Pueblo Missions National Monument in Mountainaire, NM. Shown at park center to visitors.

On the edge of the East-Central plains of New Mexico, the austere ruins of four mission churches loom above the remains of several pueblos, now buried beneath desert soil after three hundred years. The ruined churches and buried pueblos comprise Salinas Pueblo Missions National Monument where, preserved, are the physical remnants of a turbulent clash of cultures in the 17th century. The Franciscan missionaries simultaneously protected the Indians from exploitative colonial authorities, and imposed Christianity on people who already had their own highly developed culture and theology. The consequence of this well-intended experiment proved to be catastrophic for both groups.

Breath of Life was shot over two years in several locations in northern and central New Mexico. Voices of the Pueblo people and Franciscans are by Sabine Ulibarri and noted poet Simon Ortiz.

BRINGING IT ALL BACK HOME

Country USA   **Year** 1998   **Length** 55 m.   **Genre** DF
Director Chris Eyre
Producer James Luna
Distributor
Not in distribution.

In *Bringing It All Back Home*, filmmaker Chris Eyre (*Smoke Signals*) follows provocative Native performance artist James Luna as he prepares to bring his work back home. Although he has performed his ironic and controversial social commentary all over the country, until now he has not performed for his own community, the La Jolla Indian Reservation in Southern California. "We're our own toughest critics," claims Luna, in this interesting study of a unique artist among Indians.

BROKEN RAINBOW

Country USA   **Year** 1985   **Length** 70 m.   **Genre** DF
Director Maria Florio and Victoria Mudd
Producer Maria Florio and Victoria Mudd
Distributor
Facets Multimedia
www.facets.org
1 800 331-6197 [b] 773-929-5437 [f]
US $24.95 VHS or
Social Studies School Services
purch@socialstudies.com
1 800 421-4246 [b] 310 839-2249 [f]
US $35.00 VHS

Broken Rainbow is about "Relocation." It is about the Navajo Indians of
Arizona, 10,000 of whom are being moved off their land by the Federal
government to make room for energy development. Through interviews
with traditional Navajo and Hopi leaders, and with Navajo who have
already been relocated into tract houses off the reservation, we explore the
tragic and far-reaching effects of this ill-conceived program. The film
speaks for all Native people who are struggling to survive as individuals
with separate cultures in the face of Western technology and "European"
values. It is an appeal from the Earth herself, as it has become impossible,
in America today, to separate environmental issues from Native American
survival.

BROKEN TREATY AT BATTLE MOUNTAIN

Country USA   **Year** 1975   **Length** 60 m.   **Genre** DF
Director Joel L. Freedman
Producer Joel L. Freedman
Distributor
Cinnamon Productions
19 Wild Rose Road
Westport, CT 06880
203 221-0613 [b] 203 227-0840 [f]
www.nativevideos.com Nativevideos@aol.com
US $149.00 VHS institutional use
US $49.00 VHS home use

Broken Treaty at Battle Mountain is the story of the traditional Western
Shoshone Indians of Nevada — those who have sworn to uphold the
ancient ways — as they struggle to keep 24 million acres of Nevada land
originally promised to them by the Federal Goverment.

We experience the "Indian Way of Life" as the Shoshones explain what it
means to them: medicine, herb gathering, dance and prayer. We are with
the people as they confront the government officials who are tearing down
their sacred pinyon trees, allowing deer to be killed for sport, and are
offering the Indians $1.05 an acre for Mother Earth.

For those who think all Indians wear feathers and that treaties haven't been
broken for a hundred years, here is the dramatic story, filmed as it happened, of a broken treaty and a People's resistance in America.

Narrated by Robert Redford.

BROTHERS BEHIND THE WALLS

Country USA   **Year** 1994   **Length** 8 m.   **Genre** DS
Director Spencer E. Ante
Producer Spencer E. Ante
Distributor
Currently unavailable.

Brothers Behind the Walls addresses the difficulties of maintaining a traditional way of life in America, the mistreatment of Native Americans in
California's prisons, and possible solutions through the re-establishment of
ties to the Indian community.

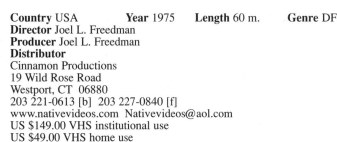

BUFFALO BILL AND THE INDIANS

Country USA   **Year** 1977   **Length** 120 m.   **Genre** FF
Director Robert Altman
Producer Robert Altman, Dino de Laurentiis
Distributor
Available on Amazon
www.amazon.com
US $16.99 VHS & DVD
Also, check local video stores or www.cdnow.com.

Buffalo Bill and the Indians marks the first collaboration between an international producer, Dino de Laurentiis one of the screen's foremost stars, Paul Newman, and one of its most important filmmakers, Robert Altman. Set in the mid 1880s tented camp of Buffalo Bill's Wild West, the film would be heralded by Wild West producer Nate Salsbury as "a historical dramedy of heroic enterprise and inimitable lustre."

Robert Altman and Dino de Laurentiis have made a film about one of the great American folk heroes, which encompasses a variety of textures, attitudes and entertainments. Both a circus and a satire, *Buffalo Bill* debunks and admires the legend of William F. Cody; questions the history and mythology of show business; examines celebrity and power, used and abused; and confronts the relationship between the Indian and White Man.

Buffalo Bill was, in effect, the first American Star, the first hero whose legend was not based on military prowess or political position, but was fabricated upon very little fact and a lot of publicity. Paul Newman brings 20 years of superstar talent to the role, as Buffalo Bill is presented as an Indian scout, buffalo hunter, adventurer, murky philosopher, ladies' man, actor, showman, and a human being trying to live up to his image. As Newman says, "I looked on Buffalo Bill as being the first movie star and went from there." Also featuring Will Sampson.

Original Release Date - 1976.

BUFFALO HUNT, THE

Country USA   **Year** 1986   **Length** 20 m.   **Genre** LS
Director Chet Kincaid
Producer Chet Kincaid
Distributor
Lucerne Media
37 Ground Pine Road
Morris Plains, NJ 07950
1 800 341-2293 [b] 973 538-0855 [f]
www.lucernemedia.com   LM@lucernemedia.com
US $99.00 VHS educational - part of "Ni'bthaska of the Umonhon" series

The Buffalo Hunt follows one family of the Omaha tribe, concentrating on the 12-year old boy, Ni'bthaska, through a summer in their lives during the year 1800. The village has traveled many miles to find the buffalo for the summer hunt. The scouts return with the whereabouts of the herd and the Herald tells the village to prepare. The hunt is successful, but Inshti'thinke, Ni'bthaska's rival, is nearly trampled by a buffalo. Ni'bthaska saves him and although Inshti'thinke tries to take credit for his bravery, eventually the true story comes out and the boys are reconciled. The program ends with a celebration dance at which Ni'bthaska decides to make a flute to woo a beautiful young woman.

BY WORD OF MOUTH

Country USA   **Year** 1999   **Length** 30 m.   **Genre** DS
Director Chris Landry
Producer Chris Landry
Distributor
Chris Landry
5842 Corbin Avenue
Tarzana, CA 91356
818 345-3944 [b]
US $14.95 VHS

For generations in the Indian world, hope, inspiration, comfort and wisdom have primarily been shared via the spoken word, thus allowing the interpretive value of the individual to digest and apply the information in their day to day circumstances. By utilizing the tools of today (electronic media) we hope to share with many that which previously has been kept amongst few, and would like to thank the Great Spirit for the opportunity to do so.

CAMP NY-MU-MAH

Country USA   **Year** 1979   **Length** 19 m.   **Genre** DS
Director Jane Stubbs
Producer Richard Trudell
Distributor
Patricia Trudell Gordon
Indian Youth of America
P.O. Box 2786
Sioux City, Iowa 51106
712 252-3230 [b]   712 252-3712 [f]
US $50.00 VHS

For three consecutive summers, the American Indian Lawyer Training Program, Inc., of Oakland, California, has conducted the Indian Youth Camp, Ny-Muh-Mah, on the Warm Springs Reservation in northeastern Oregon. Ny-Muh-Mah means "we are one people" and so states the camp's purpose: to provide a vehicle for an inter-tribal exchange between Indian youth from the reservation and urban centers, and to provide for the cultural enrichment that Indian young people need to develop their pride and self-esteem. The film, *Camp Ny-Muh-Mah* is a presentation of these children and their camp.

The film was made to aid in the ongoing fundraising process by visually demonstrating the reality and viability of the camp to its sponsors and potential sponsors.

CARVED FROM THE HEART–
A PORTRAIT OF GRIEF, HEALING AND COMMUNITY

Country USA   **Year** 1997   **Length** 30 m.   **Genre** DS
Director Ellen Frankenstein
Producer Ellen Frankenstein, Louise Brady
Distributor
New Day Films
22-D Hollywood Avenue
Ho-Ho-Kus, NJ 07423
888 367-9154 [b] 201 652-1973 [f]
orders@newday.com   www.newday.com
US $250.00 VHS universities, US $99.00 VHS community
US $65.00 VHS rental

A Tsimpsean wood carver loses his son to a cocaine overdose and decides, in his grief, to create a totem pole in his son's honor. He invites the people of Craig, Alaska to help and as the project grows, it brings people of diverse backgrounds together. The people ultimately face the problems of drug abuse and violence and try to help the community heal. *Carved From The Heart* acknowledges intergenerational grief that grows out of rapid changes in lifestyle and interruptions to the passage of tradition and knowledge with Native American communities.

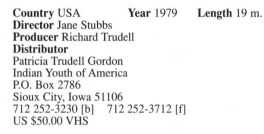

CELEBRATION

Country Canada   **Year** 1995   **Length** 9 m.   **Genre** DS
Director R. Kennedy Tuesday
Producer R. Kennedy Tuesday
Distributor
Video Pool, Inc.
#300 - 100 Authur Street
Winnipeg, Manitoba
R3B 1H3 Canada
204 949-9134 [b] 204 942-1555 [f]
vporders@videopool.org
CAD $65.00 rental - please call for sale prices

Celebration is about the Native Addictions Council of Manitoba's Annual Sobriety Pow-Wow. This particular pow-wow is held to honor and support its clients and others who have an addiction to alcohol or drugs, but are now trying to lead alcohol and drug free lifestyles.

CHANGING THE IMAGE

Country USA   **Year** 1994   **Length** 9 m.   **Genre** DS
Director Dave Wheelock
Producer Dave Wheelock and Institute of American Indian Arts
Distributor
Not in distribution - student film
IAIA
Avan Nu Po Road
Santa Fe, NM 87505
505 424-2300 [b]

This production profiles the Moving Images video field production classes at the Institute of American Indian Arts.

CHARLEY SQUASH GOES TO TOWN

Country USA   **Year** 1975   **Length** 5 m.   **Genre** ANS
Director Duke Redbird
Producer National Film Board of Canada
Distributor
National Film Board of Canada Library
22-D Hollywood Avenue
Ho-Ho-Kus, NJ 07423
1 800 542-2164 [b] 201 652-1973 [f]
US $75.00 VHS [Title code: C0169049]
For purchase within Canada visit the NFB website at www.nfb.ca
1 800 267-7710 toll free within Canada

An animated film based on an Indian comic-strip character created by Duke Redbird, telling the story of a youg Indian who leaves the reserve to make his way in the city. Eventually he returns to the reserve and the ways of his people.

CHETAN, THE INDIAN BOY

Country Germany   **Year** 1980   **Length** 93 m.   **Genre** FF
Director Hark Bohm
Producer Hark Bohm, Natalia Bowakow
Distributor
Hamburger Kino Kompanie
Friedensallee 3
D - 22765 Hamburg
Germany
0049 (0)40-39907129 [b] 0049 (0)40-3903939 [f]
DM 349.00 VHS, DM 250.00 35 &16mm

In this dubbed film from Germany, the well-worn saga of rancher/sheepherder conflict is used as the basis of an unusually portrayed relationship between a young Indian boy and a wandering sheepherder in Montana in the 1860s. The simple script and good acting make this a warmly credible account.

CHILDREN OF WIND RIVER

Country USA   **Year** 1990   **Length** 28 m.   **Genre** DS
Director Victress Hitchcock
Producer Ava Hamilton
Distributor
Chariot Distribution
1274 Lambert Circle
LaFayette, Colorado 80026
303 666-4558 [b] 303 666-5808 [f]
www.chariotdist.com   cdistribution@qwest.net
US $49.00 VHS with guide

Children of Wind River examines the problems facing children and families on the Wind River Reservation in central Wyoming. Narrated by Ava Hamilton, a member of the Arapaho Tribe, the program traces the history of Shoshone and Arapaho family life and shows how the introduction of boarding schools disrupted the continuity in a generation that did not fit in at school or at home. The emphasis on "going the white man's way" is responsible for many of the problems of low self esteem, lack of adult role modeling and a shortage of individual and community resources — problems shared by many Indian families today.

Now, the tribes on the Wind River Reservation are refocusing their efforts and resources on the needs of young children in a concerted attempt to intervene in this self-defeating cycle. One important aspect of the programs they are developing is a reintroduction of Shoshone and Arapaho language and culture through the participation of tribal elders.

CIRCLE MOVING, THE

Country Canada   **Year** 1984   **Length** 28 m.   **Genre** DS
Director Gary Nichol
Producer Gary Nichol
Distributor
Guerilla Films, Inc.
2938 Dundas Street West
P.O. Box 70517
Toronto, Ontario
M6P 4E7 Canada
info@guerillafilms.org
US $20.00 VHS
US $150.00 VHS Educational use

The Circle Moving illustrates the quiet and powerful struggle for cultural survival among Canada's Native People. The film reveals some of the hopes and dreams they have for future generations. It captures the dedication, courage and conviction of some of the men, women and children rebuilding their individual lives, and that of their communities, on a foundation of traditional values. We join them in celebrating the joy shared in every step forward.

CIRCLE OF LIFE

Country USA   **Year** 1990   **Length** 43 m.   **Genre** LS
Director Will Hommeyer
Producer Will Hommeyer
Distributor
Leech Lake Health Division
Route 3, Box 100
Cass Lake, Minnesota 56633
218 335-8260 [b]
US $50.00 VHS

Circle of Life is an American Indian video which explores teenage pregnancy. the film provides a dialogue that draws from the rich oral tradition of the American Indian culture. The topics include men's responsibilities, birth control, the effects of drugs and alcohol, parenting, and birth. The video includes real-life testimonials, interwoven with writer/poet Roberta Hill Whiteman, who tells a story about a porcupine stranger. The program is intended to empower and inform teens while allowing individuals to draw their own conclusions.

CIRCLE OF THE SUN

Country Canada   **Year** 1977   **Length** 30 m.   **Genre** LS
Director Colin Low
Producer Tom Daly
Distributor
National Film Board of Canada Library
22-D Hollywood Avenue
Ho-Ho-Kus, NJ 07423
1 800 542-2164 [b] 201 652-1973 [f]
US $195.00 VHS, call for rental information and prices.
For purchase within Canada visit the NFB website at: www.nfb.ca
1 800 267-7710 toll free within Canada

Like most Native American peoples, the Blood Indians, cousins of the Blackfoot, are losing their cultural heritage. Tribal unity and appreciation for the traditional ways of living are collapsing under the pressure of modern development. People of the Blood tribe today are caught "between two worlds." This beautiful "adventure" film shows how the reserve cannot adequately provide for the needs of the Blood people. They must leave to earn a living, but are compelled to return for the fulfillment of their spiritual needs. The filmmaker employs the oil rig and the Sundance as symbols of the two conflicting worlds between which the Bloods must live, and the tension this creates. The Owl dance, the Prairie Chicken dance, and the loop dance, along with numerous songs, are presented during the progress of this film.

CIRCLE OF VOICES

Country Canada   **Year** 2000   **Length** 45 m.   **Genre** DS
Director Doug Cuthand and Tasha Hubbard
Producer Doug Cuthand
Distributor

V-Tape (for Canada)	416 351-1317 [b]
410 Richmond St. W.	416 351-1509 [f]
Toronto, ON	CAD $200.00 VHS
M5V 3A8 Canada	CAD $100.00 VHS rental

Shenandoah (for US)	707 822-1030 [b]
538 "G" Street	707 822-1035 [f]
Arcata, CA 95512	US $200.00 VHS, US $45.00 VHS rental

Abuse, neglect, poverty, crime, racism are all issues many Canadian First Nations and Metis youth face each day. *Circle of Voices* is a pilot theater project that attempts to look at one of the causes of these issues: the residential school experience. In this documentary, youth from ages 13 to 23 learn to work together to put on a program dealing with their traditional culture.

CIRCLE OF WARRIORS

Country USA   **Year** 1990   **Length** 27 m.   **Genre** DS
Director Phil Lucas
Producer Phil Lucas
Distributor
Shenandoah Film Productions
538 "G" Street
Arcata. CA 95521
707 822-1030 [b] 707 822-1035 [f]
US $150.00 VHS, US $45.00 rental

AIDS is a disease of much concern within the American Indian community. American Indians are statistically one of the smaller minority groups within the United States, yet the rate of HIV and AIDS transmission is high. In this documentary film by Phil Lucas American Indians confront and discuss AIDS and its effects on their community.

CIRCLES

Country Canada   **Year** 1998   **Length** 58 m.   **Genre** DF
Director Shanti Thakur
Producer Don Haig, Mark Zannis
Distributor
National Film Board of Canada Library
22-D Hollywood Avenue
Ho-Ho-Kus, NJ 07423
1 800 542-2164 [b] 201 652-1973 [f]
US $129.00 VHS, call for rental information and prices.
For purchase within Canada visit the NFB webiste at: www.nfb.ca
1 800 267-7710 toll free within Canada

A film about justice and community healing, *Circles* is an inside look at sentencing circles — an alternative approach to justice in the Yukon. This traditional procedure focuses on finding ways to heal an offender, a victim and the community instead of relying solely on punishment. For some, circle sentencing is a way to re-connect with their spiritual traditions and to break away from the cycle of crime, court, and prison. The Yukon is the first jurisdiction in North America to use sentencing circles in partnership with the formal justice system. Some of the ex-offenders and victims portrayed in *Circles* are now helping to set up circle sentencing in American inner cities and suburbs.

CLEARCUT

Country Canada   **Year** 1991   **Length** 98 m.   **Genre** FF
Director Richard Bugajski
Producer Stephen J. Roth, Ian McDougall
Distributor
Available on Amazon
www.amazon.com
US $9.99 VHS
Also check www.cdnow.com

Clearcut, a disturbing and controversial drama of rage and revenge, recounts the harrowing story of Peter, a big-city lawyer who ventures into the unforgiving north to represent Native claims.

At a Native demonstration against logging, Peter comes face to face with the enigmatic and unpredictable Arthur. In contrast to Peter's overt pacifism, Arthur's rage explodes against those who are destroying the environment. After losing a court battle over Native land claims, Arthur kidnaps Peter and Bud Rickets, the local paper mill manager, and takes them on a terrifying journey, where Peter is forced to witness and comply to the unspeakable torture inflicted on Bud.

Based on M. T. Kelly's novel *A Dream Like Mine* (1987 Governor General's Award), *Clearcut* raises the issue of whether the violence lies within Arthur's acts or within the destruction of our natural heritage.

This intense human drama is directed by Richard Bugajski, whose chilling film, *Interrogation,* was a 1990 award-winner at Cannes. It stars Graham Greene, whose performance in *Dances With Wolves* garnered an Oscar nomination for Best Supporting Actor.

COLA UND KANU (COLA & CANOE)

Country Germany   **Year** 1995   **Length** 44 m.   **Genre** DS
Director Ralf Marschallek
Producer Um Welt Film
Distributor
Um Welt Film Production Company
Rosenthaler Strasse 39
10178 Berlin
Germany
49 30 282-4311 [b] 49 30 281-7564 [f]
um.welt.film@t-online.de
US $19.00 VHS

One village, one tribe, one nation. Cape Flattery, the most northwesterly point of the USA, is where the Makah tribe live. They call this place one of the "four corners of the world" and have been living here for more than two thousand years in the midst of an enormously rich and varied natural environment. In the past, they used to hunt whale and seal, but nowadays they fish for salmon and halibut off the rugged Pacific coast. The ocean is still their main source of food and livelihood. As a Makah saying has it, "when the tide comes in, the table is laid." This small Indian tribe now has only 1,200 members, most of whom live in Neah Bay, the last remaining village and port on the Makah Reservation. The Makah were, and continue to be, threatened by the encroachment of Americans and their way of life. Compulsory Christianization and schooling; greed for the many coveted objects of the land, forest, and sea; new, unknown diseases; alcohol; as well as opportunism on their own part have decimated, demoralized and fragmented their people over the last 150 years.

COLD JOURNEY

Country Canada   **Year** 1977   **Length** 75 m.   **Genre** FF
Director Martin Defalco
Producer George Pearson
Distributor
National Film Board of Canada Library
22-D Hollywood Avenue
Ho-Ho-Kus, NJ 07423
1 800 542-2164 [b] 201 652-1973 [f]
US $275.00 VHS, call for rental information and prices
For purchase within Canada visit the NFB website at: www.nfb.ca
1 800 267-7710 toll free within Canada

A tense, gripping account of one young Canadian Indian's attempt to find a place for himself. It tells of the cultural shock of an educational system that teaches him to be a white man, and of his attempts to discover a way of life more meaningful to his Indian culture and ancestry.

The stars of the film are Buckley Petawabano who played the leading role in the CBC television series, *Adventures in Pow-wow Country*; Johnny Yesno, former host of CBC Radio's *Indian Magazine* and star of Walt Disney's *King of the Grizzlies*; and Chief Dan George, Oscar nominee for his role in *Little Big Man*.

Cold Journey is a fictional story, but an engrossing and challenging one, based on experiences of life that are often all too true. The objective of education for Canada's Native people has, until recently, been seen as assimilation. In the schools, they learn a new language and a new way of life. Some Indians make the transition, but others become stranded between the traditional values of the reserve and the competitive, often unfeeling white society.

This film is the tragic story of a young Indian caught in this dilemma. He encounters many defeats, unexpected pitfalls and a sense of disillusionment that is as cruel as the bitter wind that greets him on his cold and lonely journey.

COLLIDING WORLDS

Country USA   **Year** 1980   **Length** 33 m.   **Genre** DS
Director Orie Sherman
Producer Orie Sherman
Distributor
Currently unavailable.

Like a woven basket, the lives of three Mono Indian women, representing three generations, are intertwined to form the content of this film. The focus is on the grandmother's life which represents the symbolic root of a passing generation. Knowledge is passed on to a new generation through her granddaughter.

The film shows the transitional changes that have taken place between the traditional and modern, ways which collide and clash. Change is inevitable. Even though technology changes, values and culture do not easily change.

Colliding Worlds, narrated in the Mono language with English voice-over, documents the lives of Mono People surviving in 1980.

COLVILLE TRIBAL FORESTRY

Country USA   **Year** 1990   **Length** 7 m.   **Genre** IND
Director Jim Desautel
Producer Jim Desautel
Distributor
Not in distribution.
Colville Tribes
P.O. Box 72
Nespelem, WA 99155
509 634-2332 [b]

The 11 bands that comprise the Colville Confederated Tribes developed this video to highlight the tribe's interdisciplinary team concept in managing their natural resources. This progressive management approach has allowed the Colvilles to protect and preserve their precious resources, while making studies toward economic self-sufficiency through tribally-owned and operated enterprises.

COMING TO LIGHT: EDWARD S. CURTIS AND THE NORTH AMERICAN INDIAN

Country USA   **Year** 2000   **Length** 85 m.   **Genre** DF
Director Anne Makepeace
Producer Anne Makepeace Productions and WNET
Distributor
Bullfrog Films
P.O. Box 149
Oley, PA 19547
610 779-8226 [b]   610 370-1978 [f]
www.bullfrogfilms.com   info@bullfrogfilms.com
US $295.00 VHS, US $95.00 VHS rental

Edward S. Curtis (1868-1952) was a driven and charismatic pioneer photographer who set out in 1900 to document traditional Indian life. He rose from obscurity to become the most famous photographer of his time, created an enormous body of work (10,000 recordings, 40,000 photographs) and died poor and forgotten. His work was rediscovered in the 1970s and he is now synonymous with the photography of American Indians.

Coming to Light tells the dramatic story of Curtis' life, the creation of his monumental work, and his changing views of the people he set out to document. The film also gives Indian people a voice in the discussion of Curtis' images. Hopi, Navajo, Blackfeet, Crow, Blood, Piegan, Suquamish, and Kwakiutl people who are descended from Curtis' subjects or who are using the photographs for cultural preservation respond to the pictures, tell stories about the people in the photographs, and discuss the meaning of the images.

Coming to Light presents a complex, dedicated, flawed life, and explores many of the ironies inherent in Curtis' story: the often controversial nature of his romantic images and the value of the photographs to Indian people and to all Americans today.

COMPUTER GRAPHICS AT IAIA

Country USA   **Year** 1994   **Length** 4 m.   **Genre** DS
Director Dana Dupris
Producer Dana Dupris and Institute of American Indian Arts
Distributor
Not in distribution - student film
IAIA
Avan Nu Po Road
Santa Fe, NM 87505
505 424-2300 [b]

This production profiles the Computer Graphics classes at the Institute of American Indian Arts. It focuses on one student who is enrolled in the classes.

CONTRARY WARRIORS: A STORY OF THE CROW TRIBE

Country USA   **Year** 1985   **Length** 60 m.   **Genre** DF
Director Pamela Roberts, Constance Poten
Producer Pamela Roberts
Distributor
Rattlesnake Productions
P.O. Box 266
Bozeman, MT 59771
406 586-1151 [b]
US $99.00 VHS, US $59.00 VHS rental

Contrary Warriors is a contemporary and historical film about the Crow Indians of southeastern Montana. The film turns around two major themes: the struggle to keep Crow lands and the abiding strength of Crow family, clan and culture. Like many Native Americans, the Crows live on an isolated reservation, cut off from the mainstream of American life. What most people, even Montanans, know of the Indians living within their state is limited and full of misconception. *Contrary Warriors* offers a bridge of understanding and communication between two cultures: Indian and White. Focusing on the life and career of 97-year-old Crow Indian leader and statesman, Robert Yellowtail, the film weaves the past through the present. Throughout his life, Yellowtail has battled to hold together the land and its people. Even now, almost a century old, Yellowtail still fights alongside a new generation of Crows for economic recover, racial equality and the preservation of Crow country. Robert Yellowtail's story illuminates the proud and bitter history of the Crow people. The lives of several contemporary Crows also reveal the different ways people have adapted to reservation life today.

COPPERMINE

Country Canada   **Year** 1992   **Length** 56 m.   **Genre** DF
Director Ray Harper
Producer Jerry Krepakevich, Graydon McCrea
Distributor
National Film Board of Canada Library
22-D Hollywood Avenue
Ho-Ho-Kus, NJ 07423
1 800 542-2164 [b] 201 652-1973 [f]
US $195.00 VHS, call for rental information and prices.
For purchase within Canada visit the NFB website at: www.nfb.ca
1 800 267-7710 toll free within Canada

Coppermine is about the consequences of two cultures coming to live together in the same place.

The people who lived around the Coronation Gull and on Victoria Island in Canada's central arctic were called the Copper Inuit. When southern Canadians, Americans and British moved into the area in the early 1900s, they established a settlement at the mouth of the Coppermine River which became known as Coppermine.

For thousands of years every spring and fall, the nomadic Inuit came to this spot to fish. The whites came for many different reasons: mining exploration, the fur trade, law enforcement, scientific research, even adventure. Missionaries came to spread the word of God and to compete for the souls of the Inuit. While their motives may have differed, the whites had one thing in common: they carried with them diseases that were previously unknown to the Inuit and to which they had no resistance.

Whenever a boat came, people would get sick. It was expected. They even had a name for it: ship's illness, the boat cold. But in 1929 a virulent form of tuberculosis arrived with the boat. And this time it was different: those who got sick didn't get better.

CORN IS LIFE

Country USA   **Year** 1983   **Length** 16 m.   **Genre** DS
Director Patricia Barey
Producer Patricia Barey
Distributor
UC Extension Center for Media and Independent Learning
2000 Center Street, Fourth Floor
Berkeley, CA 94704-1223
510 642-0460 [b] 510 643-9271 [f]
cmil@uclink.berkeley.edu
US $47.00 VHS rental (a day)

In the concluding scene of *Corn is Life*, a five year old Hopi child crouches in a field of dry, rustling cornstalks and struggles to pull off a ripened ear of purple corn. Nearby, young Hopis go along the rows, level one stalk after another with a blow from the foot, tear off the ears and heap them into piles. Walking uncertainly among the stalks that still stand, a ninety year old great-grandfather carries a small bundle of corn he has gathered and drops it onto one of the piles. It is the end of a season.

"Life dies," says the Hopi narrator speaking in English, "and life is left behind. The cornstalks die but the seed is left behind... to become another cornstalk, another field, another generation." The moment provides a fitting close to a film that explores the central roles that corn has played in the life of every Hopi, young and old, for centuries: it has been and continues to be an essential food, a holy substance used in every ritual of Hopi complex religious life, and a major symbol of Hopi culture.

COYOTE SPEAKS

Country USA   **Year** 1995   **Length** 18 m.   **Genre** LS
Director Vladan Mijailovic
Producer George Amiotte
Distributor
Heaven Fire Productions, Inc. / Exclusive Pictures
15951 Arminta Street
Van Nuys, CA 91406
818 901-1392 [b] 818 904-9004 [f]
www.ExclusivePictures.com   sales@ExclusivePictures.com
US $19.95 VHS

George Amiotte (Coyote) presents the Lakota legend of creation with an artistic futuristic twist that pierces our hearts and causes us to reconsider our environmental actions and attitudes.

In this video we see that Coyote is rooted deep in the legends of the Redman and has always been present. He is one of the messengers between this world and the world of the unseen. It is said that Coyote is God's dog. According to the legend, Coyote had four ages to teach man these sacred teachings and for man to understand and master the divine mysteries hidden here on earth. Three of these ages have come and gone and now it is the eleventh hour.

We are at a point in time that the Native American legends speak of as a "world out of balance." Man is devouring the earth's resources at an astronomical rate. Man has annihilated seventy percent of the animal species and deforested almost all of the ancient forests on the planet. He has broken every natural and spiritual law given to him. Coyote speaks of these enlightening experiences for the body, mind and spirit. Where are you on the great medicine wheel of life? Who are you? What are you doing here? Perhaps Coyote has a message for you.

CRAZY HORSE RETURNS

Country USA   **Year** 1994   **Length** 4 m.   **Genre** DS
Director Paul Aguilar
Producer Paul Aguilar
Distributor
Currently unavailable.

The warrior and leader Crazy Horse became a symbol for the Indian people because of his fight to preserve the beauty of his people's culture, tradition, and spiritual beliefs. He was asked many times to go to Washington, D. C. to talk to the leaders of the white nations. He did not go, for he knew if he had, they would kill him. In *Crazy Horse Returns*, Crazy Horse comes back in Spirit to tell us what he would have said, had he gone to Washington, D. C. It is a message that will ring out for all time. Written by and starring Stuart "Proud Eagle" Grant.

CRAZY HORSE: SPIRIT BEHIND THE NAME

Country USA   **Year** 2000   **Length** 27 m.   **Genre** DS
Director David R. Anderson and Nick Guroff
Producer David R. Anderson and Nick Guroff
Distributor
Oyate Music Group Productions
4647 NDCBU, 5200 Placitias Road
Taos, NM 87571
505 758-7286 [b] 505 770-4409 [f]
www.oyatemusic.com   oyatemusic@msn.com   tony@oyatemusic.com
US $24.95 VHS

Crazy Horse: Spirit Behind the Name chronicles the court battle currently taking place between the corporate power structure of the Arizona Iced Tea Company and the descendants of Crazy Horse, who currently reside on the Rosebud Reservation in South Dakota. The film approaches the case by giving a historical perspective on the tenets of Lakota Indian culture, cultural imperialism, and alcoholism in the Native community. Relying on this framework the question is raised, "Does a corporation have the right to profit from such a product as Crazy Horse Malt Liquor?" A legalistic and ethical battle is already underway that could determine how Native rights are honored in modern America.

CREE WAY

Country Canada　　　　**Year** 1978　　**Length** 26 m.　　　**Genre** DS
Director Tony Ianzelo
Producer Peter Katadotis, Mark Zannis
Distributor
National Film Board of Canada Library
22-D Hollywood Avenue
Ho-Ho-Kus, NJ　07423
1 800 542-2164 [b]　201 652-1973 [f]
US $175.00 VHS, call for rental information and prices.
For purchase within Canada visit the NFB website at:　www.nfb.ca
1 800 267-7710 toll free within Canada

Concern for the quality of education in Native communities has been growing ever since the National Indian Brotherhood published its working paper "Indian Control of Indian Education" in 1972. The number of educational programs responsive to local needs and Native communities has also been on the increase. Success of the different programs has been measured by the way they reflect the character of the communities in which they are introduced. The Cree Way Project at Rupert House, a small Indian village on Quebec's James Bay coast, provides one such example.

The community has initiated a unique curriculum development project and learning center. The introduction of locally-produced teaching materials into the classroom has modified the entire school system and has made local control of education a reality.

At Cree Way, over 200 books have been designed and printed locally, most of them in eight Cree dialects. Many of the books contain the stories of elders which might otherwise be lost forever as well as accounts of the Cree hunting culture. In this way, the children of Rupert House have a unique opportunity to know the author and publisher of the books they use in school.

Often the community leaders give classroom lessons. Local artifacts are shown and explained. For older residents, this is an opportunity to contribute to the community's well being; for the children, it is an occasion to learn from the experienced.

Another innovation is that the school year at Rupert House has been modified to take into account the hunting seasons. In the spring, the school is closed for several weeks, yet teaching continues within the family, the traditional educational system of the Cree.

CROSSING THE RAINBOW BRIDGE

Country USA　　　　**Year** 2000　　**Length** 28 m.　　　**Genre** DS
Director Kat High
Producer Kat High
Distributor
Oyate
2702 Mathews Street
Berkeley, CA　94702
510 848-6700 [b]　510 848-4815 [f]
www.oyate.org
US $25.00 VHS

In the winter of 1971, Acho'mawi elder Craven Gibson related the story of the ancient connection between the Native people of Northeastern California and the Native Hawaiians to Darryl (Babe) Wilson. This oral history was the springboard for a series of reconnections for several California Indian/Hawaiian families and a two-year internet connection between students at Sherman Indian School in Riverside, California and Anuenue (Rainbow) Hawaiian Language Immersion School in Honolulu, Hawaii.

CROW-MAPUCHE CONNECTION, THE

Country USA   **Year** 1992   **Length** 15 m.   **Genre** DS
Director Arvo Iho
Producer Susan Stewart
Distributor
Currently unavailable.

The Crow-Mapuche Connection is a unique collaboration between Crow artist Susan Stewart and the acclaimed Soviet director Arvo Iho. It is a film about art and international solidarity for Native people. The film features a "Painting performance" wherein artist Stewart shows her "spiritual and real-life connections" with the Mapuche Indians of Argentina.

DANCE ME OUTSIDE

Country Canada   **Year** 1994   **Length** 87 m.   **Genre** FF
Director Bruce McDonald
Producer Brian Dennis & Bruce McDonald
Distributor
Available on Amazon
www.amazon.com
US $13.99 VHS

Director Bruce McDonald has concocted a feisty adaptation of novelist W.P. Kinsella's *Dance Me Outside* - a contemporary look at life on an Indian reserve and its environs. Bolstered by a winning, youthful cast, the film is a droll ensemble piece that makes its serious points skillfully and effortlessly.

Central to the story is Silas Crow (Ryan Rajendra Black), a teen living on a Northern Ontario reserve whose goal is to take a mechanic's course in Toronto with his buddy Frank Fencepost (Adam Beach). Part of his entrance requirement is to write a story about his home, and the film's narrative serves as the basis of that tale.

The incident that focuses the characters is the rape and murder of Little Margaret Wolfchild. The killer, Clarence Gaskill (Hugh Dillon), is a rowdy who hangs out at the Blue Quill pool hall. His conviction for manslaughter, for which he is sentenced to two years, has a powerful impact on individuals and the community as a whole.

The orbiting vignettes tend to be humorous or poignant. When Silas' sister Illianna (Lisa LaCroix) returns home with her Anglo husband, Robert (Kevin Hicks), the ensuing tension is less about cultural differences than their childlessness. When it's revealed that Robert has a low sperm count, a plan is hatched to couple Illianna with an ex-boyfriend (Michael Greyeyes) while the buddies enlist friends to stage a bogus ritual in which Robert will be inducted in the tribe. The latter section is a comic delight, as Robert dons war paint and proclaims himself the spirit of the wolverine.

Without wearing its sentiment on its sleeve, *Dance Me Outside* subtly conveys the nature of Indian-White tension from the Native's perspective. The Indians are neither noble nor savage, but an abused minority with quite understandable and deep-seated resentment toward the colonists.

DANCES WITH WOLVES

Country USA   **Year** 1990   **Length** 180 m.   **Genre** FF
Director Kevin Costner
Producer Jim Wilson and Kevin Costner
Distributor
Dances With Wolves is widely available on VHS and DVD at local video stores (for rental and purchase).

Dances With Wolves opens in the midst of the Civil War in 1863 Tennessee. Union Lieutenant John Dunbar (Kevin Costner), as a reward for an act of supposed heroism, chooses reassignment to the Western frontier only to find that Fort Sedgewick has been abandoned and he is its sole inhabitant. Soon he comes in contact with the Sioux — particularly the Holy Man, Kicking Bird (Graham Greene), and the warrior, Wind in His Hair (Rodney A. Grant) — and gradually, through Dunbar's real acts of bravery and honesty, they begrudgingly develop a mutual respect and admiration. Suspenseful to the end, *Dances with Wolves* reaffirms the Native Americans' abiding reverence for the wilderness and faithfully recaptures their struggles against the onslaught of outsiders. Ultimately Lieutenant Dunbar must make a final irrevocable decision about his own destiny and which way of life he will pursue.

Three years in the making, and filmed on location in South Dakota, the movie captures the untamed West with historical and cultural veracity. Two hundred period costumes were created, over 2500 buffalo stampeded, and Costner as well as all the Native American actors with speaking parts learned Lakota, the Sioux language spoken during the period.

Also starring: Mary McDonnell, Floyd Red Crow Westerman, Tantoo Cardinal, and Jimmy Herman.

DANCING BOY: CELEBRATIONS OF THE SALISH, KISANKA AND PEND O'REILLES

Country USA   **Year** 2000   **Length** 12 m.   **Genre** DS
Director Pat Matt, Jr.
Producer Salish Kootenai College - Media Center
Distributor
Salish Kootentai College - Media Center
P.O. Box 117
Pablo, MT 59855
406 675-4800 ext 283 [b] 406 675-4801 [f]
US $20.00 VHS retail, US $15.00 VHS wholesale

Dancing Boy is a short documentary of two summer Pow Wows on the Flathead Indian Reservation in western Montana. The confederated tribes, now known as the Salish, Kootenai, and Pend d'oreilles, hold two summer Pow Wows on the reservation. These tribes host their own Pow Wows with their own personalities. Two Native reporters and three crewmen embark on the mission of interpreting the modern Pow Wow experience for an audience of all nations and creeds.

DANCING WITH PHOTONS

Country USA   **Year** 1998   **Length** 27 m.   **Genre** DS
Director Beverly Morris
Producer Beverly Morris
Distributor
Lucerne Media
37 Ground Pine Road
Morris Plains, NJ 07950
1 800 341-2293 [b] 973 538-0855 [f]
www.lucernemedia.com   LM@lucernemedia.com
US $99.00 VHS educational

Is it possible for an American Indian to pursue a career in science while maintaining one's cultural identity? Dr. Fred Begay, who holds a Ph.D. in nuclear physics shows how to make this possible. *Dancing With Photons* tells the story of a modern man who also carries on the wisdom of the old. Dr. Begay is a role model and mentor for minority students, especially Native Americans, who are interested in pursuing science and technology careers without losing the connections to their cultures. Dr. Begay's colleagues in science and education, Navajo educators and leaders, and science students from the Navajo Nation tell us why it is as important to develop traditional cultural knowledge as it is to pursue higher education.

DAWN RIDERS

Country USA   **Year** 1978   **Genre** DS
Distributor
Currently unavailable.

From its beginning in ancient petroglyphs to vivid contemporary works, Native American Art is examined in this documentary-style film essay. Early Indian artists, both in prehistoric times and after the dawn of recorded history, often used their art not only as an expression of religious symbolism but as a record of significant events in the life of the tribe. In a profound sense they were dawn riders, timekeepers, carrying forward for unseen generations the memories of their people.

As America moved into modern times, the role of the Indian artist shifted and at the same time began to grow in importance. By the early 20th Century, this development was taking place at a phenomenal rate of speed, and ultimately gave rise to a new art form entirely indigenous to America: Contemporary Indian Painting.

The Dawn Riders explores the fascinating world of Indian Painting today, showing how it is both rooted in the oldest cultural traditions on the continent, and possessed with great vitality as an ongoing creative stream. Dialogues with three internationally recongnized Indian artists- Blackbear Basin, Dick West and Woodrow Crumbo- reflect the intensity and truthfulness of this art movement, as well as the nature of its hopes and potential future directions.

DEAD MAN

Country USA   **Year** 1995   **Length** 120 m.   **Genre** FF
Director Jim Jarmusch
Producer Demetra MacBride
Distributor
Miramax Home Video
Also available on Amazon
www.amazon.com
US $13.99 VHS, US $25.99 DVD

Dead Man is the story of a young man's journey, both physically and spiritually, into a very unfamiliar terrain. William Blade (Johnny Depp) travels to the extreme western frontiers of America sometime in the second half of the nineteenth century. Lost and badly wounded, he encounters a very odd, outcast Native American, named "Nobody," (Gary Farmer) who believes Blake is actully the dead English poet of the same name. The story, with Nobody's help, leads Blake through situations that are in turn comical and violent. Contrary to his nature, circumstances transform Blake into a hunted outlaw, a killer, and a man whose physical existence is slowly slipping away. Thrown into a world that is cruel and chaotic, his eyes are opened to the fragility that defines the realm of the living. It is as though he passes through the surface of a mirror, and emerges into a previously unknown world that exists on the other side.

DEBBY AND SHARON: THE RECOVERY SERIES

Country Canada   **Year** 1989   **Length** 15 m.   **Genre** DS
Director Moira Simpson
Producer John Taylor, Jennifer Torrance
Distributor
National Film Board of Canada Library
22-D Hollywood Avenue
Ho-Ho-Kus, NJ 07423
1 800 542-2164 [b] 201 652-1973 [f]
US $125.00 VHS, call for rental information and prices.
For purchase within Canada visit the NFB website at: www.nfb.ca
1 800 267-7710 toll free within Canada

Like their parents, Debby and Sharon became alcoholics. Also like their parents, they are now recovering alcoholics. The two sisters talk about their battle to shake the addictions that began when they were teenagers, and of their feelings of self-worth now that they are alcohol and drug free. Of special importance to maintaining their sobriety has been a renewed commitment to their Native Indian culture. This is one of a series of films about women recovering from drug and/or alcohol dependency.

DEEP INSIDE CLINT STAR

Country Canada   **Year** 1999   **Length** 89 m.   **Genre** DF
Director Clint Alberta
Producer Silva Basmajian, Louise Lore
Distributor
National Film Board of Canada Library
22-D Hollywood Avenue
Ho-Ho-Kus, NJ 07423
1 800 542-2164 [b] 201 652-1973 [f]
US $295.00 VHS, call for rental information and prices.
For purchase within Canada visit the NFB website at: www.nfb.ca
1 800 267-7710 toll free within Canada

Director Clint Alberta takes us on a hilarious and bittersweet journey into the hearts and minds of some very ordinary and extraordinary young Canadians. Clint, taking on the role of "Clint Star," seeks out his far-flung buddies, young Natives like himself. They talk about sex and life, love and abuse, and 500 years of oppression, with humor, grace and courage. Hugo plays in a punk band. Tawny Maine used to wonder about her Egyptian-Swedish ancestry but now wants to go to university, marry and "live happily ever after." Harvey feels he has yet to live, but he's finally accepted his homosexuality. Michael is fiercely protective of his cultural and sexual identity. Becky seems to have been through it all, but she's ready for a second chance. Gerald left school and is letting life lead him where it may. *Deep Inside Clint Star* explores issues of identity, sexuality and intimacy, while retaining the creative and playful style of a director who is not afraid of turning the camera on himself. This engaging documentary will draw you out of yourself and deep inside Clint Star.

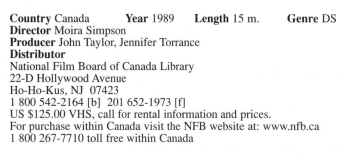

DENE FAMILY

Country Canada   **Year** 1981   **Length** 20 m.   **Genre** DS
Director John & Joan Goldi
Producer John & Joan Goldi
Distributor
Currently unavailable.

The Dene are the northern Athapaskan Indians of the North Western Territories, the Yukon, Northern Alberta, Saskatchewan, Manitoba, and British Columbia.

This film is narrated by Elizabeth, a ten year old Indian girl, who gives us a positive and intimate look at the day-to-day life of her family. The family lives in a small isolated northern community.

We see her Dad at work on a new road, then we visit the school where her Mom teaches Chipewan, the local Native language. Later the whole family works together on the log house that they are building.

The girls teach the youngest to make bannock on the wood stove and to sew with beads. After the chores are done the youngest is rocked to sleep in her hammock while her Mom hums a lullaby.

Then we go with the family into the bush where, among other things, the boys learn to set a net and catch a big trout and the girls learn to prepare duck soup, for this is a family that still depends on the bush for much of their food.

Throughout the film Elizabeth explains that "life has changed for our people," but shows us the many ways that old traditions, skills, and values are still alive.

DENE FAMILY FROM THE EVERYWHERE SPIRIT

Country Canada   **Year** 2000   **Length** 28 m.   **Genre** DS
Director Don Marks
Producer Curtis Johnnie and Don Marks
Distributor
Native Multimedia Productions, Inc.
#36 - 40 Osborne Street
Winnipeg, Manitoba
R3L 1X9 Canada
204 231-1524 [b] 204 231-5555 [f]
Please call for pricing

The Everywhere Spirit is a five part series which presents the history of five of Canada's First Nations. For the first time, this story is told from an Aboriginal perspective by elders in their own language. Each of the First Nations endured hardship because of forced relocation. However, their spirit remains within them wherever they are and that spirit sustains them. The "Dene Family" episode covers the forced relocation of the Dene from Duck Lake to Churchill, Manitoba where, deprived of their traditional way of life, 56 Elders died in the first year and many Dene froze to death or died in boating or train accidents. Forced to live off food from the town garbage dump, many Dene turned to alcohol. Finally, the Elders moved their people back to their traditional caribou hunting grounds.

DENE NATION

Country Canada **Year** 1980 **Length** 30 m. **Genre** DS
Director Rene Fumoleau
Producer Rene Fumoleau
Distributor
Not in distribution.

This film is about the history of Dene people. It shows us how they view themselves, in the past and in the present, through the use of interviews, documents, photographs, drawings and articles. Topics discussed include treaty negotiations, land claims, aboriginal rights, government policies and education.

DETOUR: OR HOW I SPENT MY WEEKEND

Country USA **Year** 1994 **Length** 28 m. **Genre** LS
Director Deron Twohatchet
Producer Deron Twohatchet
Distributor
Third World Newsreel
545 8th Avenue
New York, NY 10018
212 947-9277 [b] 212 594-6417 [f]
twn@twn.org
US $175.00 VHS, US $60.00 VHS rental

The video is documented around and about the lives of two mismatched drifters, Jim and James. The narrative is perpetually challenged, provoked and finally disregarded in favor of a hard-boiled, Hechtian-Brechtian dialogue among subjectivities of the homo/hetero, red/white, personal/political, and textual/meta-textual varieties. The documentary suffers an excess of sincerity during an objective critique of the Exotic American Trickster figure, and collapses into the convention of experimental video. A sudden return to the origins of traditional narrative (oral history) signals the end of the beginning.

DIABETES: LIFETIME SOLUTIONS

Country Canada **Year** 1998 **Length** 30 m. **Genre** PS
Director Peter von Puttkamer
Producer Peter & Sheera von Puttkamer
Distributor
Gryphon Productions Ltd.
P.O. Box 93009, 5331 Headland Drive
West Vancouver, BC
V7W 3C0 Canada
604 921-7627 [b] 604 921-7626 [f] gryphon@telus.net
US $148.00 VHS, CAD $175.20 VHS

This half-hour documentary is about the prevention, care and maintenance of diabetes in First Nations communities. The video looks at the history and present day factors contributing to diabetes, the fastest rising disease among North American Aboriginals. This culturally sensitive video covers not only the basics of diabetes and its causes, but discusses factors unique to Native communities.

DINEH NATION

Country USA   **Year** 1990   **Length** 30 m.   **Genre** DS
Director Russell Richards
Producer Russell Richards
Distributor
Filmakers Library
124 East 40th St.
New York, NY 10016
212 808-4980 [b]   212 808-4983 [f]
www.filmaker.com   info@filmaker.com
US $195.00 VHS, US $55.00 rental

Dineh Nation tells the story of the Dineh people and their "beauty way," which is basic to their feeling for Mother Earth; the expression of this sacred outlook in their arts and crafts; and the blow that has been dealt to their people and their culture by economic development of their land.

DINEH: THE PEOPLE

Country USA   **Year** 1977   **Length** 28 m.   **Genre** DS
Director Stephen Hornick
Producer Jonathan Renis
Distributor
Currently unavailable.

A frighteningly realistic documentary narrated by the Navajo people themselves. The main narrator, Peterson Zah, educated outside the reservation, has now returned as director of the only legal service for all the Native Americans of the Southwest. Through his vision, the film becomes a truly unique Navajo perspective on the industrial political machinery and its attempts to devour this dying civilization. Peterson takes us to his parents' home on the reservation where life has remained unchanged for over a hundred years. We see exactly how his parents satisfy their every need by living on the land, with livestock as the basis of culture and existence.

Having discovered the second largest coal deposit in the U.S. underneath the Navajo-Hopi Reservation, the government and power companies found it necessary to obtain a clear division of the land in order to strip-mine. With total disregard for these people, one of the largest strip mining efforts in America is now in progress on their land. In 1975, Congress passed the Owens Bill. The forced relocation of 5,000 Navajos is impending. This film bears witness to the fact that history is repeating itself, as Native Americans are again facing theft of their land and annihilation of their way of life.

DISCOVER INDIAN AMERICA

Country USA   **Year** 1991   **Length** 12 m.   **Genre** DS
Director Dan Jones and George Burdeau
Producer Dan Jones and George Burdeau
Distributor
Not in distribution.
Dan Jones
2647 S. Barrington Avenue, #7
Los Angeles, CA 90064
310 477-3434

This proposed series is designed as an overview to various aspects of Native American culture. This program deals with two ancient fishing techniques utilized by Plains and Mississippian cultures. The first technique, "to touch the fish," demonstrates a dangerous technique of catching catfish by hand, while the second technique of fishing "stuns" fish using native plants.

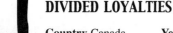

DIVIDED LOYALTIES

Country Canada   **Year** 1990   **Length** 102 m.   **Genre** FF
Director Mario Azzopardi
Producer Gerry Rochon
Distributor
Not in distribution.

Joseph Brant and many of his fellow Iroquois gather at Fort Stanwix, colony of New York, in 1878 to witness the peace treaty with the great Chief Pontiac and to take in one of the most significant land treaties ever made between Indians and whites. Joseph returns home to the Mohawk Valley with a beautiful young Oneida woman, Neggen, who becomes his wife.

White settlers and the Mohawk farm side by side along the river, and Joseph's sister Molly becomes the mistress of Sir William Johnson, the wild Irishman who administers Indian affairs from his great mansion. Crafty and cunning, fanatically loyal to the crown but always honest with the Indians, Johnson is like a father to young Joseph.

Joseph fathers a son but loses his wife to tuberculosis. New tensions are building in the American Colonies and the valley is divided between Loyalists and Patriots. The Mohawk and the other tribes of the Six Nations try to remain neutral, but old alliances draw them toward the crown.

Starring Jack Langedijk, Tantoo Cardinal, Raoul Trujillo, and Dennis Lacroix.

DIVIDED TRAIL, THE

Country USA   **Year** 1979   **Length** 83 m.   **Genre** DF
Director Jerry Aronson
Producer Jerry Aronson
Distributor
Not in distribution.

The Divided Trail, a documentary by filmmaker Jerry Aronson, clearly falls outside the voyeurism of the traditional non-Indian accounts of Indian life. Aronson happened to be present at one of the first Indian activist protests conducted in Chicago by a discontented group of urban Indians and was inspired to begin the film. Instead of immediately transforming his film footage into a symbolic "message" film, Aronson became interested in the continuing growth and experiences of urban Indians and the problems they confront at various stages of their stay in the cities.

Over a period of eight years, Aronson returned again and again to record the experiences, attitudes, beliefs and emotions of three Indians as they moved through the vocational and social alternatives with which activism presented them from the 1960s to the 70s. Aronson was able to show this prolonged time of exploration, choices, and decisions with vivid scenes and memorable footage. These Indians have moved from a century-long inertia into militant concern for their culture and identity and finally into a more mature and reasoned perspective on what it means to be an Indian today. This extended temporal dimension makes *The Divided Trail* unique in the history of documentary films regarding the contemporary Indian experience, since time itself becomes the ultimate narrator of the story.

DO:GE: GAGWE:GO O'JAGWADA' (WE STOOD TOGETHER)

Country USA **Year** 1994 **Length** 31 m. **Genre** DS
Director Allan Jamieson
Producer Allan Jamieson / Seneca Nation and Honor Indian Treaties
Distributor
Seneca Nation Tribal Council Office
1490 Route 438
Irving, NY 14081
716 532-4900 [b]
US $25.00 VHS

This program represents the Seneca People's first effort at documenting their contemporary history on video.

When New York State, in July of 1992, sought to extend its taxation arm into the sovereign territory of the Seneca Nation of Indians, the two reservation communities unified in protest. Citing the *Buffalo Creek Compromise Treaty of 1848*, the plain language of which promised no New York State taxes for any purpose on the Seneca reservations, the Seneca people mobilized and eventually occupied two State highways passing through their lands.

What began as a peaceful picketing process escalated into a confrontation between the Senecas and riot forces of the New York State police.

The six-day protest ended when the New York State Attorney General finally ordered a stay on enforcement of the Attea Decision pending its appeal. Approximately one year later, New York's highest court unanimously overturned the 1992 decision.

DONALD MARSHALL YOUTH CULTURAL CAMP

Country Canada **Year** 1998 **Length** 26 m. **Genre** DS
Director Rod Carleton
Producer Rod Carleton
Distributor
Currently unavailable.

What role does ancestry have in determining the future? In the case of troubled and at-risk youth, it's been proven to have a large role. This documentary looks at the Donald Marshall Youth Cultural Camp, which since 1994 has been assembling groups of troubled Mik'maq youth, young offenders and kids who are heading for trouble and teaching them the ways of their ancestors. The documentary captures the activities of this camp, tells the story of what led Marshall to create the project, and demonstrates how a cultural approach to dealing with young people can make a difference.

DOORS FACING EAST

Country USA **Year** 1994 **Length** 13 m. **Genre** DS
Director Margot Dubin
Producer Margot Dubin
Distributor
Currently unavailable.

Navajo legends tell us the first mud hogan was built for Changing Woman, the principal Navajo deity, by her spouse, the Sun. The hogan was made of wooden beams and wet earth. Changing Woman's hogan was modeled after Huerfano Mountain, a table shaped butte in New Mexico that suggested the form of a hexagonal cribbed-roof hogan.

Over time, hogan-builders have incorporated modern materials into hogan architecture. Plywood, electrical fixtures, plumbing pipes, carpet, even solar panels increase the comfort and efficiency of a hogan without fundamentally altering its structure. Like the legendary first hogan, modern hogans are built with six sides, a smoke hole in the center of the domed roof, and the door facing east, to greet the rising sun. Because of the hogan's intimate link with Navajo deities, ritual songs and prayers accompany its construction.

Doors Facing East documents the construction of a modern-style hogan.

DREAMER

Country USA   **Year** 2000   **Length** 10 m.   **Genre** LS
Director Raymond E. Spiess, Jr.
Producer Raymond E. Spiess, Jr.
Distributor
Apollo Cinema
1160 Alvira Street
Los Angeles, CA 90035
323 939-1122 [b] 323 939-1133 [f]
www.apollocinema.com   carol@apollocinema.com
US $150.00 VHS educational, US $19.99 VHS home video
Also distributed by Shenandoah Films (Arcata, CA)

In 1926, in the desert territory that would eventually become the Western
United States, a Native American (Saginaw Grant) has a prophetic dream
of the alarming future of Mother Earth. Awakened abruptly from this
dream, he asks the Great Spirit about the validity of his visions.
Confirming the reality of his dream, the Great Spirit then performs a
Native American dance symbolizing the strength of the Indian people, the
visions that are yet to come, and the care we must take with our precious
planet.

DRUM MAKING

Country USA/Canada   **Year** 1996   **Length** 29 m.   **Genre** DS
Director Gilles Tasse-La Fountaine
Producer Gilles Tasse-La Fountaine
Distributor
Currently unavailable.

Drum Making provides a step by step explanation on how to make traditional hand drums. The audience is taught by Joe and Judy Charlo from
Yellowknives Dene First Nation in Canada. Mr. Charlo explains which
trees can be used, how to shave the wood into the frame of the drum, and
later shape it into a circle. Mrs. Charlo demonstrates how to prepare the
caribou hide and gives insights into the best time of year to harvest hides
for drums. Finally, Mr. Charlo spreads the prepared hide over the wood
frame and secures it with glue and snew.

DRUM SONG

Country Canada   **Year** 1994   **Length** 52 m.   **Genre** DD
Director Ron Braun, Brian Stethem
Producer Ron Braun, Kippah Productions
Distributor
L.M. Media
115 Torbay Road, Unit #8
Markham, Ontario
L3R 2M9 Canada
909 475-3750 [b] 909 475-3756 [f]
lmmedia@the-wire.com
US $25.00 VHS

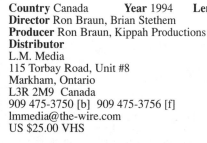

After spending three years in prison, Russell Bear desperately wants his
life to change. He accepts a parole back to the home he left as a young
man in the hope that it might help.

On his return, Russell discovers that his community has also felt the need
to make a change. Not knowing where to begin, the people looked to their
Elders for directions. From that hopeful first step, an alternative justice
approach based upon traditional community healing was developed.

Agreeing to supervise Russell's parole is a big step for the community, and
for Russell. But with the guidance of Leonard, an Elder in the community,
Russell learns that he has the ability to alter the self-destructive course of
his life.

DRUMBEAT FOR MOTHER EARTH

Country USA   **Year** 1999   **Length** 54 m.   **Genre** DF
Director Joseph DiGangi, Amon Giebel
Producer Joseph DiGangi, Amon Giebel, Tom Goldtooth, & Jackie
Warledo
Distributor
Bullfrog Films
P.O. Box 149
Oley, PA 19547
1 800 543-3764 [b] 610 370-1978 [f]
www.bullfrogfilms.com info@bullfrogfilms.com
US $250.00 VHS, US $85.00 VHS rental

Many scientists and tribal people consider persistent toxic chemicals to be
the greatest threat to the long-term survival of Indigenous Peoples.
Drumbeat for Mother Earth explores how these chemicals contaminate the
traditional food web, violate treaty rights and travel long distances. Toxins
are also passed from one generation to the next during pregnancy, causing
cancer, learning disabilities, and other serious health problems.

Indigenous Peoples' connection to Mother Earth places them on a collision
course with these chemicals. Continued survival within a contaminated
environment means making life and death decisions that could alter whole
cultures, diets, ceremonies and future generations.

Currently, the Unted Nations is negotiating a worldwide treaty on a group
of 12 of these chemicals, including PCBs, DDT, and dioxin. The UN
involvement reflects the ability of these chemicals to travel long distances
across international borders. Unfortunately, the official U.S. position does
not support elimination of these compounds. Many tribal people consider
this to be a continuation of the government's genocidal history.

The video features testimony from a variety of Indigenous Nations in the
U.S., Central America, and the Arctic as well as interviews with scientists,
activists and the chemical industry.

DUNCAN CAMPBELL SCOTT:
THE POET AND THE INDIANS

Country Canada   **Year** 1995   **Length** 56 m.   **Genre** DF
Director James Cullingham
Producer Michael Allder & James Cullingham
Distributor
First Run / Icarus Films
32 Court Street, 21st Floor
Brooklyn, NY 11201
718 488-8900 [b] 718 488-8642 [f]
www.frif.com
US $390.00 VHS

Duncan Campbell Scott (1862-1947) is best known as one of Canada's
prominent early literary figures. That he was also a federal civil servant,
who rose through the bureaucracy to become one of the most powerful
heads of the Indian Department, is not well known. From 1913-1932,
Scott was responsible for implementing one of the most repressive and
brutal assimilation program Canada ever levied against First Nations
Peoples. This film explores the apparent contradiction between Scott, the
sensitive and respected poet, and Scott, the insensitive enforcer of
Canada's most tyrannical Indian polices.

EAGLE AND THE RAVEN, THE: PURIFICATION BY BANISHMENT

Country USA   **Year** 1996   **Length** 60 m.   **Genre** DF
Director Vladan Mijailovic
Producer George Amiotte
Distributor
Heaven Fire Productions, Inc. / Exclusive Pictures
15951 Arminta Street
Van Nuys, CA 91406
818 901-1392 [b]   818 904-9004 [f]
www.ExclusivePictures.com   sales@ExclusivePictures.com
US $19.95 VHS

Two teenage boys were sentenced to banishment on two separate islands by a Tlingit tribal court in Klawock, Alaska, for severely beating and robbing a delivery man in Everett, Washington two years ago. The Washington state goverment turned the boys over to the Tlingit tribal court after they spent nearly one year in Snohomish County Jail. *The Eagle and the Raven* tells the story of the first time in history that a criminal case was referred to a tribal court for punishment. The banishment was a precedent setting move that has the potential to alter the way our current judicial and penal systems handle juvenile criminals.

ECHOES OF OUR PAST

Country USA   **Year** 1992   **Length** 24 m.   **Genre** DS
Director Vern Korb
Producer Vern Korb
Distributor
Shenandoah Film Productions
538 "G" Street
Arcata, CA 95521
707 822-1030 [b]   707 822-1035 [f]
Not in distribution.

This film depicts the history of the California Indian from pre-European contact up to the present. Events such as the invasion of Spanish explorers and the building of the missions are recreated using artists' renderings, historic photos, and sound effects.

ECHOES OF THE SISTERS - FIRST NATIONS WOMEN: BREAST CANCER

Country Canada   **Year** 1996   **Length** 24 m.   **Genre** PS
Director Richard Hersley
Producer Renae Morriseau
Distributor
First Nations Breast Cancer Society
Rm. D311, BC Women's Health Center
4500 Oak Street, Box 75
Vancouver, BC
V6M 3N1 Canada
604 875-3677 [b]   604 875-2445 [f]
CAD $75.00 VHS, CAD $6.00 VHS rental

Breast cancer exists and is growing at an alarming rate in our First Nations communities due to a lack of education. Aboriginal women are not getting examined regularly by physicians because they may neither understand the medical procedures nor know how to go about getting an examination. *Echoes of the Sisters- First Nations Women: Breast Cancer* is designed to educate Native Women on breast cancer and treatment through the stories of four women. "It is our hope that education may replace feelings of doubt amongst women and that we may start to save lives for generations to come."

EDUCATION OF LITTLE TREE, THE

Country USA   **Year** 1998   **Length** 117 m.   **Genre** FF
Director Richard Friedenberg
Producer Jake Eberts
Distributor
Paramount Pictures
5555 Melrose Avenue
Hollywood, CA 90038
323 956-1837 [b] 323 862- 0171 [f]
US $9.95 VHS

To grow up is to find your place in the world. For eight year old Little Tree, the task will not be easy. Having suffered the loss of his mother and his father, he goes to live with his grandparents in the backwoods of East Tennessee.

Enveloped by the warmth and wisdom of these two caring souls, he experiences for the first time the awesome beauty and wonder of nature, and the wisdom of the Cherokee Way. *The Education of Little Tree* is a magical story of a young boy growing up and finding the home his heart longed for.

Starring Joseph Ashton, Graham Greene, Tantoo Cardinal and James Cromwell

ERNIE PEPION AND THE ART OF HEALING

Country USA   **Year** 1994   **Length** 28 m.   **Genre** DS
Director Terry Macy
Producer Daniel Hart
Distributor
Native Voices
Padelford 514C - Box 345305
University of Washington
Seattle, WA 98195
206 616-7498 [b] 206 616-3122 [f]
US $39.95 VHS home use, US $99.95 VHS educational use
US $39.95 VHS rental
Teachers study guide available for US $4.00

Ernie Pepion and the Art of Healing is a video portrait of handicapped artist, veteran, and Blackfeet Indian, Ernie Pepion. The video centers upon Ernie's surreal and autobiographical paintings, and portrays the therapeutic healing power of art within Ernie's life.

The film contains interviews with Ernie and friends, photographs, observational video, old 8mm film footage, and computer scanned images of Ernie's 1993 show, "Dream on Wheels."

ESTHER SHEA: THE BEAR STANDS UP

Country USA   **Year** 1998   **Length** 29 m.   **Genre** DS
Director Ward Serrill
Producer Ward Serrill
Distributor
Woody Creek Productions
P.O. Box 31968
Seattle, WA 98103
206 547-2318 [b]
US $24.95 VHS

The Bear Stands Up is a portrait of Tlingit elder Esther Shea of the Tongass Bear Clan, who has dedicated her life to teaching the language, songs, and values of Tlingit traditional life in Southwest Alaska. This short film follows her history, starting at her childhood home. Later, she attended mission school, where she was forced to keep her culture locked inside. Many years later, she set out to rediscover her cultural identity and reawakened traditions long in hibernation.

FACES YET TO COME

Country USA   **Year** 1997   **Length** 10 m.   **Genre** PS
Director David W. Stamps
Producer David W. Stamps
Distributor
Opportunity Productions
2506 N. Jefferson
Enid, OK 73701
1 800 443-3827 [b] 580 242-8273 [f]
vincent@opi2001.com
US $35.00 VHS

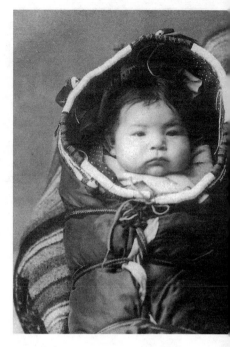

Faces Yet to Come is a ten minute video that informs viewers about Fetal
Alcohol Syndrome. It shows how Native views of spirituality, the earth
and the significance of the Seventh Generation promote the well-being of
future generations. *Faces Yet to Come* presents the view that taking care of
the earth and ourselves are two sides of the same coin, especially regarding
the health of the children yet to come.

FACING THE WIND –
A SONG FOR YELLOW THUNDER CAMP

Country USA   **Year** 1982   **Length** 60 m.   **Genre** DF
Director Chuck Banner, David Hopper
Producer Chuck Banner, David Hopper
Distributor
Currently unavailable.

In June 1980, the United States Supreme Court ruled that the Black Hills
of South Dakota had unjustly been taken from the Lakota (Sioux) Nation.
Facing The Wind documents the establishment of the Yellow Thunder
Camp in the Black Hills, combining today's primary environmental and
human rights issues, as well as touching insights into Lakota life, traditions
and spirituality.

FAMILY OF THE GREAT MYSTERY

Country USA   **Year** 1990   **Length** 28 m.   **Genre** DS
Director Na Bahe Keedinihii
Producer Na Bahe Keedinihii
Distributor
Currently unavailable.

This film recounts the problems surrounding the Hopi and Dineh tribes in
the Joint-Use Area (JUA) in Northern Arizona.

"My intention for this program is to bring to focus a statement by Dineh
people that is always overlooked. This justifies that sovereignty (of the
Dineh) is more ancient than what anthropologists theorize." -Na Bahe
Keedinihii

FARTHER WE RUN, THE CLOSER WE GET, THE

Country USA   **Year** 1979   **Length** 28 m.   **Genre** DS
Producer The Drug Alliance
Distributor
Currently unavailable.

The film is set against the backdrop of the Sound-to-Narrows Run, and follows Cathy, Cecilia and John La Pointe as they train for the race and finally join 4,000 other runners at the starting line.

The runners and their parents talk about why they run, and how running has affected their sense of themselves and their relationships with each other.

The Drug Alliance produced *The Farther We Run, The Closer We Get* in an effort to create an effective prevention tool without an over-powering anti-drug message. Pre-release screenings to adolescents, physicians, court workers and the general community indicate success. The film deals with the quality of life, and the pain and excitement of challenging ourselves. Through the film, running becomes a metaphor for the foot paths and trails of growing up.

FEATHER OF HOPE

Country Canada   **Year** 1992   **Length** 30 m.   **Genre** DS
Director Gil Cardinal
Producer Gil Cardinal
Distributor
Currently unavailable.

Ken Ward was the first Native person in Canada to go public as a carrier of the AIDS-HIV virus. *Feather of Hope* is the deeply-felt, revealing story of Ken's commitment to use his personal tragedy to create healing and awareness among his people.

FEATHERS IN THE SUN

Country USA   **Year** 1982   **Length** 28 m.   **Genre** DS
Director Ray Baldwin Louis
Producer Ray Baldwin Louis
Distributor
Currently unavailable.

Feathers In The Sun is a film about recreation among Navajo people. It takes a look at Navajo youth and what they are doing today.

The film brings into perspective the cultural values of the Navajo people and how they have adapted in modern times to meet the challenges of youth development and goal setting on the Navajo Reservation.

FEDERAL INDIAN LAW

Country USA   **Year** 1980   **Length** 19 m.   **Genre** DS
Director Joel L. Freedman
Producer Joel L. Freedman
Distributor
Not in distribution.

Narrated by Kirke Kickingbird (Kiowa), attorney and founder of the
Institute for the Development of Indian Law, this film traces the develop-
ment of Federal Indian Law through treaties, statutes and court decisions.
By using real life examples, it illustrates the impact that Federal Indian
Law can have on tribal economies and community lifestyles and how law
can be made to work for tribes.

FIRST NATION BLUE

Country Canada   **Year** 1996   **Length** 48 m.   **Genre** DS
Director Daniel Prouty
Producer Kent Martin
Distributor
National Film Board of Canada Library
22-D Hollywood Avenue
Ho-Ho-Kus, NJ 07423
1 800 542-2164 tele 201 652-1973 fax
$150.00US VHS, call for rental information and prices.
For purchase within Canada visit the NFB website at: www.nfb.ca

First Nation Blue takes us behind the bulletproof vest to uncover the
changing attitudes of the Native and non-Native police officers who serve
First Nations communities in Ontario. The film features three officers who
show that instead of being outsiders forcing the people to change, police
are now adapting themselves to address the needs of Native people.
Intercutting actual patrol footage with at-home interviews, this powerful
documentary shows first-hand the intimate relationships the officers have
developed with the people they serve, how they deal with delicate and
potentially violent situations, and what effect their work has on their private lives. In close-knit communities, where officers may find themselves
forced to arrest neighbors and relatives, police work is particularly difficult. That difficulty is compounded for police working among First
Nations people dealing with high rates of suicide, substance abuse and
child neglect while struggling to maintain their cultural integrity. Despite
the depth of the social problems portrayed, *First Nation Blue* remains
hopeful, showing how the First Nations of Canada are shaping their own
destiny.

FIRST NATIONS: BREAST SELF EXAMINATION

Country Canada   **Year** 1998   **Length** 18 m.   **Genre** PS
Director Jacqueline Davis
Producer Tony Wade
Distributor
First Nations Breast Cancer Society
Rm. D311, BC Women's Health Center
4500 Oak Street, Box 75
Vancouver, BC
V6M 3N1 Canada
604 875-3677 [b] 604 875-2445 [f]
CAD $45.00 VHS

The video was made to help Aboriginal women learn how to perform
breast self-examination on themselves. It is also for health professionals
both non-Native and Native, to help teach Native women how to do the
exam, and to show compassion and patience.

The video has an all Native cast made up of breast cancer survivors, all of
whom dealt with the disease successfully, and introduces other knowledge-
able guests. Graphic designs of the different types of breast cancer surgery
are shown to let women know that this can happen to them too if they
don't practice monthly breast self-examinations and have regular mammo-
grams.

The First Nations Breast Cancer Society is dedicated to getting breast cancer education out to Aboriginal women so that they don't have to die need-
lessly due to lack of education.

FISH: A SPECIAL RELATIONSHIP
FROM FIRST NATIONS PORTRAITS SERIES

Country Canada   **Year** 1994   **Length** 6 m.   **Genre** PS
Director Peter von Puttkamer
Producer Peter von Puttkamer
Distributor
Gryphon Productions, Ltd.
P.O. Box 93009 / 5331 Headland Drive
West Vancouver, BC
V7W 3C0 Canada
604 921-7627 [b] 604 921-7626 [f]   gryphon@telus.net
US $148.00 VHS series - US $35.00 VHS single segment
CAD $175.20 VHS series

Fish examines the age-old relationship between the Nuu-cha-nulth people and the fish which swim in their waters off the west coast of Vancouver Island. To the Nuu-chah-nulth, fish are much more than just food; there are stories about fish, songs about fish, and fish masks, not to mention a myriad of uses for every part of the fish. A cultural historian shares with us the things he learned as a youngster from his elders: caring for the salmon roe, respecting the unborn fish yet to come. An elder woman is seen cutting up fish with two generations of her family. She speaks of the importance of passing on fish preparation techniques to her granddaughter.

The purpose of the video is to show the deep connection - culturally, spiritually and physically which Nuu-chah-nulth peoples have with fish.

FISH HAWK

Country USA   **Year** 1980   **Length** 93 m.   **Genre** FF
Director Donald Shebib
Producer Jon Slan
Distributor
Available on Amazon
www.amazon.com
US $7.95 VHS

Fish Hawk, a nature-adventure-drama, is based on the novel *Old Fish Hawk* by Mitchell Jayne. Will Sampson stars as an Osage Indian who regains his identity as an Indian and dignity as a man. As a young boy, Fish Hawk was raised by a white couple in a small community after his own parents were killed by soldiers in a raid. Now in the autumn of his years, he is tired of being regarded as just a "drunken Indian" by the townspeople and longs to return to his homeland to die in peace. Before leaving, he is hired by a farmer to kill a fierce bear and becomes friends with the farmer's young son. Through his friendship with the young boy, he rediscovers his identity as an Indian in seeking to teach the enthusiastic boy everything he can. Fish Hawk finally comes to terms with his own personal integrity and returns to his homeland.

Original Release Date - 1979.

FISHING PEOPLE: THE TULALIP TRIBE

Country USA   **Year** 1980   **Length** 17 m.   **Genre** DS
Director Heather Oakson
Producer Heather Oakson
Distributor
Tulalip Tribes - Communications Department
6729 Totem Beach Road
Marysville, WA 98271-9714
360 651-3332 [b] 360 651-4334 [f]
seeyahtsub@aol.com
Replacement videos available - please call for information.

This film depicts the relations between the U.S. and the Tulalip Tribe in regard to its land, fishing rights and mutual treaties. Despite their strenuous efforts at objectivity and reserve, there is inevitable indignation and anger on the part of the filmmakers. Careful details, an absence of stridency and a comprehensive attitude make this work more powerful, more socially activating than a propaganda film would have been. Clearly, an ongoing struggle is implied in which the viewer is invited to participate.

FIVE O'CLOCK WORLD ARTIST: HAL KETCHUM

Country USA   **Year** 1998   **Length** 3 m.   **Genre** MV
Director Glen DiVencenzo
Producer Sallie DiVincenzo
Distributor
Not available for distribution.

Based on a song by Hal Ketchum, this music video is about a country boy who must leave the ambient atmosphere of his ranch for his eight to five job as a welder on a high rise construction site in the city.

His pickup truck is seen winding through dusty country roads which give way to major freeways that ultimately take him to his job. He stands uninspired before a steel high rise. Reluctantly, he trades his cowboy hat for a hard hat.

Perched high on a steel girder with the city skyline in the background, his welding torch gives off a blinding arc that reflects off of his shield as he pauses for a moment. His thoughts take him away to the world of the Cowboy Palace where his entrance is met by a couple of lady admirers and his girlfriend who becomes a little jealous and irritated at the attention he receives from the ladies.

Knowing she is angry with him, he hopes to make it up to her by asking her to dance. Reluctantly, she accepts. He woos her and by the end of the dance, he wins her back. They embrace, kiss and walk off arm in arm as his daydream ends and he returns to the tedium of his work and the real world.

FOLLOW ME HOME

Country USA   **Year** 1997   **Length** 99 m.   **Genre** FF
Director Peter Bratt
Producer Peter Bratt, Benjamin Bratt, Alan Renshaw, Irene Romero
Distributor
Currently unavailable, for more information contact:
Kifaru Productions
23852 Pacific Coast Hwy. #766
Malibu, CA 90265
1 800 400-8433 [b] 310 457-2688 [f]
www.kifaru.com kifaru1@aol.com

Four young artists (two Chicano, one African American , and one Native American) embark upon a cross country journey with the intent to paint a mural on the walls of the White House. Along the way they meet a mysterious African American woman. Together, the four men and the woman encounter racism, sexism, internal conficts and finally redemption as they discover their common humanity.

Starring Jesse Borrego, Benjamin Bratt, Calvin Levels, Steve Reevis and Alfre Woodard.

FOLLOW THE CHILDREN / ONE BRIGHT DAY
ARTIST: CARLOS REYNOSA

Country USA   **Year** 1997   **Length** 8 m.   **Genre** MV
Director Carlos Reynosa
Producer Carlos Reynosa
Distributor
Shenandoah Film Productions
538 "G" Street
Arcata, CA 95521
707 822-1030 [b] 707 822-1035 [f]
US $125.00 VHS, US $45.00 VHS rental
These music videos can be found in the program
"Life, Love, and Earth."

A music video from singer Carlos Reynosa, who has been called by one critic, the "Cat Stevens of the '90s." "Follow the Children" is a tribute to children everywhere.

FOLLOW YOUR HEART'S DESIRE ARTIST: ULALI

Country USA   **Year** 1995   **Length** 4 m.   **Genre** MV
Director Ramin Ninmi
Producer Rosemary Richmond, Rob Kitson
Distributor
Currently unavailable.
MRA
P.O. Box 8322
Silver Spring, MD 20910
301 589-9654 [b]

Pura Fe, Soni and Jennifer comprise Ulali. These three Native women
acapella singers deliver a mystical and sweeping sound that evolves from
blending a variety of traditional and contemporary indigenous music styles
of the Americas. Internationally recognized and critically acclaimed, Ulali
travels and performs throughout the Americas at cultural festivals, conferences and concert halls in Europe and throughout the world.

The group has performed at the gala opening of the Smithsonian's
National Museum of the American Indian in New York City and at the
United Nation's 4th World Pre-Conference on Women, where they
received an overwhelming response by those in attendance.

FONSECA: IN SEARCH OF COYOTE

Country USA   **Year** 1984   **Length** 30 m.   **Genre** DS
Director Mary Louise King
Producer Mary Louise King
Distributor
Currently unavailable.

Harry Fonseca is a Native American of Portuguese, Hawaiian and
Nisenan-Maidu descent. He was born and raised in Northern California,
majored in fine art at California State University in Sacramento, and now
lives and works in Albuquerque, New Mexico. His favorite theme is
"Coyote," the trickster of Native American legend – which becomes trans-
formed in these paintings and drawings into an anthropomorphic figure.
Recently, "Coyote" has been joined by a female friend, "Rose." Fonseca's
primitive style with modern overtones has become famous coast-to-coast.
The roster of his shows include the C.N. Gorman Museum at the
University of California, Davis; Southwest Museum, Los Angeles; Artist
Embassy Gallery, Santa Fe, New Mexico; and American West Gallery,
Chicago, Illinois. The documentary is a romp through Fonseca's paintings
and drawings with commentary by the artist.

Fonseca: In Search of Coyote was independently produced by Shoshoni
Films for the ten-year retrospective exhibition of the artist's work at the
Wheelwright Museum of the American Indian in Santa Fe.

FOR ANGELA

Country Canada   **Year** 1994   **Length** 21 m.   **Genre** LS
Director Daniel Prouty, Nancy Trites Botkin
Producer Joe MacDonald, Nancy Trites Botkin, Ches Yetman
Distributor
National Film Board of Canada Library
22-D Hollywood Avenue
Ho-Ho-Kus, NJ 07423
1 800 542-2164 [b] 201 652-1973 [f]
US $195.00 VHS, call for rental information and prices.
For purchase within Canada visit the NFB website at: www.nfb.ca
1 800 267-7710 toll free within Canada

A dramatic story of racism and empowerment, inspired by the experience
of Rhonda Gordon and her daughter, Angela. A bus ride changed their
lives in a way no one could have foreseen. When three boys harass
Rhonda and Angela, Rhonda finds the courage and determination to take a
unique and powerful stand against ignorance and prejudice. A great discussion starter on racism and its impact. Teacher's Guide included.

FORGOTTEN WARRIORS

Country Canada   **Year** 1996   **Length** 51 m.   **Genre** DF
Director Loretta Todd
Producer Michael Doxtater, Carol Geddes, Jerry Krepakevich, Graydon McCrea
Distributor
National Film Board of Canada Library
22-D Hollywood Avenue
Ho-Ho-Kus, NJ 07423
1 800 542-2164 [b] 201 652-1973 [f]
US $129.00 VHS, call for rental information and prices.
For purchase within Canada visit the NFB website at: www.nfb.ca
1 800 267-7710 toll free within Canada

Although they could not be conscripted, when World War II was declared, thousands of Canadian Aboriginal men and women enlisted and fought alongside their non-Native countrymen. While they fought for freedom for others, ironically the Aboriginal soldiers were not allowed equality in their own country. As a reward for fighting, the Canadian Soldier Veteran's Settlement Act allowed returning soldiers to buy land at a cheap price. However, many of the Aboriginal soldiers were never offered nor told about the land entitlement. Some returned home to find the government had seized parts of their own reserve land to compensate non-Native war veterans. Whole First Nations communities still mourn the loss of the thousands of acres of prime land they were forced to surrender. With narrator Gordon Tootoosis providing a historical overview, Aboriginal veterans poignantly share their unforgettable war memories and their healing process. We join them as they travel back to Europe to perform a sacred circle for friends left behind, but not forgotten, in foreign grave sites.

FORT GOOD HOPE

Country Canada   **Year** 1978   **Length** 47 m.   **Genre** DS
Director Ron Orieux
Producer John Taylor
Distributor
National Film Board of Canada
1 800 267-7710 toll free within Canada
For purchase within Canada visit the NFB website at: www.nfb.ca
For US distribution information call the NFB at:
212 629-8890 [b]

Shot during the Berger Inquiry into the Mackenzie Valley pipeline, this film presents the Native people's point of view. The majority feel that pipeline development would destroy their ancient hunting grounds and upset the balance of nature, and that Canada's title to the land is far from settled. This film raises important questions about northern development in general.

FOSTER CHILD

Country Canada   **Year** 1987   **Length** 43 m.   **Genre** DS
Director Gil Cardinal
Producer Jerry Krepakevich, Graydon McCrea(exec), Tom Radford(exec)
Distributor
National Film Board of Canada Library
22-D Hollywood Avenue
Ho-Ho-Kus, NJ 07423
1 800 542-2164 [b] 201 652-1973 [f]
US $195.00 VHS, call for rental information and prices.
For purchase within Canada visit the NFB website at: www.nfb.ca
1 800 267-7710 toll free within Canada

At age thirty-five, Gil Cardinal searches for his natural family and an understanding of the circumstances that led to his coming into foster care as an infant. *Foster Child* is a documentary--unstaged and unrehearsed--about the process of that discovery, beginning with his fruitless attempt to see his own file. In his search, Gil encounters frustration and loss, but eventually finds his natural family and a renewed sense of his Métis culture.

FOUR

Country Canada   **Year** 1983   **Length** 30 m.   **Genre** DS
Producer Potlatch Theater and Film Society
Distributor
Currently unavailable.

Four is an exciting multi-media drama presenting over one hundred years of Northwest Coast art in dance, music, mime and art forms. It was narrated by the late Chief Dan George and his son Len George. "Chief Dan George was in great demand from the film studios at this time, but always had time to support young people in developing their talents. In respect to his age, and commitments, we asked him to tape the narrative so he would not have to attend the taxing nightly performances. He was there on opening night and continued attending regular performances strengthening the young members of the cast. We are dedicating this performance to his memory, a fine leader of his people, artistically, spiritually, and an inspiration to all people," says Melrose Moilliet of Potlatch Theater & Film Society.

FOUR CORNERS: A NATIONAL SACRIFICE AREA?

Country USA   **Year** 1983   **Length** 59 m.   **Genre** DF
Director Christopher McLeod
Producer Glenn Switkes, Randy Hayes, Christopher McLeod
Distributor
Bullfrog Films
P.O. Box 149
Oley, PA 19547
1 800 543-3764 [b] 610 370-1978 [f]
www.bullfrogfilms.com   info@bullfrogfilms.com
US $ 29.95 VHS Rental also available

Narrated by Peter Coyote, this film documents cultural and ecological impacts of energy resource development in the American Southwest. It features interviews with governors, energy company officials, ranchers, and Native American leaders, including Thomas Banyaca, spokesperson for the traditional Hopi religious leaders, Peterson Zah, Navajo Chairman, former Chairman Peter McDonald, and others who have had their lives affected by rapid development of the coal and uranium resources in their area.

FOUR DIRECTIONS: A CANOE FOR THE MAKING

Country Canada   **Year** 1995   **Length** 22 m.   **Genre** DS
Director George Bloomfield
Producer Bonita Siegel, Roxana Spicer, Canadian Broadcasting Corp.
Distributor
Canadian Broadcasting Corporation, Non-Broadcast Sales
P.O. Box 500, Station A
Toronto, Ontario
M5W 1E6 Canada
416 205-6384 [b] 416 205-3482 [f]
edsales@toronto.cbc.ca
US $115.00 VHS, US $395.00 VHS (series of 4)

Four Directions is a series of programs about First Nations people made for Canadian television.

A grandfather, Simon Paul, discovers that his granddaughter has been badly beaten by her husband, Norman Loon. Simon Paul tricks Norman Loon into coming with him to a remote Northern Ontario island where they must build a canoe in order to return home. During the month of building and talking and surviving on the island, Norman begins the process of healing himself and his marriage.

FOUR DIRECTIONS: BORDERS

Country Canada   **Year** 1995   **Length** 22 m.   **Genre** LS
Director Gil Cardinal
Producer Duncan Lamb, Canadian Broadcasting Corporation
Distributor
Canadian Broadcasting Corporation, Non-Broadcast Sales
P.O. Box 500, Station A
Toronto, Ontario
M5W 1E6 Canada
416 205-6384 [b] 416 205-3482 [f]
edsales@toronto.cbc.ca
US $115.00 VHS, US $395.00 VHS (series of 4)

Four Directions is a series of programs about First Nations people made for Canadian television.

Olivia lives on a reserve at the base of the Rockies with her young son, Luke. Her daughter has left the reserve to seek her fortune in the United States. Something prevents Olivia from visiting her daughter. Olivia's cousin, Gloria, traps her into going to the States and their interesting journey begins.

When they reach the U.S. Border, Olivia declares her citizenship as Blackfoot. She is cajoled by the gaurds, but refuses to change her declaration, and they are sent back to Canada.

Again she declares her citizenship as Blackfoot at the Canadian border, and again she is refused entry. Back and forth between borders they go, much to Luke's confusion.

Finally, Olivia reveals her reasoning, their predicament comes to a head, and this story of passive resistance and pride comes to an interesting end.

FOUR DIRECTIONS: FLAT MOUNTAIN TAXTALES

Country Canada   **Year** 1995   **Length** 22 m.   **Genre** LS
Director Kit Hood
Producer Duncan Lamb, Canadian Broadcasting Corporation
Distributor
Canadian Broadcasting Corporation, Non-Broadcast Sales
P.O. Box 500, Station A
Toronto, Ontario
M5W 1E6 Canada
416 205-6384 [b] 416 205-3482 [f]
edsales@toronto.cbc.ca
US $115.00 VHS, US $395.00 VHS (series of 4)

Four Directions is a series of programs about First Nations people made for Canadian television.

In the shadow of the Yukon mountains, an older couple, Mary and Henry, live a simple life on a trapline. One day a letter arrives from the tax department in far-off Vancouver.

Mary walks to the nearest pay phone only to discover that their case worker is out to lunch. Even when Mary reaches her the next day, they don't come close to an understanding. Henry does his best to make light of this frustrating situation.

This is a charming tale, which shows all too clearly how systems are separated by more than miles from the people they are supposed to serve.

FOUR DIRECTIONS: THE HERO

Country Canada   **Year** 1995   **Length** 22 m.   **Genre** LS
Director Gary Farmer
Producer Duncan Lamb, Canadian Broadcasting Coroporation
Distributor
Canadian Broadcasting Corporation, Non-Broadcast Sales
P.O. Box 500, Station A
Toronto, Ontario
M5W 1E6 Canada
416 205-6384 [b] 416 205-3482 [f]
edsales@toronto.cbc.ca
US $115.00 VHS, US $395.00 VHS (series of 4)

Four Directions is a series of programs about First Nations people made
for Canadian television.

Two young friends from the reserve come to the the city to seek a new life.
When they arrive, they learn much about themselves and each other.
Charlie gets himself a job, a suit and responsibilities. Frank becomes a
"professional" activist, depending on Charlie for life's necessities.

This arrangement is not without tension. Charlie wishes that Frank would
grow up and learn to pay his share; Frank worries that his friend is becoming "white." He seeks to reacquaint Charlie with his heritage.
Unexpectedly, he gets assistance from the Spirit of a Clanmother.
Ultimately, Charlie learns the importance of his heritage.

FRENCH MAN, NATIVE SON

Country Canada   **Year** 1997   **Length** 27 m.   **Genre** DS
Director Monika Ille
Producer Colette Blanchard, Gilles Peloquin
Distributor
National Film Board of Canada Library
22-D Hollywood Avenue
Ho-Ho-Kus, NJ 07423
1 800 542-2164 [b] 201 652-1973 [f]
US $175.00 VHS, call for rental information and prices.
For purchase within Canada visit the NFB website at: www.nfb.ca
1 800 267-7710 toll free within Canada

When 16-year-old Jean-Luc Battuz met Lonnie and Theresa Selam's family on the Yakima Reservation in Washington State, he immediately felt he
was where he belonged. Over a decade later they would adopt him as their
son, and he would move to British Columbia in order to live near them.
Though he is white and European, Jean-Luc's affinity with the spiritual
values of North American Native cultures drew him into a relationship
with the Selam family. *French Man, Native Son* recounts the unique
exchange between Jean-Luc, now 28, and his adoptive parents. He will
always retain his original heritage, even while actively participating in the
life, responsibilities, and traditions of the family who have welcomed him
into their lives.

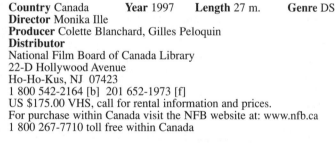

FRITZ SCHOLDER: A FILM PROFILE

Country USA   **Year** 1979   **Length** 28 m.   **Genre** DS
Distributor
Facets Multi-Media, Inc.
1517 W. Fullerton Avenue
Chicago, IL 60614
773 281-9075 [b] 773 929-5437 [f]
www.facets.org   sales@facets.org
US $39.95 VHS

Fritz Scholder, a California Mission Indian, is an artist who creates paintings and prints that depict today's American Indian, caught between modern society and traditional life.

Scholder was born in Breckenridge, Minnesota in 1937. He traces his Native ancestry back to his great grandmother, a Cupeño, who married his German born great grandfather. Their son, also a Fritz, married a Luiseño from Southern California.

Scholder studied Art at California State, Sacramento earning a BA. He has taught at the University of Arizona in Tucson and at the Institute of American Indian Art. He has been the recipient of such awards as the Ford Foundation Purchase, 1962 and the Grand Prize at the Scottsdale Indian National, 1969.

FROG MONSTER, THE

Country USA   **Year** 1994   **Length** 10 m.   **Genre** ANS
Director Joshua M. Vermette, Indian Island School students
Producer Michael E. Vermette
Distributor
Indian Island School
1 River Road, Penobscot Reservation
Old Town, ME 04468
207 827-4285 [b] 207 827-3599 [f]
US $29.95 VHS for "The Frog Monster and Other Penobscot Stories" (20 min).

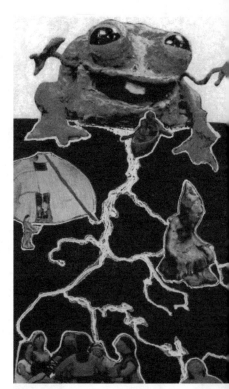

The Frog Monster is a video which utilizes the latest innovations in student animation at The Indian Island School. It combines paper cut-outs with clay animation and involves more than ten different set combinations used for backgrounds. The video starts out with the school theme song, which was written by Wabanaki musician and storyteller John "Bear" Mitchell, for this production.

The story was retold by John and translated into video by the Indian Island School's Fifth, Sixth, Seventh and Eighth graders. This Penobscot legend describes how the Penobscot River came to be, as well as the origin of the Penobscot Water Clans. The video contains Native people, a pure man, a variety of animals, and the Penobscot legendary hero Koluscap, who battles with the huge Frog Monster who insists on keeping all the water for himself.

This animation was made for a general audience and grades K-12, and holds a powerful moral message on respecting our waterways and the Water Clans within them. This animation was also a winner of the Maine Student Film and Video Festival in 1994.

FROM FOUR DIRECTIONS: A CALL TO CONSCIOUSNESS

Country USA   **Year** 1992   **Length** 52 m.   **Genre** DF
Director Mark Halfmoon
Producer Mark Halfmoon
Distributor
Mark Halfmoon
P.O. Box 2693
Santa Cruz, CA 95063
831-457-9754 ext.1788 [b]
US $19.99 VHS

Dineh elders at Big Mountain in northeastern Arizona tell their story of
forced relocation by the U.S. government. Responding to a letter from the
Dineh, a group of Vietnam veterans organize a nation-wide convoy to support the elders in their resistance to relocation.

FROM THE ROOTS:
CALIFORNIA INDIAN BASKETWEAVERS

Country USA   **Year** 1997   **Length** 28 m.   **Genre** DS
Director Sara Greensfelder
Producer Sara Greensfelder
Distributor
California Indian Basketweavers Association
P.O. Box 2397
Nevada City, CA 95959
530 478-5660 [b]   530 478-5662 [f]
ciba@ciba.org   www.ciba.org
US $20.00 VHS home video
For educational purchase call UC Extension: 510 642-0460 [b]

Basketweaving was once an integral part of daily life among California's
many tribes. It also provided a vehicle for artistic and technical excellence
in the hands of the finest weavers. The destruction of Native life during the
post-contact years nearly led to the demise of weaving traditions. Today,
new generations of weavers are working to preserve and continue the
ancient knowledge required of their art. In *From the Roots*, California
Indian basketweavers speak eloquently of their traditions, techniques and
plants, as well as the challenges facing them today. These include restrict-
ed access to plant gathering, as well as the use of hazardous pesticides in
areas where plants are gathered.

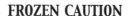

FROZEN CAUTION

Country Canada   **Year** 1988   **Length** 12 m.   **Genre** DS
Director Elizabeth C. Moes
Producer Elizabeth C. Moes
Distributor
Currently unavailable.

This is the story, told in the first person, of the Temagami Natives, who
have been fighting for recognition of their aboriginal rights for over 100
years. Their story is typical of the colonial usurpation of aboriginal history
and rights around the world. Although the Temagami Band never surren-
dered their land in treaty, the Province of Ontario went ahead and sold land
to mining, lumber, tourist and hydro companies. Their case is headed for
the Supreme Court of Canada and an important precedent for Native land
claims across the country will be set as a result of that ruling.

Produced in cooperation with the "Teme-Augama Anishnabai," this film
describes the history of aboriginal rights to land in Canada, the history of
their plight, their current court case and their vision of self-government
and land control.

FRY BREAD - JUST SAY NO

Country USA   **Year** 1994   **Length** 9 m.   **Genre** DS
Director Pam Belgarde
Producer Pam Belgarde
Distributor
Please contact Pam Belgarde at:
pam@wellnative.com   www.wellnative.com
Price upon request.

This video focuses on a young man who maintains a healthy lifestyle and his feelings about fry bread.

GABRIEL WOMEN: PASSAMAQUODDY BASKETMAKERS

Country USA   **Year** 1999   **Length** 28 m.   **Genre** DS
Director Michael Sacca & Robert Atkinson
Producer Robert Atkinson
Distributor
Center for the Study of Lives, University of So. Maine
400 Bailey Hall
Gorham, ME 04038
207 780-5078 [b] 207 780-5043 [f]
atkinson@usm.maine.edu
US $20.00 VHS

One of the most accomplished and giving basketmakers of the Waponahki peoples, Mary Gabriel was born in the Passamaquoddy Indian Township of Princeton, Maine in 1908. She was honored as a National Heritage Fellow in 1994. Here she tells her inspiring story of learning the centuries-old tradition from her grandmother, and of passing it on to her two daughters, Sylvia and Clare, who are also master basketmakers. Adding a broader perspective to their story are Theresa Hoffman, executive director of the Maine Indian Basketmaker Alliance; Joseph Nicholas, curator of the Waponahki Museum in Pleasant Point, Maine; and Kathleen Mundell, traditional and community arts associate of the Maine Arts Commission.

GERONIMO: AN AMERICAN LEGEND

Country USA   **Year** 1993   **Length** 110 m.   **Genre** FF
Director Walter Hill
Producer Neil Canton, Walter Hill, Michael S. Glick (exec.)
Distributor
Columbia TriStar
10202 W. Washington Blvd.
Culver City, CA 90232
310 244-4000 [b]
Also available at local video and rental stores and on www.amazon.com

An American legend comes to breathtaking life in this explosive epic western starring Jason Patrick, Robert Duvall, Gene Hackman, Matt Damon, and Wes Studi as Geronimo.

Studi gives a stunning performance as the fearless warrior who was the last Indian leader to surrender to the white man. Betrayed by the Army's legendary "Indian fighter" General George Crook (Hackman), Geronimo leads a small band of warriors in escape. Pursued by a principled officer (Patric), a grizzled army scout (Duvall), and a gung-ho West Point graduate (Damon), Geronimo evades capture through brilliant military strategy and cutthroat courage. His true stroy is both an action adventure and a spiritual journey through the heart of a warrior.

GERONIMO JONES

Country USA   **Year** 1975   **Length** 21 m.   **Genre** DS
Distributor
Phoenix Learning Group
2349 Chaffee Dr.
St. Louis, MO 63146
314 569-0211 [b]   314 569-2834 [f]
www.phoenixcoronet.com
phoenixfilm@worldnet.att.net
US $75.95 VHS

Geronimo Jones is a young Indian boy living on a Papago Reservation in Arizona and searching for his own identity in American society. His grandfather, a descendant of the great Apache chief Geronimo tells the boy stories of the Indians' past greatness and one morning hands him down a treasured Apache medallion. Visiting town after school, Geronimo is persuaded by a storeowner to trade his medallion for a television set for his grandfather. When the set is turned on to a western, rifle shots fill the air, and Geronimo and his grandfather watch Indians, as "the enemy," being mowed down in the name of civilization. The grandfather looks away in grief, and Geronimo wanders outside, shaken and bewildered. Now without his medallion, uncertain of his heritage and his future, he still is eager for life and goes off to look at the moon with his cousin.

GHOST DANCE

Country USA   **Year** 1991   **Length** 9 m.   **Genre** DS
Director Tim Scwab, Christina Craton
Producer Tim Scwab, Christina Craton
Distributor
New Day Films
22-D Hollywood Avenue
Ho-Ho-Kus, NJ 07423
888 367-9154 [b] 201 652-1973 [f]
www.newday.com   orders@newday.com
US $99.00 VHS, US $45.00 VHS rental

Ghost Dance is a poetic film on the meaning and consequences of the Wounded Knee Massacre. The film uses poetry and paintings inspired by the massacre and its aftermath to convey despair, and offer insight and hope. *Ghost Dance* was filmed on location at the site of Wounded Knee on the Pine Ridge Indian Reservation, and at Cuny Table, a high plateau of prairie rising above the Badlands, where the largest Ghost Dance ceremonies in the area took place.

After providing a historical overview, the narrators describe the serenity of the Native Americans as they performed their religious dance in the face of oncoming white attackers. Confident that their ceremony would bring back their old life, they clung to the hope that they would live again, despite the onslaught of bullets. Evoking the poignant stories of some of those who fell, this sensitively constructed short suggests that the South Dakota landscape echoes with the names of those who died in 1890.

GIFT OF CHOICE - YOU CHOOSE

Country USA   **Year** 1992   **Length** 18 m.   **Genre** PS
Director Vern Korb
Producer Larry Murillo
Distributor
Shenandoah Film Productions
538 "G" Street
Arcata, CA 95521
707 822-1030 [b] 707 822-1035 [f]
A 29min. version of this film is available at US $200.00 VHS
US $45.00 VHS rental
Under the title - You Choose Tobacco, A Gift of Choice

This presentation centers around tobacco use and abuse, and is designed to discourage youth from smoking and chewing tobacco. The film carries a theme of respect and love for oneself, the earth, and other people regarding the use of tobacco.

GIFT OF THE GRANDFATHERS, THE

Country USA   **Year** 1997   **Length** 44 m.   **Genre** DS
Director Doug Cuthand
Producer Jerry Krepakevich, Graydon McCrea, Jerry McIntosh, June Morgan
Distributor
National Film Board of Canada   1 800 267-7710 toll free within Canada
For purchase within Canada visit the NFB website at: www.nfb.ca

For US purchase contact:
Shenandoah Films
538 "G" Street
Arcata, CA 95521
707 822-1030 [b] 707 822-1035 [f]
Please call for pricing.

The Aboriginal peoples who travelled the Great Plains by horseback some three centuries ago were Canada's first cowboys. Today, horsemanship remains a vibrant part of Western First Nations culture; it is one of the gifts of the grandfathers. Tracing the colorful history of North American Indian cowboys and rodeos through to the present day, *The Gift of the Grandfathers* trails along with Sandra Crowchild and Richard Bish, Indians from the Tsuu T'ina Nation in Southern Alberta who were born to the rodeo life. Travelling to the four corners of the Great Plains, the video charts their progress as they make their way to the all-important Indian National Finals Rodeo in Saskatchewan, held in Canada for the first time in 20 years. Saddle up for a ride on the First Nations rodeo circuit--the source of a strong sense of history and pride, as well as heaping helpings of plain, old-fashioned good times.

GIFT, THE

Country Canada   **Year** 1998   **Length** 49 m.   **Genre** DS
Director Gary Farmer
Producer Jerry Krepakevich
Distributor
National Film Board of Canada Library
22-D Hollywood Avenue
Ho-ho-kus, NJ 07423
1 800 542-2164 [b] 201 652-1973 [f]
US $129.00 VHS, call for rental information and prices.
For purchase within Canada visit the NFB website at: www.nfb.ca
1 800 267-7710 toll free within Canada

Ever since it was first nurtured from a grass by the Maya, corn has held a sacred place in the lives of Indigenous peoples in the Americas. Before colonization, corn was widely used as a beverage, a food staple, an oil and a ceremonial object. It was respected and revered as a critical part of creation. *The Gift* explores the powerful bond and spiritual relationship that continues to exist between people and corn. The video begins in North America on the traditional lands of the Six Nations Confederacy (in southern Ontario and northern New York state) where we witness the planting of the corn and all the work and humor that accompany the community harvest. Next we travel to southern Mexico, from San Cristobal to the lowlands of the rain forests, for the green corn and seed corn harvests. Mayan culture is inconceivable without corn--and NAFTA's threat to the Maya's right to grow maize became a central issue in the Zapatista uprisings. Through interviews, dance and song, *The Gift* is a beautiful exploration of the intertwined lives of people and corn, capturing the traditional, spiritual, economic and political importance of this sacred plant.

GIFT TO ONE, A GIFT TO MANY –
JAMES JACKSON SR., OJIBWE MEDICINE MAN

Country USA   **Year** 1993   **Length** 58 m.   **Genre** DF
Director Phillip Norrgard, Lorraine Slabbaert-Norrgard
Producer Lorraine Slabbaert-Norrgard
Distributor
Fond du Lac Human Services Division
927 Trettel Lane
Cloquet, MN 5572
lnorrgard@hotmail.com
218 879-1227 [b]   218 879-8378 [f]
US $20.00 VHS, home use
US $85.00 VHS, institutional use

This film explores the life and work of Ojibwe Medicine Man, James Jackson Sr., who practiced in Minnesota, Wisconsin and Michigan and was known throughout the midwest and Canada for his vast knowledge of Ojibwe culture and his gift as a healer. This program provides a rare and intimate view of the role and life of an Ojibwe medicine man in today's society.

Mr. Jackson requested that this program be made so that all people could learn more about the Ojibwe people. He speaks candidly and insightfully about his life and his work. During the final weeks of this life, Mr. Jackson appealed to Indian people to learn their language, use tobacco, and get an Indian name. In its final scenes, the program captures testimonials at Mr. Jackson's funeral.

GOING BACK TO THE BLANKET

Country Canada   **Year** 1990   **Length** 28 m.   **Genre** DS
Director Michael Doxtater
Producer Michael Doxtater
Distributor
Currently unavailable.

During the 1800s and 1900s, hundreds of church run, government controlled residential schools were set up on reserves across Canada and the United States. Their purpose was to "Christianize" the Native "Heathens" and to educate them in the ways of the white man. The methods used to obtain this end were often cruel and un-Christian — resulting in a chilling cultural schizophrenia.

Going Back to the Blanket is a contemporary half hour documentary about the Canadian Native residential school experience. Through personal stories and interviews, *Going Back to the Blanket* explores the ongoing struggle within the Native community to re-unite a culture torn apart by these white Christian educational institutions. The negative impact of residential schools reverberates through many generations.

GOLDEN SEAL, THE

Country USA   **Year** 1983   **Length** 94 m.   **Genre** FF
Director Frank Zuniga
Producer Samuel Goldwyn
Distributor
Available on Amazon.com
www.amazon.com
US $9.94 VHS

One stormy night, on the island of Unak in the far-off Aleutian Islands, a boy named Eric came face-to-face with a golden seal. He had heard about this rare creature for the first time that very day. A wise old man said the seal used to live among the Aleut people as a benevolent, protective spirit, but when man began to hunt her, she vanished. According to legend, she will come back one day, to someone pure in heart, in the middle of a ferocious storm, like the one which sent Eric stumbling into the shelter where lay the shimmering seal.

This privileged moment in the film *The Golden Seal* begins a modern parable of love, greed and violence in a part of the world most people have never glimpsed, even in a photograph — the Aleutian Islands. As the story unfolds, a child's innocence is placed in direct conflict with the failed dreams, pride and ordinary greed of adults, most significantly his own father. By its conclusion, everyone has changed, including the boy, and the mythical seal has returned to her natural place in the depths of the ocean. A lesson has been learned, balance restored.

GOOD MEDICINE

Country USA   **Year** 1995   **Length** 21 m.   **Genre** DS
Director Tamsin Orion Seidler
Producer Tamsin Orion Seidler
Distributor
Shenandoah Film Productions
538 "G" Street
Arcata, CA 95521
707 822-1030 [b] 707 822-1035 [f]
US $200.00 VHS, US $45.00 rental

The American Indian's holistic approach to healing is the subject of *Good Medicine*, a documentary film that examines the perceptual differences between modern western medicine and the centuries-old healing art of the Native American.

Filmed on location in South Dakota and Arizona, *Good Medicine* sensitively explores the design and effect of highly complex Indian healing ceremonies never before recorded on film.

Good Medicine's "Indianess" is affirmed by its narrator and host, John Belindo, the former executive director of the National Congress of American Native Indians. A full-blooded Native American — half Kiowa, half Navajo — Belindo defines the fundamental difference between the two perceptions of healing: "To the white man," Belindo explains, "the symptom — be it a cold or a tumor — is the disease; to the Indian, the symptom is a sign of a deeper, spiritual disturbance."

As the documentary reveals, these "disturbances" are identified and treated by traditional Indian medicine men in amazingly intricate ceremonies rarely observed by non-Indians and never captured on film - until now.

GOOD MEDICINE

Country USA   **Year** 1981   **Length** 48 m.   **Genre** DS
Director Christopher Gaul
Producer Christopher Gaul
Distributor
Currently unavailable.

Good Medicine looks at traditional and Western medicine on the Navajo reservation. It explores how these very different health care systems interact in the modern world. Where they interact and where they diverge are crucial questions for the Navajo health workers featured, who choose to use both approaches in their caregiving.

GRAND AVENUE

Country USA   **Year** 1996   **Length** 165 m.   **Genre** FF
Director Dan Sackheim
Producer Tony To
Distributor
Available on Amazon.com
www.amazon.com
US $17.98 VHS

Grand Avenue, the HBO mini-series written by Greg Sarris, chronicles the lives of three Native American contemporary families, struggling to find their place in American society. Shot on location in Santa Rosa, California, the presentation has a blockbuster lineup of talent.

Its stars include three time Emmy winner A. Martinez (*L.A. Law, Pow Wow Highway*), Irene Bedard (Voice of Pocahontas, *Lakota Woman*), Tantoo Cardinal (*Lakota Woman, Dances With Wolves*), Sheila Tousey (*Thunderheart*), and Diane Debassige (*Loyalties, War Party*) and newcomers Deeny Dakota, Sam Vlahos, Alexis Cruz, and Jenny Gago. Both behind and in front of the cameras, Native Americans from many tribes in Northern California participated in the project.

Sarris, who was adopted at birth, and raised in both Indian and White families, previously served as Chief of the Coast Miwok tribe. Receiving his M.A. and Ph.D. from Stanford University, he is currently a tenured professor at UCLA where he teaches Indian literature and creative writing. Sarris is also a prolific writer about his heritage and personal experiences.

GRAND CIRCLE, THE

Country USA   **Year** 1995   **Length** 12 m.   **Genre** LS
Director Pierre Lobstein, Richard Whitman
Producer Pierre Lobstein (exec), Richard Whitman, Joe Nevaquaya
Distributor
Sun Circle Productions
121-24th Avenue, NW   PMB 120
Norman, OK   73069
405 495-4759 tele   405 329-4442
tsoyah@usa.net
$50.00US VHS, $25.00US VHS rental

In *The Grand Circle*, two brothers travel across Oklahoma, Louisiana, the Mississippi River and Alabama on their way to Georgia, through states of pervasive indifference. Returning to the homelands, to ourselves, we remember the removal, the land runs, the ancestors, the future. Mounds and other evidence of our continuance inspire reverence and wonder. We are part of something ancient. Our spirit, humor, and faith cannot be stolen.

There is no narrative in the film, no voice, no translation - only the imagery, the text, and the audio. It is a collaboration between brothers, ancestors, the land, and the viewer.

GRANDFATHER SKY

Country USA   **Year** 1993   **Length** 50 m.   **Genre** LS
Director Victress Hitchcock
Producer Suzanne Benally, Victress Hitchcock
Distributor
Chariot Distribution
1274 Lambert Circle
LaFayette, CO 80026
303 666-4558 [b]   303 666-5808 [f]
www.chariotdist.com   cdistribution@qwest.net
US $89.00 VHS with guide

This hour long drama tells the story of Charlie Lone Wolf (played by Dana White Calf), a troubled urban Lakota/Navajo youth whose journey from Denver to the home of his sheepherder uncle (played by Benjamin Barney) in Lukachukai, is at the heart of his discovery of what it means to be Navajo.

Charlie's emerging knowledge of his heritage and his struggle to find his identity provides us with a sense of the importance of family and place to the Dineh. His journey awakens us to what it means to be a human being... living in the present and at home with the past.

GREAT SPIRIT WITHIN THE HOLE, THE

Country USA   **Year** 1983   **Length** 60 m.   **Genre** DF
Director Chris Spotted Eagle
Producer Spotted Eagle Productions
Distributor
Not in distribution.
Spotted Eagle Productions
2524 Hennepin Avenue, South
Minneapolis, MN 55405-3567
612 377-4212 [b] and [f]
cseagle@tc.umn.edu

"They think we're still playing Indians," says a Choctaw inmate. "They don't think we're for real. But we've been real since the beginning of time. The spirit of the beginning is still here."

That intensity is shared by many American Indians imprisoned across the nation, who are discovering — some for the first time — their own inherited religion. *The Great Spirit Within the Hole* is a one-hour film documentary, produced and directed by Chris Spotted Eagle for KTCA-TV, Minneapolis/St. Paul, Minnesota.

The program describes how the practice of ancient rites has inspired inmates to discover a new self-identity and provides a means to survive the devastating prison experience.

GREAT WOLF AND LITTLE MOUSE SISTER FROM WALKING WITH GRANDFATHER SERIES, PROGRAM 3 "THE MOUNTAIN"

Country USA   **Year** 1984   **Length** 26 m.   **Genre** DS
Director Phil Lucas
Producer Phil Lane, Jr.
Distributor
Lucerne Media
37 Ground Pine Road
Morris Plains, NJ 07950
1 800 341-2293 [b]   973 538-0855 [f]
www.lucernemedia.com   LM@lucernemedia.com
US $99.00 VHS educational, "Walking With Grandfather" series

The Great Wolf and Little Mouse Sister is one of the stories that Joshua Lowdog tells and is about how the Little Mouse sacrificed to help the Great Wolf and after a long and difficult journey, was transformed into a higher being.

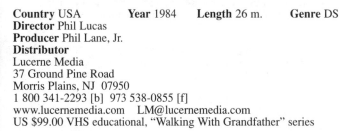

GREY OWL

Country USA   **Year** 1999   **Length** 117 m.   **Genre** FF
Director Richard Attenbourough
Producer Jake Eberts and Richard Attenbourough
Distributor
Columbia TriStar
10202 W. Washington Blvd.
Culver City, CA 90232
310 244-4000 [b]
US $14.95 VHS, US $24.99 DVD
Available for rent at local video stores.

A biopic about Archibald Belaney (Pierce Brosnan), born in Hastings, England in 1888, who at 17 immigrated to Canada, where he began to reinvent himself. Claiming to be part Apache Indian, he called himself Grey Owl and took on the old ways of First Nations People, living in the wilderness, hunting and trapping, and later hiring himself out as park ranger. Archie Grey Owl, during the dark days of the Depression, made his living as a hunter in the untamed north woods of Canada, until he fell in love with a beautiful young Mohawk woman who inspired him to quit trapping. He turned to writing and became the best known "Indian" in the world, a pioneer conservationist, a best-selling author, and celebrated lecturer. He toured the world in beaded buckskins and feathers, meeting with heads of states and kings and queens. But the more famous he became, the more people began to ask questions about his past, a secret past that threatened to take away everything that was dear to him. This is a story about the triumph of love, searching for the truth, and living in harmony with nature. Archie Grey Owl died a premature death at 49 but his story continues to fascinate, and his legacy lives on. Through his books, still in print today some 60 years later, and his famed lectures, Grey Owl became one of the first defenders of nature and an outspoken conservationist.

Quebec actress Annie Galipeau – who is First Nations Matawaki – plays the role of Pony.

GRIZZLY ADAMS AND THE TREASURE OF THE BEAR

Country USA   **Year** 1995   **Length** 101 m.   **Genre** FF
Director John Huneck
Producer Link Wyler
Distributor
Currently unavailable.

This is the story of Grizzly Adams (Tom Tayback) and his quest to rescue his close friend Professor Brummette, who has fallen into the hands of evil men - led by Professor Hunnicutt (Joseph Campanella) - who are seeking to rob the sacred burial grounds of the ancient Indian Tribe known as the Bear People.

Along the way he encounters a group of lost orphans and Gentle Storm (Selina Jayne), a pregnant Indian woman whose husband has been murdered by the very men who have taken the Professor. Over his protests, Grizzly Adams finds himself on an adventurous and perilous journey to Dark Mountain with orphans, Gentle Storm, and the professor's wife and daughter in tow.

Adams and Samson (his bear) guide this young troupe safely through the dangerous wilderness to Dark Mountain where Gentle Storm must have her baby to fulfill an ancient prophecy. There they meet up with the thieves who have kidnapped the Professor, but they also discover the secrets of Dark Mountain. A giant golden spirit bear and three Indian shamans (medicine men) rise up to protect the sacred ground and the innocent ones. Gentle Storm gives birth to a son, and then joining her husband, passes on to her final resting place, thus fulfilling the prophecy.

Adams enlists the aid of the Brummettes to help with the baby. The Brummettes also decide to adopt two of the orphans, Jacob and Lydia, while Adams takes Gabe (the orphaned young man) to live with him. The group watches as Gentle Storm and her husband, having overseen the fulfillment of the prophecy, are free to go to their final resting place over Dark Mountain.

GROUND ZERO / SACRED GROUND

Country USA   **Year** 1998   **Length** 9 m.   **Genre** ANS
Director Karen Aqua
Producer Karen Aqua
Distributor
Shenandoah Film Productions
538 "G" Street
Arcata, CA 95521
707 822-1030 [b] 707 822-1035 [f]
US $75.00 VHS, US $45.00 VHS rental

Ground Zero/Sacred Ground explores two opposing forces, their often
uneasy coexistence and the effects they have on each other. The locale is
the high desert of South-Central New Mexico, which is host to two distinct
sites. Three Rivers is a Native American rock art site where over 10,000
petroglyphs were created by the Jornada Mogollon people between 900
and 1400 AD. Thirty-five miles away, on the White Sands Missile Range,
the world's first atomic bomb was detonated in 1945. The juxtaposition of
these two sites points to the striking contrast between the two worlds
which created them: one which accepts and reveres the power of the natural world, and the other which strives to control and manipulate the forces
of nature.

GROWING UP NAVAJO - TEENS ON THE REZ

Country USA   **Year** 1999   **Length** 52 m.   **Genre** DF
Director Heather Spaulding
Producer Heather Spaulding
Distributor
Navajo Nation Television (NNTV)
P.O. Box 2310
Window Rock, AZ 86515
520 871-6655 [b]
Please call for local broadcast information on this program over NNTV.

Growing Up Navajo follows four teenagers on their search for individual
and cultural identity on the Navajo reservation.

We first meet Marshall, a basketball champion and community hero, who
is as committed to college scholarships and academics as he is to Navajo
tradition. Then Christina explains how she balances high school with raising a toddler. By sharing her personal struggle with a delinquent boyfriend
and family alcoholism, she reveals serious issues regarding family structure and the need to communicate love. The third teen is Wayne, a Cobra
gang member, who is more culturally devoted than most elders may realize. Both he and his older brother Randy (one of the Cobras' founding
fathers) explain how kids on the reservation join gangs, the fact that gang
violence is growing, and the desperate need for community to support and
empower its youth. Finally, Rosephena, a senior at the local high school
that emphasizes cultural preservation, shares her talent and love for Navajo
tradition. Through song and dance, she stresses the importance of preserving "the old ways."

Between youth segments, we hear from the adult community. Great-grand-
mothers, social services reps, police officers, and youth advocates express
their own concerns and hope for today's teens.

The object of *Growing Up Navajo* is to promote open and honest dialogue
between youth and community. It serves as a reminder that in order to preserve culture for posterity, the Navajo community must begin by understanding its most precious resource: their proud and promising children.
Truly, this is a message for not only other Native American peoples, but
for all communities.

HAIRCUTS HURT

Country USA **Year** 1995 **Length** 10 m. **Genre** LS
Director Randy Redroad
Producer Randy Redroad
Distributor
Third World Newsreel
545 8th Avenue
New York, NY 10018
212 947-9277 [b] 212 594-6417 [f]
twn@twn.org
US $200.00 VHS, US $45.00 VHS rental

A Native American woman and her young son encounter everyday racism
when they visit a local barbershop in, as filmmaker Redroad calls it,
"Redneck USA." The son's resistance, combined with the music of a
Native American street musician, sets the background for reflections on the
mother's childhood, the meaning of "haircut" for Native Peoples, and what
it means for her to cut her son's hair.

HAND GAME

Country USA **Year** 2000 **Length** 66 m. **Genre** DF
Director Lawrence Johnson
Producer Lawrence Johnson
Distributor
Lawrence Johnson Productions
P.O. Box 14384
Portland, OR 97293
503 284-1019 [b] 503 294-0912 [f]
www.ljproductions.com ljp@teleport.com
US $29.95 VHS

Unknown to most Americans, hand game, also called stick, grass, or bone
game, is a guessing game played by teams and accompanied by betting.
Once played by over eighty tribes, it is still the most widely played Native
gambling game in North America. Every year thousands of American
Indians pack their lawn chairs and game sets and hit the "hand game trail,"
competing in tournaments and games on reservations throughout the west.
Historically, hand game played an important part in inter-tribal relations.
Hand game was played at fishing grounds and summer trade fairs. Today it
is played in homes and at powwows and tournaments. Despite attempts by
churches and courts to suppress it, hand game has remained a widespread
phenomenon and significant expression of "Indianness."

Hand game is usually played between two teams of any number of players
with two pairs of small marked and unmarked cylinders (bones) that are
concealed in the hands. Some tribes use elk teeth. The guessing team
attempts to guess through hand signs which of the hiders' hands hold the
unmarked cylinders. Songs are sung to instill power in the people that are
hiding the bones. Songs may be composed, gained through dreams or
learned. Many people today tape-record their games to learn the other
team's songs. Hand game requires concentration, endurance, confidence
and memory.

Directed and produced by Lawrence Johnson, the film is framed by a traditional coyote story relating the origins of death and the hand game. Seven
years in the making, *Hand Game* opens at a tournament in Arlee, Montana
on the Flathead Indian Reservation, then travels across the Northwest to
the Crow, Blackfeet, Makah, Spokane, Coeur d' Alene, and Walker River
Northern Paiute Reservations. The film takes the viewer on a journey
through Indian Country, a journey full of humor, riveting music and engaging characters.

HANDS OF HISTORY

Country Canada   **Year** 1994   **Length** 52 m.   **Genre** DF
Director Loretta Todd
Producer Margaret Pettigrew, Ginny Stikeman
Distributor
National Film Board of Canada Library
22-D Hollywood Avenue
Ho-Ho-Kus, NJ 07423
1 800 542-2164 [b] 201 652-1973 [f]
US $195.00 VHS, call for rental information and prices.
For purchase within Canada visit the NFB website at: www.nfb.ca
1 800 267-7710 toll free within Canada

Doren Jensen, Rena Point Bolton, Jane Ash Poitras and Joanne Cardinal-Schubert are First Nations artists who seek to find a continuum from traditional to contemporary forms of expression.

These women, who are master artists, have sought paths through which their world views and their experiences could find expression in the act of creating. Their experiences, from the mundane to the profound, are revealed: their philosophies as artists, their techniques and creative styles, how they raised their families, and the exultation felt in the act of creating.

Hands of History explores their lives on their journey to become artists, the obstacles they have had to overcome, and the works they have created.

HANTAVIRUS: REDUCING THE RISK

Country USA   **Year** 1993   **Length** 10 m.   **Genre** IND
Director Judy Preston
Producer Olivia Romero
Distributor
National Indian Video of America
4212 San Andres NE
Albuquerque, NM 87110
505 881-8546 [b]
US $9.95 VHS

The primary goal of this production is to protect the well-being of the public at large by informing, instructing and empowering the individual to take control of a previously out-of-control situation: the spread of hantavirus.

The secondary goal of this production is to restore the strong sense of pride and dignity among the Navajo people, this pride has been damaged as a result of the misdirected and biased media spotlight on the Navajo Nation due to the epidemiological prominence of Hantavirus on Navajo land.

Total cooperation between traditional medicine people, the Navajo Nation and western medicine has successfully created this video mechanism, which will be utilized nationally to communicate to all people that Hantavirus is not an "Indian Virus" and that public awareness of this killer can save lives.

HAROLD OF ORANGE

Country USA   **Year** 1984   **Length** 30 m.   **Genre** LS
Director Richard Weise
Producer Dianne Brennan
Distributor
Lucerne Media
37 Ground Pine Road
Morris Plains, NJ 07950
1 800 341-2293 [b] 973 538-0855 [f]
www.lucernemedia.com   LM@lucernemedia.com
US $99.00 VHS educational

A group of Minnesota Indians receive a foundation grant to develop a strain of miniature oranges that they can grow on their reservation. When they're ready to market their produce, the logo they put on the orange crates is a white man in a suit and tie. Charlie Hill is cast as Harold Sinseer, the title character, leader of a group of Indians who, after having met all the grant requirements for the orange growing scheme, are now back for a new grant to start coffee houses on Minnesota reservations. The coffee they propose to serve will be made from pinch beans, a native Minnesota crop "that saved America in the Great War when pinch bean coffee was served to GIs."

Director Richard Weise states, "Harold is a trickster, a historical figure in Indian lore, and a storyteller. The trickster has been important to Indian culture since before the white man came. He is a compassionate trickster; not a hero, but a smart survivor who lives by his wit and imagination. He doesn't set out to hurt anybody. The screenplay is based on stories from Indian lore. The script pokes fun at both cultures, the Indians and the foundation people."

HAUDENOSAUNEE: WAY OF THE LONGHOUSE

Country USA   **Year** 1982   **Length** 13 m.   **Genre** DS
Director Bob Stiles
Producer John Akin
Distributor
First Run / Icarus Films
32 Court Street, 21st Floor
Brooklyn, NY 11201
718 488-8900 [b] 718 488-8642 [f]
www.frif.com
US $160.00 VHS, US $35.00 VHS rental

Haudenosaunee tells about the ways and attitudes of the people of the Longhouse—the Haudenosaunee, also known as the Six Nations Iroquois Confederacy. The league of the Haudenosaunee, established some one thousand years ago, is one of the oldest continuously functioning governments in the Western Hemisphere. It is based on a comprehensive and interrelated code of principles and concepts known as the Great Law of Peace. This film explores some of those concepts as it frames a portrait of the contemporary Haudenosaunee peoples and their professions, schools and organizations—a synthesis of the old and the new: the essence of survival.

HE WHO DREAMS:
MICHAEL GREYEYES ON THE POWWOW TRAIL

Country Canada   **Year** 1997   **Length** 53 m.   **Genre** DF
Director Alan Burke
Producer Alan Burke, Canadian Broadcasting Corporation
Distributor
Currently unavailable.
Canadian Broadcasting Corporation, Non-Broadcast Sales
P.O. Box 500, Station A
Toronto, Ontario
M5W 1E6 Canada
416 205-6384 [b] 416 205-3482 [f]
edsales@toronto.cbc.ca

Actor/Choreographer Michael Greyeyes is profiled in this feature documentary that doubles as the story of one man's quest and as an informative look at the powwow, its culture and rituals. Greyeyes, who began his career as a ballet dancer with the National Ballet of Canada and with Eliot Feld in New York, was forced to retire from the dance stage due to a recurrent shin injury. Ultimately, he came to prominence through acting in films such as *Crazy Horse* and *Dance Me Outside*, but he never lost the desire to dance.

He Who Dreams: Michael Greyeyes on the Powwow Trail reveals Greyeyes facing his need to dance again and exploring powwow dancing as an outlet to fullfill that need. The documentary shows Greyeyes traveling from powwow to powwow, collecting the pieces for his regalia and learning the foundation of traditional dancing. It culminates with a dance he choreographed to simultaneously honor his past and look to the future.

HEALING JOURNEY

Country Canada   **Year** 1994   **Length** 25 m.   **Genre** DS
Director Greg Coyes
Producer Laszlo Barna
Distributor
Currently unavailable.

Healing Journey explores the high rate of suicide among young people in Native communities by focusing on a particular group of teenagers and the efforts of their community to help and heal. The film was shot on location on the reserves near Kenora, Ontario and is narrated by Tantoo Cardinal.

HEALING OF NATIONS

Country Canada   **Year** 1994   **Length** 48 m.   **Genre** DS
Director George Amiotte & Peter von Puttkamer
Producer George Amiotte & Peter von Puttkamer
Distributor
Gryphon Productions, Ltd.
P.O. Box 93009, 5331 Headland Drive
West Vancouver, BC
V7W 3C0 Canada
604 921-7627 [b] 604 921-7626 [f] gryphon@telus.net
US $155.00 VHS
CAD $197.60 VHS

Healing of Nations looks at cultural revival in Native American and Canadian First Nations communities. Filmed in two countries over a one year period, the film focuses on youth empowerment, the value of traditional ceremonies and teachings and the impact these traditions are having on young Native people. Lakota cultural leader Max Bear is seen guiding young people through sweat lodge and tobacco ceremonies. Several Native cultural leaders from a diverse group of tribes speak eloquently about the importance of traditional practices. Co-produced and co-directed with Native cultural educator George Amiotte (Guardian of the Oglala Sundance Society), this production is presented and spoken in the words of the Native American spiritual leaders and youth. The program also features a Canadian Native urban education program, where young people are using traditions to rediscover inner strengths; and a young Salish paddling team that is preparing physically and spiritually for a 500 mile canoe journey (and an international gathering of seagoing peoples) using traditional Native ceremonies.

HEAR ME ARTIST: TUDJAAT

Country Canada   **Year** 1997   **Length** 5 m.   **Genre** MV
Director Larry Carey
Producer Randall Prescott
Distributor
Sony Music Canada
1121 Leslie Street
Toronto, ON
M3C 2J9 Canada
416 391-1960 [b]
Note: This music video is currently sold out. However, once there is a sufficient demand more will be produced.

Canadian singing duo Tudjaat specialize in the ancient Inuit art of throat singing. The video, "Hear Me," combines elements of this traditional art with modern hip-hop sensibilities.

HEART OF THE PEOPLE:
LIFE, DEATH AND REBIRTH OF A GREAT RIVER

Country Canada   **Year** 1996   **Length** 59 m.   **Genre** DF
Director Peter von Puttkamer
Producer Sheera and Peter von Puttkamer
Distributor
Gryphon Productions, Ltd.
P.O. Box 93009, 5331 Headland Drive
West Vancouver, BC
V7W 3C0 Canada
604 921-7627 [b]   604 921-7626 [f]   gryphon@telus.net
US $155.00 VHS, personal copy US $29.95
CAD $197.60 VHS, personal copy CAD $29.95

Heart of the People tells of Vancouver Island's Huu-ay-aht people's centuries old relationship to the river, before and after the clear-cutting of their valley. Once numbering close to 8,000 people, the Huu-ay-ahts, great whalers of the past, are today a community of 486 people. Flowing through their territory is the Sarita River. The Huu-ay-aht name, which means "white with the sperm of Salmon," recalls an era in the not too distant past when the river was teeming with millions of fish. Over-fishing began at the mouth of the Sarita with the arrival of a large scale commercial fishing fleet at the turn of the century. Elders in the film recollect the days when logging companies bulldozed their homes until they were forced to move from their land. Today, the Huu-ay-ahts are seeking support from local non-Natives to join them in restoring the Sarita River Watershed. They have succeeded in starting a watershed restoration program with McMiliam-Bloedel logging corporation and the British Columbia government.

HEART OF THE SPIRIT

Country USA   **Year** 1997   **Length** 36 m.   **Genre** LS
Director Robert Ybanez
Producer Yoeme Heritage Partnership
Distributor
Currently not in distribution. However, some copies can be made available under special circumstances for donation.
Please call 520 930-5671 [b]

Rudy has recently been initiated into a Yaqui street gang. One night, Rudy meets his match when he is contacted by his inner voice, the Guardian Spirit, who takes him on a journey that will change his life forever. An unusual look into the world of Native American gang life, *Heart of the Spirit* sends out a strong message against violence to Native communities.

HIDDEN MEDICINE

Country USA   **Year** 1999   **Length** 15 m.   **Genre** LS
Director Robby Romero
Producer Roland Joffe
Distributor
Eagle Thunder Enterprise
P.O. Box 1115
Taos, NM 87571
505 737-2855 [b]   505 737-2856 [f]
redthunder@eaglethunder.com
US $18.00 VHS home video,
US $400.00 35mm or Beta SP rental

Hidden Medicine is a film special in support of legislation now pending in Congress to protect the remaining 4% of our national forests. *Hidden Medicine* premiered at a special screening during the 1999 Sundance Film Festival with a keynote address by Robert Redford. The film was produced by Roland Joffe, executive produced by Horst Rechelbacher, co-written by Chief Oren Lyons and written and directed by Robby Romero. *Hidden Medicine* was shot on location at the Onondaga Nation using Robby's unique film style, seamlessly weaving together music, poetry, dance and vital information.

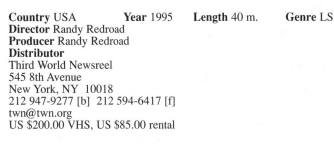

HIGH HORSE

Country USA   **Year** 1995   **Length** 40 m.   **Genre** LS
Director Randy Redroad
Producer Randy Redroad
Distributor
Third World Newsreel
545 8th Avenue
New York, NY 10018
212 947-9277 [b]   212 594-6417 [f]
twn@twn.org
US $200.00 VHS, US $85.00 rental

All over the city, dislocated Native People are reclaiming what has been stolen from them. Calling on the Ancestors to guide them as they leave the artificial world of the Colonizers, they catch a spirit ride to their true identities. The People are returning Home, as it is known in their culture, land and language. *High Horse* is a freedom myth, alive within the rhythms of natural justice: a Native kick in the Colonial ass.

HISTORY OF THE LUISEÑO PEOPLE: LA JOLLA INDIAN RESERVATION – CHRISTMAS 1990

Country USA   **Year** 1993   **Length** 27 m.   **Genre** LS
Director Isaac Artenstien
Producer James Luna
Distributor
Video Data Bank
37 South Wabash Avenue
Chicago, IL 60603
312 345-3550 [b]   312 541-8073 [f]
US $200.00 VHS, US $50.00 VHS rental

Remarks director Isaac Artenstien, "The 'Luiseño Christmas' video is part of an on-going series of interdisciplinary work focusing on my vision of and for my Luiseño people.

"In the work there is a thin line between what is fictional and what is non-fiction, and what is real emotion and what is art. These opposing elements are what draw viewers to the work.

"As in all of my artwork, there is a cultural element where I let (or seem to) people in on American Indian cultures. What we see and feel are the things that I promote. There are also elements in the work about American culture that everyone can identify with and that makes for an understanding that we are all more alike than different."

HIV/AIDS NATIVE FOCUS

Country USA **Year** 1998 **Length** 2 m. **Genre** PS
Director Frank Tyro
Producer Confederated Salish Kootenai Tribes
Distributor
Not in distribution.

These spots were focused on Native Americans in Montana and run on broadcast stations and cable networks throughout the state. Through the use of images and words, Native American viewers are encouraged to think about the risks HIV/AIDS pose in their communities and to examine possible destructive personal behaviors.

HOCAK YOUTH LEADERSHIP CAMP AND NIKJAGI'U

Country USA **Year** 1998 **Length** 9 m. **Genre** DS
Director Daryl Lonetree, Marlon White Eagle
Producer Hocak Wazijoci Language Cultural Program
Distributor
Not in distribution.
Hocak Wazijoci Language and Cultural Association
P.O. Box 390 / N4895 Hwy 58
Mauston, WI 53948
608 847-5694 [b] 608 847-7203 [f]

At the Summer Youth Leadership Camp, the Hocak youth learn, among other things, the Hocak language, how to be leaders, and how to become better, more well-rounded individuals while encouraging the independent spirit of Hocak people. This video was made to promote the importance of the program, which is undergoing changes and budget cuts that might limit its effectiveness.

HOLLOW WATER

Country Canada **Year** 2000 **Length** 48 m. **Genre** DS
Director Bonnie Dickie and Tina Mason
Producer Joe MacDonald
Distributor
National Film Board of Canada Library
22-D Hollywood Avenue
Ho-Ho-Kus, NJ 07423
1 800 542-2164 [b] 201 652-1973 [f]
US $129.00 VHS, call for rental information and prices.
For purchase within Canada visit the NFB website at: www.nfb.ca
1 800 267-7710 toll free within Canada

Hollow Water, Manitoba is home to 450 people, two-thirds of them victims of sexual abuse. The offenders — mothers, fathers, aunts, uncles, and cousins — have left a legacy of pain and denial, addiction and suicide. *Hollow Water* follows the journey of one family who participates in the healing circle to confront their past. Their story of hope is a testament to one community's ability to change.

HOME

Country USA   **Year** 1999   **Length** 15 m.   **Genre** LS
Director Elizabeth Downer
Producer Kathy Paschal
Distributor
Shenandoah Film Productions
538 "G" Street
Arcata, CA 95521
707 822-1030 [b] 707 822-1035 [f]
US $175.00 VHS, US $45.00 VHS rental

Home is about a Native American woman's search for her family. As a child, she and her brother were taken by social workers and put up for adoption in non-Native homes. After years of separation, she still dreams of her brother and the love they once shared. She decides to return to the reservation to seek out her relatives and ultimately, to find her brother. Though her intentions are good, she finds that healing such deep wounds is harder than she had imagined.

HOMELAND

Country USA   **Year** 2000   **Length** 58 m.   **Genre** DF
Director Hank Rogerson and Jilann Spitzmiller
Producer Hank Rogerson and Jilann Spitzmiller
Distributor
UC Extension Center for Media and Independent Learning
2000 Center Street, Fourth Floor
Berkeley, CA 94704
510 642-0460 [b] 510 643-9271 [f]
cmil@uclink.berkeley.edu
US $250.00 VHS, US $90.00 VHS rental

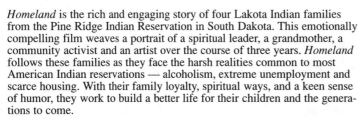

Homeland is the rich and engaging story of four Lakota Indian families from the Pine Ridge Indian Reservation in South Dakota. This emotionally compelling film weaves a portrait of a spiritual leader, a grandmother, a community activist and an artist over the course of three years. *Homeland* follows these families as they face the harsh realities common to most American Indian reservations — alcoholism, extreme unemployment and scarce housing. With their family loyalty, spiritual ways, and a keen sense of humor, they work to build a better life for their children and the generations to come.

In the interviews and footage of *Homeland's* four families, there is a palpable yearning for self-reliance and personal freedom — freedom from tribal corruption, freedom from the government's grip. They are searching for space that is theirs alone, where they don't feel watched or constricted. For some families, this freedom is a return to family land that is outside of town, far from cluster housing. For others, freedom is looking for educational and employment opportunities off the reservation. The goal of *Homeland* is to overturn destructive stereotypes and to reveal the complexities of contemporary Native American life as few documentaries have done before.

HONEY MOCCASIN

Country Canada   **Year** 1998   **Length** 49 m.   **Genre** LS
Director Shelley Niro
Producer Shelley Niro
Distributor
Women Make Movies
462 Broadway, 5th Floor
New York, NY 10013
212 925-0606 [b] 212 925-2052 [f]
info@wmm.com
US $250.00 VHS, US $75.00 VHS rental,
US $125.00 16mm rental

The locale for *Honey Moccasin* is Reservation X, otherwise known as the
Grand Pine Indian Reservation. But it could be any Indian Reserve. The
story revolves around two rival bars: the Smokin' Moccasin, owned by
Honey (Tantoo Cardinal) and the Inukshuk Café owned by Zachary John
(Billy Merasty). Zachary feels cheated out of a lot of money because he
feels Honey bought her establishment from his father, Johnny John, for a
lot less than it is worth. Woven through are Honey's relationships with
best friend Bernelda Birch (Bernelda Wheeler), a journalist and a singer
for Honey and the Mock-a-Sins; her daughter Mabel (Florene Belmore),
who is going to university to study filmmaking and is also a singer in the
band; and Beau (Kelly Henhawk), the Smokin' Moccasin's bouncer and
Honey's protector. A quasi-Native American "roadhouse movie", *Honey
Moccasin* is a showcase for many talents from the Native/multi-cultural
communities.

HONORABLE NATIONS

Country USA   **Year** 1991   **Length** 54 m.   **Genre** DF
Director Chana Gazit & David Steward
Producer Chana Gazit & David Steward
Distributor
Filmakers Library
124 East 40th Street
New York, NY 10016
212 808-4980 [b] 212 808-4983 [f]
www.filmakers.com info@filmakers.com
US $395.00 VHS, US $75.00 rental

Nestled in the picturesque hills of New York State's Allegheny region sits
the sleepy town of Salamanca. It is difficult to imagine a setting more
serene, nor one more unlikely to be the center of dramatic and unpredictable events that would pit landlord against tenant, put at risk an
American town, and alter the course of America's relationship to Indian
Nations.

For 99 years, the residents of Salamanca have rented the land under their
homes for an average of $1/year from the Seneca Indians, under terms of a
lease imposed by Congress. Now, as the lease is about to expire, a century
of bad business must be renegotiated. The film follows the unfolding
drama as the survival of an American town and justice for the Senecas
appear to be in conflict.

HONORING KUMAT

Country USA   **Year** 2000   **Length** 13 m.   **Genre** DS
Director Daniel Golding
Producer Daniel Golding and Ah Mut Pipa Foundation
Distributor
Ah Mut Pipa Foundation
P.O. Box 160
Bard, CA 92222
760 572-5334 [b]
US $125.00 VHS educational use
US $75.00 VHS community organizations

The Glamis Gold Company of Canada is seeking to lease land from the Bureau of Land Management, land adjacent to the Fort Yuma Reservation in southern California. The proposed gold mine will employ the Running Man site, a place of religious importance to the Quechan and other Colorado River tribes. In the winter of 1998, a group of Quechan youth organized by concerned Quechan tribal members decided to run on one of their traditional running trails. This trail passes directly through the proposed mine site. This was not to be a run of protest, but one of empowerment, to show the creator, Kumat, that he was not forgotten.

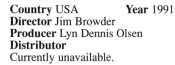

HONORING THE PAST, SHAPING THE FUTURE

Country USA   **Year** 1991   **Length** 6 m.   **Genre** IND
Director Jim Browder
Producer Lyn Dennis Olsen
Distributor
Currently unavailable.

Northwest Indian College was established by the Lummi Indian Business Council in 1983. It is the third largest and fastest growing of the 27 tribal colleges established since 1968.

The mission of Northwest Indian College is to provide post-secondary opportunities for Indian people. The college curriculum includes academic and vocational education, cultural education, community service, and continuing education, including adult basic education.

HOPI PROPHECY

Country Japan   **Year** 1987   **Length** 75 m.   **Genre** DF
Director Kiyoshi Miyata
Producer Kiyoshi Miyata
Distributor
Currently unavailable.

A prophecy warning of the destruction of Hiroshima and Nagasaki by "grounds full of ashes" was engraved on a Hopi stone tablet. *Hopi Prophecy* traces the thread that ties the ancient wisdom of the Hopi and the Hiroshima experience. The film, which begins with a scene of Hiroshima on August 7, 1945, depicts the long struggle of the Hopi and Navajo to save the Earth from human destruction.

The director, Kiyoshi Miyata, spent 7 years completing this film, which has been shown in every city and major television station in Japan.

HOPI: SONGS FROM THE FOURTH WORLD

Country USA   **Year** 1983   **Length** 58 m.   **Genre** DF
Director Pat Ferrero
Producer Pat Ferrero
Distributor
New Day Films
22-D Hollywood Avenue
Ho-Ho-Kus, NJ 07423
888 367-9154 [b] 201 652-1973 [f]
www.newday.com   orders@newday.com
US $199.00 VHS, US $75.00 VHS rental

The first in-depth film experience of the meaning of the Hopi way—a philosophy of living in balance with nature. The film describes the Hopi philosophy of life, death, and renewal as revealed in the interweaving life cycle of humans and corn plants.

The film opens with the Hopi story of the Emergence and follows their destiny to the mesa tops of Northeast Arizona, where they have lived for over 1,000 years. The Hopi believe they were led to this spot to fulfill their destiny as guardians of the land. Their survival has depended on a precarious balance between the dry soil and the rain, and their farming is infused with prayer and spiritual practice.

Storytelling is a vital part of their tradition, and the film includes stories told by a farmer, a religious elder, a grandmother, a painter, a potter, and a weaver. Their stories reveal a living philosophy integrating art and daily life.

HOPILAVAYI

Country USA   **Year** 1993   **Length** 18 m.   **Genre** DS
Director T. Bart Hawkins
Producer T. Bart Hawkins
Distributor
Not in distribution.

Hopilavayi is about the Hopi Indians of Arizona and their plea for the revival of Hopilavayi, their Native language. With photography officially banned in 1917, this Native American Nation, rich in cultural tradition and spirituality, remains a mystery to much of the world.

HORSE SONG

Country USA   **Year** 2000   **Length** 56 m.   **Genre** FF
Director Norman Patrick Brown
Producer Norman Patrick Brown, Gayle Williamson, Stuart Noble
Distributor
4 Directions Health Communications
P.O. Box 160
Shiproack, NM 87420
Michele Hayes - contact
505 368-6499 [b]
505 368-6324 [f]
Purchase Price: Free to All Native Health, Cultural, Community, Educational Organizations

A drama in the Navajo language, *Horse Song* tells the story of Jack White, a Navajo man diagnosed with diabetes. Jack's denial and refusal to seek help for himself results in the disruption of his job and his family. His grandparents, wife and children struggle to understand the emotional effects of this disease, and with their support, Jack comes to understand the healing effects of Navajo traditional medicine and Western medicine.

HOUSE MADE OF DAWN

Country USA **Year** 1977 **Length** 88 m. **Genre** FF
Director Richardson Morse
Producer Richardson Morse, Edward Teets
Distributor
Available on Amazon.com
www.amazon.com
US $9.98 VHS

House Made of Dawn is a Pulitzer-Prize winning story of the American Indian, a stranger in his Native land. This film is about Abel and his two worlds—that of his fathers, wedding him to the rhythm of the seasons, and that of the 20th century, leading him into a compulsive cycle of alcohol, weakness and dissipation.

House Made of Dawn is the past, present, and future. Abel, a soldier and murderer, must face the unwelcomed white man's world as a punishment for his wrongdoing. But his link to his Native life never escapes him. The tug-of-war between these unique cultures never ceases.

Starring Larry Littlebird, Judith Doty, Jay Varela and Mesa Bird.

HOUSE OF PEACE

Country USA **Year** 1999 **Length** 30 m. **Genre** DS
Director Cathleen Ashworth
Producer G. Peter Jemison
Distributor
Friends of Ganondagan
P.O. Box 113
Victor, NY 14564
716 742-1690 [b] 716 742-2353 [f]
US $129.95 VHS with guide, US $79.95 VHS

The story of what happened to the Seneca village of Ganondagan 300 years ago can be told in many different ways. It can be told from the point of view of the invaders, the French, or it can be told from the point of view of the Senecas. *House of Peace* tells the story from a Seneca perspective because both the producer and writer are Seneca. *House of Peace* focuses on the longhouse, a traditional Iroquois dwelling, that was built 1997-98 at the New York State Historic Site where the 16th century village of Ganondagan stood. The video documents the building of the new longhouse as well as the importance of the longhouse as a way to understand a culture. The longhouse is not only a place to live, it is also a symbol of the Iroquois Confederacy, which still exists today.

HOW PANTHER GOT HIS TEARMARKS

Country USA **Year** 1992 **Length** 12 m. **Genre** ANS
Director Vern Korb
Producer Sarah Supahan
Distributor
Not in distribution.
Shenandoah Film Productions
538 "G" Street
Arcata, CA 95521
707 822-1030 [b] 707 822-1035 [f]

How Panther Got His Tearmarks is a Northern California Karuk tribal legend combining human and animal characters. A young man leaves his wife and family to venture over the mountain and explore neighboring tribes. Not coming back until years later, he is punished by seeing his wife turn into a tree and his son into a rock. As he cries, he himself is turned into a panther.

HUCHOOSEDAH: TRADITIONS OF THE HEART

Country USA **Year** 1996 **Length** 57 m. **Genre** DF
Director Katie Jennings
Producer Katie Jennings
Distributor
Lucerne Media
37 Ground Pine Road
Morris Plains, NJ 07950
1 800 341-2293 [b] 973 538-0855 [f]
www.lucernemedia.com LM@lucernemedia.com
US $99.00 VHS educational

Today, fewer than a dozen people are fluent in Lushoosteed, the language of the Skagit tribe of Western Washington state. But one woman is diligently working to preserve Lushootseed as a living language. *Huchoosedah: Traditions of the Heart* chronicles of the effort of 77 year-old Upper Skagit elder, Vi Hilbert, to ensure the survival of her people's language and traditional stories. Vi, a tribal historian, scholar, and teacher, pursues her work with single-minded dedication—sometimes even in the face of opposition—because "without the language, there is no culture."

HUNT, THE

Country Canada **Year** 1997 **Length** 10 m. **Genre** LS
Director Tamara Bell
Producer Tamara Bell
Distributor
Tamara Bell
604 251-6244 [b] 604 251-1986 [f]
tamarab@3web.net
US $15.00 VHS, CAD $20.00 VHS

Three hunters lost in the woods form the basis of this piece of Native humor. When a genie appears and grants each of them a wish, the results are both ironic and hilarious.

I AM ALCOHOL

Country Canada **Year** 2000 **Length** 33 m. **Genre** LS
Director Don Burnstick
Producer Alan Bibby
Distributor
Burnstick Promotions
499 Banting Drive
Winnipeg, Manitoba
R3K 1C6 Canada
204 832-2913 [b] 204 888-2818 [f]
redskin@mb.sympatico.ca
CAD $40.00 VHS

I Am Alcohol is a vivid portrayal of a man's painful journey as he battles his loneliness and fear with alcohol. This moving drama demonstrates the importance of surrendering the mask of alcohol, drugs, sexual promiscuity, peer pressure, and falseness and reclaiming our true spiritual destinies.

I AM DIFFERENT FROM MY BROTHER

Country USA   **Year** 1981   **Length** 20 m.   **Genre** LS
Director Tony Charles
Producer Tony Charles
Distributor
Lucerne Media
37 Ground Pine Road
Morris Plains, NJ 07950
1 800 341-2293 [b] 973 538-0855 [f]
www.lucernemedia.com   LM@lucernemedia.com
US $99.00 VHS educational

This real life docu-drama depicts the actual Name-Giving ceremony of three young Flandreau Dakota Sioux Indian children.

Filmed in March, 1981, at Flandreau, South Dakota, it is the story of two sisters and their brother, Winona, Jody, and Hep, who in the tradition of the Dakota Tribe come of age by receiving their traditional Indian names from their grandparents with the ceremonial blessing of the Keeper of The Pipe.

I HEARD THE OWL CALL MY NAME

Country USA   **Year** 1977   **Length** 78 m.   **Genre** FF
Director Daryl Duke
Producer Daryl Duke
Distributor
Available on Amazon.com
www.amazon.com
US $17.99 VHS

A sensitive and moving drama about a man's awakening to life in the face of death. A young Anglican priest, unaware that he has only a short time to live, is sent by his bishop to a remote Indian village in British Columbia, ostensibly to help the Indians, but actually to learn from them "enough about life to be ready to die."

I Heard the Owl Call My Name is a warming, human story of the understanding that develops between people of different cultures as well as a fascinating portrayal of the values, traditions, and concerns for human dignity of the Native Americans.

Starring Tom Courtenay, Dean Jagger, Paul Stanley and Marianne Jones.

Original Release Date - 1973.

I NEVER GAVE UP HOPE ARTIST: LORRIE CHURCH

Country Canada   **Year** 2000   **Length** 5 m.   **Genre** MV
Director Darryl Kesslar
Producer Eaglehill Music / George Atcheynum
Distributor
Eaglehill Music
Box 145
Gallivan, Sask.
S0M 0X0 Canada
360 937-7796 [b]
www.lorriechurch.com   1 877 256-7743 [b]
US $13.95 VHS, CAD $19.95 VHS

Lorrie Church is a singer/songwriter from the Sweetgrass First Nation Indian Reserve in the province of Saskatchewan. She shares a heritage of both Metis and Cree elements. Although her music is mainstream country she draws a lot of strength from her rich cultural background, hence her Cree name which means Grey Feathers.

"I Never Gave Up Hope" is the title track off of Lorrie's 1999 album of the same name.

I' TUSTO: TO RISE AGAIN

Country Canada   **Year** 2000   **Length** 54 m.   **Genre** DF
Director Barb Cranmer
Producer Barb Cranmer and Cari Green
Distributor
Magpie Releasing Inc.
2 - 284 Wellington Cresent
Winnipeg, Manitoba
R3M 0B5 Canada
204 453-1915 [b] 204 233-2610 [f]
www.magpiereleasing.com   nola@magpiereleasing.com
CAD $25.00 VHS

On August 29, 1997 the 'Namgis First Nation of Alert Bay was rocked to its core. The Bighouse, where traditional ceremonies were held, was engulfed in flames. *I 'Tusto: To Rise Again* recounts the events resulting from this horrific act of arson, while retracing the cultural significance of the Bighouse to the 'Namgis First Nation people.

I WILL FIGHT NO MORE FOREVER

Country USA   **Year** 1977   **Length** 106 m.   **Genre** FF
Director David L. Wolper
Producer David L. Wolper
Distributor
Available on Amazon.com
www.amazon.com
US $17.99 VHS

The words "I will fight no more forever," are taken from the speech of surrender made by Chief Joseph to General Howard of the U.S. Army in 1877. Joseph was a peace loving man who had always counseled patience with the white man's encroachments, but when the situation became intolerable, he proved a superb military tactician. Forced by a "trail of broken treaties" to take up arms, Chief Joseph attempted to fight his way to freedom in Canada. In a running battle still studied in military science at West Point, Joseph led his band of 300 braves and their women and children 1,600 miles in 11 weeks, simultaneously fighting to a standstill ten separate commands of the U.S. Army. He was within 30 miles of the Canadian border when, surrounded by his dead comrades, Joseph conceded defeat in a poetic speech that summed up the tragic confrontation of two cultures.

With the surrender of the Nez Perce, the military conquest of the Native Americans in the United States was almost complete. The brilliant original screenplay by Jeb Rosebrook and Theodore Strauss manages at once to portray all the parties as human beings, with doubts and failings, and at the same time creates a vivid reminder of the government policies that herded Indians together for eventual extinction on reservations that were little more than cultural prisons.

Staring Ned Romero, Sam Elliot, Nick Ramus and James Whitmore.

Original Release Date 1975.

I'LL TAKE MANHATTAN

Country USA   **Year** 1994   **Length** 30 m.   **Genre** LS
Director Robin M. Craig
Producer Robin M. Craig
Distributor
Currently unavailable.

Native Americans—college grads—decide to take over the First New York Office Building in New York City in order to reclaim their land in Manhattan. This leads to a meeting between an uptight yuppie stockbroker, trying to get into his office on a Sunday morning, and a Native American medicine man.

IF IT CAN HAPPEN TO ME, IT CAN HAPPEN TO YOU

Country USA   **Year** 1994   **Length** 27 m.   **Genre** DS
Director Harlan McKosato
Producer Harlan McKosato
Distributor
Chariot Distribution
1274 Lambert Circle
LaFayette, CO 80026
303 666-4558 [b] 303 666-5808 [f]
www.chariotdist.com   cdistribution@qwest.net
US $50.00 VHS

In July 1992, Lisa Tiger was informed she was HIV positive. Lisa, a
Muscogee Creek/Cherokee from Oklahoma, did not hesitate in committing
herself to educating other Native Americans, especially youth, about this
lethal virus she had acquired.

The true story of this courageous young woman offers strength and inspiration. Her story has raised awareness throughout Indian Country, not only
about about HIV/AIDS but also the encompassing reality that lives with
Native American youth of today.

The 29 year-old Tiger has continued her mission and expanded her vision
to raising the life expectancy of all Native Americans. Her message has
just begun to truly impact the lives of thousands.

IKWE

Country Canada   **Year** 1987   **Length** 57 m.   **Genre** FF
Director Norma Bailey
Producer Norma Bailey, Michael Scott (exec), Ches Yetman (exec)
Distributor
National Film Board of Canada Library
22-D Hollywood Avenue
Ho-Ho-Kus, NJ 07423
1 800 542-2164 [b] 201 652-1973 [f]
US $150.00 VHS, call for rental information and prices.
For purchase within Canada visit the NFB website at: www.nfb.ca
1 800 267-7710 toll free within Canada

It is 1770 in the Canadian Northwest, the scene an isolated Ojibway village on the shores of Georgian Bay. Ikwe, a young Ojibway girl on the
threshold of womanhood, awakens from a terrifying dream. She envisions
a strange man whose presence evokes haunting images of sadness and desolation. The arrival of a young Scottish trader transforms her dreams into
reality.

Ikwe believes that her marriage to this stranger has been ordained and she
leaves her home and family to begin a new life. The union promises prosperity for her tribe but it also means hardship and isolation for Ikwe. It
soon becomes apparent that their individual values and divergent customs
are not in harmony. There are differences that cannot be ignored.

In the end, the images that haunted Ikwe's dream unfold with tragic clarity.
It is she who becomes the unwilling messenger of desolation and despair,
but it is also she who provides a harbinger of hope for a dying people.

Starring Hazel King, Gladys Taylor and Geraint Wyn-Davies.

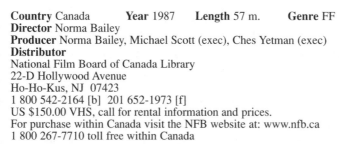

IMAGES OF INDIANS: THE GREAT MOVIE MASSACRE

Country USA   **Year** 1980   **Length** 30 m.   **Genre** DS
Director Phil Lucas
Producer Robert Hagopian
Distributor
Oyate
2702 Mathews Street
Berkeley, CA 94702
510 848-6700 [b] 510 848-4815 [f]
www.oyate.org
US $50.00 VHS

No other minority in American history has been so long feared, gawked at, or hated than the American Indian. This first segment of the five part series *Images of Indians* looks at the Indian's warrior image. Clips are shown from Robert Altman's *Buffalo Bill and the Indians*, starring Paul Newman, and William Wellman tells a sad, ironic story of attempting to tell the true story of Buffalo Bill.

IN MACARTHUR PARK

Country USA   **Year** 1977   **Length** 90 m.   **Genre** FF
Director Bruce Schwartz
Producer Bruce Schwartz
Distributor
Not in distribution.

A ninety-minute social documentary on the problems of an American Indian in Los Angeles, fictionalized and presented dramatically.

The film focuses on the activities of Triam Lee, a 29 year old Mojave Indian and Colorado River fisherman. The opening sequence is a stark murder he commits in daylight in MacArthur Park.

The rest of the film delineates the reasons behind the murder, his activities afterwards, and his life as a frightened fugitive in an urban environment with which he cannot cope, as well as a wife and child back on the reservation who he is responsible for and yet he cannot support. Doomed by a society which chooses not to deal responsibly with its minority citizens, we watch him as he moves through a world of seedy fourth-class hotels, train depots and bus stations, funky bars, hookers and transients. The film attempts to actively detail this particular world and its problems.

Starring James Espinoza, Marcy Eudal and Pete Homer.

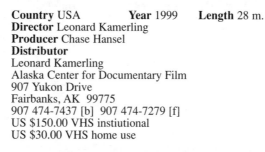

IN OUR OWN IMAGE: ALASKA NATIVE DOLL-MAKERS AND THEIR CREATIONS

Country USA   **Year** 1999   **Length** 28 m.   **Genre** DS
Director Leonard Kamerling
Producer Chase Hansel
Distributor
Leonard Kamerling
Alaska Center for Documentary Film
907 Yukon Drive
Fairbanks, AK 99775
907 474-7437 [b] 907 474-7279 [f]
US $150.00 VHS instiutional
US $30.00 VHS home use

The film takes us into the world of Eva Heffle, Inupiaq Dollmaker, and six other renowned Alaska Native doll makers, where we learn first hand the traditional, spiritual, cultural and financial realities of being a contemporary Alaska Native artist. "I'm trying to keep our culture alive through my dolls," Eva tells us. "When I'm dead and gone, the kids that haven't learned about their culture can look at my dolls—and they'll know. They'll understand that we take pride in what we do, because we survived this country."

Alaska Native People have fashioned human figurines out of stone, bone, ivory, trade cloth, and many other materials—for play and ceremonial purposes—for more than a thousand years. *In Our Own Image* explores this ancient tradition and the way Alaska Native women and men have transformed it into a vibrant, much in demand modern art form.

IN THE BEST INTEREST OF THE CHILD

Country USA   **Year** 1982   **Length** 20 m.   **Genre** DS
Director Carol & Vern Korb
Producer Carol & Vern Korb
Distributor
Shenandoah Film Productions
538 "G" Street
Arcata, CA 95521
707 822-1030 [b]   707 822-1035 [f]
US $200.00 VHS, US $45.00 rental

Narrated by Will Sampson, the film portrays the effects of state child protective practices on Indian youngsters and families, prior to the passage of the Indian Child Welfare Act.

IN THE BLUE GROUND: A NORTH OF 60 MOVIE

Country Canada   **Year** 1998   **Length** 94 m.   **Genre** FF
Director Alan Simmonds
Producer Doug Mac Leod, Tom Dent-Cox
Distributor
Alliance Atlantis (for Canadian Sales) contact: Doug Smith
121 Bloor Street, E Suite 1500
Toronto, Ontario
M4W 3M5 Canada
415 967-1174 [b]
For purchase outside of Canada:
Alliance Atlantis (contact: Maria Sanchez)
184-192 Drummond Street, Suite 200
London, England NW13HP   011 44 207 391-6900 [b]

North of 60, one of Canada's most popular television series, defies many odds. It seemed inconceivable that a program about a small Native town in the Northwest Territories would succeed on primetime television. Yet this compelling drama attracts approximately 1.4 million viewers weekly. *In The Blue Ground: A North of 60 Movie* builds on the weekly drama and becomes a gripping contemporary police thriller set against the striking backdrop of the Canadian North. When a geologist on the verge of a major diamond find is murdered and town nurse Sara Birkett disappears under mysterious circumstances, Mounties James Harper (Peter Kelly Gaudreault) and Michelle Kenidi (Tina Keeper) find themselves tracking a deadly phantom in the desolate bush. Also featuring Michael Horse.

IN THE LAND OF THE WAR CANOES (1914)

Country USA   **Year** 1977   **Length** 47 m.   **Genre** DS
Director Edward S. Curtis
Producer Seattle Film Company
Distributor
Milestone Film and Video
P.O. Box 128
Harrington Park, NJ 07640-0128
1 800 603-1104 [b]   201 767-3035 [f]
milefilms@aol.com
US $39.00 VHS & DVD, US $200.00 for public performace rental.
Please call for more information.

Best known as one of the premiere photographers of the 20th century, Edward S. Curtis devoted his life to documenting the disappearing world of the American Indian. In this film, originally entitled *In the Land of the Headhunters*, Curtis retold a story of love and revenge among the Kwakiutl Indians of Vancouver Island. Curtis spent three years with the Kwakiutl to meticulously recreate their way of life before the white man came. In addition to the magnificent painted war canoes of the title, the film features wonderful Native costumes, dancing and rituals — including a powerful scene of a vision quest.

In 1972, the only surviving print of this film was carefully restored and an original score of music and chants was recorded by the Kwakiutls themselves. Although some of the material suffers from nitrate damage due to its age, *In the Land of the War Canoes* still presents a magnificent image of a lost world.

IN THE LIGHT OF REVERENCE

Country USA   **Year** 2000   **Length** 72 m.   **Genre** DF
Director Christopher McLeod
Producer Christopher McLeod, Malinda Maynor
Distributor
Bullfrog Films
P.O. Box 149
Oley, PA 19547
1 800 543-3764 [b] 610 370-1978 [f]
www.bullfrogfilms.com   info@bullfrogfilms.com
Pricing for educational and institutional use TBA

Across the United States, Native Americans are struggling to protect their sacred places. Religious freedom, so valued in this country, is not guaranteed to those who practice land-based religion. Every year more sacred sites - the land based equivalent of the world's great cathedrals - are being destroyed. Strip mining and development cause much of this destruction. But rock climbers, tourists and New Age religious practitioners are part of the problem too. The biggest problem is ignorance.

In the Light of Reverence is a film that will change that ignorance. This feature-length documentary tells the story of three indigenous communities and the land they struggle to protect: the Hopi of the Four Corners area, the Wintu of Northern California, and the Lakota of the Great Plains.

Producers Toby McLeod and Malinda Maynor have taken the time to film *In the Light of Reverence* with careful attention to creating true partnerships with Native communities. They are working closely with the Seventh Generation Fund, a Native American-controlled grassroots organization. Together, they will make the film the centerpiece of a grassroots movement - Religious Freedom 2000 - seeking increased respect for land-based religion and legal protection for sacred lands.

IN THE SPIRIT OF OUR FOREFATHERS

Country Canada   **Year** 1979   **Length** 32 m.   **Genre** DS
Producer Saskatchewan Indian Cultural Center
Distributor
Currently unavailable.

This vivid portrayal of the Treaty Six Centennial depicts the entire scope of commemoration activities, ranging from the formal ceremonies near Fort Carlton to contemporary sporting events at the summer game; from gatherings of elders advising the young to the less serious parleys of hand-game gamblers.

IN THE WHITE MAN'S IMAGE

Country USA   **Year** 1992   **Length** 59 m.   **Genre** DF
Director Christine Lesiak
Producer Matthew Jones, Christine Lesiak
Distributor
Not in distribution
Native American Public Telecommunications
P.O. Box 8311
Lincoln, NE 68501
402 472-3522 [b]

The program explores the federal goverment's greatly flawed experiment to turn American Indians away from their own culture and assimilate them into white culture during the late 19th and early 20th centuries.

IN WHOSE HONOR? AMERICAN INDIAN MASCOTS IN SPORTS

Country USA   **Year** 1998   **Length** 46 m.   **Genre** DS
Director Jay Rosenstein
Producer Jay Rosenstein
Distributor
New Day Films
22-D Hollywood Avenue
Ho-Ho-Kus, NJ 07423
888 367-9154 [b] 201 652-1973 [f]
www.newday.com   orders@newday.com
US $189.00 VHS, US $80.00 VHS rental

Amazing how taking your family out to a college basketball game can change your life forever, but that is exactly what happened to Charlene Teters.

Teters (Spokane) took her two daughters to see a University of Illinois basketball game and was horrified at the antics of the hometeam's mascot, Chief Illiniwek. Her sense of shame and dismay compelled her to take action and speak out against this insult. The film takes a critical look at the long-running practice of "honoring" American Indians by using them as team mascots and nicknames in sports. In Whose Honor? follows the remarkable story of Charlene Teters and her impassioned transformation from a graduate student into a national movement leader. Along the way she is spat on, threatened and even assaulted, yet she never wavers in her mission to protect and preserve her cultural identity for her children.

IN-BREAKER

Country Canada   **Year** 1975   **Length** 91 m.   **Genre** FF
Director Bob Elliot, James Margellos
Producer George McCowan
Distributor
Not in distribution.

The inbreaker of this story is Chris McRae, a student anxious to be his own man but dependent on money sent to him by his fisherman brother Roy. Searching for work and wanting to pay off his debt of gratitude, Chris leaves his prairie home and goes to join Roy in a Pacific Coast fishing village. But he finds that Roy cannot provide a job. And when he tries by himself, he is turned down because he is so green…until he is taken on as an inbreaker by Muskrat, a brawling Indian fisherman who is Roy's hated rival.

Chris' loyalty is now divided between his brother and his employer. When Roy and Muskrat fight, Chris manages to force them to settle their grudge in a fishing contest. The outcome only inflames their antagonism further and leads to a violence Chris failed to foresee and independence he did not anticipate.

Starring Johnny Yesno, Christopher George and Johnny Crawford.

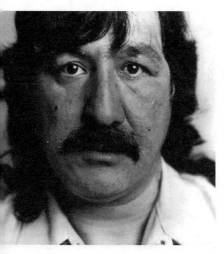

INCIDENT AT OGLALA

| **Country** USA | **Year** 1992 | **Length** 90 m. | **Genre** DF |

Director Michael Apted
Producer Arthur Chobanian
Distributor
Miramax Home Video.
Also available at local video and rental stores.

Robert Redford is the executive producer, and narrator, of this documentary feature that deals with the events surrounding the 1975 fatal shootings of two FBI agents and one American Indian on the Pine Ridge Indian Reservation in South Dakota.

The film follows the subsequent persecution of American Indian Movement activist Leonard Peltier, who was charged, tried and sentenced to two life terms for the deaths of the FBI agents - despite evidence which showed, beyond a shadow of a doubt, that he was not the gunman.

Director Michael Apted (*Thunderheart*) uses interviews with American Indians, Federal officials and lawyers to give details into the case, including persuasive ballistic evidence.

The film ends with the hope that an appeal will allow new evidence to be heard in Peltier's case. If not he remains encarcerated for a crime the filmmakers believe he did not commit.

INDIAN

| **Country** USA | **Year** 1977 | **Length** 86 m. | **Genre** FF |

Director Kieth Merrill
Producer Kieth Merrill, Dagney Merrill
Distributor
Currently unavailable.

Indian is a subjective exploration of what it is to be Indian in America. It is a stream of consciousness as seen and felt by one man, one Indian.

Raymond Tracey was born in a hogan and grew up on an Indian reservation. Until he was eight years old, the only world he knew was the hills and valleys of his home. He thought that all people were like his people. He left the reservation to attend white schools and learn the "other" ways. At 22, he looks back and wonders about the historical legacy of questions left unanswered. Who am I? Where do I belong in the world? Is there a purpose with my life? During one summer Raymond Tracey traveled 27,000 miles across America in search of the answers.

The film documents Tracey's random and diverse experiences as he searches for his roots in the fathers before him, recalls his past and the teachings of his grandfather, meets and interacts with a variety of different tribes involved in many different things, and discovers in all of them, a part of being Indian.

INDIAN ACT: THE FACTS, THE FEARS, AND THE FUTURE
– A Nation in Transition

Country Canada   **Year** 1989   **Length** 26 m.   **Genre** DS
Director Kem Murch
Producer Kem Murch
Distributor
Walpole Island Heritage Center / Dean Jacobs (Ex. Director)
Rural Route 3
Wallaceburg, Ontario
N8A 4K9 Canada
519 627-1475 [b] www.bkejwanong.com
Please call or visit the website for video information.

This is a story about the Indian Act (Canada), and is meant to clarify and open discussion about what the Indian Act is, how it affects Native people, and whether/how to abolish/change it.

From the time you're born and registered as an "Indian," to the time that you die — nothing will affect your life as much as the Indian Act.

Yet many people don't understand the implications of self-government, nor the ways in which the Indian Act affects them. Others are wary of change, of losing government supports with no system to replace them.

Without an understanding of the powers of the Act or the possibilities for change through self-government, Native people cannot discuss or negotiate their own futures.

INDIAN BLOOD

Country USA   **Year** 1992   **Length** 35 m.   **Genre** DS
Director Milton L. Brown
Producer Milton L. Brown
Distributor
Bama Boy Productions, Inc.
mlbrrown@ddyne.com
251 343-3124 [b]
Price upon request.

Indian Blood is the story of the Mowa Band of Choctaw Indians of Alabama, and their struggle for Federal recognition.

INDIAN COUNTRY

| **Country** USA | **Year** 1988 | **Length** 60 m. | **Genre** DF |

Director Michael Kirk
Producer Michael Kirk
Distributor
Currently unavailable.
Frontline
125 Western Avenue
Boston, MA 02134
617 300-3500 [b]

To his supporters, Joe DeLaCruz is a valiant, modern day warrior fighting an insensitive bureaucracy and the tragic reservation conditions that threaten to destroy his Quinault Indian Nation. To his detractors, he has become a puppet of the very bureaucracy he condemns, posing as a national Indian figure instead of leading his tribe.

"Indian Country," a *Frontline* documentary, examines life on the Quinault Indian Reservation in Washington State and assesses the successes and failures of its leader Joe DeLaCruz, over the last 20 years.

"This documentary asks why this Indian Nation, with strong leadership, federal financial support, and tribal independence has been unable to significantly improve the quality of life for its people," says *Frontline* executive producer David Fanning. The Quinaults' dilemma provides fresh understanding of the struggle facing many Indian tribes across the country.

INDIAN POSSE: LIFE IN ABORIGINAL GANG TERRITORY

| **Country** Canada | **Year** 1999 | **Length** 39 m. | **Genre** DS |

Director Katerina Cizek, Catherine Bainbridge
Producer Katerina Cizek, Catherine Bainbridge
Distributor
Wild Heart Productions
5505 St-Laurent, Suite 3018A
Montreal, Quebec
H2T 1S6 Canada
514 272-8241 [b]

Drugs, theft, drive-by shootings and 10-year-old prostitutes. Welcome to Winnipeg's North End — home to Indian Posse, the most powerful gang in the hood. *Indian Posse* is a daring exploration into the lives of three North End families as they struggle to live in the face of gang violence and try to stop the trend of losing their kids to gangs. Paul Lacasse Sr., a resident of the North End for the past 23 years, has watched his neighborhood deteriorate. He has lost three sons to gang life and is on the verge of losing a fourth. Will 14-year-old Paul Jr. follow in his brother's footsteps? Enter Trevor Sinclair, Paul Sr.'s 19-year-old son. A member of Indian Posse for four years, Trevor has been in and out of jail since the age of 12. Now a father himself, he is trying to turn his life around through his work with Winnipeg Native Alliance, an organization dedicated to keeping kids off the street. But with most of his friends still in gangs, will he be able to keep it together? Marie Kelly, a mother of six, is fed up with living in gang territory. Her 12-year-old daughter Claire is already a victim of gang violence. What will happen to Marie's children if they stay in the North End? How can she protect them from gang life? Filmmakers Katerina Cizek and Catherine Bainbridge follow Paul Sr., Trevor, Marie and their families over an entire summer. The result is a shocking glimpse into the everyday lives of three families fighting to overcome the tragedies and violence that surround them.

INDIAN RIGHTS-INDIAN LAW

Country USA   **Year** 1978   **Length** 28 m.   **Genre** DS
Director Joe Consentino
Producer Joe Consentino / Ford Foundation (NY)
Distributor
Not in distribution.
Native American Rights Fund
1506 Broadway
Boulder, CO 80302
303 447-8760 [b]

The Native American Rights Fund (NARF) is the only national nonprofit
Indian law firm devoted to the protection of Indian rights. Since it was
founded in 1971, NARF's major emphasis has been upon the preservation
of tribal existence and resources and the fulfillment of the nation's long-
standing obligations to Indian people.

Indian Rights — Indian Law focuses on the work of NARF's lawyers,
most of whom are Indians, in such cases as the fight between fourteen
tribes and Washington State officials over treaty fishing rights along the
Pullayup River, the struggle of the Paiute Tribe against the diversion of
water from Pyramid Lake in Nevada, the religious rights of Indian prisoners, more equitable treatment for Indian schoolchildren, and the land
claims suits of the Passamaquoddy and Penobscot Tribes in Maine. NARF
also played a major role in helping to restore the Menominee Tribe in
Wisconsin to Federal trust status.

Indian Rights — Indian Law provides a rare glimpse of the litigation
process and insight into why land, resources, and tribal sovereignty are so
important in preserving Indian identity.

INDIAN TIME I

Country Canada   **Year** 1988   **Length** 48 m.   **Genre** PS
Director David Devine
Producer Don Marks, Curtis Jonnie
Distributor
Native Multimedia Productions, Inc.
#36 - 40 Osborne Street
Winnipeg, Manitoba
R3L 1X9 Canada
204 231-1524 [b] 204 231-5555 [f]
Available for large broadcast licence only, please call for more informa-
tion.

An hour-length television variety special featuring the comedy, music and
dance of North America's finest Native performing artists.

"We set out to produce *Indian Time* with one goal in mind: to provide an
alternative to what's been served in the past. Our focus is solid, contemporary entertainment. In this case, it is being provided by North America's
finest Native performing artists. We want our audience to laugh at the
poignant humor of Charlie Hill as he laughs at himself, his people and others. We meant our audience to simply appreciate the richness of the
melodies and lyrics of our musical artists. Maybe there's a message. But it
won't get through unless our audience is thoroughly entertained and wants
more. That's what *Indian Time* is all about. *Indian Time* was developed to
open up your mind, explore new kinds of entertainment and find new ways
to think about the world we share".
— Curtis Jonnie, Don Marks, Producers

INDIAN TIME II - FLY WITH EAGLES

Country Canada **Year** 1992 **Length** 48 m. **Genre** PS
Director Don Marks
Producer Don Marks, Curtis Jonnie
Distributor
Native Multimedia Productions, Inc.
#36 - 40 Osborne Street
Winnipeg, Manitoba
R3L 1X9 Canada
204 231-1524 [b] 204 231-5555 [f]
Available for large broadcast licence only, please call for more information.

Indian Time 2 is a television variety show featuring the music, comedy, dance and drama of North America's top aboriginal entertainers.

Set at the Forks Site in Winnipeg, a historical meeting place for aboriginal people at the junction of the Red and Assiniboine Rivers, *Indian Time 2* showcases the talents of Quebec folk-rockers Kashtin, comedian Charlie Hill, actors and singers Tom Jackson, Shingoose, Joanne Shenandoah, and Margo Kane.

INDIAN TRIBAL GOVERNMENT

Country USA **Year** 1980 **Length** 16 m. **Genre** DS
Director Joel L. Freedman
Producer Joel L. Freedman
Distributor
Not in distribution.

Narrated by Ernie Stevens (Oneida) and filmed on location at the Gila River Indian Reservation, this film shows how effective tribal governments operate and what tribal members should expect from their governments. Governmental processes and staffs, courts and police are seen meeting everyday needs as well as planning for the future.

INNU TOWN ARTIST: CLAUDE McKENZIE

Country Canada **Year** 1999 **Length** 4 m. **Genre** MV
Director Michel Brault
Producer Katia Paradis
Distributor
Currently unavailable.

"Innu Town" is the debut single off of Claude McKenzie's first solo album, also entitled Innu Town. McKenzie, a Canadian Native from a reserve in Northern Quebec, sings in his Native language Montagnais. A language only spoken by 12,000 people.

He is formerly of the singing duo Kashtin.

INSTITUTE FOR THE DEVELOPMENT OF INDIAN LAW SERIES

Country USA   **Year** 1979   **Length** 35 m.   **Genre** DS
Director Joel L. Freedman
Producer Joel L. Freedman
Distributor
Not in distribution.

"Indian Jurisdiction"
"A Question of Indian Sovereigny"
"Indian Treaties"
"Indians and the U.S. Government"
"The Federal-Indian Trust Relationship"

Five short films made by the Institute for the Development of Indian Law to explain the legal rights of Indian Nations and the federal /Indian relationship.

INUIT KIDS

Country USA   **Year** 1987   **Length** 15 m.   **Genre** DS
Director Paulle Clark
Producer Paulle Clark
Distributor
Bullfrog Films
P.O. Box 149
Oley, PA 19547
1 800 543-3764 [b] 610 370-1978 [f]
www.bullfrogfilms.com info@bullfrogfilms.com
US $49.00 VHS, US $20.00 VHS rental

The different lives of Jeffrey and Peter, two Inuit boys living in the Arctic, are examined. Peter speaks only Inukitut, is training to be a hunter and lives in the outcamp in traditional ways. Jeffrey speaks both Inukitut and English, lives in the town and attends school.

INUPIATUN

Country Canada   **Year** 1981   **Length** 55 m.   **Genre** DF
Director Peter Haynes, Harold Tichenor
Producer Peter Haynes, Harold Tichenor
Distributor
Crescent Entertainment, Ltd.
555 Brooksbank Ave, Building 9, Suite 330
North Vancouver, BC
V7J 3S5 Canada
604 983-5992 [b]   604 983-5015 [f]
www.crescent.ca   htichenor@crescent.ca
Price upon request.

Jacob Archie, son of Head Point Archie Erogaktoak, the great hunter, was born in a tent at King Point as the family was travelling from Alaska to Aklavik. It was a long trip, taking many years.

Jacob, married now 20 years to Elizabeth, is a hunter and the best trapper in the Mackenzie Delta region. His is not a grandiose living. It is a very hard living, continually frustrated by the vicissitudes of the game and the weather, and by the ever-changing market for furs. But it is an honorable life, which has its roots in the age old way of the Eskimo. It takes from the 20th century only the things that it needs. Jacob says, "Old ways, new ways, makes no difference—always the animals are the same."

Jacob and Elizabeth are some of the last Inuit prepared to face the vast unyielding land and the predatory weather to preserve their pride.

Sadly, *Inupiatun* may be the final document of the Eskimo way.

INVISIBLE PEOPLE-
GENOCIDE OF THE TRADITIONAL NAVAJOS

Country USA   **Year** 1999   **Length** 12 m.   **Genre** DS
Director Marrissa Kelley
Producer Marrissa Kelley
Distributor
Currently unavailable.

American Indian history continues to repeat itself in remote northern
Arizona as the US government, fueled by mining interests, forcibly
removes traditional Navajo elders and their families from their ancestral
homelands, which they have occupied continuously for centuries. In this
documentary short, these fiercely traditional people tell us their story.

ISAAC LITTLEFEATHERS

Country Canada   **Year** 1985   **Length** 95 m.   **Genre** FF
Director Les Rose
Producer Gerald M. Soloway
Distributor
Available at CD Now
www.cdnow.com
US $6.79 VHS

During the summer of 1947, in a small prairie town, five year old Issac
Littlefeathers is abandoned by his Indian mother at Abe Kapp's corner grocery store. Nine years later, his white father, Jesse, an ex-professional
hockey player, returns to the prairies. Issac, now 14 years old, has grown
up in the care of Abe, a widowed, ex-stage magician. Their relationship
has evolved from the vagueness of strangers to the closeness of father and
son. Nevertheless, problems do exist.

To the parents of Issac's Jewish friends, Issac is a "goy." To the neighborhood toughs, the Varco brothers, he is a half-breed called "Chief" who presents a formidable one man defense league for his friends—victims of the
Varco's anti-Semitic, anti-minority prejudices. To Abe's daughter, Golda,
Issac is a trouble-making street fighter. Issac cannot understand the passiv-
ity of the Jewish nature, that "Jewish kids don't fight" as Abe says.

Abe believes that what Issac needs is a solid background. Karen, from the
Children's Aid Society, thinks Issac should learn more about his Indian
culture.

Issac continues his vendetta against the Varcos, despite run-ins with the
police and almost everybody else. A truce seems inconceivable—even a
boxing 'grudge' match in an arena between Issac and Bill Varco fails to
end the vengeance. The crimes that Issac and the gang perpetuate against
each other escalate to more and more destructive heights, leading to a final
dramatic confrontation.

Starring William Korbut, Lou Jacobi and Scott Hylands.

ISHI: THE LAST OF HIS TRIBE

Country USA   **Year** 1979   **Length** 130 m.   **Genre** FF
Director Robert Ellis Miller
Producer Edward & Mildred Lewis Productions
Distributor
Not in distribution.
Ira Englander
330 Washington Blvd., Suite 400
Marina del Rey, CA 90292
310 574-0889 [b]   310 574-3846 [f]

Ishi: The Last of His Tribe is a made for television special based on the
book by Theodora Kroeber. Kroeber's anthropologist husband Alfred was
the man who, in 1911, discovered the last surviving member of the Yahi
Indian tribe hiding in a barn in Oroville, California. Dennis Weaver plays
Professor Fuller, the Kroeber counterpart who befriends the Native
American Ishi and learns his language (much of the film is subtitled). Ishi
is played by Joseph Running Fox as a teenager and Eloy Phil Casados as
an adult. This informative and deeply moving project was conceived for
TV by Dalton Trumbo, who died in 1976 before finishing his script, which
was completed by his son Christopher Trumbo.

ISHI, THE LAST YAHI

Country USA   **Year** 1992   **Length** 60 m.   **Genre** DF
Director Jed Riffe, Pamela Roberts
Producer Jed Riffe, Pamela Roberts
Distributor
UC Center for Media and Independent Learning
2000 Center Street, 4th Floor
Berkeley, CA 94704
510 642-0460 [b] 510 643-9271 [f]
cmil@uclink.berkeley.edu
US $295.00 VHS, US $75.00 VHS rental
Also avilable at www.cdnow.com for home use.

Ishi, The Last Yahi tells the story of Ishi, who came to be known as the "last wild Indian in North America." His sudden appearance in 1911 stunned the country. His tribe was considered extinct, destroyed in bloody massacres during the 1860s-70s.

Narrated by Academy Award winning actress Linda Hunt, *Ishi, The Last Yahi* offers a unique window to aboriginal life in America. For the first time, a broad national audience will hear Ishi speaking in his own voice on Alfred Kroeber's original wax recordings, and will enter Ishi's world through archival motion picture footage and hundreds of photographs taken by Kroeber and others.

IT CAN'T RAIN ALL THE TIME

Country USA   **Year** 1996   **Length** 35 m.   **Genre** LS
Director Lance Richmond
Producer Lance Richmond
Distributor
AICH Productions
708 Broadway, 8th Floor
New York, NY 10010
212 598-0100 [b] 212 598-4909 [f]
akwesasne@aol.com
Please call for pricing and rental information.

Rates of suicide and substance abuse are at tragic levels among Native American youth, 600 percent higher than the rest of the nation. *It Can't Rain All the Time* addresses issues of youth suicide and substance abuse in an entertaining and inspiring method, by focusing on teenager Dani's (Irene Bedard) struggle growing up while coping with the tragic death of her beloved older sister.

IT STARTS WITH A WHISPER

Country Canada   **Year** 1993   **Length** 27 m.   **Genre** LS
Director Shelley Niro & Anna Gronau
Producer Shelley Niro & Anna Gronau
Distributor
Women Make Movies
462 Broadway, 5th Floor
New York, NY 10013
212 925-0606 [b] 212 925-2052 [f]
info@wmm.com
US $275.00 VHS, US $80.00 VHS rental,
US $115.00 16mm rental

It Starts With a Whisper tells the story of eighteen year old Shanna, who has grown up on the Six Nations Reserve and now must decide what path to follow in life. The choice between traditional and contemporary values seems impossible. She feels all alone, yet she is watched over by ancestral spirits—three "matriarchal clowns"—who sometimes appear as her outrageous aunts, Emily, Molly and Pauline. The aunts take Shanna on a mythic journey to Niagara Falls. The waters that whispered along the banks of the Grand River, that runs through the Six Nations Reserve, have become the thundering torrent Niagara Falls, as Native people around the world celebrate their cultures and gain empowerment.

Her aunts' warmth and humor, and a dream-like encounter with a well known Native leader, help Shanna realize she is loved and is entitled to live her life, remembering and respecting the people of the past and traditional ways.

ITAM HAKIM HOPIIT

Country USA   **Year** 1984   **Length** 58 m.   **Genre** DF
Director Victor Masayesva, Jr.
Producer Victor Masayesva, Jr.
Distributor
IS Productions
P.O. Box 747
Hotevilla, AZ 86030
520 734-6600 [b]
prods@infomagic.com
US $175.00 VHS

Itam Hakim Hopiit translates directly as "we, someone, the Hopi People." Indirectly, the phrase, as used by the narrator, Ross Macaya, reflects ancient heritage here on the North American Continent: we came here as unknown bands to fullfill our destiny of a united Hopi Nation. It is the process of becoming, this journey to the heart of the North American Continent which is Macaya's story.

JAY SILVERHEELS: THE MAN BESIDE THE MASK

Country Canada   **Year** 2000   **Length** 44 m.   **Genre** DS
Director David Finch and Maureen Marovitch
Producer Great North International
Distributor
History TV Canada
1 877 843-9371 [b] for North America
www.historytelevision.com

Mohawk actor Jay Silverheels played the monosyllabic, stoic Tonto (of Lone Ranger fame) with poker faced perfection. In 1949, at age 35, he became the first aboriginal actor to play a Native American on television, and he became the symbolic Indian to a generation. While the handsome actor would later play alongside some of Hollywood's finest, found a school for Native actors, and prove himself a talented thespian, he would never escape being typecast as the Indian brave.

Jay Silverheels left behind an important legacy that is still being felt, and fought for, by a new generation of Native artists. Aboriginal actors Tina Keeper, Michael Horse, Peter Kelly Gaudreault and Tom Jackson speak about how Silverheels inspired them and helped forge a path that is still being followed, and improved upon, by Native actors, writers and directors today.

JENNY

Country Canada   **Year** 1989   **Length** 48 m.   **Genre** LS
Director Ray Ramayya
Producer Ray Ramayya
Distributor
Ray Ramayya
P.O. Box 1494, 432 East Cres
La Ronge, Saskatchewan
S0J 1L0 Canada
306 425-3792 [b] and [f]
ray.ram@sk.sympatico.ca
Call for pricing information.

This contemporary drama is the story of Jenny, a Canadian Native girl with a beautiful singing voice who lives in the Northern lake country with her husband, Henry, and young son, Billy. Jenny sings, and Henry plays the flute. But Jenny hates the "bush ghetto" and longs to go south to the big city.

Her desire to leave intensifies when Billy narrowly escapes drowning in the rapids. When she is discovered by a record producer, and moves to the city, Jenny's dreams seem about to be fulfilled. Anxious to make it in the music business, she neglects her family, and Henry leaves her. How Jenny becomes reconciled to her past and her northern roots forms the climax to this moving story.

JOE PANTHER

Country USA　　　　**Year** 1977　　**Length** 110 m.　　**Genre** FF
Director Paul Krasny
Producer Stewart H. Beveridge
Distributor
Currently unavailable.

Joe Panther (Ray Tracey) is proud to be a Seminole with his rich heritage in the Florida Everglades, but he wants more. He wants the best of what the white man's world can offer also. He knows that he can never be content with just wrestling alligators for the amusement of tourists—he must move beyond the hanging cypress trees, beyond the alligator pits, beyond the quiet Seminole village. He wants to achieve manhood in the modern world, and he is willing to pay the price.

But he must prove himself. He wants desperately to get a job on the charter fishing boat of Captain Harper (Brian Keith). To prove to the captain that he is trustworthy and dependable, and to help the captain's brother stock his alligator farm, Joe captures an 11-foot alligator in the Glade swamps. Because of his dependability, he is hired as a helper in the boat.

But the price he pays is almost more than he can bear. His best friend, Billy Tiger (A Martinez) is killed in trying to help him succeed in a society that seems bent on building barriers for him and his kind.

Depressed, hurt and blaming himself for Billy's death, Joe is ready to abandon his dream, ready to withdraw from the outside world. But the wise advice of an old Seminole, Turtle George (Ricardo Montalban), snaps Joe back from depression. Kneeling in the dirt, Turtle tells Joe, "We too die just a little when someone we love dies. But the time for mourning is over."

The rapport between the wise, old Seminole and the young restless youth transcends all despair. Joe finds a new inner source of strength, and rising from his knees, he knows that he can succeed in the outside world.

Overcoming difficulties and obstacles, Joe "walks into his tomorrows" with courage, perseverance and greater awareness. He begins to realize the fulfillment of this dream, and in the final scene he is back on the fishing boat—as Captain Harper's mate.

JOHNNY GREYEYES

Country Canada　　　**Year** 2000　　**Length** 80 m.　　**Genre** FF
Director Jorge Manzano
Producer Jorge Manzano, Timothy L. Hill, Phylis Ellis
Distributor
Wolf Video
P.O. Box 64
New Almanden, CA 95042
408 268-6782 [b]
US $39.95 VHS, US $24.95 DVD
www.nepantla.com

Johnny Greyeyes embraces a tightly woven narrative of memories, dreams, and the desires of Johnny, a Native woman in her early thirties, and those of her family, who are displaced by addiction, abuse and the prison experience. The story takes place during Johnny's last year in Kingston's maximum-security prison for women.

Johnny has spent most of her life in one form of prison or another. Since the shooting death of her father, she's been in and out of correctional services. Taken away to reform school at the age of 15, Johnny falls through the cracks of life and eventually ends up in a maximum-security prison. Her life in prison revolves around her relationship with her lover Lana, her fellow inmates and her family: her mother Leona and younger brother Daytona.

Johnny's strength guides the lives of those around her, embodying the love and courage that she was denied in her young life. A journey through her own history and pain lead Johnny to love, a sense of spiritual purpose, and resolve with her past. In essence the film plays with universal themes: the importance of family, identity and the need to belong, to have a place to call home. Staring Gail Maurice, Jonathan Fisher, Columpa C. Bobb and Gloria May Eshkibok.

JOURNEY HOME

Country Canada   **Year** 1995   **Length** 39 m.   **Genre** PS
Director Peter von Puttkamer
Producer Peter von Puttkamer / Kecia Larkin
Distributor
Gryphon Productions, Ltd.
P.O. Box 93009 / 5331 Headland Drive
West Vancouver, BC
V7W 3C0 Canada
604 921-7627 [b] 604 921-7626 [f] gryphon@telus.net
US $148.00 VHS
CAD $175.20 VHS

Across North America, Native Indian communities are struggling to come
to terms with HIV and AIDS. Some communities have been supportive of
PHAs (Persons with HIV or AIDS) while others have responded with
ignorance, fear and denial. *Journey Home* examines issues facing three
Native PHAs in rural and urban community settings in Canada. The video
follows the lives of these three people and looks at ways in which they are
finding support from their communities, friends and relatives. In a small
Ontario community, Chris, a young woman who is HIV infected, finds
strength from the strong traditional values of her community and leadership. On a reserve in Quebec, Roland, a young man with AIDS, returns
home and finds a community-run medical program to help him with his
physical and emotional needs. In downtown Vancouver, Ray, a man who
first contracted the virus ten years ago, speaks about creating his own support network in his urban environment. The purpose of the video is to
motivate and inspire Native Indian communities and Urban health/social
programs into supporting and helping PHAs in their area. It is hoped the
video will combat fear and ignorance of HIV/AIDS by presenting communities and leaders who have decided to treat PHAs as equal and participating members of society instead of persons to be feared.

JOURNEY TO MEDICINE WHEEL

Country USA   **Year** 1998   **Length** 52 m.   **Genre** DF
Director Raymond Chavez
Producer Raymond Chavez
Distributor
Currently unavailable.

Journey to Medicine Wheel is a compelling one-hour documentary film
that presents an extraordinary portrait of the Native American Crow Tribe,
the Absaroka, or "Children of the Long-Beaked Bird." The story is told
primarily from the perspective of one particular Crow family and clan, the
Old Elks, and follows four generations of the Old Elk family and other
clan members who have gathered together for the annual Crow Fair Pow
Wow with 4,000 Native people along the banks of the Little Big Horn
River in Montana. The film interweaves the story of the Crow tribe with
the stories of the Old Elk family members, as the spectacular pow-wow
dances, songs, drum-circles, and rodeo unfold at Crow Fair. After the
pow-wow celebrations conclude, we follow the Old Elks as they take their
daughter, Deneta, up in to the Big Horn Mountains to the site of the sacred
Medicine Wheel. Here, they enact a rite of passage ritual, and ask their
ancestors for continued blessings and guidance for Deneta's passage into
womanhood and the next phase of her life.

JOURNEY TO SPIRIT ISLAND

Country USA   **Year** 1988   **Length** 93 m.   **Genre** FF
Director Laszlo Pal
Producer Bruce Clark
Distributor
Pal Productions, Inc.
4056 North East 174th Street
Seattle, WA 98155
206 361-9366 [b] 206 363-9575 [f]
palpal@wolfnet.com
Call for current distribution information.
Check www.Amazon.com and local video rental stores.

Journey to Spirit Island is a family adventure film rich in Native American folklore with a dash of suspense. The film tells the story of Maria (Bettina Bush), a young Nahkut Indian girl living on a reservation, who has been brought up in two worlds. She is nurtured in the old ways by her grandmother, a tribal elder and shaman, who is the spiritual center of the film. Maria also has school, television, and friends who have little interest in their heritage. And there is the newest controversy on the reservation: a young, ambitious but ruthless tribe member convinces the people to sell part of their sacred island to developers. During a summer kayaking trip, Maria, her brother and two young friends from Chicago become involved in an unforgettable adventure involving the island, the corrupt tribe member, an ancient curse and a magic canoe. Their survival depends on Maria bridging the gap between the old Indian ways and the contemporary world. Filmed in Washington State on the rugged Olympic Peninsula coastline and picturesque San Juan Island by Academy Award winning director of photography, Vilmos Zsigmond.

JUSTICE OR JUST US

Country Canada   **Year** 1989   **Length** 55 m.   **Genre** DF
Director Don Marks
Producer Don Marks, Curtis Jonnie
Distributor
Native Mulimedia Productions, Inc.
#36 - 40 Osborne Street
Winnipeg, Manitoba
R3L 1X9 Canada
204 231-1524 [b] 204 231-5555 [f]
Please call for pricing

Aboriginal people make up 3 to 5 percent of the Canadian population. Natives account for 60 to 80 percent of the inmates in Manitoba's jails. *Justice or Just Us* examines the disproportionate representation of Native people in the criminal justice system.

The hour long documentary special focuses on the people most affected by this issue. Native inmates provide the reasons for their dilemma and ways to solve their problems. *Justice or Just Us* also reaches far beyond the well-known problem of poverty to examine racism and the culture clash between Indian and mainstream North American societies.

Justice or Just Us presents more than just the facts. This documentary was produced to force action on the issue of Aboriginal people in conflict with the law. Questions raised and the solutions offered by *Justice or Just Us* are being considered by lawmakers and political activists throughout Canada.

KABLOONAK

Country Canada   **Year** 1994   **Length** 105 m.   **Genre** FF
Director Claude Massot
Producer Georges Benayoun, Paul Rozenberg, Pierre Gendron
Distributor
Lions Gate (for Canadian purchase)
376 Victoria Street, Suite 300
Westmount, Quebec
H3Z 1C3 Canada
514 906-4196 [b]   514 336-0607 [f]

Bloom Films (US and International purchase)
55 Sanite Ziateur East
Montreal, Quebec
H2T 1A4 Canada
514 274-8499 [b]

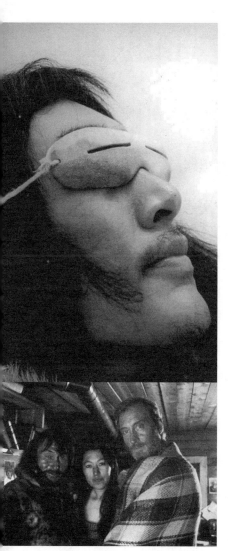

In 1922, a tiny man with wrinkled eyes and a child-like laugh won over movie audiences in New York, London, Paris, and Moscow, stealing the limelight from some of the biggest movie stars of the day. Yet nothing about Inuk Nanook's life prepared him such unexpected fame.

Two years earlier, Robert Flaherty, an American of Irish ancestry, had arrived in Port Harrison, Hudson Bay. He brought with him a camera, processing equipment and a projector. In those days, it was an insane undertaking. The few white men to venture to the far North were merchants. Relations between them and the Inuit were simple: they traded fox fur for white man's goods.

Flaherty spent a year filming in the tiny community, showing a passionate interest, incomprehensible to the Inuit, in various aspects of their lifestyle. Throughout the film, humorous anecdotes alternated with the shared hardships of a pitiless life in one of the world's most beautiful yet hostile environments.

Back in New York, after completing the editing of his movie, Flaherty encountered general indifference from distributors. It was Charles Pathe who finally agreed to distribute it as part of a double-bill with Harold Lloyd's *Grandma's Boy*. The film was an immediate success, quickly earning legendary status.

But as they watched the tiny image of Nanook moving across the screen, fascinated audiences all over the world could hardly suspect that, thousands of miles away, somewhere near Hudson Bay, the Inuk was in a final battle struggling for his survival.

Indeed, while Flaherty was earning worldwide recognition for the introduction of a new cinematographic genre—the documentary—Nanook and his community were victims of a great famine. The annual mail delivery from the Inukjuak outpost brought Flaherty news of Nanook's death. Kabloonak is the story of this legendary movie. Through the friendship of two men, it also tells of a passionate meeting of two worlds.

Starring Adamie Inukpuk, Charles Dance and Seporah Q. Ungalag.

KAINAI

Country Canada   **Year** 1977   **Length** 27 m.   **Genre** DS
Director Raoul Fox
Producer Colin Low
Distributor
National Film Board of Canada Library
22-D Hollywood Avenue
Ho-Ho-Kus, NJ 07423
1 800 542-2164 [b]   201 652-1973 [f]
US $175.00 VHS, call for rental information and prices.
For purchase within Canada visit the NFB website at: www.nfb.ca
1 800 267-7710 toll free within Canada

On the Blood Indian Reserve, near Cardston, Alberta, a hopeful new development in Indian enterprise is underway. Once rulers of the western plains, the Bloods live on a 1,300-square-kilometer reserve. Many have lacked gainful employment and now pin their hopes on a pre-fab factory they have built. Will the production line work and wages fit into their cultural pattern of life? The film shows how it is working and what the Indians themselves say about their venture.

KAMIK

Country Canada   **Year** 1991   **Length** 15 m.   **Genre** DS
Director Elsie Swerhone
Producer Jow MacDonald, Ches Yetman
Distributor
National Film Board of Canada Library
22-D Hollywood Avenue
Ho-Ho-Kus, NJ 07423
1 800 542-2164 [b] 201 652-1973 [f]
US $150.00 VHS, call for rental information and prices.
For purchase within Canada visit the NFB website at: www.nfb.ca
1 800 267-7710 toll free within Canada

A tradition that has existed for over five thousand years is in danger of extinction. It is a tradition that embodies more than the preservation of cultural heritage.

For Ulayok Kavlok, an expert hunter and seamstress, the making of a pair of seal skin boots can mean the difference between life and death in the harsh climate of Canada's Arctic. Ulayok is one of the last of a generation of Inuit, born and bred on the land, but her skills in making the seal skin boots called Kamik may soon be lost in the cultural transformation overtaking her community.

Ulayok and her family, like many Inuit today, strive to balance two very different worlds. *Kamik* offers a glimpse of those worlds and the thread one woman weaves between them.

KANATA: LEGACY OF THE CHILDREN OF AATAENTSIC

Country Canada   **Year** 1999   **Length** 52 m.   **Genre** DF
Director Rene Sioui LaBelle
Producer Jacques Menard, Jacques Vallee
Distributor
National Film Board of Canada Library
22-D Hollywood Avenue
Ho-Ho-Kus, NJ 07423
1 800 542-2164 [b] 201 652-1973 [f]
US $250.00 VHS, call for rental information and prices.
For purchase within Canada visit the NFB website at: www.nfb.ca
1 800 267-7710 toll free within Canada

On a rigorous and passionate quest, Huron-Wendat director René Siouï Labelle retraces the path of his ancestors and surveys their territories, recording images of stunning beauty. He unveils a historical journey known to very few as he reflects upon the identity of the Wendat Nation. In the 1600s, when the Wendat met Europeans, they were a prosperous society. They had been living on the shores of the Saint Lawrence River and around the Great Lakes for centuries. Tragically, the arrival of foreigners created massive upheavals that led to the disintegration of the great Wendat Confederation. A spiritual energy emanates from the men and women we encounter in this film, most of them from Wendake, 8 km north-west of Stadacona, which Chief Donnacona described to Jacques Cartier as the great village, or Kanata.

KANEHSATAKE: 270 YEARS OF RESISTANCE

Country Canada   **Year** 1993   **Length** 119 m.   **Genre** DF
Director Alanis Obomsawin
Producer Wolf Koenig, Colin Neale, Alanis Obomsawin
Distributor
National Film Board of Canada Library
22-D Hollywood Avenue
Ho-Ho-Kus, NJ 07423
1 800 542-2164 [b] 201 652-1973 [f]
US $275.00 VHS, call for rental information and prices.
For purchase within Canada visit the NFB website at: www.nfb.ca
1 800 267-7710 toll free within Canada

For 78 days in the summer and early fall of 1990, the world watched as Mohawks rose up to defend their land in armed standoff with the Quebec police and the Canadian army. Powerful images of the opposing forces glaring at each other across the barbed wire dominated the news, captivating public interest. Suddenly, the area just kilometers away from downtown Montreal resembled a war zone. The crisis at the Mohawk village of Kanehsatake, near the town of Oka, forced Native issues into the spotlight where they could no longer be ignored.

Kanehsatake: 270 Years of Resistance is award winning filmmaker Alanis Obomsawin's first hand account of the conflict. Riveting in its behind-the–barricades depiction of the standoff, the feature length documentary shows tension escalating to the breaking point, sometimes with violent results.

Obomsawin's detailed portrayal of the Mohawk community places the Oka crisis within the larger context of Mohawk land rights, disregarded by white authorities for centuries and destined to culminate in the 1990 standoff. The evocative portrait of the Mohawk people focuses on the human dimension of the conflict, exploring the conviction that motivated the Mohawks and the spirit that enabled them to stand firm.

This historic documentary examines the role of the federal and provincial politicians, the police and military in the Oka conflict and offers a startling depiction of the manipulation of the news media by authorities.
Kanehsatake: 270 Years of Resistance is an intricate and revealing account of a standoff that marked a turning point for Canada's Native peoples.

KASHTIN ETERNAL DRUM ARTIST: KASHTIN

Country Canada   **Year** 1993   **Length** 47 m.   **Genre** DS
Director Jean-Jacques Sheitoyan
Producer Les Productions Avanti Cine Video
Distributor
Currently unavaiable.

A fascinating look at one of Canada's national treasures: the richness and diversity of legends within the American Indian culture. In this soulful video, Native rock group KASHTIN uses the traditional drum as a link between Native nations from across Canada. As it holds great knowledge, the drum opens the door to the power of music.

KEEP THE CIRCLE STRONG

Country Canada   **Year** 1991   **Length** 28 m.   **Genre** DS
Director Joel Bertomeu, Luc Cote, Robbie Hart
Producer Luc Cote, Robbie Hart
Distributor
The Cinema Guild, Inc.
130 madison Avenue, 2nd Floor
New York, NY 10016
212 685-6242 [b] 212 685-4717 [f]
thecinemaguild@aol.com
US $250.00 VHS, US $50.00 VHS rental
Also distributed by the NFB of Canada: www.nfb.ca

Keep the Circle Strong follows the life of Mike Auger, a Cree from
Northern Canada who embarks on a five month journey to Bolivia, South
America. He goes there to live and work with the Aymara Indians,
Bolivia's largest indigenous group. Through his journey, we witness the
story of one man and his quest to recover his Native culture, as well as the
story of two Native peoples and the striking parallels between them.

KEEPERS OF THE FIRE

Country Canada   **Year** 1994   **Length** 55 m.   **Genre** DF
Director Christine Welsh
Producer Michael Chechik, Ian Herring, Signe Johansson, Joe
MacDonald, Christine Welsh
Distributor
National Film Board of Canada
1 800 267-7710 toll free within Canada
For purchase within Canada visit the NFB website at: www.nfb.ca
Omni Film (US Distributor)
Suite 204, 111 Water Street
Vancouver, BC
V6B 1A7 Canada
604-681-6543 [b] 604-688-1425 [f]
Please call for pricing.

For half a millennium, First Nations Women have been at the forefront of
aboriginal peoples' resistance to cultural assimilation. Today, Native
women are still fighting for the survival of their cultures and their peoples
on many different fronts—in the rainforest and the city, in the courts and
legislatures, and in the longhouse and the media. From the Mohawk
women who stood at the barricades during the "Oka crisis" to the Haida
women who defended Lyell Island, *Keepers of the Fire* profiles Canada's
Native "warrior women"—the storytellers and the dreamers, the healers
and the fighters, those who are protecting and defending their land, their
culture and their people in the time honored tradition of their foremothers.

KEEPERS OF THE WATER

Country USA   **Year** 1997   **Length** 38 m.   **Genre** DS
Director Al Gedicks
Producer Al Gedicks
Distributor
Mining Center
210 Avon Street, #4
La Crosse, WI 54603
608 784-4399 [b] 608 785-8486 [f]
US $50.00 VHS, US $15.00 VHS rental

Viewable on a variety of levels, *Keepers of the Water* is an inspiring story
of how an environmental issue affects everyone, Indians and whites alike,
in their fight against corporate America. Set against the pristine backdrop
of Northern Wisconsin, *Keepers of the Water* focuses on the fight of the
residents of the area against the Exxon Corporation and its efforts to open
a copper mine and toxic waste dump at the headwaters of the Wolf River,
one of the last wild and clean rivers left in the Midwest. Aware that the
proposed mine would have disastrous affects on fish, wildlife and human
life in this unspoiled area, white residents have joined the local Sokaigon
Chippewa tribe to prevent this from happening. In presenting the potential
consequences to the region, tribal leaders, local residents, and Wisconsin
governmental officials come together to form the largest, broadest multira-
cial environmental alliance ever formed over a single issue in Wisconsin.

KEETOOWAHS COME HOME, THE

Country USA   **Year** 1996   **Length** 26 m.   **Genre** DS
Director Larry Foley
Producer Frank Scheide
Distributor
Currently unavailable.

The Keetoowahs Come Home is an exploration of the United Keetoowah Band of Cherokees' forced removal to Oklahoma in 1828 and their hope to relocate to Arkansas today. On September 10, 1991, Chief John Ross and the council of the United Keetoowah Band of Cherokee Indians participated in a ceremonial march cross the Oklahoma-Arkansas state line. Cherokee member Jim Henson narrates the story, which profiles the history and hopes of the tribe, in both English and Cherokee.

KINAALDA, NAVAJO RITE OF PASSAGE

Country USA   **Year** 1999   **Length** 57 m.   **Genre** DF
Director Lena Carr
Producer Lena Carr
Distributor
Indian Summer Films
10705 Benito S.W.
Albuquerque, NM 87121
505 836-1336 [b]

Kinaalda, Navajo Rite of Passage is a documentary about the coming-of-age ceremony for a young Navajo girl, Tanya. Navajo families and their community give the Kinaalda when their daughters get their first menses. It is their way of guiding their daughters from childhood to adulthood. The story of Tanya's ceremony is paralleled to the personal story of a Navajo woman who, as a young girl, did not have a Kinaalda. She searches for answers to why she was not given the gift meant for every Navajo girl.

KING OF THE GRIZZLIES

Country USA   **Year** 1975   **Length** 93 m.   **Genre** FF
Director Ron Kelly
Producer Winston Hibler, Robert F. Metzler (exec), Erwin L. Verity (exec)
Distributor
Not in distribution.

At a Ranch owned by the Colonel (Chris Higgins), the Indian foreman, Moki (John Yesno), befriends a baby grizzly bear. Years later, the now mature bear returns to the ranch and threatens the livestock in Moki's care. The Colonel wants the bear killed, but Moki refuses to hurt his old friend. Moki must find another way to appease the grizzly's hunger.

Original Release Date - 1970.

KOLUSKAP AND HIS PEOPLE

Country USA   **Year** 1992   **Length** 7 m.   **Genre** ANS
Director Joshua M. Vermette
Producer Indian Island School Students
Distributor
Indian Island School
1 River Road, Penobscot Reservation
Old Town, ME 04468
207 827-4285 [b] 207 827-3599 [f]
US $29.95 VHS for "The Frog Monster and Other Penobscot Stories' (20 min).

Based on an adaptation of the story taken from *Legends of the Wabanaki Indians: Glooscap and His Magic*, sixth graders explore all aspects of paper cut-out animation, including developing artwork and characters, filming, and adding the soundtrack.

KUPER ISLAND: RETURN TO THE HEALING CIRCLE

Country Canada   **Year** 1997   **Length** 45 m.   **Genre** DS
Director Peter C. Campbell, Christine Welsh
Producer Christine Welsh
Distributor
National Film Board of Canada Library
22-D Hollywood Avenue
Ho-Ho-Kus, NJ 07423
1 800 542-2164 [b] 201 652-1973 [f]
US $225.00 VHS, call for rental information and prices.
For purchase within Canada visit the NFB website at: www.nfb.ca
1 800 267-7710 toll free within Canada

For almost a century, hundreds of Coast Salish children were sent to the Kuper Island Residential School that stood on a remote island off the coast of British Columbia. Some died trying to escape across the water on logs and many more died later from the after effects of alcoholism and the ills spawned by the horror of their broken childhoods. Throughout the years, only a few of the survivors spoke openly about their ordeal. In *Kuper Island: Return to the Healing Circle*, the former residents of Kuper Island embark on an extraordinary healing journey and reflect on their experiences at the school they referred to as Alcatraz. Although the stories of abuse are horrifying, *Kuper Island: Return to the Healing Circle* is ultimately uplifting as it shows how far the survivors have come.

KUSAH HAKWAAN

Country USA   **Year** 1999   **Length** 75 m.   **Genre** FF
Director Sean Morris
Producer Sean Morris and Erik Wolford
Distributor
Currently unavailable.

The film takes its name from the Tlingit Indian legend of a demon that lives in the spirit worlds of Southeast Alaska.

Filmed entirely on location in Alaska, the production explores the traditions of Native American storytelling. In the dark, fire-lit Clan House, the Tlingit Elder walks between fantasy and reality as he reveals the centuries-old legend of Kusah Hakwaan. He spins a tale of mysticism, telling of two brothers, Shawn and Yuntun, who set out to conquer this monster threatening their village. While interviewing Tlingit Elders for the making of this project, one expressed concern that the tradition of storytelling was disappearing and that his generation may be the last to remember these important myths. In today's modern film arena of dazzling special effects, intense sound, and quick-cuts editing, the simple power of stories told around a fire can be eclipsed.

Kusah Hakwaan bridges these two worlds by combining tradition with technology. The project weaves innovative visual effects, compelling action scenes, and breathtaking footage together with the authentic Tlingit creation myth. The resulting story echoes the Tlingits' esteemed tribal values, ancient traditions, and influence of the all-knowing spiritual world. *Kusah Hakwaan* strives to spark a new interest of traditions and legends in the imagination of the next generation of storytellers.

KWA'NU'TE': MICMAC AND MALISEET ARTISTS

Country Canada   **Year** 1992   **Length** 41 m.   **Genre** DS
Director Catherine Martin, Kimberlee McTaggart
Producer Sami Fareed Ahmed, Kent Nason, Germaine Wong
Distributor
National Film Board of Canada Library
22-D Hollywood Avenue
Ho-Ho-Kus, NJ   07423
1 800 542-2164 [b] 201 652-1973 [f]
US $195.00 VHS, call for rental information and prices.
For purchase within Canada visit the NFB website at: www.nfb.ca
1 800 267-7710 toll free within Canada

KWA'NU'TE' is a chant that carries the power of creation. It is a vehicle to the spirit world. Its purpose is to bring back visions of healing. When KWA'NU'TE' is sung, it honors and thanks those spirits that have shared their visions and dreams. The film celebrates Micmac and Maliseet artists who have transformed those dreams and visions into reality.

This film profiles a number of Micmac and Maliseet artists from Nova Scotia and New Brunswick, showing their similarities and differences, samples of their work and the sources of their inspiration. It offers a remarkable look at Native art and spirituality in Atlantic Canada.

KWEKANAMAND: THE WIND IS CHANGING

Country Canada   **Year** 2000   **Length** 54 m.   **Genre** DF
Director Carlos Ferrand
Producer Stephanie Larrue and Yves Bisaillon
Distributor
National Film Board of Canada Library
22-D Hollywood Avenue
Ho-Ho-Kus, NJ   07423
1 800 542-2164 [b] 201 652-1973 [f]
US $250.00 VHS, call for rental information and prices.
For purchase within Canada visit the NFB website at: www.nfb.ca
1 800 267-7710 toll free within Canada

Annie Smith St. Georges is an Algonquin mother of four. She led a largely uneventful life until February 10, 1990 when Yanik, her eldest son, ended his own life. Annie's world was shaken to its roots. Her life became a living hell until the day she had a vision of a glass teepee, ten stories high, in downtown Ottawa. In memory of her son and for all those young Native people struggling to find meaning in life, Annie set out on her mission to erect this monument.

LA GUAJIRA

Country Venezuela   **Year** 1984   **Length** 58 m.   **Genre** DF
Director Calogero Salvo
Producer Calogero Salvo
Distributor
Chip Taylor Communications
2 Eastview Drive
Derry, NH   03038
1 800 876-2447 [b] 603 432-2723 [f]
www.chiptaylor.com   sales@chiptaylor.com
Price upon request.

The Guajiros are a people who have survived the harsh elements of their desert environment and intervention of outside cultures. Through the centuries they have learned to interpret the values and laws of those cultures to assure perpetuation of their race. In this film, their art and ancient ceremonies are intermingled with the economic and socio-political realities existing in Latin America today.

By special AIFI invitation.

LACROSSE: THE CREATOR'S GAME

Country Canada   **Year** 1995   **Length** 25 m.   **Genre** DS
Director Kem Murch
Producer Scott Calbeck, Kem Murch
Distributor
Magic Lantern Communications, Ltd.
10 Meteor Drive
Toronto, ON
M9W 1A4 Canada
416 675-1155 [b]   416 675-1154 [f]
www.magiclantern.ca video@magiclantern.ca
CAD $49.00 VHS Institutional   CAD $25.00 VHS home

This video examines the roots of North America's oldest team sport, played by Native Americans before Columbus arrived on the continent. The game had a cultural and spiritual element that European settlers had no way of relating to, yet in Canada they wasted no time wrestling control of lacrosse from the Natives that taught them to play.

Lacrosse was billed as the national sport of the new country when Canada was created in 1867, but by 1880 Native players were banned from amateur competition. Clearly, the concept of "national sport" did not apply to everyone. It was not until the 1930s that Native players were once again allowed to compete at all levels.

The Six Nations Reserve enjoyed national lacrosse success in 1992 and 1994, and the video documents both the rise to prominence of Native lacrosse players and the rediscovery of traditional values in the game.

LADIES OF THE INLET

Country Canada   **Year** 1996   **Length** 27 m.   **Genre** DS
Director Annie Fraziér Henry
Producer Annie Fraziér Henry
Distributor
Video Out Distribution
1965 Main Street
Vancouver, BC
V5T 3C1 Canada
604 872-8449 [b]   604 876-1185 [f]
videoout@telus.net
Call for pricing (purchase and rental available)

Ladies of the Inlet is a sensitive, personal journey with the six oldest Sechelt women as they travel up the Jarvis Inlet in British Columbia and visit the deserted villages where they once lived. Through a collage of historic photos, interviews, and a dramatic re-enactment their stories unfold. The women recount childhood legends and sing Native songs as we visit them on their reserve on the Sunshine Coast of British Columbia.

LAKOTA QUILLWORK: ART & LEGEND

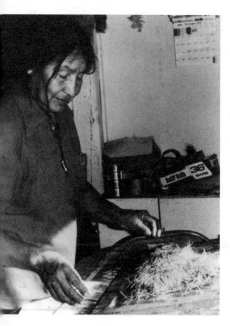

Country USA   **Year** 1985   **Length** 27 m.   **Genre** DS
Director H. Jane Nauman
Producer H. Jane Nauman
Distributor
Sun Dog Films
P.O. Box 232
Custer, SD 57730
650 673-4065 [b]
US $29.95 VHS home video
US $110.00 VHS institution

Lakota Quillwork: Art & Legend describes the nearly lost art of porcupine quillwork of the Lakota Sioux.

Through historic footage, special effects, and the paintings of Sioux artist Oscar Howe, the film portrays the legend of Double Woman, who first brought the art of porcupine quilling to Lakota women from the spirit world.

Double Woman was said to sing from rock cliffs, but was never seen except in dreams. When tanned robes were brought to her tipi, they were returned with fine quilled designs. Some said she was a crazy woman who laughed uncontrollably. Others said she was an enchantress and no man was equal to her spell. But all said that she was wakan, sacred, and that those who dreamed of Double Woman became expert quillworkers.

In this film, singer Nellie Two Bulls brings back an old song of Double Woman from the early stories recorded at the Pine Ridge Reservation.

LAKOTA STRAIN

Country USA   **Year** 1994   **Length** 5 m.   **Genre** LS
Director Richard L. Rohrer, Jr.
Producer Richard L. Rohrer, Jr.
Distributor
For more information on this film e-mail Rich Rohrer at
mail@richrohrer.com

The conflict between the white settlers and the Native Americans of the great North American plains was widespread. In every corner of this beautiful and sacred land, battles were won and lost, stories and legends were created. One story, *Lakota Strain,* reveals a Lakota warrior and a white woman's struggle for peaceful coexistence. Ignorant of each other's culture, they strain to understand. Their personal struggleis a metaphor for the greater conflicts of the Great Plains and Rocky Mountains that deafened millions of crying and angry spirits.
Featuring Stuart "Proud Eagle" Grant and Liz Green.

LAKOTA WOMAN: SIEGE AT WOUNDED KNEE

Country USA   **Year** 1994   **Length** 110 m.   **Genre** FF
Director Frank Pierson
Producer Lois Bonfiglio (ex), Hanay Geiogmah, Fred Berner
Distributor
Available on Amazon.com
www.amazon.com
US $13.99 VHS
Also available on www.cdnow.com

Lakota Woman: Siege at Wounded Knee stars Irene Bedard in the title role as Mary Crow Dog. The film chronicles the life of Mary from her youth on the reservation, her years in bording school, her increasing political activism and her time spent at Wounded Knee during the 1973 occupation. Mary spent 71 days at Wounded Knee, and it is this event that is at the core of *Lakota Woman.*

Also starring August Schellenberg, Joseph Running Fox, Floyd Red Crow Westerman, Pato Hoffman, Michael Horse and Tantoo Cardinal.

LAND IS OURS, THE

Country USA   **Year** 1996   **Length** 57 m.   **Genre** DF
Director Laurence Goldin
Producer Laurence Goldin
Distributor
Aurora Films
P.O. Box 022955
Juneau, AK 99802
907 586-6696 [b]
larygoldin@aol.com
US $250.00 VHS educational, US $29.95 VHS home video

The Land is Ours is a historical documentary about the Tlingits and Haidas of southeast Alaska. Though they resisted the Russian Empire for a century, American imperialism brought awesome gunships, epidemics, and discrimination. However, they would not remain victims. Using cultural strengths to launch America's first civil rights movement, the Tlingits and Haidas in the 1920s won voting rights, school integration, and economic opportunity. *The Land is Ours* is also the story of how a young attorney challenged the powerful canned salmon industry, prosecuted landmark civil rights cases, and faced a vindictive white power elite.

William Paul, Sr. was a brilliant Tlingit attorney and the first Native elected to the territorial legislature. Amidst conflicting cultures, the very strengths that made William Paul a legal warrior offended many of his own people and cost him their love. In the end, he proved his own undoing, even as he launched the land claims suit that changed Alaska forever.

LAND OF THE WANNABE FREE
ARTIST: ROBBY BEE AND THE BOYZ

Country USA   **Year** 1995   **Length** 5 m.   **Genre** MV
Director Tom Bee
Producer Robby Bee
Distributor
SOAR Corporation (for CD information)
5200 Constitution NE Avenue
Albuquerque, NM 87110
505 268-6110 [b]

We have tried to create a video that paints what contemporary America is all about today. Very little has changed for Native Americans, and our struggles continue to be just that, our struggles. We are POWs in a country that is quick to promote life, liberty and justice for all. The invisible ink reads, but not for Indians. The school system teaches our children to believe that Christopher Columbus was a hero, never bothering to mention that he was also responsible for making Indians the first slaves in our own country. To Native Americans, George Washington is not our father, and Christopher Columbus is certainly not a hero. Why doesn't America set aside a day honoring all of the Great Chiefs? They certainly honor their own chiefs! We are living in a land of the wanna be free.

LAND RIGHTS FROM STORYTELLERS OF THE PACIFIC

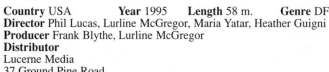

Country USA   **Year** 1995   **Length** 58 m.   **Genre** DF
Director Phil Lucas, Lurline McGregor, Maria Yatar, Heather Guigni
Producer Frank Blythe, Lurline McGregor
Distributor
Lucerne Media
37 Ground Pine Road
Morris Plains, NJ 07950
1 800 341-2293 [b] 973 538-0855 [f]
www.lucernemedia.com   LM@lucernemedia.com
US $99.00 VHS educational - part of "Storytellers of the Pacific" series

"Slaves of the Harvest," set on the Pribiloff Islands of Alaska with Larry Merculieff representing the Aleut people, tells of almost two hundred years of virtual slavery, first by the Russians and then by the Americans.

"Stranger in Our Own Homeland," set in Guam with Angel Santos representing the Chamoru people, documents their struggle to regain control over their own homeland.

LANDS OF OUR ANCESTORS

Country USA   **Year** 1994   **Length** 42 m.   **Genre** DS
Director Allan Forbes, Jr.
Producer Seneca Nation, Sheila Kenjockety (project coordinator)
Distributor
Seneca Nation
1490 Route 438
Irving, NY 14081
716 532-4900 [b]

In 1964, the interest of Allan Forbes, Jr. an independent filmmaker from Cambridge, MA, was captured by the plight of a small Indian tribe in Western New York state which was on the verge of having one-third of its reservation inundated to serve as a reservoir for a federal dam project. Forbes, a non-Indian filmmaker, moved with his wife and infant daughter to the reservation and set about documenting the struggle of the Senecas. For more than a year, Forbes and his wife observed and recorded the lifestyle and sentiments of community members dwelling in the "take area" and were still recording when the Army Corps of Engineers moved in to raze their homes, churches, burial grounds and schools in preparation for the flooding. The film was shot without sound; the interviews and wild track audio were recorded separately on reel-to-reel audio tape.

For years, Forbes was unable to interest a sponsor in subsidizing the post-production of his film. The black and white footage, audiotapes and photographs were boxed and eventually stored in his attic in Cambridge. There the properties remained for nearly 30 years. Finally, in March of 1993, the 73 year old Forbes contacted the Seneca Nation of Indians to inquire whether the tribe might wish to subsidize completion of the film. A period of negotiation followed, and in May of 1994, the Tribal Council of the Seneca Nation of Indians, in an unprecedented move, appointed the funds necessary to transfer the rapidly deteriorating 16mm film to Beta, to complete the documentary and acquire all the original properties and exclusive rights to the name. The tribe took control of the project and hired Forbes as director. A six-person Seneca steering committee (all members of the community displaced by the reservoir) served as an advisory board to the post production team.

LAST DAYS OF OKAK, THE

Country Canada   **Year** 1986   **Length** 24 m.   **Genre** DS
Director Anne Budgell, Nigel Markham
Producer Barry Cowling, Kent Martin
Distributor
National Film Board of Canada Library
22-D Hollywood Avenue
Ho-Ho-Kus, NJ 07423
1 800 542-2164 [b] 201 652-1973 [f]
US $150.00 VHS, call for rental information and prices.
For purchase within Canada visit the NFB website at: www.nfb.ca
1 800 267-7710 toll free within Canada

Only grass-covered ruins remain of the once-thriving town of Okak, an Inuit settlement on the northern Labrador coast. Moravian missionaries evangelized the coast and encouraged the growth of Inuit settlements, but it was also a Moravian ship that brought the deadly Spanish influenza during the world epidemic of 1919. The Inuit of the area were decimated, and Okak was abandoned. Through diaries, old photos and interviews with survivors, this film relates the story of the epidemic, with its accompanying horrors, as well as examining the relations between the Natives and the missionaries.

LAST OF THE DOGMEN

Country USA   **Year** 1995   **Length** 118 m.   **Genre** FF
Director Tab Murphy
Producer Joel B. Michaels
Distributor
Available on amzon.com
www.amazon.com
Also available at local video stores for rental or purchase.

Tom Berenger is Lewis Gates, a bounty hunter haunted by the past, hired to track down three escaped convicts in the Oxbow region of the Rockies. Their trail leads him to a secluded spot and signs of a struggle, but no bodies - only a strange arrow shaft remains. Gates takes the arrow to an expert in Native American culture, Lillian Sloan (Barbara Hershey), and together they set off in search of an impossible mystery - a tribe they believe cannot exist, massacred over 100 years ago. What they discover deep in the Oxbow may prove an answer to both Lillian's dreams and Lewis' nightmares. But for now, it's a desperate race against time if they are to save the last of the Dogmen from the destructive forces of the modern world.

Starring Steve Reevis, Kurtwood Smith, and Eugene Blackbear.

LAXWESA WA - STRENGTH OF THE RIVER

Country Canada   **Year** 1995   **Length** 54 m.   **Genre** DF
Director Barb Cranmer
Producer Barb Cranmer, Michael Doxtater, Cari Green
Distributor
National Film Board of Canada 1 800 267-7710 toll free within Canada
For purchase within Canada visit the NFB website at: www.nfb.ca

Nimpkish Wind Productions, Inc. (US distribution)
#107 2772 Spruce Street
Vancouver, BC
V6H 2R2 Canada
604 731-8044 [b] 604 731-8011 [f]

As distinct fishing societies of great spiritual, cultural and economic wealth, First Nations have always respected the resources of their rivers and oceans. But within their own lifetime, they have watched governments "manage" the fishery into a state of crisis. Now it's time for people to listen to what Natives have to say. Filmmaker Barb Cranmer, a member of the 'Namgis First Nation, explores the rich fishing traditions of the Sto:lo, Heiltsuk and 'Namgis peoples of Canada's west coast in *Laxwesa Wa - Strength of the River*. With over fifteen years experience fishing Johnstone Strait with her father, Cranmer presents rarely heard stories of traditional fishing practices and documents Native peoples' efforts to build sustainable fishery for the future.

LAY YOUR BURDEN DOWN ARTIST: TIGER TIGER

Country USA   **Year** 2000   **Length** 4 m.   **Genre** MV
Director Lee Tiger and Tom Bea
Producer Tiger Tiger and Seminole Tribe of Florida
Distributor
Sound Of America Records
P.O. Box 8606
Albuquerque, NM 87198
954 370-3900 [b] 954 370-3999 [f]
US $8.00

Tiger Tiger is comprised of two brothers Stephen and Lee Tiger, from the Miccouskee Tribe of Florida. They are proud of their Indian roots, and equally proud of their redefined musical sound, which they hope will not only portray a positive awareness of their culture, but also carry this awareness over into the world of pop music.

"Lay Your Burden Down" is the first single off Tiger Tiger's 2000 album Southern Exposure.

LEARNING PATH, THE

Country Canada   **Year** 1991   **Length** 56 m.   **Genre** DF
Director Loretta Todd
Producer James Cullingham, Cari Green, Kent Martin, Peter Raymont
Distributor
National Film Board of Canada
1 800 267-7710 toll free within Canada
For purchase within Canada visit the NFB website at: www.nfb.ca

For US distribution information contact the NFB at:
212 629-8890 [b]

Native control of Native education is the motivating idea of *The Learning Path*. Director Loretta Todd introduces the viewer to three remarkable educators. In their own unique ways, Edmonton elders Ann Anderson, Eva Cardinal, and Olive Dickason are leading younger Natives along *The Learning Path*. The Native educators recount their own harrowing experiences at residential school, memories which fueled their determination to preserve their languages and identities. Todd uses a unique blend of documentary footage, dramatic reenactments, and archival film interweaving the three women's life stories. We see them at work in the schools of Edmonton and the nearby Saddle Lake Reserve. These unsung heroines are making education relevant in today's Native communities.

LEARNING PLACE, THE

Country USA   **Year** 1997   **Length** 15 m.   **Genre** IND
Director Bill N. Baker
Producer Pamela Jennings
Distributor
North Slope Borough School District / TV Studio
P.O. Box 169
Barrow, AK 99723
907 852-0215 [b] 907 852-2145 [f]
US $20.00 VHS

The Learning Place follows the emotional and physical journeys of Stephanie, Madi and Scott, high school graduates from small Alaskan communities, as they embark on their new lives as college students in Anchorage, Fairbanks and Sitka. Commissioned by the North Slope Borough School District, *The Learning Place* was made to encourage Alaska Native high school students to pursue college education.

LEGEND OF THE LONE RANGER, THE

Country USA   **Year** 1981   **Length** 98 m.   **Genre** FF
Director William A. Fraker
Producer Walter Coblenz
Distributor
Available on Amazon.com
www.amazon.com
US $9.98 VHS

Michael Horse stars as Tonto in *The Legend of the Lone Ranger*, an action-adventure story dealing with the legend of the man behind the mask.

When young Texas Ranger, John Reid, is the only surviving member of an ambush by the outlaw Butch Cabendich, he is rescued by his old childhood friend Tonto. After recoving from his injuries, he decides to dedicate his life to fighting outlaws like Butch Cabendich. John Ried then takes on the mask of the Lone Ranger. With the help of Tonto, the pair rescue the President of the United States from Cabendich's clutches.

LEONARD PELTIER ARTIST: LITTLE STEVEN

Country USA   **Year** 1989   **Length** 4 m.   **Genre** MV
Director Hart Perry
Producer Hart Perry
Distributor
Perry Films
530 West 25th Street, 3rd Floor
New York, NY 10001
212 989-2880 [b] 212 989-3262 [f]
hart@perryfilms.com   www.perryfilms.com
US $25.00 VHS

Leonard Peltier is a Native American political prisoner. He is currently
serving two life sentences in the Leavenworth Federal Prison for the
deaths of two FBI agents on the Pine Ridge Indian Reservation in 1975.
However, his trial and conviction were full of inconsistencies and corruption. In this music video by Little Steven, Peltier's story is told with the
hopes of his eventual freedom.

LIFE SPIRIT

Country USA   **Year** 1993   **Length** 24 m.   **Genre** DS
Director Fidel Moreno
Producer Fidel Moreno
Distributor
Native Visions
320 Central So. West
Albuquerque, NM 87102
505 242-2300 [b] 505 242- 4880 [f]
US $29.95 VHS

Life Spirit speaks of the inherent ancestral power, breathed into songs,
prayers, and ceremonies of the American Indian. Eagle feathers, pipes,
bundles, drums, masks, and all ceremonial materials are given the knowledge to heal, the knowledge to guide, the knowledge to keep every life
form in harmony. They are necessary for the spiritual worship of these living cultures, and belong to them.

Life Spirit features interviews with outstanding Native leaders. Reuben
Snake, Spiritual Leader (Winnebego), Sara James (Gwich'in), Clark
Tenakhongva (Hopi), Elmer Blackbird (Omaha), Chief Jake Swamp
(Mohawk), Johnny WhiteCloud (Otoe), Michael Haney (Seminole), Oren
Lyons, Faithkeeper (Onondoga), and Marilyn Youngbird (Arikara-Hidasta)
express the importance of the repatriation of ceremonial material, its value
to their living culture and to all of life.

LIGHTING THE 7TH FIRE

Country USA   **Year** 1994   **Length** 41 m.   **Genre** DS
Director Sandra Sunrising Osawa
Producer Sandra Sunrising Osawa
Distributor
Upstream Productions
6850 35th Avenue NE #11
Seattle, WA 98115
206 526-7122 [b] 206 526-7127 [f]
US $30.00 VHS home video

A unique and innovative video that weaves together spearfishing treaty
rights issues in Wisconsin, the Chippewa prophecy of the seventh fire, and
profiles of some of the people who have helped to bring back the tradition
of spearfishing. This video captures a transition from loss to victory with
insights on law, culture, and history as seen from a tribal perspective.
Although racism is shockingly evident, it is countered by the strong spiritual persistence of people who believe that the time prophesized as the
seventh fire, when traditions will return, is very near. Directed and produced by Native American Producer, Sandra Johnson-Osawa.

LIKE THE TREES

Country Canada   **Year** 1975   **Length** 14 m.   **Genre** DS
Director Kathleen Shannon
Producer Len Chatwin, Kathleen Shannon
Distributor
National Film Board of Canada Library
22-D Hollywood Avenue
Ho-Ho-Kus, NJ 07423
1 800 542-2164 [b] 201 652-1973 [f]
US $125.00 VHS, call for rental information and prices.
For purchase within Canada visit the NFB website at: www.nfb.ca
1 800 267-7710 toll free within Canada

Rose is a Metis from Northern Alberta, a woman who has lifted herself out
of an anguished existence in the city by rediscovering her roots among the
Woodland Cree. "I've left everything . . . I'm just being myself . . . Like
the trees, we belong here." A film of interest to all.

LISTEN TO THE DRUM

Country USA   **Year** 1990   **Length** 14 m.   **Genre** IND
Director Victor Romero
Producer Victor Romero
Distributor
Not in distribution
US Census Bureau / Public Information Office
4700 Silver Hill Road
Suitland, MD 20746
301 457-3045 [b] 301 457-6611 [f]

American Indians telling American Indians why the 1990 census is important: that was the intent when two American Indian producers set out for
Laguna, NM; Bismarck, ND; Chicago, IL; and Tahlequah, OK, to inform
leaders about the need for accurate population and housing numbers.

LITTLE BIG MAN

Country USA   **Year** 1975   **Length** 150 m.   **Genre** FF
Director Arthur Penn
Producer Stuart Millar
Distributor
Available on Amazon.com
www.amazon.com
US $9.95 VHS
Also check local video stores.

Little Big Man follows the history of the Wild West through the eyes of
Jack Crabbe (Dustin Hoffman), a white orphan adopted and raised by the
Cheyenne and the sole white survivor of Custer's Last Stand. The story is
told in flashbacks by the 121 year-old Crabbe, who recounts his upbring-
ing as a "Human Being" among the Cheyenne. His mentor, Old Lodge
Shins (Chief Dan George), gives him the name "Little Big Man" and
teaches him about living in harmony with nature. As a young man, Crabbe
is thrust back into the white world, and from one misadventure to another.
He finds, after witnessing the white man's folly and destruction first hand,
that he prefers life as a "Human Being." Also starring Thayer David, Faye
Dunaway, Jeff Corey, Martin Balsam, and Richard Mulligan.

Original Release Date - 1970.

LITTLE ROCK'S RUN

Country USA   **Year** 1998   **Length** 59 m.   **Genre** DF
Director James LuJan
Producer James LuJan
Distributor
Contact 505 751-3380 [b]
US $49.95 VHS

Lakota activist Timothy "Little Rock" Reed has been called the most wanted man in America today. Over forty states joined the state of Ohio in the
effort to put him behind bars. His crime? He violated his parole by leaving
Ohio six days before his parole was completed. Six days. Why did he flee
Ohio when he was so close to freedom? And why has Ohio pursued him
with a zeal usually reserved for more violent criminals? More interestingly,
why did the state of New Mexico try to grant him asylum? The answers to
these questions are addressed in the fascinating, startling documentary,
"Little Rock's Run."

LITTLE TRAPPER, THE

Country Canada   **Year** 1999   **Length** 25 m.   **Genre** DS
Director Dorothy Schreiber
Producer Jerry Krepakevich, Graydon McCrea
Distributor
National Film Board of Canada Library
22-D Hollywood Avenue
Ho-Ho-Kus, NJ 07423
1 800 542-2164 [b] 201 652-1973 [f]
US $129.00 VHS, call for rental information and prices.
For purchase within Canada visit the NFB website at: www.nfb.ca
1 800 267-7710 toll free within Canada

Robert Grandejambe, Jr. is a unique and industrious 13-year old kid. While
his peers are adopting a more modern, urban lifestyle, Robert is continuing
the traditions of his Cree forebears. Equally at home in town or in the
bush, the young boy is *The Little Trapper*, hunting, fishing, and living off
the land. His knowledge and skills are the heritage and inheritance passed
down from his parents and grandfather. Robert has a genuine motivation
to continually learn more about the traditional lifestyle and the beliefs of
his ancestors.

Robert's sense of responsibility and initiative, his great love and enthusi-
asm for the bush, and his respectful approach to hunting and trapping are
all qualities that make him unique and special, and a model for others his
age.

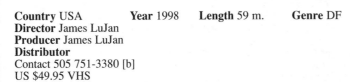

LIVE AND REMEMBER

Country USA   **Year** 1988   **Length** 30 m.   **Genre** DS
Director Henry Smith
Producer Richard Muller, Solaris Lakota Project
Distributor
Clearvue/eva, Inc.
6465 N. Avondale Avenue
Chicago, IL 60631
773 775-9433 [b]   773 775-9855 [f]
1 800 444-9855 [b]
www.clearvue.com   custserv@clearvue.com
US $50.00 VHS

A glimpse of the culture of the Lakota Sioux, filmed on South Dakota's
Rosebud Reservation.

The half-hour documentary features intimate interviews with Lakota Sioux
elders, medicine men and traditional dancers. It touches on such topics as
the role of women in modern Indian society and the acculturation of
Indians into white society. But the bulk of the program deals with the traditions of the Lakota Sioux: their spirit world, ceremonies, music and
dance; their oral tradition; their traditional medicine; and the interaction
between humans and nature in their culture.

LIVING WITH TRADITION

Country USA   **Year** 1979   **Length** 28 m.   **Genre** DS
Director Anthony Brown
Producer Anthony Brown
Distributor
Lucerne Media
37 Ground Pine Road
Morris Plains, NJ 07950
1 800 341-2293 [b] 973 538-0855 [f]
www.lucernemedia.com   LM@lucernemedia.com
US $99.00 VHS educational - part of the "Forest Spirits" series

This film tells the story of how the Menominee managed to maintain traditions when the U.S. Government ended their protected status as an Indian
tribe and how the 1973 return to tribal status has begun to reverse the
process. This film is one of a seven part series entitled "Forest Spirits." It
was filmed on location in Wisconsin.

LONG WAY FROM HOME, A

Country USA   **Year** 1994   **Length** 9 m.   **Genre** DS
Director Bernice Dahl
Producer Bernice Dahl and Institute of American Indian Arts
Distributor
Not in distribution - student film
IAIA
Avan Nu Po Road
Santa Fe, NM 87505
505 424-2300 [b]

This presentation was produced for Alaskan students thinking about
attending the Institute of American Indian Arts in Santa Fe, New Mexico.
It examines the environmental and cultural differences that might be
encountered while going to the Institute.

LONGBOAT

Country Canada   **Year** 1993   **Length** 23 m.   **Genre** DS
Director David Storey
Producer David Storey
Distributor
Shenandoah Film Productions
538 "G" Street
Arcata, CA 95521
707 822-1030 [b] 707 822-1035 [f]
US $150.00 VHS, US $45.00 rental

Longboat examines the life, times and misunderstandings of turn of the century long distance runner Tom Longboat. Based on Bruce Kidd's book, *In Defense of Tom Longboat*, it focuses on a chance meeting between Toronto Star reporter Jimmy McKearney and Longboat years after his career had ended. Curmudgeondy McKearney wants to hear the rags to riches to rags stereotype reinforced, but he is surprised when Longboat gives him the real story. An insightful examination of North American 20th century society and its values is the subtext of this fascinating story of one of the Iroquois Nations most famous athletes.

Starring Denise Lacroix.

LOOKS INTO THE NIGHT

Country USA   **Year** 1996   **Length** 37 m.   **Genre** LS
Director Lorraine Norrgard
Producer Roger Ellis, Valerie Red-Horse
Distributor
Lorraine Norrgard
345 Prevost Rd.
Cloquet, MN 55720
218 879-2288 [b]
218 724-4269 [f]
US $29.95 VHS

A dramatic look at the lives of four American Indian women dealing with issues of culture, spirituality, and education. Based on a true story and filmed on location at the Chumash Tribe of Southern California, *Looks Into the Night* breaks new cinematic ground in featuring Indian women and contemporary issues.

Laura (Valerie Red-Horse), is a medical school student in Los Angeles, of Chumash Tribal descent, who was separated from her family at the time of her parent's death. Disturbing dreams and visions propel Laura on a journey of self-discovery. Through a twist of events, she is reunited with her family and culture where she learns "we're never alone, not ever!"

Also featuring Tantoo Cardinal, Kimberly Norris and Patricia Van Ingen.

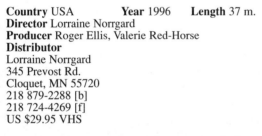

LOYALTIES

Country USA   **Year** 1986   **Length** 98 m.   **Genre** FF
Director Anne Wheeler
Producer William Johnston, Ronald Lillie, Michael Peacock, Mamoun Hassan
Distributor
Oasis International
6 Pardee Avenue, Suite 104
Toronto, Ontario
M6K 3H5 Canada
416 588-6821 [b] 416 588-7276 [f]
info@oasispictures.com
Please call for pricing

Loyalties is the story of an unlikely friendship between two women of vastly different backgrounds and circumstances. Nurturing of their children and the children themselves provides the first bond, the first bridge between the women.

Lily Sutton (Susan Wooldridge) is an upper middle class English woman who has followed her husband (Kenneth Welsh) to a medical practice in Lac La Biche, Alberta. She's a woman of impeccable taste and breeding whose approach to misfortune is to be ever more cheerful and well-mannered and polite than she was before. The Suttons and three of their four children, have just moved into a large expensive home on the lakeside. Rosanne Ladouceur (Tantoo Cardinal) is a Metis woman whose family has lived in or near Lac La Biche for several generations. She is poorly educated but bright and aggressive. She deals with everything straight on, often to her own detriment.

Underlying the dramatic story and momentum of LOYALTIES, is the detailed accuracy given to the portrayal of life in a small town in northern Alberta, circa 1985. The film emphasizes the extended Metis household, with low-rents, the people are poor but thriving, where Rosanne and her children are living; on the other hand the Suttons with their inclination for tasteful acquisition and style. Equally important is the detail afforded to the business of women living day to day surrounded by the raising of small children.

MAHEO'S RACE

Country USA   **Year** 1990   **Length** 9 m.   **Genre** ANS
Director Sharon Altman
Producer Sharon Altman
Distributor
Currently unavailable.

Maheo, the Great Spirit, challenges the animals to a race to capture the sun. The prize is power.

MAHK JCHI ARTIST: ULALI

Country USA   **Year** 1995   **Length** 4 m.   **Genre** MV
Director Victor Ginzburg
Producer Gary Ramano & Jessica Falcon
Distributor
Currently unavailable.
MRA
P.O. Box 8322
Silver Spring, MD 20910
301 589-9654 [b]   301 589-3819 [f]

Pura Fe, Soni and Jennifer comprise Ulali. These three Native women acappella singers deliver a mystical and sweeping sound that evolves from blending a variety of traditional and contemporary indigenous musical styles. Critically acclaimed, Ulali travels and performs worldwide at cultural festivals, conferences and concert halls.

The group has performed at the gala opening at the Smithsonian's National Museum of the American Indian in New York City, and at the United Nation's 4th World Conference on Women, where they received an overwhelming response by those in attendance.

Singing about the Native struggle and prophecies, the work of Ulali is a form of personal and historic expression.

MAKAH: THE WHALE HARVESTERS

Country USA/Germany **Year** 2000   **Length** 117 m.   **Genre** DF
Director Ralf Marshalleck
Producer Ralf Marshalleck and Um Welt Film
Distributor
Makah Tribal Council
P.O. Box 115
Neah Bay, WA 98357
360 645-2201 [b] 360 645-2788 [f]
Please call for pricing.

The Makah of Cape Flattery, on the U.S. Northwest Coast, are an ocean-fishing tribe who, with the support of the U.S. Government, decided to resume their tradition of whaling. This brought conflict with environmental protectionists and animal rights activists. The traditional Indian way of life, often held up as the model for environmental awareness, suddenly became the opponent.

"My idea of this project was to make it a joint venture with the Makah tribe as a natural consequence of the intercultural dialog I have intended to generate. The Makah have contributed to the production of the film. For this they own the distribution rights for North America. That gives them the chance to earn some money to support traditional tribal activities by their own means." -- Ralf Marshalleck

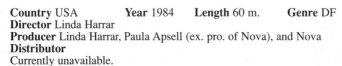

MAKE MY PEOPLE LIVE:
THE CRISIS IN INDIAN HEALTH

Country USA   **Year** 1984   **Length** 60 m.   **Genre** DF
Director Linda Harrar
Producer Linda Harrar, Paula Apsell (ex. pro. of Nova), and Nova
Distributor
Currently unavailable.

Make My People Live is an episode from the PBS television series *Nova*. Indian health workers and Indian Health Service (IHS) administrators talk about Indian values and a perspective of health that is distinctly different from Western medicine's. Health, they say, is a state of harmony with the environment; physical and spiritual welfare must be united. One alcoholism worker among the Navajo suggests that his sensibility makes his people especially vulnerable to mental distress. Despite this, Everett Rhoades, the IHS' first Indian director, maintains that American medicine as a whole stands to learn from the Indian concept of health.

In *Make My People Live*, *Nova* also investigates the state of health care for Indians who have been relocated to cities. Over half of America's Native population now live in urban centers, often isolated and unassimilated. These people receive medical care through special urban clinics — currently funded through the Indian Health Care Improvement Act.

MAKING A DIFFERENCE

Country USA   **Year** 1980   **Length** 30 m.   **Genre** DS
Director Barbara Alexander
Producer Ira Englander
Distributor
Currently unavailable.
Ira Englander
330 Washington Blvd., Suite 400
Marina del Rey, CA 90292
310 574-0889 [b]   310 574-3846 [f]

Making a Difference is a film about the largest gathering of American
Indian youth in history. On August 16, 1979, over 300 Native American
young people converged on Washington, D.C. to participate in the first
national Annual Indian Youth Leadership Conference. Sponsored by the
Division of Indian and Native American Programs of the Department of
Labor, this conference included youth from tribes and reservations from all
over the country.

We watch as the young people attend a reception on the White House
Lawn and meet President Carter, speak to government officials, and learn
about the governmental economic processes which are vital to Indian
groups today. We also see them on a tour of the capital city and as they
discuss the problems which face them and their tribes.

Most importantly, we see them emerge from the conference with a sense of
their own potential as leaders and of their importance in the future of their
people.

MAKING A NOISE: A NATIVE AMERICAN MUSICAL JOURNEY WITH ROBBIE ROBERTSON

Country USA   **Year** 1998   **Length** 57 m.   **Genre** DF
Director Dana Heinz Perry
Producer Dana Heinz Perry
Distributor
Perry Films
530 W. 25th Street
New York, NY 10001
212 989-2880 [b] 212 989-3262 [f]
www.PerryFilms.com
US $25.00 VHS
CD's of soundtrack also available

*Making A Noise: A Native American Musical Journey with Robbie
Robertson* is an extraordinary new music documentary featuring the former leader of the 60's rock group, The Band. The film documents
Robertson's reunion with relatives and childhood friends on the Six
Nations Reserve where he spent his childhood summers. During this musical journey, Robertson absorbs the Native rhythms of his youth and blends
them with contemporary rock, jazz and blues to create a rich, exciting new
sound.

But the journey is not solely Robertson's. He forms a loose collective of
Native American musicians that includes Rita Coolidge, Buffy Sainte-
Marie and poet/activist John Trudell. Together, they create songs that are
redolent of their heroic past yet possess a contemporary sensibility. *Making
A Noise: A Native American Musical Journey with Robbie Robertson* documents Robertson's personal explorations of his musical past and present
and combines them into an inspiring program.

MAN, THE SNAKE AND THE FOX, THE

Country Canada   **Year** 1979   **Length** 12 m.   **Genre** LS
Director Tony Snowsill
Producer Tony Snowsill
Distributor
National Film Board of Canada Library
22-D Hollywood Avenue
Ho-Ho-Kus, NJ 07423
1 800 542-2164 [b]   201 652-1973 [f]
US $99.00 VHS, call for rental information and prices.
For purchase within Canada visit the NFB website at: www.nfb.ca.
1 800 267-7710 toll free within Canada

The Man, the Snake and the Fox combines live action and puppetry. The film unfolds a poignant Ojibway legend that deals the concepts of sharing and promises. It is set in a traditional story-telling framework, with Basil Johnston of the Royal Ontario Museum's Ethnology Department relating the legend to a group of Indian children. Shortly after the story begins, we merge with the puppet world as large puppets act out the tale. The puppets are fully articulated, with moving heads, arms, legs, mouths and eyes. The audience of children featured in the film come from the Wandering Spirits Survival School in Toronto, and the title song is sung in Ojibway by Edna Manitouwabi.

MATTER OF RESPECT, A

Country USA   **Year** 1992   **Length** 29 m.   **Genre** DS
Director Ellen Frankenstein
Producer Ellen Frankenstein, Sharon Gmelch
Distributor
New Day Films
22-D Hollywood Avenue
Ho-Ho-Kus, NJ 07423
888 367-9154 [b]   201 652-1973 [f]
www.newday.com   orders@newday.com
US $150.00 VHS university, US $79.00 VHS community
US $55.00 VHS rental

A Matter of Respect is a stereotype-breaking documentary about the meaning of tradition and change. From a young drummer and dancer guiding tourists through a museum, to a silver carving radio D.J., to a Tlingit elder teaching at a summer fish camp, this engaging video portrays modern Alaska Natives expressing and passing on their culture and identity.

MATTER OF TRUST, A

Country Canada   **Year** 1998   **Length** 35 m.   **Genre** DS
Director Rod Carleton
Producer Rod Carleton
Distributor
Contact Richard Moore at:
Aboriginal Justice Learning Network / Department of Justice
284 Wellington Street
Ottawa, Ontario
K1A 0H8 Canada
613 946-6615 [b]

A Matter of Trust is the story of an innovative policing operation with the City of Vancouver Police Department. The Vancouver Police and Native Liaison Society was established 7 years ago to attempt to create a more cohesive relationship between the Native people living on the East Side skid row and the Vancouver Police Department. Since the establishment of the Liaison office, the relationship between Indians and the Police Department (which once could be described as tenuous, at best) experienced a remarkable turnaround. The Vancouver Police and Native Liaison Society is now established as a key partner with the province of British Columbia justice system. *A Matter of Trust* tells the story of how this was accomplished.

MAZERUNNER: THE LIFE AND ART OF T.C. CANNON

Country USA   **Year** 1993   **Length** 7 m.   **Genre** DS
Director Phillip Albert
Producer Phillip Albert
Distributor
Not in distribution.

Mazerunner is a short experimental documentary based on the life and work of Native American artist and poet T.C. Cannon. A large body of Cannon's paintings and drawings are utilized, as well as two of his poems. The piece concentrates on three basic areas of Cannon's life. The first deals with Cannon's strong reaction to the history of Native Americans since Columbus. The second refers to his own tour of duty in Vietnam. The third area alludes to his premonition of an early death. He is generally regarded as one of the most influential Native American artists of this century.

MEDICINE FIDDLE

Country USA   **Year** 1992   **Length** 81 m.   **Genre** DF
Director Michael Loukinen
Producer Michael Loukinen
Distributor
UC Extension Center for Media and Independent Learning
2000 Center Street, Fourth Floor
Berkeley, CA 94704-1223
510 642-0460 [b] 510 643-9271 [f]
cmil@uclink.berkeley.edu
US $195.00 VHS purchase US $75.00 VHS rental

A lively, foot-stomping documentary about the fiddling and dancing traditions of Native and Metis families in Northern Michigan, Wisconsin, North Dakota, Ontario and Manitoba, Canada. The fiddle was introduced to Native peoples by French fur traders and later by Irish and Scottish trappers and lumberjacks. Over the past two centuries this music became deeply imbedded in the cultural memory of descendants.

Unlike the coercive assimilation imposed by the Euro-American clerical and govermental authorities, Native people chose to play the fiddle and dance. Native influence occurs in the uneven, unpredictable phrasing that ethnomusicologists have found in traditional drum music. Names of fiddle tunes — "Sitting Bull," "Buffalo Gal," "Lonesome Indian," and "Devil, Shake a Half-Breed" reflect the creative contributions of the Ojibway, Menominee, Ottawa, and Metis. A rich underworld of Native mythology supports and interprets this expressive tradition.

Medicine Fiddle weaves tunes, dance and stories to restore the inner life, and remind us that we are all connected to a much older and broader multicultural version of the past.

MEDICINE MEN

Country USA   **Year** 1990   **Length** 18 m.   **Genre** LS
Director Gary Maynard
Producer Gary Maynard
Distributor
The Gary Paul Agency
84 Canaan Ct., Suite 17
Stratford, CT 06614
203 336-0257 [b] and [f]
www.thegarypaulagency.com   gcmaynard@aol.com
Price upon request.

Twenty nine year old Joseph Standing Bear (Albert Bowen) is an American Indian who is working as an intern at a city hospital and assists the hospital's paramedic squad. On a routine call, Joe and his partner discover a tribal medicine man, John Makes Face (George American Horse), trying to cure a heart attack victim with a medicine necklace. Joe and his partner intervene and deliver the sick man to the hospital.

Upon their arrival, Joe's partner discovers the medicine man's necklace in the van. He gives it to Joe for safe keeping. Curious of the necklace and its owner, Joe decides to visit John.

During his visit, Joe discovers that John is a member of his tribe and that he knows his grandfather, Abraham Standing Bear (Frank Salcedio). He also tells the young doctor-to-be that there is a mystery surrounding him that involves Joe as his messenger of death. Joe demands an explanation to the old Indian's story, but John tells him that Abraham has the answers and that he should ask him.

The medicine man's words propel Joe into a journey of self-examination, where he must trust his own vision in order to honor his friend and make peace with his grandfather and himself.

MEDICINE RIVER

Country Canada   **Year** 1993   **Length** 94 m.   **Genre** FF
Director Stuart Margolin
Producer Stuart Margolin
Distributor
Barbara Allinson (for US)
baj@1direct.com
416 532-5765 [b]   416 532-5759 [f]
For foreign purchase contact:
Alliance Atlantis in Toronto, Ontario Canada
416 967-1174 [b]

Graham Greene stars as Will, an international photojournalist who returns to Medicine River to be with his brother for their mother's funeral in the Blackfoot community he left behind twenty years ago. Upon his arrival, Will is confounded by his brother's whereabouts and the idiosyncrasies of the small community, where everyone knows everyone else's business better than their own. He falls prey to Harlen Big Bear, portrayed by Tom Jackson, whose unique style of community planning draws Will into a series of situations that turn his life upside down. Will is coerced into helping Harlen parlay a van to transport Native leaders into a photo study of wildlife migration patterns that turns into new uniforms for the basketball team resulting in the need to produce a calendar that is quickly becoming a book... and then Will meets Louise, played by Shiela Tousey.

As Will waits for the return of his brother, Harlen benevolently misleads Will into the mystifyingly interconnected lives of the Native community. In the process, Will comes to know much more than he ever expected about the hearts and minds of *Medicine River*.

MEDICINE WHEEL, THE

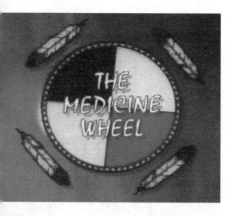

Country Canada   **Year** 1995   **Length** 25 m.   **Genre** DS
Director Richard Hersley
Producer Richard Hersley, Renae Morriseau
Distributor
Motion Visual
Suite 503 - 130 W. Keith Road
No. Vancouver, BC
V7M 1L5 Canada
604 990-9337 [b] coyote@uniserve.com
US $99.00 VHS, US $49.00 VHS rental

The wheel has neither beginning nor ending. It has always been. For aboriginal people, the circle represents the journey of human existence. It con-
nects us to our past, to our present and to our future. Within the periphery
of the circle lies a key to Native philosophy, values, traditions and perhaps
part of the very essence of Native thought. All things living, past, present
and future depend upon its equilibrium.

The Medicine Wheel signifies a joining of races, the red race. It speaks
about the responsibility of these Nations to work together as custodians for
the preservation of the Earth. Many aboriginal teachings — the Cree, the
Navajo, the Siksika (Blackfoot), the Salish, the Maori of New Zealand, the
Tibetan, for example — speak of the circle, and the need to re-evaluate our
existence in healing, and preserving the Mother Earth.

Although the specifics of the wheel may change from Nation to Nation,
the importance of this concept is synonymous. There are aboriginal communities in Canada that are developing local economies and life-styles,
based on its teaching. There are several healing centers in Canada that utilize the Medicine Wheel for helping people cope with grief, drug and alcohol addiction, and HIV/AIDS.

The Medicine Wheel concept has its origins from the great plains of North
America. Many aboriginal communities in B.C. have utilized its teachings
and recognize the similarities within their own specific teachings. *The
Medicine Wheel* is a concept that evolves within the eyes of the beholder.
It is movement. It is sound. It is a way of life.

MENOMINEE NATION POWWOW, THE

Country USA   **Year** 1994   **Length** 44 m.   **Genre** DS
Director Martha Gilespie
Producer Martha Gilespie / Verna deLeon
Distributor
Currently unavailable.

Powwows are social events celebrated by Native Americans throughout the
United States and Canada. It is colorful pageantry, unparalleled any other
place in the world.

The Powwow is a social gathering of friends, relatives and tribes to renew
acquaintances, dance, feast and to welcome all people as they enjoy
eachother's company.

The Annual Menominee Nation Pow Wow is considered to be a major cultural highlight in the Midwest. It takes place in the beautiful Woodland
Bowl, a natural amphitheater in Keshena, WI.

MESA VERDE: LEGACY OF STONE AND SPIRIT

Country USA   **Year** 1997   **Length** 23 m.   **Genre** DS
Director Gray Warriner
Producer Gray Warriner
Distributor
Camera One
8523 15th Ave. NE
Seattle, WA 98115
206 523-3456 [b]   206 523-3668 [f]
cameraone@prodigy.net
US $19.95 VHS

Also available through Shenandoah Film Productions, Arcata, CA.
707 822-1030 [b]   707 822-1035 [f]

Mesa Verde is not only one of America's most important parks preserving
the prehistoric past, it is a United Nations World Heritage Site. Discover
the fascinating story of ancient America and the Pueblo builders who made
this remote high plateau their home so long ago. *Mesa Verde: Legacy of
Stone and Spirit* shows the viewer a place that transcends international
boundaries as well as time.

MI'KMAQ FAMILY: MIGMAEIO OTJIOSOG

Country Canada   **Year** 1995   **Length** 32 m.   **Genre** DS
Director Catherine Anne Martin
Producer Marilyn A. Belec, Shelagh Mackenzie
Distributor
National Film Board of Canada Library
22-D Hollywood Avenue
Ho-Ho-Kus, NJ 07423
1 800 542-2164 [b] 201 652-1973 [f]
US $195.00 VHS, call for rental information and prices.
For purchase within Canada visit the NFB website at: www.nfb.ca
1 800 267-7710 toll free within Canada

Migmaeio Otjiosog means "Roots so deep they can't be pulled..."

When Mi'kmaq people speak of "the old ways" of child rearing, they are
referring to customs, values and practices which existed before European
settlement. The Mi'kmaq were the first of the First Nations people to feel
the impact of European culture. The Indian Act, the policy of resettlement
onto reserves and the residential school regime all weakened the fabric of
Mi'kmaq society.

Now, however, as a matter of survival in the face of social, cultural and
economic problems, First Nations people are rediscovering the old ways
and once again passing them onto the next generation. Many traditional
child rearing customs of the Mi'kmaq are shared by all First Nations people, and can provide valuable lessons today in the areas of nurturing, disci-
pline and the meaning of kinship and social support.

MIND OF A CHILD, THE

Country Canada   **Year** 1995   **Length** 60 m.   **Genre** DF
Director Gary Marcuse
Producer Svend-Erik Eriksen, Gary Marcuse, Lorna Williams
Distributor
Face to Face Media
1818 Grant Street
Vancouver, BC
V5L 2Y8 Canada
604 251-0770 [b] 604 251-9149 [f]
Available in English and in French
US $60.00 VHS

The Mind of a Child follows the work of Lorna Williams, a teacher from a
First Nations reserve on the west coast of Canada, and her search for help
for the aboriginal children who have lost belief in themeselves. Lorna was
hired by the Vancouver schools to help the 2,000 aboriginal children in the
inner city schools. Too many of them are dropping out, or get out onto the
streets, where drugs, abuse and violence are waiting.

In Jerusalem, Lorna discovered the extraordinary work of an Israeli child
psychologist, Reuven Feuerstein, who began his work 50 years ago, helping children who had survived the Holocaust.

The heart of Feuerstein's approach is his belief that all cultures prepare
children to be competent, adaptable adults. Lorna looks at the history of
aboriginal people in North America and in her own community, and shows
how suppression and misunderstanding over the last 100 years can lead to
learning problems in children today.

MINO-BIMADIZIWIN: THE GOOD LIFE

Country USA   **Year** 1998   **Length** 59 m.   **Genre** DF
Director Deb Wallwork
Producer Deb Wallwork, Mary John
Distributor
Lucerne Media
37 Ground Pine Road
Morris Plains, NJ 07950
1 800 341-2293 [b] 973 538-0855 [f]
www.lucernemedia.com LM@lucernemedia.com
US $99.00 VHS educational

Mino-Bimadiziwin: The Good Life is about the tradition of wild rice harvesting among the Ojibwes of Minnesota. This warm and intimate documentary provides an unusual glimpse into life on the reservation, and
background interviews illuminate both the economic and spiritual aspects
of this ancient tradition. The story centers on Dorothy and Darwin Stevens,
who have been ricing together for over 40 years. Darwin Stevens himself
is the last of the old rice caretakers, whose job it was to watch over the
lake, raise and lower the water levels, and enforce decisions pertaining to
the harvest. Despite cultural losses and financial hardship, elders like the
Stevens made a living out of what they had: knowledge of the land, and an
infinite faith in the Creator. The program uses these issues as a springboard
into the underlying economic, social, and philosophical issues of sustainable land use.

MISTRESS MADELEINE

Country Canada　　　　**Year** 1987　　**Length** 57 m.　　　**Genre** FF
Director Aaron Kim Johnston
Producer Norma Bailey, Ches Yetman (exec)
Distributor
National Film Board of Canada Library
22-D Hollywood Avenue
Ho-Ho-Kus, NJ 07423
1 800 542-2164 [b]　201 652-1973 [f]
US $150.00 VHS, call for rental information and prices.
For purchase within Canada visit the NFB website at: www.nfb.ca
1 800 267-7710 toll free within Canada

The time is 1850 and the Hudson Bay Company has the monopoly on the fur trade in Canada. Angered by the restrictions of the Company and frustrated by low prices, the Métis have begun to trade with the Americans. They have also begun to establish their own communities in the heart of the Canadian West. It is within this context of free trade and land rights that the drama of *Mistress Madeleine* unfolds.

Madeleine, the wife of a Hudson Bay Company Clerk, is content with life at the Company Trading Post. Her husband's career is flourishing and her position as wife and mother is a secure and happy one. But she is also caught in the middle of a power struggle, divided by her loyalty to her brother, a free trader, and to her husband.

Madeleine's dilemma is soon overshadowed by a more devastating reality. Company policy is changing and a new order is called for, one that has no place for Madeline and her children. Tumbled into a shattering world of broken dreams and uncertainty, Madeleine must decide not only for her future but her real identity.

Starring Mireille Deyglun, Neil Munro and Harry Daniels

MOON'S PRAYER, THE

Country USA　　　　**Year** 1991　　**Length** 50 m.　　　**Genre** DS
Director John deGraf
Producer John deGraf, Nick Freeman, KIRO TV
Distributor
The Video Project
P.O. Box 77188
San Francisco, CA 94107
1 800 475-2638 [b]　415 821-7204 [f]
videoproject@videoproject.net
US $85.00 VHS

Beginning with an impassioned oratory in the Tulalip reservation longhouse, *The Moon's Prayer* takes viewers throughout western Washington to explore threats to our spectacular, but fragile environment, and the efforts of Washington's first people to protect and restore our land.

The program focuses on the environmental devastation and its impact on the state's salmon and timber populations over time, and how that in turn has affected the Native Americans in Washington.

MORE THAN BOWS AND ARROWS

Country USA   **Year** 1979   **Length** 56 m.   **Genre** DF
Director Gray Warriner
Producer Cinema Associates Inc.
Distributor
Camera One
8523 15th Ave. NE
Seattle, WA 98115
206 523-3456 [b] 206 523-3668 [f]
email: cameraone@prodigy.net
US $19.95 VHS

Also available through Shenandoah Film Productions, Arcata, CA
707 822-1030 [b] 707 822-1035 [f]

More than Bows and Arrows traces the contributions made by Native Americans to the development of the United States. Viewers experience such wonders as the cliff dwellings of Mesa Verde, the recreated colony at Jamestown, the Iroquois Confederacy, the frozen north of the Eskimo and the buffalo-filled Great Plains. Narrated by Pulitzer prize winning author N. Scott Momaday.

MOTHER OF MANY CHILDREN

Country Canada   **Year** 1977   **Length** 58 m.   **Genre** PS
Director Alanis Obomsawin
Producer Don Hopkins, Douglas Macdonald, Alanis Obomsawin
Distributor
National Film Board of Canada Library
22-D Hollywood Avenue
Ho-Ho-Kus, NJ 07423
1 800 542-2164 [b] 201 652-1973 [f]
US $150.00 VHS, call for rental information and prices.
For purchase within Canada visit the NFB website at: www.nfb.ca
1 800 267-7710 toll free within Canada

This film is an album of Native womanhood, portraying a proud matriarchal society that for centuries has been pressured to adopt different standards and customs. All of the women featured share a belief in the importance of tradition as a source of strength in the face of change.

MOTHER'S CHOICE, A

Country Canada   **Year** 1996   **Length** 26 m.   **Genre** PS
Director Peter von Puttkamer
Producer Sheera and Peter von Puttkamer
Distributor
Gryphon Productions, Ltd.
P.O. Box 93009 / 5331 Headland Drive
West Vancouver, BC
V7W 3C0 Canada
604 921-7627 [b] 604 921-7626 [f] gryphon@telus.net
US $148.00 VHS
CAD $175.20 VHS

A Mother's Choice presents the tragedy of Fetal Alcohol Syndrome and Fetal Alcohol Effect from the perspective of Native American mothers, who speak about emotional issues and memories which lie at the root of drinking and drugging. These mothers deliver heartfelt messages to aboriginal men and women to consider the health of their unborn child. Designed as a prevention tool, the production touches on the medical definitions of F.A.S. and presents methods so that people with addictive problems can seek help before they consider having children.

MOVIN' UP

Country USA   **Year** 1980   **Length** 22 m.   **Genre** PS
Director Shawnee Brittan
Producer Shawnee Brittan
Distributor
Not in distribution.

Movin' Up depicts how an American Indian family may participate in the Department of Housing and Urban Development's Mutual Help Housing Program. The film was funded through a grant from the Federal Agency to the SAC & Fox Housing Authority.

Filmed against a background of authentic hogans, pueblos and tipis, the film's narrator (Richard Wilson-Santee Sioux) explains how Indian families may obtain adequate housing. To illustrate Housing and Urban Developments Mutual Help Program, the film follows the Riddle family (Choctaw-Chickasaw) as they go through the process of getting a new home. Crowded into a tiny house with no plumbing and only a wood burning stove for heat, the Riddles turn to their Tribal Housing Authority. With the help of their housing counselor, they qualify for the Mutual Help Program. Soon the entire family is assisting a professional construction crew in building a new home. After moving in, the Riddles reflect on their experiences and offer down-to-earth advice to other Indian families who may be considering the Mutual Help Housing Program.

MUCKLESHOOT: A PEOPLE AND THEIR LANGUAGE

Country USA   **Year** 2000   **Length** 50 m.   **Genre** DS
Director Scott Ross
Producer Scott Ross / Ethereal Motion Pictures
Distributor
Not in distribution.
Muckleshoot Tribal College / Language Program
5602 Auburn Way S.
Auburn, WA 98092-7347
253 735-6647 [b]   253 735-6739 [f]

A journey following the history of the xwəlsucid language, as demonstrated by the people of the Muckleshoot Indian Tribe, and renown storyteller Vi Herbert, an Upper Skagit elder. Their language is traced back to it's beginnings and revisited through the eyes and voices of it's teachers today, and students.

Though the language has been asleep for many years, the Muckleshoot Tribe sees the reawakening of its language as a vital part of living their culture. Share the vision as you listen to the elders reflect about their memories, and growing up in a different time when the language was spoken everyday.

MY LAND IS MY LIFE

Country Canada   **Year** 1987   **Length** 55 m.   **Genre** DS
Director Joan Goldi
Producer Joan Goldi
Distributor
Currently unavailable.

This film gives a sympathetic view of northern Indian family life year round, as it relates to the wilderness and wildlife in the remote north of Canada. By showing that Indians still have strong ties to the land, the film hopes to counter opposing claims by animal rights extremists.

MY NAME IS KAHENTIIOSTA

Country Canada   **Year** 1995   **Length** 30 m.   **Genre** DS
Director Alanis Obomsawin
Producer Don Haig, Alanis Obomsawin
Distributor
Women Make Movies
462 Broadway, 5th Floor
New York, NY 10013
212 925-0606 [b] 212 925-2052 [f]
info@wmm.com
US $195.00 VHS, US $60.00 VHS rental

For purchase in Canada visit the NFB website at: www.nfb.ca

Arrested after the 78-day armed standoff during the 1990 Oka crisis, Kahentiiosta, a young Mohawk woman proud of her centuries-old heritage, is detained four days longer than the other women. Her crime? The prosecutor representing the Quebec government will not accept her aboriginal name. From the perspective of Kahentiiosta, we witness the arrest and detention of those who withdrew to the Kanehsatake Treatment Centre after the Canadian Army advanced, and we learn why Kahentiiosta was prepared to die to protect the land and trees sacred to the Mohawk people of Kanehsatake.

MY NATIVE SELF

Country Canada   **Year** 1998   **Length** 54 m.   **Genre** DF
Director Marco Mascarin
Producer Marco Mascarin
Distributor
Currently unavailable.

Through the eyes of director Marco Mascarin, the viewer is told the story of a young man's search for identity through the complex territories of shame, sexuality and acceptance within Native culture. *My Native Self* tells of the friendship between Marco and David Forlines, a traditional carver on the Quileute reservation in La Push, Washington. Forlines is gay and HIV positive. His final wish is for an "International" canoe to be paddled 1,200 miles to an upcoming indigenous gathering in Bella Bella, British Columbia. David's canoe is to be paddled by people of different ethnic backgrounds, to celebrate diversity and the acceptance of differences.

As the canoes prepare for the trip north, some Quileute Tribal members oppose David's International canoe, on the grounds that only Native people should be paddle participants. The arguments threaten to pull the community apart. In one volatile meeting, a Quileute man insists that non-Natives have no place in the canoes, while a white paddler from the International canoe suggests that being "Native" has nothing to do with the color of one's skin.

Throughout the filming, as his friendship with David grows and he becomes more involved in the reservation community, Marco must face his own questions about shame and acceptance. At an emergency meeting for the International canoe, he is asked whether he will continue to film amid growing hostilities. At that moment, Marco walks into the story and acknowledges: "It was time to leave the safety of my camera." Ultimately, by the time of the film's close, Marco's story ceases to be merely about canoes and culture when he learns the devastating news about the death of David Forlines.

MY VILLAGE IN NUNAVIK

Country Canada   **Year** 2000   **Length** 46 m.   **Genre** DS
Director Bobby Kenuajuak
Producer Nicole Lamothe
Distributor
National Film Board of Canada Library
22-D Hollywood Avenue
Ho-Ho-Kus, NJ 07423
1 800 542-2164 [b] 201 652-1973 [f]
US $129.00 VHS, call for rental information and prices.
For purchase within Canada visit the NFB website at: www.nfb.ca
1 800 267-7710 toll free within Canada

Bobby Kenuajuak was born in 1976 in the village of Puvirnituq on the
shores of Hudson Bay in northern Quebec. He won a National Film Board
contest for Aboriginal filmmakers at the age of 23, which allowed him to
learn his craft at the NFB's Montreal headquarters, where he spent 18
months producing *My Village in Nunavik*.

Shot during three seasons, Kenuajuak's documentary tenderly portrays village life and the elements that forge the character of this people: their history, the great open spaces and their unflagging humor.

Though Kenuajuak appreciates the amenities of southern civilization that
have made their way north, he remains attached to the traditional way of
life and the land: its vast tundra, the sea teeming with Arctic char, the sky
full of Canadian geese. *My Villlage in Nunavik* is an unsentimental film by
a young Inuk who is open to the outside world but clearly loves his village.

MYSTERY OF THE LOST RED PAINT PEOPLE, THE

Country USA   **Year** 1987   **Length** 60 m.   **Genre** DF
Director T.W. Timreck & William Goetzman
Producer T.W. Timreck & William Goetzman
Distributor
Bullfrog Films
P.O. Box 149
Oley, PA 19547
1 800 543-3764 [b] 610 370-1978 [f]
www.bullfrogfilms.com   info@bullfrogfilms.com
US $250.00 VHS, US $90.00 VHS rental

Did you know that a seafaring American tribe explored the shores of North
American 7,000 years ago? Or that these ancient Americans rivalled their
European counterparts in navigational skills several millennia before the
Vikings?

The Mystery of the Lost Red Paint People follows U.S., Canadian and
European scientists from the barrens of Labrador - where archaeologists
uncover an ancient stone burial mound - to sites in the U.S., France,
England and Denmark, and to the vast fjords of northernmost Norway
where monumental standing stones testify to links among seafaring cultures across immense distances.

NANIBAA'

Country USA   **Year** 1999   **Length** 18 m.   **Genre** LS
Director David Grotell
Producer Rock Point School
Distributor
Currently unavailable. For more information, contact:
Rock Point School
Highway 1910
Rock Point, AZ 86545

Nanibaa' is a 16-year old Navajo girl from Rock Point, Arizona, a small farming community in the Four Corners area of the Navajo Nation. Rock Point is an extremely remote community that retains a lot of its traditional Navajo culture. The Navajo language is spoken as a first language of the elders in the community. Nanibaa' is part of the younger generation, which is tantalized by "the outside world." She has applied to and been accepted by a prep school off the "rez"; however, when she asks for her parents' permission to attend this school, she is flatly denied. She subsequently steals the family car and, with a friend, comes across an ingratiating Navajo street girl and looks up someone she met in a chat room on the Internet. After a terrifying experience in this stranger's hotel room, she and her friend return to Rock Point where Nanibaa' has an epiphany of sorts. She receives a message from the "Holy People" and thereby realizes that Rock Point, Arizona is exactly where she is supposed to be in the world.

NANOOK TAXI

Country Canada   **Year** 1978   **Length** 90 m. **Genre** FF
Director Edward Folger
Producer Jeffrey Hayes
Distributor
Not in distribution.

Nanook Taxi is more than a drama about a man who goes off to taste the attractions of the "city" - it is also an intimate and revealing look at a people whose life and way of thinking are in the process of profound change.

At the beginning of the drama, Ningiusksiak (Joanasie Salomonie), an Inuit fron Cape Dorset, is tempted to try another kind of life, so he decides to fly to Frobisher Bay to make some money. Ningiusksiak has a cousin, Ashoona (Mickey Turqtug), in Frosbisher Bay. Ashoona, a somewhat urbanized Inuit who makes a living as a construction worker, knows nothing about the Inuit way of life in the far North. Ashoona takes Ningiusksiak in hand and helps him to find a job driving a taxi. Ningiusksiak has difficulties adapting to "city" ways, and, one night with his cousin, causes raised eyebrows when he orders and eats a raw, frozen fish at a fancy restaurant.

Increasingly unhappy and bewildered, Ningiusksiak takes to spending his money on liquor and his time in seedy nightclubs. One night, half-heartedly trying to show that he is having a good time, he looks up and sees his wife. She has come to take him home to Cape Dorset.

NATION IS COMING, A

Country Canada   **Year** 1996   **Length** 24 m.   **Genre** LS
Director Kent Monkman
Producer Kent Monkman
Distributor
V-Tape
401 Richmond Street, West
Toronto, Ontario
M5V 3A8 Canada
416 351-1317 [b] 416 351-1509 [f] www.vtape.org

A Nation is Coming resurrects a Ghost Dancer as a symbol of hope in a world threatened by new diseases and rapidly changing technologies. With the millennium fast approaching, *A Nation is Coming* draws upon Native prophecy to present an alternative to the (European) apocalyptic vision of the future. Four separate dance sequences follow one man's journey through memory and vision to a spiritual awakening: a down and out urban Indian struggles with illness; in hope of a renewed world, a ghost dancer is transported to another realm; a colonized Indian searches for identity in an unstable world; and finally, the dancer reclaims his traditions in a celebration of contemporary Native culture.

Featuring Michael Greyeyes.

NATIONAL MUSEUM OF THE AMERICAN INDIAN – NATIONAL CAMPAIGN VIDEO

Country USA   **Year** 1993   **Length** 10 m.   **Genre** IND
Director Lisa Donner
Producer Dan Jones (exec), Lisa Donner
Distributor
Not in distribution.
Cultural Resources Center
4220 Silver Hill Road
Suitland, MD 20746
301 238-6624 [b]

An introduction to the National Museum of American Indian, the newest museum of the Smithsonian Institution and the last building ever to be constructed on the National Mall in Washington D.C. When Congress established the museum in 1989, it mandated that one-third of the construction cost of the Mall site be raised from the private sector.

National Museum of the American Indian provides an overview of the new museum and its funding needs. The film is targeted at prospective donors to the museum's fund-raising campaign. It is intended to educate the viewer about the unique mission of the museum, to convince the viewer that this long-overdue cultural institution is worthy of his or her investment of time and money, and to make an appropriately dramatic and emotional appeal for support.

Dan Jones, a member of the Ponca tribe of Oklahoma, served as Executive Producer of the film, to make certain that all aspects of the production reflect an appropriate portrayal of Native American values and cultures.

NATIVE AMERICAN RIGHTS: PLUNDERED OR PRESERVED

Country USA   **Year** 1992   **Length** 58 m.   **Genre** DF
Director Bill Fogarty, Judy Uphouse
Producer Bill Fogarty, Judy Uphouse
Distributor
Currently unavailable.

Controversy surrounds 237 skeletal remains of a prehistoric Native American tribe, on display since 1927 at the Dickson Mounds State Museum in Illinois.

Although the State Museum Board recommended closing the exhibit in 1989, it has remained open, in spite of the current national trend by museums and universities to return ancestral remains to Native American tribes for reburial. Native Americans have requested that the remains of their ancestors be reburied with respect to their cultural and religious beliefs. The State of Illinois feels reburial would jeopardize scientific studies of the prehistoric remains.

NATIVE ENCOUNTER, THE

Country USA   **Year** 1995   **Length** 6 m.   **Genre** LS
Director Veronica Smith, Pamela Hurley
Producer SIPI College Bound
Distributor
Not in distribution.
SIPI College
P.O. Box 10146
Albuquerque, NM 87184
505 346-2340 [b]

In a Native American spoof on the Grey Poupon commercials, Indian students encounter two new age women in their pursuit of Grey Poupon for their fry bread sandwich.

NATIVE FOODS DAY

Country USA   **Year** 1994   **Length** 7 m.   **Genre** DS
Director Shamino Taylor
Producer Shamino Taylor and Institute of American Indian Arts
Distributor
Not in distribution - student film
IAIA
Avan Nu Po Road
Santa Fe, NM 87505
505 424-2300 [b]

This video profiles a popular event held at the Insititute of American
Indian Arts, Native Foods Day!

NATIVE VETERANS: A WARRIOR'S STORY

Country Canada   **Year** 1998   **Length** 40 m.   **Genre** DS
Director Joe Beardy
Producer Joe Beardy
Distributor
Currently unavailable.

Native Veterans: A Warrior's Story deals with Native Veterans from the
First and Second World Wars through the Korean War of the 1950s. It
examines the contributions Native Canadians made to these wars and highlights some of the great Native war heroes who emerged. The production
also highlights the neglect and racism Canadian Native Veterans faced
upon returning to Canada after their tours of duty overseas.

NATURALLY NATIVE

Country USA   **Year** 1998   **Length** 108 m.   **Genre** FF
Director Jennifer Wynne Farmer and Valerie Red-Horse
Producer Mashantucket Pequot Tribal Nation
Distributor
Red-Horse Releasing
6028 Calvin Avenue
Tarzana, CA 91356
818 705-2588 [b]   818 705-4969 [f]
redhorse88@aol.com
US $21.95 VHS home video, US $1,500.00 35mm screening rental

A first in many respects, *Naturally Native* is the first film about Native
American women written, directed, produced and starring Native
American women. It is also the first mainstream dramatic feature film to
be funded by an American Indian tribal nation: the Mashantucket Indian
Tribe of Connecticut.

One of the first features to explore Indians' relationship with corporate
America, *Naturally Native* follows the lives and loves and pain and joy of
three sisters (Valerie Red-Horse, Irene Bedard and Kimberly Norris) as
they attempt to start their own Native cosmetics business (hence the film's
title). The film examines each sister's own identity issues, different career
paths and attempts to overcome obstacles both in the business world and in
the home. A touching love story of family and culture, *Naturally Native*
delivers a subtle but strong wakeup call regarding the treatment of Indians
in the corporate environment.

NAVAJO CODE TALKERS

Country USA **Year** 1982 **Length** 28 m. **Genre** DS
Director Tom McCarthy
Producer New Mexico Film Video
Distributor
Shenandoah Film Productions
538 "G" Street
Arcata, CA 95521
707 822-1030 [b] 707 822-1035 [f]
US $125.00 VHS, US $45.00 rental

Navajo Code Talkers is a documentary film using interviews and archival footage to show the vital role a small group of Navajo Marines played in the South Pacific during World War II. Includes 1940s archival footage of Navajo life as well as scenes of World War II.

NAVAJO MEDICINE: WE DO THE WORK

Country USA **Year** 1994 **Length** 29 m. **Genre** DF
Producer Edwin Herzog, Jon Farmer
Distributor
Currently unavailable.

This half-hour documentary profiles Navajo health care workers who, with limited resources, are on the front lines to provide health care services for the Navajo people.

Hosted by actor Wes Studi, *Navajo Medicine* visits hospitals and health care facilities on the Navajo reservation, where mortality rates from tuberculosis, alcoholism and diabetes are dramatically higher than the overall U.S. population.

The program tells the stories of Navajo health care workers like Lorraine Thomas, a registered nurse who works twelve hour shifts at the Kayenta Diabetes Clinic; Marilyn Yazee, a Navajo Community Health Representative as she makes the rounds in the Chinle region comforting elders in their hogans; and the doctors and nurses who make a difficult two hour trip, along unpaved roads, to a remote health clinic at the foot of Navajo Mountain to care for their people.

NAVAJO NATION:
MEETING THE CHALLENGE TO DEVELOP

Country USA **Year** 1982 **Length** 16 m. **Genre** DS
Director Ken Kauffman
Producer Ken Kauffman
Distributor
Currently unavailable.

This film presents a positive, factual overview of the Navajo region, culture, and economy emphasizing the achievements, problems and plans of Navajo economic development. The film is designed to be used by tribal representatives when they conduct negotiations with businessmen, government officials, and financiers in order to secure their participation in the development of Navajo resources.

Assuming that this business oriented audience will know little of Navajo culture and economy, the approach taken is necessarily introductory and broad. This broad approach also allows the Tribes flexibility in its use of the film. Not only will it be used externally to attract outside participation in Navajo economic development, the film will also be made available through free-loan distribution to any interested parties, and it will also be used internally as an educational tool explaining tribal economic plans to the Navajo people.

Realizing that resource development is controversial, the filmmakers have made every effort to present the subject as evenhandedly as possible. The decision as to which specific development projects are to be embarked upon is for the Navajo Tribe to decide for itself.

NAVIGATE ARTIST: WAYQUAY

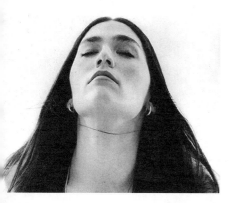

Country USA   **Year** 1997   **Length** 4 m.   **Genre** MV
Director Andrew Unangst
Producer Andrew Unangst, Wayquay
Distributor
Currently unavailable.

Wayquay, a recording artist of Ojibway/Anishanabe descent, combines rhythms and chants from her Native American background with the grooves of blues, rock, and rap to form a unique style. "Navigate," a cut from her album *Tribal Grind*, retraces steps on the path left by her ancestors to bring "messages of simplicity, sharing and honor."

NEGUAGUON – LAC LA CROIX/ WHAT WE'RE ASKING

Country Canada   **Year** 1988   **Length** 60 m.   **Genre** DF
Director Judith Doyle
Producer Judith Doyle
Distributor
Currently unavailable.

In this hour-long documentary, Ojibway Band Members of the Neguaguon (Lac La Croix) Reserve tell the story of their struggle to continue earning a livelihood by guiding on their ancestral lands. This isolated air-access-only community of 240 is completely surrounded by wilderness parkland—Quetico Provincial Park in Canada, and Superior National Forest in upstate Minnesota. The village is located on the Canada-US boundary waters, and laws banning outboard motors threaten to rob the Native people of their economic base—taking tourists fishing using small motorboats. A cross-section of the community, including Elders, guides, teachers, young people and the Chief, speak of their history, community developments such as laws banning alcohol and welfare abuse, and traditional culture. Award winning director Judith Doyle collaborated with the Lac La Croix Band over two years to produce a film which portrays their way of life and political battle, and which represents their views.

NEW INDIANS, THE

Country USA   **Year** 1977   **Length** 60 m.   **Genre** DF
Director Terry Sanders
Producer Terry Sanders & Freida Lee Mock
Distributor
Not in distribution.
National Geographic Society
Washington, DC
202 857-7000 [b]

Narrated by Robert Redford and hosted by E.G. Marshall, *The New Indians* is a documentary on contemporary Indian life seen through four perspectives: The Navajo, Miccocukee (Florida), Kwakiutal, and intertribal.

The Navajo segment features the encroachment onto tribal land by power companies and strip mining companies. The Miccocukee, living in the Everglades, are also threatened by a dwindling land base; they are shown living much the same way as their ancestors and how they make a living now. The Kwakiutal of the Pacific Northwest are shown at a potlatch, longhouse and carving. In the final segment, the film follows a group of urban Indians from Chicago as they attend an international treaty conference in Canada.

NEW PATH OF HOPE, A – NATIONAL AMERICAN INDIAN LISTENING CONFERENCE

Country USA   **Year** 1995   **Length** 17 m.   **Genre** DS
Director Nedra Darling
Producer Nedra Darling
Distributor
Currently unavailable.

A New Path of Hope was created as the opening statement for the American Indian Listening Conference in Albuquerque, NM, May 5, 1994. The video contains footage of the historic White House meeting on April 29, 1994, of President Clinton with tribal leaders from over 500 tribal nations in the U.S. Mr. Clinton was the first president to invite all the tribal leaders to meet at the White House in over 100 years. *A New Path of Hope* contains current issues and policies that affect Native Americans and the struggle for survival we face everyday.

NEW TRAILS

Country USA   **Year** 1978   **Length** 25 m.   **Genre** DS
Producer Ira Englander (exec)
Distributor
Ira Englander
330 Washington Blvd., Suite 400
Marina Del Rey, CA 90292
310 574-0889 [b]   310 574-3846 [f]
Price upon request.

The transition from the reservation to the city is a difficult one for most Native Americans. It is this emotional upheaval which is dramatically illustrated in the opening montage of *The New Trails*.

For those Indians making the transition, as well as for those already in the city, the adjustment is further complicated by the economic problems of finding a job.

This film deals with the ways in which a model Urban Indian CETA Center can reach these people and help them find satisfying work and is intended to help the staff of the CETA Centers be more effective in helping the many people who come to them for assistance.

NEWE SOGOBIA IS NOT FOR SALE! – THE STRUGGLE FOR WESTERN SHOSHONE LANDS

Country USA   **Year** 1993   **Length** 28 m.   **Genre** DS
Director Jesse Drew
Producer Jesse Drew
Distributor
Video Data Bank
112 S. Michigan Avenue
Chicago, IL 60603
312 345-3550 [b] 312 541-8073 [f]
info@vdb.org
US $200.00 VHS, 3/4"   US $50.00 VHS, 3/4" rental

Newe Sogobia is Not For Sale depicts the battle between Western Shoshone land activists Mary and Carrie Dann and the US Government's Bureau of Land Management. This ongoing conflict is over who will control the Western Shoshones' ancestral lands in Northeastern Nevada. This video lets the Shoshones speak about their ties to the land and their determination to keep it at any cost.

NEZ PERCE: PORTRAIT OF A PEOPLE

Country USA   **Year** 1984   **Length** 23 m.   **Genre** DS
Director Phil Lucas
Producer Phil Lucas
Distributor
Lucerne Media
37 Ground Pine Road
Morris Plains, NJ 07950
1 800 341-2293 [b]   973 538-0855 [f]
www.lucernemedia.com   LM@lucernemedia.com
US $99.00 VHS educational

This documentary traces the history of the Nez Perce people from the first peaceful interactions with the Louis and Clark expedition through the tribe's parital conversion to Christianity and resulting spiritual schism, to the 1860 Gold Rush and the eventual takeover of more than 90% of Nez Perce land by whites.

NIKJAGI'U (DOLLS)

Country USA   **Year** 1998   **Length** 15 m.   **Genre** DS
Director Daryl Lonetree, Marlon White Eagle
Producer Hocak Wazijoci Language Cultural Program
Distributor
Not in distribution.
Hocak Wazijoci Language and Cultural Association
P.O. Box 390 / N4895 Hwy 58
Mauston, WI 53948
608 847-5694 [b]   608 847-7203 [f]

Nikjagi'u is a video about the importance of dolls in Hocak culture. Two tribal elders, Kenneth Funmaker, Sr. and his niece Pauline, discuss doll-making and the need to take care of the dolls. Interspersed with the elders' descriptions are scenes reenacting the doll stories.

NO ADDRESS

Country Canada   **Year** 1989   **Length** 56 m.   **Genre** DF
Director Alanis Obomsawin
Producer Marrin Canell, Colin Neale (exec), Alanis Obomsawin
Distributor
National Film Board of Canada Library
22-D Hollywood Avenue
Ho-Ho-Kus, NJ 07423
1 800 542-2164 [b]   201 652-1973 [f]
US $150.00 VHS, call for rental information and prices.
For purchase within Canada visit the NFB website at: www.nfb.ca
1 800 267-7710 toll free within Canada

In the spring of 1988, the official estimate for the number of homeless in Montreal stood at 12,000. *No Address* focuses on the young Native people who make up part of this swelling population.

Some of these young people leave troubled communities; others leave because their families have already scattered. Eventually the young people drift into cities such as Montreal, beckoned by the glamour of city life, and the vague hope of finding roots.

Their hopes are soon shattered. Whatever money they have soon runs out. To apply for welfare, they need a permanent address. Those who manage to make the welfare rolls soon find that the monthly $188.00 for people under 30 is not enough to pay for a room, let alone food. They sleep where they can: outdoors, in lobbies, in condemned buildings, occasionally at shelters or with friends. This documentary tells their stories.

NO MORE SECRETS

Country Canada   **Year** 1996   **Length** 23 m.   **Genre** PS
Director Loretta Todd
Producer Loretta Todd
Distributor
Contact the National Film Board of Canada for distribution information:
1 800 267-7710 toll free within Canada
212 629-8890 [b] in the US

No More Secrets is an in-depth portrayal of solvent abuse among young people. Through dramatic reenactments, interviews, and group discussions, the film traces the family history of solvent abuse and the possible reasons youth seek this dangerous high.

NO SURRENDER

Country Canada   **Year** 1995   **Length** 52 m.   **Genre** DF
Director Shelia Jordan
Producer Shelia Jordan
Distributor
Distribution La Fete
387 St. Paul West
Montreal, Quebec
H2Y 2A7 Canada
514 848-0417 [b] 514 848-0064 [f]
info@lafete.com
US $11.95 or CAD $14.95 VHS purchase

No Surrender tells an alarming story: 50 years ago, a Canadian multinational corporation flooded 800 square kilometers of land to produce electricity and aluminum, uprooting the Cheslatta Nation from its ancestral home.

Today, the Cheslattas' rivers now flow in the white man's direction in the name of progress, and their nation finds itself on the brink of extinction; their ancestors' tombs float on the waters alongside the dying salmon that once thrived in the Nechako river. And there is even more at stake than the fate of a nation - the delicate ecosystem of an entire river valley, home to a multitude of species, has been turned upside down, and thousands of caribou, moose and grizzly drowned. In the considerably lower waters of the Nechako, disturbed by frequent and sudden reservoir flushes, the populations of Chinook and Sockeye salmon are dwindling to dangerously reduced levels.

It would be easy to give up - too easy. But not for the Cheslatta, whose position is clear: there can be *No Surrender*.

NO TURNING BACK

Country Canada   **Year** 1997   **Length** 47 m.   **Genre** DS
Director Gregory Coyes
Producer Michael Doxtater, Carol Geddes, Jerry Krepakevich, Graydon McCrea
Distributor
National Film Board of Canada Library
22-D Hollywood Avenue
Ho-Ho-Kus, NJ 07423
1 800 542-2164 [b] 201 652-1973 [f]
US $225.00 VHS, call for rental information and prices.
For purchase within Canada visit the NFB website at: www.nfb.ca
1 800 267-7710 toll free within Canada

On November 21, 1996, the Royal Commission on Aboriginal Peoples delivered its recommendations on the status of Canada's First Nations. For five years, the commission traveled to more than 100 communities and heard from more than 3,000 representatives. The Royal Commission focused its inquiry on sixteen Aboriginal issues and became a sounding board for all the past government injustices, including the slow process of land claim settlement, the reluctance to recognize Aboriginal self-government, the inequity of Aboriginal prisoners held in jail, and the legacy of residential schools. For two-and-a-half years, Edmonton director Greg Coyes worked with teams of Native filmmakers, following the Commission on its journey from coast to coast. The video weaves the passionate and articulate voices of Indian, Inuit, and Métis people with the history of Canada's relationship with its First Nations peoples. In this video, Canadian Aboriginal voices are heard collectively, providing a valuable tool for informing both non-Native and Native people about their living conditions and their history.

O'SIEM

Country Canada   **Year** 1996   **Length** 54 m.   **Genre** DF
Director Gilliam Darling Kovanic
Producer George Johnson, Tamarin Productions
Distributor
National Film Board of Canada Library
22-D Hollywood Avenue
Ho-Ho-Kus, NJ 07423
1 800 542-2164 [b] 201 652-1973 [f]
US $250.00 VHS, call for rental information and prices.
For purchase within Canada visit the NFB website at: www.nfb.ca
1 800 267-7710 toll free within Canada

O'Siem is a biographical film about the life of Gene Harry, Spiritual Healer, Indian Shaker Church Minister, Eagle Dancer in the Salish Long House, canoe paddler, and devoted father. Gene's life is full of the demands of work, church, community, family, and his rigorous athletic training. With his busy schedule, the only time Gene has available to train for paddling is at his job at a car wash. Between cars he works out with weights on his wrists and paddles. He flexes, stretches, does sit ups, and practices paddling technique. As his story unfolds, the audience realizes Gene's life has had its hardships. With courage, honesty, and dignity, Gene discusses the trials that have befallen him and the means of his healing that enable him to help others.

OCTOBER STRANGER

Country Canada   **Year** 1985   **Length** 26 m.   **Genre** LS
Director Alan Collins
Producer Christopher Lowry
Distributor
Alfa Nova Productions
139 Booth Avenue
Toronto, Ontario
M4M 2M5 Canada
416 778-4307 [b]   carabas@visinet.ca
CAD $30.00 VHS

The lakes and forests of Northern Ontario form the setting for this story of a young Indian at odds both with his own heritage and the dominant white culture. John Askewe is a 22 year old Ojibwe who has been educated in a residential school away from the Reserve. On completing his education, he is estranged from the traditional life of his people, yet he has a natural gift for storytelling. His favorite authors are Dylan Thomas and Leonard Cohen. To create a Native literature beyond legends and "touristy stuff" is his ambition, but he is not clear how to achieve his goal. There are no precedents in Native culture.

One summer an idealistic young English teacher, Ann Kelly, comes to teach a course in creative writing on the Reserve. She encourages John to become a professional writer, When she returns to Toronto, John wants to follow her, seeking his fame and fortune. First he must say goodbye to his Indian girlfriend, Ida, to whom he is engaged to be married. Ida is furious because she correctly suspects that one reason for his trip is to pursue an affair with Ann and not just his writing. She warns him, if he leaves, she will find someone else. He is offered a job as Band Administrator but turns it down, saying he is not interested in politics. On a hunting trip with his father, he shows more interest in photographing the moose than in using his rifle. His father gently mocks him for his poor showing as a hunter. The next morning he oversleeps and fails to say goodbye when his father leaves early to guide some Americans on a fishing trip. With his artist friend Peter, he takes the float plan south on the first stage of his struggle to become one of Canada's first published Native authors.

OH CANADA

Country USA   **Year** 1994   **Length** 7 m.   **Genre** DS
Director Rebeca Wolfchild
Producer Rebeca Wolfchild and Institute of American Indian Arts
Distributor
Not in distribution - student film
IAIA
Avan Nu Po Road
Santa Fe, NM 87505
505 424-2300 [b]

This video presentation compares the different perspectives of Native students about Canadians.

OJIGWANONG:
ENCOUNTER WITH AN ALGONQUIN SAGE

Country Canada   **Year** 2000   **Length** 26 m.   **Genre** DS
Director Andre Gladu
Producer Lucie Ouimet
Distributor
National Film Board of Canada Library
22-D Hollywood Avenue
Ho-Ho-Kus, NJ 07423
1 800 542-2164 [b] 201 652-1973 [f]
US $175.00 VHS, call for rental information and pricing.
For purchase within Canada visit the NFB website at: www.nfb.ca
1 800 267-7710 toll free within Canada

William Commanda, from the Manniwaki Reserve in Quebec, spent much
of his life working and creating Indian Nation government in North
America. Serving as chief of the Maniwaki Reserve from 1951 to 1970, he
devoted himself to the reconciliation of peoples and cultures. Accordingly,
he first set out to reconcile the Algonquins and Iroquois. His message,
although directed to his own peoples, was universal in scope. For this old
sage, healing was the main priority, and this healing could only be
achieved through forgiveness and tolerance.

OKIMAH

Country Canada   **Year** 1998   **Length** 51 m.   **Genre** DF
Director Paul M. Rickard
Producer Sally Bochner, Germaine Wong
Distributor
National Film Board of Canada Library
22-D Hollywood Avenue
Ho-Ho-Kus, NJ 07432
1 800 542-2164 [b] 201 652-1973 [f]
US $225.00 VHS, call for rental information and prices.
For purchase within Canada visit the NFB website at: www.nfb.ca
1 800 267-7710 toll free within Canada

Since time immemorial, the goose hunt has been of central importance to
the Cree people of the James Bay coastal regions. Today, the goose is no
longer a major nutritional staple for the people, but the hunt plays an
increasingly important role in the transmission of Cree culture, skills and
ethics. Filmmaker Paul Rickard takes us along with his family on a fall
goose hunt in the surrounding areas of Moose River in Northern Ontario.

Through the hunt, we see how the traditional land management system is
practiced. The Okimah are the hunting leaders, whose life experiences and
observations as hunters enable them to teach customary rules for exploit-
ing the resource base. We see how these hunting excursions are not only
about harvesting, but about the need to respect the land, the animals and
the transmission of the Okimah's knowledge from one generation to the
next.

ON AND OFF THE RES' WITH CHARLIE HILL

Country USA   **Year** 2000   **Length** 58 m.   **Genre** DF
Director Sandra Osawa
Producer Sandra Osawa
Distributor
Upstream Productions
6850 35th Avenue NE #11
Seattle, WA 98115
206 526-7122 [b] 206 526-7127 [f]
US $30.00 VHS home video.

On and Off the Res With Charlie Hill is a one-hour documentary that
delivers a stunning knock out punch to the stereotype of the stoic Indian.
This straight ahead, inspiring story about America's foremost Indian comedian, Charlie Hill, will not only make you laugh, but will raise your consciousness in the process. There are precious few portraits of contemporary
American Indians, a motivating fact for award winning
director Sandy Osawa (Makah Tribe), best known for her stories that capture the heartbeat of Indian America.

We learn how Hill developed an early "secret wish" to become a comedian, and how that wish carried him from an Indian reservation in Wisconsin
to the nightclubs in Los Angeles, where Hill currently works. Hill's honesty is engaging as he shares his struggles to enter the world of stand up
comedy and in the process is told that "an Indian comedian is an oxy-
moron." We come to understand that becoming a comedian for an Indian is
no laughing matter, as noted author Vine Deloria, Jr. declares that "Charlie
is fighting centuries of stereotypes." We see how Hill uses material from
his own life, such as being beaten in school or being thrown out of the
Alamo, and then works his frustrations into his routines as a way to "turn
the poison into medicine."

Performance clips reveal how Hill finally landed in the national spotlight
on such influential shows as *The Tonight Show With Johnny Carson*, *The
Richard Pryor Show*, *The Big Show with Steve Allen*, and the television
series *Moesha* and *Rosanne*. Hill's last gift from his father was a book on
Will Rogers and the program pays tribute to Rogers, who is also of Indian
descent. Hill's mentors, comedian Dick Gregory and author Deloria extend
the theme of Indian humor wih Deloria noting that "Indian humor has been
the central aspect of Indian life." Present day clips reveal a still gutsy Hill
saying that one day his father took him up to the mountain-top and said,
"See all that land son? Do you realize that one day NONE of this will be
yours?!"

ON THE WINGS OF TOMORROW

Country USA   **Year** 1994   **Length** 13 m.   **Genre** IND
Director Bill Baker
Producer Pamela Jennings
Distributor
North Slope Borough School District / TV Studio
P.O. Box 169
Barrow, AK 99723
907 852-0215 [b] 907 852-2145 [f]
US $20.00 VHS

On the Wings of Tomorrow is the story of the most northern school district
in America, the North Slope Borough School District, which covers 80,000
square miles of Northern Alaska. The eight villages comprising the district
are hundreds of miles apart and seven are large enough for only one school
serving all grades. How were they to offer the more advanced classes that
would prepare their children for college? A boarding school in Barrow
looked like the only answer, but the parents' memories of Indian boarding
schools forced them to look for other solutions. Their unique answer was a
highly technological distance education system that allows the students to
stay at home, have the advantages of the best teachers, and get the courses
they need to go on to college.

ONE FLEW OVER THE CUCKOO'S NEST

Country USA   **Year** 1982   **Length** 129 m.   **Genre** FF
Director Milos Forman
Producer Saul Zaentz and Michael Douglas
Distributor
Available at local video and rental stores.

Director Milos Forman brings to the screen Ken Kesey's boisterous, brawling novel about a hellraising free spirit and his adventures in a mental ward. It's the story of McMurphy (Jack Nicolson), whose rebelliousness pits him against Nurse Ratched (Louise Fletcher) and the full spectrum of insitutional repression, and whose vital charm wins him the loyalty of his fellow inmates. Also starring Will Sampson in the role of Chief Bromden.

Original Release Date - 1975.

ONE HEART, ONE SONG

Country Canada   **Year** 1994   **Length** 23 m.   **Genre** DS
Director Kelly Parker
Producer Saskatchewan Indian Cultural Centre
Distributor
Saskatchewan Indian Cultural Centre
120 - 33rd Street, East
Saskatoon, Sasketchewan
S7K 0S2 Canada
306 244-1146 [b] 306 665-6520 [f]   www.sicc.sk.ca
CAD $19.95 VHS, call for rental fees

One Heart, One Song was produced with the dream of providing a tool for young Indigenous athletes to become aware of the inner self, that was always aware to our people in the past. The second North American Indigenous Games were held in Prince Albert, Saskatchewan in the summer of 1993. This video project, undertaken by the Saskatchewan Indian Cultural Centre, captured the events, people and especially the feeling that was present with our people gathering for this special occasion.

OTHER SIDE OF THE LEDGER, THE:
AN INDIAN VIEW OF THE HUDSON'S BAY COMPANY

Country Canada   **Year** 1977   **Length** 42 m.   **Genre** DS
Director Martin Defalco, Willie Dunn
Producer George Pearson
Distributor
National Film Board of Canada Library
22-D Hollywood Avenue
Ho-Ho-Kus, NJ 07423
1 800 542-2164 [b] 201 652-1973 [f]
US $225.00 VHS, call for rental information and prices.
For purchase within Canada visit the NFB website at: www.nfb.ca
1 800 267-7710 toll free within Canada

The Hudson's Bay Company's 300th anniversary celebration was no occasion for joy among the people whose lives were tied to the trading stores. This film, narrated by George Manuel, president of the National Indian Brotherhood, presents the view of spokesmen for Canadian Indian and Métis groups. There is a sharp contrast between the official celebrations, with Queen Elizabeth II among the guests, and what Indians have to say about their lot in the Company's operations.

OUR CHILDREN ARE OUR FUTURE

Country Canada   **Year** 1982   **Length** 51 m.   **Genre** DF
Director Tony Snowsill
Producer Direction Films
Distributor
Currently unavailable.

Thanksgiving Day, 1981. Over a thousand British Columbia Native Indians converge on Vancouver to protest the apprehension of their children by provincial child welfare authorities. Chief Wayne Christian, organizer of the Indian Child Caravan, wants those children back. The socio-economic problems which plague his tiny reserve in the Okanogan Valley are typical of those experienced by Indian people across Canada. This is a compelling and disturbing film that takes an intimate look at the studies behind the statistics. The film avoids the contentions of external narrative, relying on the characters to tell their stories in their own words, in their own way.

OUR DANCES

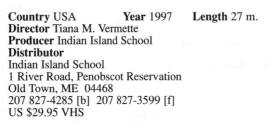

Country USA   **Year** 1997   **Length** 27 m.   **Genre** DS
Director Tiana M. Vermette
Producer Indian Island School
Distributor
Indian Island School
1 River Road, Penobscot Reservation
Old Town, ME 04468
207 827-4285 [b] 207 827-3599 [f]
US $29.95 VHS

Our Dances, directed by Tiana Vermette, an 8th grade student at Indian Island School, Penobscot Nation, Indian Island, Maine, features the Penobscot Student Dance Troupe. The video is about the cultural importance of these dances to the students of Indian Island School.

OUR DEAR SISTERS

Country Canada   **Year** 1977   **Length** 15 m.   **Genre** DS
Director Kathleen Shannon
Producer Len Chatwin, Kathleen Shannon
Distributor
National Film Board of Canada Library
22-D Hollywood Avenue
Ho-Ho-Kus, NJ 07423
1 800 542-2164 [b] 201 652-1973 [f]
US $125.00 VHS, call for rental information and prices.
For purchase within Canada visit the NFB website at: www.nfb.ca
1 800 267-7710 toll free within Canada

Alanis Obomsawin, a North American Indian who earns her living by singing and making films, is the mother of an adopted child. In *Our Dear Sisters* she talks about her life, her people, and her responsibilites as a single parent. Alanis' observations shake some of our cultural assumptions.

OUR LIVES IN OUR HANDS

Country USA   **Year** 1987   **Length** 49 m.   **Genre** DS
Director Harald Prins, Sponsor: Aroostook Micmac Council
Producer Harald E.L. Prins and Karen Carter
Distributor
Documentary Educational Resources
101 Morse Street
Watertown, MA 02172
617 926-0491 [b] www.der.org
US $245.00 VHS & 16mm, US $70.00 16mm rental
Within Maine call Northeast Historic Film 1 800 639-1636 P.O. Box 900
Bucksport, ME 04416 - US $29.95 VHS

Our Lives in Our Hands concerns an examination of the traditional Native American craft of splint ash basketmaking as a means of economic and cultural survival for Aroostook Micmac Indians of northern Maine. A documentary of rural off-reservation Indian artisans, this 49 minute color film aims at breaking down stereotypical images of these people.

OUR PAST IS OUR FUTURE

Country USA   **Year** 1999   **Length** 17 m.   **Genre** DS
Director Daniel Jumper, Robert Frank, Jeannette Cypress
Producer Seminole Tribe of Florida
Distributor
Seminole Broadcasting, Seminole Tribe of Florida
6300 Stirling Road
Hollywood, FL 33024
954 967-3417 [b] 954 967-3485 [f]
Please call for pricing.

This documentary was created in an attempt to capture the historical and cultural significance of Susie Jim Billie. She is a member of the Seminole Tribe of Florida, who are surviving in today's society while maintaining their distinct and unconquered identity that brought them to where they are today. Susie's vast wisdom is exemplified by her continued active contribution of passing on her culture in her day to day living.

Susie acquired her knowledge from her elders and ancestors in various ways, from just watching crafts being made, to listening to her elders make medicine to heal her people. No matter what she was learning, she was always told how important it was for her to pass on what she had learned. Since the Seminoles are a matriarchal society, it was even more important for Susie to learn and pass on to her children to ensure that her lineage and her people would survive long after she is gone. Susie's 100+ years have been dedicated to healing and helping her people survive into the next millenium.

OUR SACRED LAND

Country USA   **Year** 1985   **Length** 28 m.   **Genre** DS
Director Chris Spotted Eagle
Producer Chris Spotted Eagle, KTCA-TV
Distributor
Spotted Eagle Productions
2524 Hennepin Avenue, South
Minneapolis, MN 55405-3567
612 377-4212 [b] and [f]
cseagle@tc.umn.edu
Please call for pricing and rental information.

Although the Fort Laramie Treaty of 1868 set aside the Black Hills in perpetuity, the Oglala Sioux are still fighting for their legal and moral rights to the land. For Indian people, the land, traditional ways of life, their religion and the universe are inseparable. Bear Butte and the Black Hills in Southwestern South Dakota are two of the most sacred areas to the Sioux Nation. But since the 1877 Gold Rush in the Black Hills, the Sioux have been denied unrestricted access to their religious sites. Our Sacred Land is an insightful look into American Indian religious freedom and treaty issues.

OUR TOTEM IS THE RAVEN

Country Canada **Year** 1975 **Length** 21 m. **Genre** LS
Producer King Screen Productions
Distributor
Phoenix Films and Video
2349 Chaffee Drive
St. Louis, MO 63146
314 569-0211 [b] 314 569-2834 [f]
www.phoenixcoronet.com phoenixfilm@worldnet.att.net
US $89.95 VHS
US $58.00 VHS 3 day rental

Fifteen-year old David, an urban Indian boy, has little interest in his cultural heritage. His grandfather, portrayed by Academy Award nominee Chief Dan George, takes David into the forest to give him an understanding of the ways of his forefathers. This award winning drama of a boy's ordeal of endurance and ritual ascent to manhood underscore the problems Native Americans face, as customs clash with 20th century values.

OUTLAW JOSEY WALES, THE

Country USA **Year** 1979 **Length** 135 m. **Genre** FF
Director Clint Eastwood
Producer Robert Daley
Distributor
Available on Amazon.com
www.amazon.com
US $12.99 VHS, US $16.99 DVD
Also check local video stores.

Clint Eastwood's 26th feature film, *The Outlaw Josey Wales*, is the story of a man hounded by soldiers and bounty hunters while on his own bloody mission of revenge.

The western adventure drama takes place in the border area between Kansas and Missouri immediately following the Civil War, where out-of-war soldiers, aided by renegade gunfighters, bounty hunters and wanted men, banded together to kill and destroy. One group of ruthless guerillas kills the wife and young son of farmer Josey Wales, while the leader of the gang sabers Josey and leaves him for dead. Josey survives, takes up arms and seeks his revenge. For Eastwood, the role is a return to the tough, tight-lipped, violent Western hero which had initially brought him international fame.

The film was shot on location in Arizona, Utah and northern California against a background of nature which is sometimes gentle, but always awesome in its reality.

Chief Dan George co-stars as an old and very civilized Cherokee Indian who joins forces with Josey Wales. Also co-starring in the film are Sondra Locke, newcomer Geraldine Keams, Paula Trueman, John Vernon, Bill McKinney, Sam Bottoms and Will Sampson.

Original Release Date - 1976.

OVERWEIGHT WITH CROOKED TEETH

Country Canada **Year** 1997 **Length** 5 m. **Genre** LS
Director Shelley Niro
Producer Shelley Niro & Dan BigBee Jr.
Distributor
Shenandoah Film Productions
538 "G" Street
Arcata, CA 95521
707 822-1030 tele 707 822-1035 fax
$75.00US VHS, $25.00US rental

For home use check www.oyate.org

Based on a poem by Michael Doxtater, this video creation pokes fun at Indian stereotypes. The poet himself plays the principal roles of Sitting Bull and Chief Joseph.

PAHA SAPA: THE STRUGGLE FOR THE BLACK HILLS

Country USA   **Year** 1998   **Length** 60 m.   **Genre** DF
Director Mel Lawrence
Producer Mel Lawrence
Distributor
Shenandoah Film Productions
538 "G" Street
Arcata, CA 95521
707 822-1030 [b] 707 822-1035 [f]
US $175.00 VHS, US $45.00 VHS rental

The Black Hills of South Dakota are to the Lakota Sioux and Cheyenne Indians what Mount Sinai is to the Jews, the Vatican is to Roman Catholics, and Mecca is to Muslims. Sacred to the Indian — but not to the white man — the Black Hills have come to symbolize the misappropriation of Indian lands by the U.S. government.

In 1973, a mass demonstration at Wounded Knee, site of the 1890 massacre, signaled the beginning of a new era of hope among Indians. In 1980, after 117 years of legal battles through congress and the courts, the Supreme Court awarded the Sioux Nation $105 million as a settlement for their Black Hills claim in an unprecedented ruling. That award has since grown to more than $350 million. However, the Indians refuse to touch what they regard as the U.S. goverment's blood money. They want their sacred land back.

Paha Sapa is not only about what the Indian lost and is fighting to regain. It's also about what the white man lost, and may never regain: a primal, sacred connection with the land.

PAINTER'S SONG ARTIST: TIGER TIGER

Country USA   **Year** 1997   **Length** 5 m.   **Genre** MV
Director Stephen Tiger
Producer Stephen Tiger
Distributor
Sound Of America Records
P.O. Box 8606
Albuquerque, NM 87198
954 370-3900 [b] 954 370-3999 [f]
Call for pricing information.

Tiger Tiger is comprised of two brothers Stephen and Lee Tiger, from the Miccouskee Tribe of Florida. They are proud of their Indian roots, and equally proud of their redefined musical sound, which they hope will not only portray a positive awareness of their culture, but also carry this awareness over into the world of pop music.

"Painter's Song" depicts through music, photos, and film clips, the world of the Miccosukee Indians.

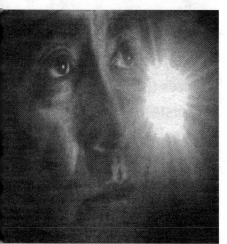

PASSAGEWAY TO THE INFINITE SELF

Country USA   **Year** 1995   **Length** 23 m.   **Genre** DS
Director Vladan Mijailovic
Producer Gayle Madaleine Randall
Distributor
Heaven Fire Productions, Inc. / Exclusive Pictures
15951 Arminta Street
Van Nuys, CA 91406
818 901-1392 [b] 818 904-9004 [f]
www.ExclusivePictures.com   sales@ExclusivePictures.com
US $19.95 VHS

Joseph Rael (Beautiful Painted Arrow) is an astonishing product of both the teachings imparted to him while growing up at Picuris Pueblo in the 1940s, and western education, including a Masters degree in political science. He is internationally recognized as a visionary, shaman and master story-teller of Ute and Pueblo heritage.

Drawing upon the teachings of his grandfather, a Native American holy man, Rael presents an extraordinary understanding of life through metaphor alongside experience.

PATRICK'S STORY

Country Canada   **Year** 2000   **Length** 24 m.   **Genre** DS
Director Doug Cuthand
Producer Lori Kuffner and Jennifer Torrance
Distributor
National Film Board of Canada   1 800 267-7710 toll free within Canada
For purchase within Canada visit the NFB website at: www.nfb.ca

Films for the Humanities and Sciences
P.O. Box 2053
Princeton, NJ 08543-2053
1 800 257-5126 [b]
US $129.00 VHS educational

Patrick Bird was "a casualty of colonialism," having walked a dark boy-hood journey of sexual abuse, neglect, foster homes, detention centers, abandonment, loss, drugs, alcohol, and self-mutilation. *Patrick's Story* explores what brought a young man to attempt suicide and what ultimately turned his life around.

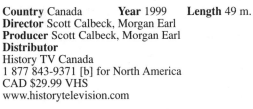

PAULINE

Country Canada   **Year** 1999   **Length** 49 m.   **Genre** DS
Director Scott Calbeck, Morgan Earl
Producer Scott Calbeck, Morgan Earl
Distributor
History TV Canada
1 877 843-9371 [b] for North America
CAD $29.99 VHS
www.historytelevision.com

Pauline Johnson was born in 1861, the daughter of a Mohawk chief and his English wife. She became one of Canada's favorite performers, reciting poetry and stories during a career on stage that lasted seventeen years. She grew up in a world of privilege, on Six Nations Territory in what is now Ontario. Her father, George Johnson, was a prosperous and influential man. He and his wife Emily raised their four children (Pauline was the youngest) in a grand house, Chiefswood, that was an important destination for visitors to the area. Alexander Graham Bell and Prince Arthur, the Duke of Connaught, were among the many people that young Pauline met.

Pauline, who had often recited poetry for the Johnson family guests and had read all the great works of literature in her family's library, began act-ing in local productions. At the age of 31, she was invited to recite at an event in Toronto. A promoter named Frank Yeigh witnessed the enthusias-tic response to Pauline and immediately booked her on a series of perfor-mances.

Taking full advantage of her dual heritage, Pauline would appear for the first act in a traditional evening dress. For the second act, she would come out in a buckskin outfit she designed, with her long hair flowing and her arms bare. It was considered risqué in the 1890s, but audiences loved her everywhere she went. She became known as "The Mohawk Princess."

PENOBSCOT: THE PEOPLE & THEIR RIVER

Country USA   **Year** 1995   **Length** 28 m.   **Genre** DS
Director David Westphal
Producer Acadia Film Video
Distributor
Penobscot Nation Museum
6 River Road
Indian Island, ME 04468
207 827-4153 [b]
US $15.00 VHS purchase

The Penobscot people have lived on the Penobscot River for thousands of years. "The river has been our highway, as well as our source of food and medicines. We consider it a living thing and gain from it our spiritual and our physical sustenance. But the river, and thereby our way of life, has been changing for the past century. It has been polluted and developed, threatening the river's very survival and thereby severely threatening our traditional way of life."

This film points out how the Penobscot Nation as well as the other people of Maine share a common interest in the health of the Penobscot River and its watershed. It also talks about what must be done — and what the Penobscot People are doing — to restore and protect the Penobscot River.

PEOPLE ARE DANCING AGAIN, THE

Country USA   **Year** 1978   **Genre** DS
Distributor
Not in distribution.
Confederated Tribes of Siletz Indians
P.O. Box 549
Siletz, OR 97380
1 800 922-1399 [b]

This sensitively produced documentary about the Confederated Tribes of Siletz in Western Oregon shows a modern Indian people, proud of both their ancient heritage and their status as Americans. Most fundamentally, it is the story of their remarkable strength in the face of profound cultural and economic change.

The history of the Siletz is chronicled from the 1850s, when coastal Indians were moved to Siletz, through 1954, when the tribe was terminated by the federal governement. All federal support was withdrawn and remaining land was sold off.

In 1970, the Siletz people began working to regain federal recognition of their tribal status. In the long, difficult process of working for restoration, there has been a rebirth of the tribe's spirit and of the people's own sense of their value as Indians in modern America.

PEOPLE OF THE KLAMATH: PRESERVING A WAY OF LIFE

Country USA   **Year** 1988   **Length** 28 m.   **Genre** DS
Director James Culp
Producer James Culp
Distributor
The Film History Foundation
650 5th Street, Suite 202
San Francisco, CA 94107
415 777-1020 [b]   415 777-3453 [f]
US $79.95 VHS

When 76-year-old Karuk Indian Lew Wilder grew up, virtually all of the elements of his culture were under attack. He was forced to attend a Bureau of Indian Affairs school hundreds of miles from his home. There, he was ridiculed for using his Native language, back home, the co-called "Indian Police" arrested his relatives for playing their Indian drums. Indian ceremonies were all but banned. A way of life was all but destroyed.

But Lew's childhood memories of watching the old men flake arrowheads, and of seeing the women of the tribe weaving baskets from willow sticks and bear grass were not lost. After a lifetime of working in the forests and the mines, Lew retired. However, he now found himself attracted to "the old ways." In his workshop, he began to make soapstone pipes and flake arrowheads in the manner he remembered from long ago. Soon, he attracted the attention of Leaf Hillman, a young Karuk who was interested in learning the ways of his people. Eventually, Leaf became a "carrier of culture" himself as he learned the Karuk tongue and taught it in the public schools on Northwestern California.

People of the Klamath: Preserving a Way of Life is the story of how language and the artistic elements of a culture are preserved and passed down from one generation to another within a Native American tribe. Newly discovered historic motion picture footage of Karuk life in the early part of the 20th century is contrasted with present-day activities such as salmon fishing, Indian gaming, basket making, and processing acorns for traditional Indian soup.

PEPPER'S POWWOW

Country USA   **Year** 1995   **Length** 58 m.   **Genre** DF
Director Sandra Osawa
Producer Sandra Osawa
Distributor
Upstream Productions
6850 35th Avenue NE #11
Seattle, WA 98115
206 526-7122 [b] 206 526-7127 [f]
US $30.00 VHS

This documentary opens up new territory for Native American subjects by focusing on Jim Pepper, an international jazz musician, whose musical contributions to the world of jazz have never been documented for general audiences. His life and music serve as a successful metaphor for many minorities who seek to participate in society while still maintaining their own cultural identity.

Pepper, whose name is as lively and unique as his musical contributions, was the first jazz artist to overtly use Native American themes and motifs. He was the first to directly integrate Native American dance and dance rhythms into jazz. Both Native American and tap dance rhythms are unmistakable in his phrasing and stem from his early training as a champion war dancer and a tap dancer. Pepper was also the first jazz musician to experiment with blending jazz and rock and formed a band in the mid 1960s called Free Spirits with Larry Coryell. Jazz purists did not take this form seriously, but in the past two decades the jazz rock movement has become quite pervasive. The Native American contribution to jazz can be documented as early as the 1820s in New Orleans when Blacks and Native Americans performed together and discovered they had the same pentatonic scale. Many jazz musicians performing today are of American Indian heritage. For the first time, such contributions will be made more widely known through the life of Jim Pepper, who passed away in February of 1992.

PETROGLYPHS, THE

Country USA   **Year** 1995   **Length** 1 m.   **Genre** PS
Director Pamela Hurley
Producer SIPI College Bound
Distributor
Not in distribution.
SIPI College
P.O. Box 10146
Albuquerque, NM 87184
505 346-2340 [b]

This one minute commercial implements imagery and a quote by Chief Seattle exemplifying concern for environmental justice.

PEYOTE ROAD, THE

Country USA   **Year** 1992   **Length** 59 m.   **Genre** DF
Director Fidel Moreno, Gary Rhine, Phil Cousineau
Producer Gary Rhine, Fidel Moreno
Distributor
Kifaru Productions
23852 Pacific Coast Hwy. #766
Malibu, CA 90265
1 800 400-8433 [b] 310 457-2688 [f]
www.kifaru.com   kifaru1@aol.com
US $125.00 VHS institutional, US $29.95 VHS home video
US $250.00 16mm rental

The Peyote Road addresses the recent U.S. Supreme Court "Smith" decision, which sent shock waves through religious communities around the country. In a decision of devastating impact to the Free Exercise of Religion clause of the United States Constitution, the court denied protection of the First Amendment religious liberty to the sacramental use of Peyote for Native Americans, one of the oldest tribal religions in the Western hemisphere.

This decision has put members of The Native American Church, the people who use Peyote as a sacrament, in the position of having to fear a knock on the door during their prayer ceremonies. *The Peyote Road* documents the centuries old sacramental use of Peyote, a cactus with psychedelic properties, and makes a strong argument that if this court decision is not countered by an act of Congress, then the first amendment right of freedom of religion for all Americans has been chillingly curtailed.

PICTURING A PEOPLE:
GEORGE JOHNSTON, TLINGIT PHOTOGRAPHER

Country Canada   **Year** 1997   **Length** 50 m.   **Genre** DS
Director Carol Geddes
Producer Sally Bochner, Don Haig, George Hargrave
Distributor
National Film Board of Canada Library
22-D Hollywood Avenue
Ho-Ho-Kus, NJ 07423
1 800 542-2164 [b] 201 652-1973 [f]
US $129.00 VHS, call for rental information and prices.
For purchase within Canada visit the NFB website at: www.nfb.ca
1 800 267-7710 toll free within Canada

At the age of 16, George Johnston left the Yukon community of Teslin and
trekked hundreds of miles overland to coastal Alaska in search of the history of his people. Johnston met with elders, learning as much as he could
about the Tlingit religion and the songs and dances of his people. A few
years later, Johnston did something else that was quite extraordinary: after
ordering a camera from a mail-order catalogue, he taught himself to use it
and to develop and print his own photographs. The images he recorded--of
special moments and everyday occasions--became a beacon to the young
and a testament to the golden times of the Tlingit people. Johnston's photos
lovingly portray a sense of history and a zest for life. His work as a photographer in the period from 1920 to 1945 has long been recognized in the
Native community, predating a generation of Indian and Inuit photographers. Today, as his photographs gain international recognition, the
National Film Board of Canada has released a documentary directed by
Carol Geddes, a clan relative of Johnston's. *Picturing a People: George
Johnston, Tlingit Photographer* is a unique portrait of a man who was himself a creator of portraits and a keeper of his culture. Johnston cared deeply
about the traditions of the Tlingit people, and he recorded a critical period
in the history of the Tlingit Nation. As Geddes says, his legacy was "to
help us dream the future as much as to remember the past."

PINTO FOR THE PRINCE, A

Country Canada   **Year** 1979   **Length** 17 m.   **Genre** DS
Director Colin Low, John Spotton
Producer Tom Daly, Michael Scott
Distributor
National Film Board of Canada Library
22-D Hollywood Avenue
Ho-Ho-Kus, NJ 07423
1 800 542-2164 [b] 201 652-1973 [f]
US $125.00 VHS, call for rental information and prices.
For purchase within Canada visit the NFB website at: www.nfb.ca
1 800 267-7710 toll free within Canada

In 1977, Prince Charles was inducted as honorary chief of the Blood
Indians on their reserve in southwestern Alberta. The ceremony, conducted
in the great Circle of the Sun Dance, commemorated the centennial
anniversary of the original signing of Treaty Seven by Queen Victoria.

PLACE OF THE FALLING WATERS, THE

Country USA   **Year** 1992   **Length** 90 m.   **Genre** DF
Director Roy Bigrance And Thompson Smith
Producer Frank Tyro and Daniel Hart
Distributor
Native Voices
Padelford 514C - Box 345305
University of Washington
Seattle, WA 98195
206 616-7498 [b]   206 616-3122 [f]
US $39.95 VHS home use, US $99.95 VHS educational use
US $39.95 VHS rental
Teachers study guide available for US $4.00

The Place of the Falling Waters focuses on the complex and volatile relationship between the people of the Confederated Salish and Kootenai Tribes and a major hydroelectric dam situated within the Flathead Indian Reservation. The documentary consists of three sections: a history of tribal society and culture before the dam's construction, the construction of the Kerr Dam in the 1930s and its impact on the reservation, and the hopes and dilemmas of the Salish and Kootenai people as they prepare to take over Kerr Dam during the next three decades.

PLACES NOT OUR OWN

Country Canada   **Year** 1987   **Length** 57 m.   **Genre** FF
Director Derek Mazur
Producer Norma Bailey, Ches Yetman (exec.)
Distributor
National Film Board of Canada Library
22-D Hollywood Avenue
Ho-Ho-Kus, NJ 07423
1 800 542-2164 [b]   201 652-1973 [f]
US $150.00 VHS, call for rental information and prices.
For purchase within Canada visit the NFB website at: www.nfb.ca
1 800 267-7710 toll free within Canada

By 1929, Canada's west, which had been home to generations of Métis, was taken over by the railroads and new settlers. The Métis became a forgotten people, relegated to eking out a living as best they could. In *Places Not Our Own*, Rose l'Esperance, a Métis, is determined that her children will have a normal life and an education. Her hopes reside in her daughter Flora, but the harshness of their situation culminates in a devastating and dramatic event. This film is part of the "Daughters of the Country series."

Starring Dianne Debassige, Tantoo Cardinal and Steve Isfeld.

POCAHONTAS

Country USA   **Year** 1995   **Length** 87 m.   **Genre** FF
Director Mike Gabriel, Eric Goldberg
Producer James Pentecost, Baker Bloodworth (assoc.)
Distributor
Buena Vista Pictures / Video
Also available on Amazon
www.amazon.com
US $20.99 VHS, US $25.49 DVD

Walt Disney Pictures' 33rd full length animated feature Pocahontas is an odyssey of adventure and romance, combining historical fact and folklore. Torn between duty and destiny, Pocahontas' (voice of Irene Bedard) life is forever changed when she befriends a handsome British soldier, Captain John Smith (voice of Mel Gibson). Through the eyes of this explorer, she learns to search for her dreams. And she teaches the young Captian Smith the ways of the foerest and of her people. Their mutual sacrifices unite their spirits forever in a love that trancends all time.

POINT, THE - THE LEGACY OF THE RIVER PEOPLE

Country USA   **Year** 1996   **Length** 60 m.   **Genre** DF
Director Peter Monahan
Producer Peter Monahan & Danny Kepley
Distributor
Currently unavailable.

The Point - The Legacy of the River People is a story spanning hundreds of years, culminating in the current relationships among cultures, humankind, and the land on which we live. Through dramatic images and commentary, the story unfolds of the Native people living along Nch'i-wana, the Columbia River, and investors planning a private residential community near the town of Lyle, Washington. The difference of opinions between those who view the land as sacred and ecologically unique and those who wish to transform the land into a residential and recreational haven has erupted into confrontation and legal conflict.

POISONING PARADISE

Country USA   **Year** 1996   **Length** 42 m.   **Genre** DS
Director Barb Allard, Kelly Reinhardt
Producer Dragonfly Productions
Distributor
Shenandoah Film Productions
538 "G" Street
Arcata, CA 95521
707 822-1030 [b] 707 822-1035 [f]
US $150.00 VHS purchase US $45.00 VHS rental
For purchase in Canada call:
Rainbow Bridge Communications, 780 455-7335 [b]
rainbow@web.net

The Swan Hills have been a traditional hunting, trapping, and gathering territory for the Treaty Eight First Nations for thousands of years. The Alberta Special Waste Treatment Center is Canada's largest hazardous waste incinerator — designed to be the final destination for all of Canada's toxic waste. The Alberta goverment chose one of Alberta's highest points east of the Rocky Mountains, right in the middle of Swan Hills, as the site for the ASWTC. Once again, Natives must fight to save traditional territory and way of life. *Poisoning Paradise* takes you to the heart of the battle.

POLTERGEIST II: THE OTHER SIDE

Country USA   **Year** 1987   **Length** 91 m.   **Genre** FF
Director Brian Gibson
Producer Mark Victor & Michael Grais
Distributor
Available on Amazon.com
www.amazon.com
US $9.95 VHS

Sequel to the 1982 hit, this film finds the Freeling family yet again surrounded and haunted by supernatural and ghostly entities. Will Sampson co-stars as Taylor, a Native American medicine man whose mysterious presence guides and protects the Freeling family during their terrible ordeal in *Poltergeist II*. JoBeth Williams, Craig T. Nelson, Heather O'Rourke and Oliver Robins star.

POMO BASKETWEAVERS: A TRIBUTE TO THREE ELDERS

Country USA   **Year** 1996   **Length** 59 m.   **Genre** DF
Director David Ludwig
Producer David Ludwig
Distributor
UC Extension Center for Media and Independent Learning
2000 Center Street, Fourth Floor
Berkeley, CA 94704
510 642-0460 [b] 510 643-9271 [f]
cmil@uclink.berkeley.edu
US $225.00 VHS, US $70.00 VHS rental

The baskets of the Pomo Indian women are world renowned for their appearance, range of technique, and diversity of form. *Pomo Basketweavers: A Tribute to Three Elders* provides an in-depth introduction to the history, culture and basket weaving traditions of Pomo women, focusing on the life works and achievements of three Pomo women: Laura Somersal, Elsie Allen & Magel McKay. The film shows in detail all aspects of Pomo basket weaving, including the cultivation, gathering, and curing of the necessary plants and the importance of basket weaving to Pomo culture.

POPOL VUH - COSMOGENESIS MAYA

Country USA   **Year** 1984   **Length** 12 m.   **Genre** ANS
Director Patricia Amlin
Producer Patricia Amlin
Distributor
Latin American Video Archives (LAVA)
124 Washington Place
New York, NY 10014
212 463-0108 [b] 212 243-2007 [f]
imre@igc.org
US $295.00 VHS

Popol Vuh is an ethno-animated film based on an ancient meso-American manuscript known as the Popol Vuh. This is a chronicle of the Awakening of the Quiche Maya people, the most powerful nation of the Guatemalan Highlands in pre-conquest times. This orally-transmitted legend contains, on one level, the whole evolutionary process of Quiche Maya culture: its religion, society, and economy.

By special AIFI invitation.

PORTRAITS OF LEADERSHIP

Country USA   **Year** 1990   **Length** 28 m.   **Genre** DS
Director Daniel Housberg
Producer Susan B. Andrews
Distributor
Not in distribution

Portraits of Leadership profiles two Alaska Native leaders, Chief Katlian of Sitka and Howard Rock of Point Hope.

Chief Katlian, a Tlingit Indian, led the last major battle against the Russians in Alaska in the early 1800s. Although he was defeated in battle and forced off his land, some 20 years later, he led his people back to their home in Sitka to reassert their right to be there. From then on, the Tlingits and Russians co-existed on the same soil.

Howard Rock, an Inupiaq Eskimo, founded and edited an influential statewide Native newspaper, the Tundra Times. Through his editorials, Rock was instrumental in passage of the Alaska Native Claims Settlement Act of 1971, which settled Eskimos, Indians and Aleuts' long-standing claims to their land.

POUNDMAKER'S LODGE - A HEALING PLACE

Country Canada   **Year** 1987   **Length** 29 m.   **Genre** DS
Director Alanis Obomasawin
Producer Marrin Canell, Alanis Obomasawin, Andy Thomson (exec),
Robert Verrall
Distributor
National Film Board of Canada Library
22-D Hollywood Avenue
Ho-Ho-Kus, NJ 07423
1 800 542-2164 [b] 201 652-1973 [f]
US $150.00 VHS, call for rental information and prices.
For purchase within Canada visit the NFB website at: www.nfb.ca
1 800 267-7710 toll free within Canada

Poundmaker's Lodge, named after a nineteenth-century Native leader, is a
treatment center in St. Albert, Alberta, where Native people troubled by
addiction to drugs and alcohol can come together for mutual support, to
partake of healing rituals like the sweat lodge, and to rediscover their traditions. The film places Native alcoholism in its historical and socio-cultural
contexts. It shows the despair of a people dispossessed of land, culture,
language and dignity, and their strength and courage in overcoming substance abuse.

POW WOW

Country USA   **Year** 1993   **Length** 30 m.   **Genre** DS
Director K.C. Chaimberlain
Producer K.C. Chaimberlain
Distributor
Currently unavailable.

The documentary *Pow Wow* is a look at today's world through the eyes of
the descendants of its oldest inhabitants. It examines the Indian dance
embodied in the Pow Wow events themselves. Here you meet dance con-
testants, vendors and spectators.

POWER

Country Canada   **Year** 1996   **Length** 77 m.   **Genre** DF
Director Magnus Isacsson
Producer Katherine Buck, Don Haig, Glen Salzman, Mark Zannis
Distributor
National Film Board of Canada 1 800 267-7710 toll free within Canada
For purchase within Canada visit the NFB website at: www.nfb.ca
Form Five Inc. (US disribution)
5505 Blvd. St-Laurent, Suite 3008
Montreal, Quebec
H2T 1S6 Canada
514 278-3140 [b]
US $29.99 VHS home use, US $59.99 VHS high schools,
US $249.00 VHS universities and libraries

When Hydro-Québec announced its intention to proceed with the enormous James Bay II hydroelectric project, the 15,000 Cree who live in the
region decided to stand up to the giant utility. With unprecedented access
to key figures like Cree leader Matthew Coon Come and American environmental activist Robert Kennedy Jr., *Power* is the compelling, behind-
the-scenes story of the Cree's five-year battle to save the Great Whale
River and their traditional way of life.

POWWOW

Country USA   **Year** 1984   **Length** 22 m.   **Genre** DS
Director Elaine Middletown
Producer Elaine Middletown
Distributor
Currently unavailable.

This video was produced in order to introduce the educational, social,
artistic, and religious aspects of Native Americans to students at the
University of Arkansas, Fayetteville, and to the Oklahoma community.

POWWOW HIGHWAY

Country USA   **Year** 1988   **Length** 90 m.   **Genre** FF
Director Jonathan Wacks
Producer Jan Wieringa
Distributor
Oyate
2702 Mathews Street
Berkeley, CA 94702
510 848-6700 [b] 510 848-4815 [f]
www.oyate.org
US $15.00 VHS
Also available at local video stores and on Amazon.com

It's present day on the Northern Cheyenne Indian Reservation in Lame
Deer, Montana. Buddy Red Bow (A Martinez) is a handsome, charismatic
and politically agressive activist—a man full of anger, passion and disillu-
siment working to protect the interests of his people. Philbert Bono (Gary
Farmer) is a mammoth, easy-going loner—an outsider who yearns to
become a spiritual warrior.

Buddy and Philbert are thrown together for one week in a journey against
time across the plains of America, rumbling down hundreds of miles of an
interstate highway in a beat-up '64 Buick dubbed "Protector."

So begins this offbeat story of two disparate Indians who learn much about
friendship, love and their cultural heritage as they travel down the scenic
expanse of interstate known as the "Pow Wow Highway."

POWWOW MOSH

Country USA   **Year** 1994   **Length** 9 m.   **Genre** DS
Director Eli Funaro
Producer Eli Funaro and Institute of American Indian Arts
Distributor
Not in distribution - student film
IAIA
Avan Nu Po Road
Santa Fe, NM 87505
505 424-2300 [b]

Parallels are drawn between traditional Pow Wow dancing and "thrashing"
in the "mosh circles" of hardcore punk and thrash metal concerts.

PRAYER OF PASSAGE

Country USA   **Year** 2000   **Length** 11 m.   **Genre** LS
Director Chris Zeller
Producer Gianina Carver
Distributor
Chris Zeller
800 S. Sycamore Avenue
Los Angeles, CA 90036
323 938-4355 [b] and [f]
dczell@yahoo.com
US $20.00 VHS

Gard, an Ojibwa youth, comes upon a leg trap in a stream. He destroys it
and engages in a mock battle, vanquishing the trapper intruders from his
land. Unbeknownst to the boy, Oshkikwe, who is out gathering berries,
catches him at his game and laughs. They play cat and mouse as they
make their way back to the woods. Separated for a stretch of trail, Gard
finds that Oshkikwe has stumbled into the company of two trappers,
Francois and Jean Pierre, whose trap Gard destroyed. Gard hides as the
trappers take Oshkikwe back to their camp, where they begin to assault
her. Gard crashes into their camp and attacks the trappers, but he is defeated and knocked unconscious. As he fades into the netherworld, the boy
locks eyes with Oshkikwe, who begins to pray.

Set in the Great Lakes region in the mid 1700s, *Prayer of Passage* is a
mythic American Indian tale that deals with the universal themes of innocence lost, heroism and retribution, ultimately becoming an original and
enigmatic parable about the cost of strength and spiritual transformation.

PRESERVING OUR PAST

Country USA   **Year** 1998   **Length** 60 m.   **Genre** DF
Director Ben W. Baker
Producer Ben W. Baker
Distributor
Sault Sainte Marie Tribe of Chippewa Indians Video Production
Two Ice Circle - Chi Mukwa, 2nd Floor
Sault Ste. Marie, MI 49783
906 635-7001 [b] 906 635-7005 [f]
www.stvideopro.org   qvideo@northernway.net
US $49.95 VHS

Preserving Our Past is a documentary about the Sault Sainte Marie Tribe
of Chippewa Indians in Sault Ste. Marie, Michigan. Topics such as natural
healing and tribal stories are just some of the featured areas in this life and
history of a people as told by Chippewa Tribal Elders. It was produced as a
series of five twelve minute shorts, each highlighting diverse tribal issues.

PRICE WE PAID, THE

Country USA   **Year** 1978   **Genre** DS
Director Business Council of the Colville Confederated Tribes
Producer Media Services, Yakima Indian Nation
Distributor
Not currently in distribution.
For more information call:
Colville Communication Services: 509 634-2222 [b]

The story of Grand Coulee Dam as an engineering Wonder of the World,
and the source of water and electric power which opened up the Northwest
to development, is a well known story indeed. *The Price We Paid* tells a
very different story about Grand Coulee Dam, a story little known beyond
the boundaries of the Colville Indian Reservation, a story of the ruthless
violation and destruction of the Colville way of life.

Ignoring the pleas of the Colvilles, and using their river bottom land without compensation, the Federal Government built Grand Coulee Dam
across the free flowing Columbia River. For 200 miles upstream from the
Dam stretched the Heartland, the ancestral home, of the Colvilles. As Lake
Roosevelt built up behind the dam, the beautiful river valley, which was
the center of the economic, cultural, and religious life of the Colville people, was flooded out and disappeared under the water – farms, homes,
towns, everything. They built no fish ladders in Grand Coulee Dam. The
salmon migrations, the mainstay of life for the Colvilles, were destroyed
forever. What was for the Federal Government, a brilliant stride in "development," was for the Colvilles a disaster.

PRIDE AND THE POWER TO WIN

Country USA   **Year** 1990   **Length** 28 m.   **Genre** DS
Director Dave and Cyndee Wing
Producer Dave and Cyndee Wing
Distributor
Lucerne Media
37 Ground Pine Road
Morris Plains, NJ 07950
1 800 341-2293 [b] 973 538-0855 [f]
www.lucernemedia.com   LM@lucernemedia.com
US $99.00 VHS educational

Pride and the Power to Win is about Baboquivari Jr. and Sr. High School,
located on the Tohono O'odham Reservation in Sells, Arizona. In 1983 the
O'odham educational community in Sells initiated a program to raise their
academic standings, increase expectations for student progress, decrease
problems of substance abuse and encourage community involvement in the
life of the school. The Tohono O'odham community called upon their centuries old cultural tradition of "consensus building" to turn their schools
around. The process empowered teachers, parents, students, administrators,
and community members to make decisions concerning the direction of
education in their community. Their efforts were so successful that in 1987
Baboquivari Jr. High School won the National Secondary School
Recognition Award along with 271 other secondary schools throughout the
United States. Baboquivari Jr. High was one of only three Native
American schools recognized for excellence.

PRIMAL MIND

Country USA   **Year** 1984   **Length** 58 m.   **Genre** DF
Director Don Lenzer
Producer Richard Berman
Distributor
The Cinema Guild
130 Madison Avenue, 2nd Floor
New York, NY 10016
212 685-6242 [b] 212 685-4717 [f]
thecinemaguild@aol.com
US $79.95 VHS, US $50.00 VHS rental

The Primal Mind identifies the important distinctions between Native
American and Western or European-based people. The film explores in
fascinating detail the two cultures' contrasting views of nature, time, space,
art, architecture and dance. Language itself plays a crucial role in this
regard, since languages are not simply different words for the same things
– they reflect fundamental differences in human perception, differences
which for centuries have led to serious misunderstandings.

PROBABLE PASSING OF ELK CREEK

Country USA   **Year** 1983   **Length** 60 m.   **Genre** DF
Director Rob Wilson
Producer Rob Wilson
Distributor
The Cinema Guild
130 Madison Avenue, 2nd Floor
New York, NY 10016
212 685-6242 [b] 212 685-4717 [f]
thecinemaguild@aol.com
US $350.00 VHS, US $90.00 VHS rental

Focusing on a small valley in Northern California, home to the little town
of Elk Creek (pop. 400) and the Grindstone Indian Reservation, the film
uses a contemporary controversy to explore some deeper themes. The state
government has plans to build a reservoir over the valley, which would
force the whites and the Indians to leave their homelands. The law gives
the Indians the power to decide whether or not the dam may be built,
which gives the film an ironic twist. In the last century, white settlers
forced the Indians out of the valley with the aid of the U.S. Cavalry. Now,
the descendants of those Indians have the power to force the descendants
of the white settlers to leave the valley.

PROTEIN FROM THE SEA

Country USA   **Year** 1980   **Length** 25 m.   **Genre** DS
Director Gray Warriner
Producer Gray Warriner
Distributor
Camera One
8523 15th Ave. NE
Seattle, WA 98115
206-523-3456 [b]   206-523-3668 [f]
email: cameraone@prodigy.net
US $14.95 VHS

Alaska's waters are some of the most productive in the world. It is no accident that Alaska Natives have relied upon the bounty of the sea since ancient times. The sea is part of Alaska Native's heritage. Gone are the cedar and sealskin boats of their forefathers. Traditional fishing has given way to high technology and commercial harvesting of seafood. Now, modern ships ply the frigid waters of the North in search of "protein from the sea," and Alaska Natives are playing an important role in the fishing industry.

Protein from the Sea is a film which documents the making of a dream into reality. It is the story of the construction of a 'floating factory' ship designed to compete with foreign seafood processing ships. Not only is the 338' Al-Ind-Esk-A Sea an American vessel – it is a Native American vessel. Its name means Aleut, Indian, Eskimo of Alaska, and its story is a fast-paced look into the seafood industry and what Natives are doing to keep their heritage of the sea alive. In production for a year and a half, *Protein from the Sea* follows the Al-Ind-Esk-A Sea from its construction to its stationing in Cold Bay, Alaska.

QATUWAS - PEOPLE GATHERING TOGETHER

Country Canada   **Year** 1997   **Length** 58 m.   **Genre** DF
Director Barb Cranmer
Producer Frank Brown, Barb Cranmer, George Johnson
Distributor
National Film Board of Canada Library
22-D Hollywood Avenue
Ho-Ho-Kus, NJ 07423
1 800 542-2164 [b] 201 652-1973 [f]
US $250.00 VHS, call for rental information and prices.
For purchase within Canada visit the NFB website at: www.nfb.ca
1 800 267-7710 toll free within Canada

For thousands of years, the great ocean-going canoe sustained the cultural and spiritual traditions of coastal First Nations. Yet this century has seen the virtual disappearance of these sacred vessels. In the 1980s, Native peoples of the Northwest Coast embarked on an emotional voyage of rediscovery. Reclaiming their ancient maritime heritage, they carved majestic canoes from cedars that were living hundreds of years before Europeans arrived in the Pacific Northwest. Crews from thirty First Nations then set out in 1993 on a remarkable journey, paddling hundreds of kilometers along ancient waterways to a historic gathering of more than three thousand people at Bella Bella, British Columbia. *Qatuwas - People Gathering Together* powerfully documents this rebirth of the ocean-going canoe and celebrates the healing power of tradition and the resurgence of Northwest Coast indigenous culture.

RABBIT BOSS – THE SURVIVAL OF A WASHOE INDIAN TRADITION

Country USA **Year** 1996 **Length** 27 m. **Genre** DS
Director Mark Gandolfo, JoAnne Peden, Tom King
Producer Tom King
Distributor
UC Extension Center for Media and Independent Learning
2000 Center Street, Fourth Floor
Berkeley, CA 94704-1223
510 642-0460 [b] 510 643-9271 [f]
cmil@uclink.berkeley.edu
US $150.00 VHS purchase US $50.00 VHS rental
For sales within Nevada call 775 784-6932 [b]

Every autumn, in sagebrush valleys east of the Sierra Nevada, Washoe Indians renew an ancient connection with their natural environment. When the time is right, a leader known as the "rabbit boss" assembles a group of hunters to move through the brush, driving jackrabbits before them. As in the past, the rabbits are killed for their meat and pelts. *Rabbit Boss* follows current leader Marvin Dressler on three rabbit drives in the spectacular basin-and-range country of the Washoe homeland. On site footage and historic photos show how the rabbit drive has survived the twentieth century transformation of Washoe life, and excerpts from a decades-old home movie record the making of one of the last of the magnificent rabbit skin blankets. Departing from customary documentary practice, the producers of *Rabbit Boss* chose to use no scripted narration – no scholarly, voiceover interpretation of action or meaning. Instead, Marvin Dressler (the Boss), the principal speaker, accounts the traditional rabbit drive, the weaving of a rabbit skin blanket, and the importance of rabbits in Washoe life. In a world of accelerating social uncertainty *Rabbit Boss* captures the enduring, binding strength of a tradition.

RADIOACTIVE RESERVATIONS

Country USA/UK **Year** 1995 **Length** 52 m. **Genre** DF
Director Ed Harrisman
Producer Goldhawk Film and Television Productions Limited, Robin Eastwood
Distributor
Filmakers Library
124 East 40th Street
New York, NY 10016
212 808-4980 [b] 212 808-4983 [f]
www.filmakers.com info@filmakers.com
US $295.00 VHS, US $75.00 rental

Radioactive Reservations tells a contemporary story of struggle in America's Wild West. Ron Eagleye Johnny is a Paiute Indian tribal judge from Nevada. He turns investigative reporter to travel across the United States in search of the truth behind plans to dump all of America's nuclear waste on Indian reservations.

RANCHERIA

Country USA **Year** 1998 **Length** 12 m. **Genre** LS
Director Timothy Ramos
Producer Timothy Ramos / Against the Wind Productions
Distributor
Not in distribution.

Rancheria is the story of a young Pomo man, Nick Thomas, who returns home to visit his mother, who has fallen ill. On the way home Nick reflects on the communities in which he grew up on the "rez" and the small Northern California town which borders the reservation.

REAL INDIAN

Country USA   **Year** 1996   **Length** 7 m.   **Genre** LS
Director Malinda Maynor
Producer Malinda Maynor
Distributor
Women Make Movies
462 Broadway, 5th Floor
New York, NY 10013
212 925-0606 [b] 212 925-2052 [f]
info@wmm.com
US $175.00 VHS & 16mm, US $35.00 VHS &16mm
Please call for more information on pricing.

Real Indian is a lighthearted, personal look at the meaning of cultural identity. As a Lumbee Indian, the filmmaker is constantly confronted with the fact that she does not fit any of society's stereotypes for Native Americans. Those stereotypes are imposed by both whites and other Indians, alienating the filmmaker from many of the conventional definitions of Native American identity. *Real Indian* makes the viewers question our perceptions of Native Americans, as well as the meaning of our own identities.

REASON TO FEAR:
THE CULTURAL DEFENSE OF HOOTY CROY

Country USA   **Year** 2000   **Length** 56 m.   **Genre** DF
Director Steve Patapoff
Producer Steve Patapoff and Jaime Kibben
Distributor
Intermedia, Inc.
1700 Westlake Avenue North, Suite 724
Seattle, WA 98109
1 800 553-8336 [b] 1 800 553-1655 [f]
US $189.00 VHS institutions, US $79.00 VHS non-profit
US $50.00 VHS rental

On the night of July 17, 1978, dozens of police officers engaged in a gun battle with five Northern California Indians who had a single .22 rifle. More than a hundred shots were fired. Three Indians were wounded. One policeman was killed.

After spending eight years on Death Row for the murder of the police officer, Patrick "Hooty" Croy, an Indian of Shasta-Karok descent, was granted a retrial. His new defense team, headed by J. Tony Serra, argued Croy acted in self-defense and gave supporting evidence of the genocide against California Indians that has continued since the 1850's. The strategy, known as a cultural defense, was used to explain why Croy feared for his life when he shot.

Reason to Fear: The Cultural Defense of Hooty Croy tells the story in the voices of those closest to the events: the Indians, their attorneys, witnesses, and jurors.

Introduction by Tony Serra and Steve Patapoff.

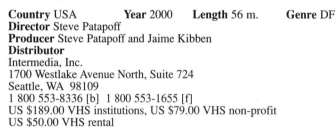

REBURIAL, THE

Country USA   **Year** 1988   **Length** 40 m.   **Genre** DS
Director Eric Mathes
Producer Eric Mathes
Distributor
Currently unavailable.

On October 13, 1987, the digging of ancestral burial grounds of the Shawnee People began on the 40 acres of land in Uniontown, Kentucky known as the Slack Farm. This area has been known and recorded, by the Smithsonian Institute, as a sacred burial site since the 1860s. The excavation and looting at the Slack Farm continued, until halted by State troopers, on December 11, 1987. During those two months, heavy mining equipment was used to unearth pottery, pipes, jewelry, and beaded artifacts, leaving in its wake over 400 "potholes," resulting in the desecration of approximately 1,200 human remains. Formal charges have been brought against the men involved. Upon visiting the site, International Treaty Council Representative, Dennis Banks stated, "this, in my estimation, is the largest single burial site in North America, and also the worst type of desecration I've seen."

RED MAN

Country USA   **Year** 1998   **Length** 7 m.   **Genre** LS
Director Will Geiger
Producer Seattle International Film Festival
Distributor
Kathleen McInnis - Cinema Seattle
6522 Phinney Avenue, North #302
Seattle, WA 98103
206 781-1077 [b] and [f]
k.mcinnis@att.net
Call for information.

"I had heard about Seattle lawmakers writing legislation to enact a law to rid the public parks of many of the homeless Native Americans who sleep there. The legislation made it illegal to lie down on a park bench." After hearing about this law, Will Greiger had a dream which gave him the idea for *Red Man*. Starring Cecil Cheeka as a Native American in search of a burial ground, *Red Man* is the result of the Fly Film Making, a program of Seattle International Film Festival in which three directors are chosen, given small crews and equipment and two days to make a film. Shown here is the resulting finished product of one of these projects.

RED ROAD TO SOBRIETY, THE

Country USA   **Year** 1994   **Length** 90 m.   **Genre** DF
Director Chante Pierce, Gary Rhine
Producer Gary Rhine, Chante Pierce
Distributor
Kifaru Productions
23852 Pacific Coast Hwy, #766
Malibu, CA 90265
1 800 400-8433 [b] 310 457-2688 [f]
www.kifaru.com   kifaru1@aol.com
US $125.00 VHS institutional
US $39.95 VHS home video

The Red Road to Sobriety is a feature length documentary examining the Contemporary Native American Sobriety Movement, which is currently flourishing throughout the United States and Canada. The program overviews the history of the Indian community's relationship with alcohol, looking carefully at the United States and Canadian government's use of alcohol in their land procurement processes. It then goes on to highlight some of the most exemplary Native-run recovery programs currently operating in North America.

For the first time, this modern cultural revitalization movement is documented, showing both the Western medical approaches, as well as the Native "grass roots" efforts, which utilize Indigenous traditions in the treatment of alcoholism.

REDSKINS, TRICKSTERS AND PUPPY STEW

Country Canada **Year** 2000 **Length** 55 m. **Genre** DF
Director Drew Hayden Taylor
Producer Silva Basmajian
Distributor
National Film Board of Canada Library
22-D Hollywood Avenue
Ho-Ho-Kus, NJ 07423
1 800 542-2164 [b] 201 652-1973 [f]
US $195.00 VHS, call for rental information and prices.
For purchase within Canada visit the NFB website at: www.nfb.ca
1 800 267-7710 toll free within Canada

Native humor has long been the best kept secret of aboriginal life. This documentary takes a look at what makes First Nations people laugh, their tradition of humor and the healing power of their laughter. Through the journey of Drew Hayden Taylor, the film travels across Canada, introducing us to Native comedians, comedy troupes, radio personalities, and elders.

RETURN OF NAVAJO BOY, THE

Country USA **Year** 2000 **Length** 56 m. **Genre** DF
Director Jeff Spitz
Producer Jeff Spitz
Distributor
UC Extension Center for Media and Independent Learning
2000 Center Street, 4th Floor
Berkeley, CA 94704
510 642-0460 [b] 510 643-9271 [f]
cmil@uclink.berkeley.edu
Please call for educational prices.
jsptv@mindspring.com www.navajoboy.com

The Return of Navajo Boy is the story of a family immortalized in the countless picture postcards of Monument Valley, and the events that unfold when they are revisited by the images of a fifty year-old documentary film. As they view the images of their parents, aunts, cousins, and themselves as children, Bernie Cly and Elsie Cly Begay tell the story of their lives behind the movie images. They recount the tales of Bernie's chronic lung disease brought on by uranium mining, Elsie's fight to preserve tribal traditions and their loss of a baby brother through a forced adoption. An emotional reunion with brother John Wayne Cly caps off this engaging look behind the Hollywood images of Native Americans.

RETURN OF THE COUNTRY

Country USA **Year** 1984 **Length** 30 m. **Genre** LS
Director Bob Hicks
Producer Bob Hicks
Distributor
Currently unavailable, for more information contact Bob Hicks:
c/o First Americans In the Arts
P.O. Box 17780
Beverley Hills, CA 90209
818 623-9529 [b]

The initial perspective of the film is that of a white female Commissioner of Indian Affairs. She has recently been named Commissioner and is all set to host a Pow Wow in honor of the President of the United States. All set, that is, until she encounters a protest by the Indians because she wants to give the president a sacred war bonnet.

Then the filmmakers' sense of surrealism guides us through a spiritual enlightenment of the Commissioner, caused by her contact with the medicine man and his pipe. The Commissioner is transported to a reverse image world where white people are watched over by an Indian run Bureau of White Affairs.

RETURN OF THE NATIVE –
THE STORY OF THE INTER TRIBAL BISON COOPERATIVE

Country USA   **Year** 1996   **Length** 21 m.   **Genre** IND
Director Sam Hurst
Producer Sam Hurst
Distributor
Inter Tribal Bison Cooperative
1560 Concourse Drive
Rapid City, SD 57703
605 394-9730 [b] 605 394-7742 [f]
itbc@enetis.net
US $15.00 VHS

Return of the Native is an inspiring depiction of multi-tribal efforts to
return American Buffalo to the daily lives of Indian people. The film tells
of the Inter-Tribal Bison Cooperative's efforts towards cultural revitalization, environmental enhancement, and sustainable culturally-driven economic development.

RETURN TO THE CIRCLE

Country USA   **Year** 1994   **Length** 10 m.   **Genre** DS
Director Emily Chavez Haack
Producer Betty Cooper, Warren Haack, Emily Chavez Haack
Distributor
Shenandoah Film Productions
538 "G" Street
Arcata, CA 95521
707 822-1030 [b] 707 822-1035 [f]
US $90.00 VHS, US $25.00 VHS Rental

Return to the Circle is a video production of the American Indian Family
Healing Center in Oakland, California. Through the inclusion of Elders
and Youth in an extended recovering family of hope, the video celebrates a
return to the wholeness of life for mothers who have been suffering from
substance abuse.

While paying attention to the spirit, mind, and body, as well as life style
changes and cultural healing, the Center provides tools, guidance, and love
for the women to go forward to a life shaped by their own most cherished
hopes.

RETURN TO THE CIRCLE: GEWI TAH BI WIN

Country USA   **Year** 2000   **Length** 35 m.   **Genre** DS
Director Richard Reeder
Producer Deb Zak, Richard Reeder
Distributor
Shenandoah Film Productions
538 "G" Street
Arcata, CA 95521
707 822-1030 [b] 707 822-1035 [f]
US $175.00 VHS, US $45.00 VHS rental

Return to the Circle: Gewi Tah Bi Win follows the journey toward wellness
of the Ojibwe Tribe in northern Minnesota. The story of the Anishinabe
people is told through the voices of tribal members and is set in the rugged
prairies and thick forests that make up the White Earth Indian Reservation.
At the heart of the documentary program is a spirit that survives hardships
and tragedy, and continues to celebrate life.
Through three generations of one family, we see the power that comes
from a commitment to community. Kim Anderson, the youngest family
member, has recently graduated from the University of Minnesota. Her
return to the Reservation to work with youth begins the circular pattern of
the program.

RETURNINGS

Country Canada   **Year** 1995   **Length** 27 m.   **Genre** DS
Director Shivon Robinsong
Producer Bill Weaver
Distributor
Currently unavailable.

Once a proud and prosperous people, the Homalco, northern-most of the Coast Salish tribe in British Columbia, were driven to alcohol and scattered to the winds by the government, culture, and the economics of the white man. *Returnings* tells the story of the determination of the Homalco to establish a new home, recover their identity, and build a new path toward the future. In doing so, the Homalco led the way to self-reliance for other First Nations in Canada.

REZ, THE (CANADIAN TV SERIES) 4 EPISODES:
STRANGE BEDFELLOWS DIR: GRAEME LYNCH
POSTER GIRL DIR: E. JANE THOMPSON
LIKE FATHER, LIKE SON DIR: TW PEACOCK
LUST DIR: JOHN L'ECUYEY

Country Canada   **Year** 1997   **Length** 116 m.   **Genre** LS
Director Greame Lynch, E. Jane Thompson, TW Peacock, John E'Ecuyey
Producer Brian Dennis
Distributor
Currently unavailable.

Based on 1995's *Dance Me Outside*, the weekly Canadian series *The Rez* continues exploring the lives of the characters from Bruce McDonald's feature film. In the four 29 minute episodes - "Strange Bedfellows," "Poster Girl," "Like Father, Like Son," and "Lust" - the show explores what happens when corporations come to the tribe, how grant money is handled, sexuality and various other situations. *The Rez* is an important look into the lives of contemporary Indians.

Featuring Jennifer Podemski, Ryan Black, Adam Beach, Tamara Podemski, Gary Farmer, Shirley Cheechoo, Herbie Barnes, Elaine Miles, Denis Lacroix and Darrell Dennis.

RICHARD CARDINAL:
CRY FROM A DIARY OF A MÉTIS CHILD

Country Canada   **Year** 1986   **Length** 29 m.   **Genre** DS
Director Alanis Obomsawin
Producer Marrin Canell, Alanis Obomsawin, Andy Thomson (exec.), Robert Verrall
Distributor
National Film Board of Canada Library
22-D Hollywood Avenue
Ho-Ho-Kus, NJ 07423
1 800 542-2164 [b] 201 652-1973 [f]
US $195.00 VHS, call for rental information and prices.
For purchase within Canada visit the NFB website at: www.nfb.ca
1 800 267-7710 toll free within Canada

"I'm skipping the rest of the years because it continues to be the same. I want to say to people involved in my life, don't take this personally. I just can't take it anymore."

Not long after he wrote these words, Richard Cardinal, 17, hanged himself from a birch tree on a hot June day in 1984.

Richard Cardinal: Cry from a Diary of a Métis Child is a loving tribute to the memory of a sensitive, articulate young man who finally ran out of hope. This film is based on a diary he left behind that contains his inner-most feelings and fears. Alone, friendless, he had nowhere to turn but inward. To hear his words is to share the profound loneliness and suffering of another human being.

Richard was Métis. By the time he died, he had lived in sixteen foster homes, plus twelve group homes, shelters and lock-ups throughout Alberta. His life had been a nightmare of brutality, neglect and indifference. Nobody could cope with a Métis child who developed a bedwetting problem. He might have been "just another dead Indian" were it not for his diary and the concern of his last foster parents, who knew him briefly and refused to let his death go unremarked.

Richard had been removed from his home at the age of four because of alcoholism in the family. He was one of eight children and, except for sporadic contact with one brother and a sister, he never saw his family again. His diary is filled with a longing to be reunited with them. He finally got his wish when the family was brought together for his funeral.

In death, Richard received the attention that so eluded him in life. His suicide prompted changes in child welfare administration and, for the first time, an acknowledgement that Native people are capable of caring for their own children.

Due in part to the new Welfare Act, numerous tribes, including the Métis, have either taken control of their own social services or are in the process of doing so.

RIDE TO WOUNDED KNEE, THE

Country USA   **Year** 1992   **Length** 86 m.   **Genre** DF
Director Robert Clapsaddle
Producer Carol Wolman
Distributor
Cinnamon Productions
19 Wild Rose Road
Westport, CT 06880
203 221-0613 [b] 203 227-0840 [f]
www.nativevideos.com Nativevideos@aol.com
US $149.00 VHS institutional use
US $49.00 VHS home use

This feature documentary tells the true story of a two-week period in 1890. Starting with the killing of Sitting Bull on December 15th at Standing Rock, North Dakota, the film traces the path of his followers as they fled the pursuing U.S. Cavalry. They took refuge with Chief Big Foot at Cherry Creek, South Dakota, 100 miles to the south. He and his people, in turn, were captured, escaped, fled 150 miles to south to Pine Ridge, and were finally taken prisoner at Wounded Knee Creek by Custer's old regiment, the Seventh Cavalry. On December 29th, about 300 men, women and children were massacred.

In 1989, a ceremonial reenactment of the flight of 1890 was filmed by the Lakota People to commemorate the centennial of the massacre. They rode from Standing Rock to Wounded Knee in minus 70-degree weather during the same two-week period in December. This beautiful footage dramatizes the 1890 events. A location shoot in September 1990 used some staging, costuming, and steady cam work to obtain additional live footage for the flight.

Interviews and comments from leaders of the Memorial Ride and participants add great insight into the historical events and their meaning to the Lakota people today. Elders whose parents or grandparents survived the massacre – Isaac Long, Burdell Blue Arm and Celane Not Help Him – tell the stories that they heard as children, in the tradition of Lakota oral history.

RIVER PEOPLE: BEHIND THE CASE OF DAVID SOHAPPY

Country USA   **Year** 1990   **Length** 51 m.   **Genre** DF
Director Michal Conford & Michele Zaccheo
Producer Michal Conford & Michele Zaccheo
Distributor
Filmakers Libaray
124 East 40th Street
New York, NY 10016
212 808-4980 [b] 212 808-4983 [f]
www.filmmakers.com info@filmakers.com
US $295.00 VHS, US $75.00 rental

River People follows the story of David Sohappy, a Native American spiritual leader who was sentenced to a five-year prison term for selling 317 salmon out of season. Sohappy is a symbol of resistance for Native Americans in the Northwest of the United States: for 20 years he has fished in open defiance of all state and federal fishing laws. He claims he has an ancestral right to fish along the Columbia River.

The case of David Sohappy is a window into the history, religion and way of life of the last community of Native fishermen still living along the Columbia.

ROCK ART TREASURES OF ANCIENT AMERICA

Country USA   **Year** 1983   **Length** 25 m.   **Genre** DS
Director Dave Caldwell
Producer Dave Caldwell
Distributor
Not in distribution.

Rock Art Treasures of Ancient America is a 25 minute survey on the subject of the ancient rock carvings, paintings, and desert figures as created by the First Americans.

Three major rock art sites located in Southern California are studied: The Shoshone petroglyphs at the national Historical Landmark, China Lake; The Mojave intaglios along the southern end of the Colorado River; and the Chumash cave paintings in the Santa Barbara area.

ROCKIN' WARRIORS

Country USA   **Year** 1997   **Length** 56 m.   **Genre** DF
Director Andy Bausch
Producer L.M. Hall
Distributor
For further information, contact:
NAPT
P.O. Box 883111
Lincoln, NE 68501
402 472-3522

Rockin' Warriors explores Native American rock n' roll not only as an indigenous phenomenon but also as a highly popular musical form in Europe. This eclectic production is the result of Luxembourg director Andy Bausch's longtime passion for Native American rock. The four primary subjects of Rockin' Warriors span the spectrum of 1960's folk to world music of the 1990s.

The film combines standard documentary procedures (i.e. interview, live footage) with other ways of looking at Indian rock, including dramatic scenes inspired by the featured artists' lives. It was shot on location at reservations in Arizona, at concerts in Germany and in the New Mexico desert by a crew of Americans, Germans and Luxembourgers. The artists profiled in this film through interview and performance footage include: Buffy Sainte-Marie, Robert Mirabal, Joy Harjo & Poetic Justice, John Trudell, Ulali, Keith Secola, Song Catchers and Tom Bee.

RUN, APPALOOSA, RUN

Country USA   **Year** 1975   **Length** 48 m.   **Genre** FF
Director Larry Lansburgh
Producer Walt Disney
Distributor
Available for rent through
www.modernsoundpictures.com
US $35.00 16mm 1 day rental
Currently unavailable for purchase.

An Indian girl, Mary Blackfeather, and her horse bring honor and glory to the Nez Perce Indian Nation of the Northwest. Wild rodeo action and a challenge of endurance in the suicide race of Hell's Mountain Relay. Featuring Adele Palacios, Wilbur Balugher, Jerry Gatlin, Walter Cloud, Jack Keran, and Ray Patnaude.

Original Release Date - 1966.

RUN OF THE SACRED HOOP

Country USA   **Year** 1999   **Length** 33 m.   **Genre** DS
Director Aggie Lukaszewski
Producer Aggie Lukaszewski
Distributor
Paha Sapa Films
19775 Avenue 256
Exeter, CA 93221
US $29.95 VHS

The film depicts the Lakota Nation's annual *Run of the Sacred Hoop*, a 500-mile run around the Black Hills. The five day endeavor is run relay style mostly by members of the Lakota Nation, but other Native teams participate as well. The action is addressed through interviews with Lakota elders and the runners themselves.

The interview reveals the many changes taking place today, in the aftermath of the domination of the Lakota by a foreign culture over a 150-year period. Some of the concerns of the elders expressed in the film are: the loss of the language in the younger people, and the loss of vast amounts of traditional land which has been steadfastly seized when treaties have been broken by the US government. The Lakota elders also ask for some of the land to be returned to the Lakota people, specifically the Black Hills of South Dakota. The film addresses the many attempts of the Lakota to seek justice in the courts of the U.S. The film also shows Lakota children in reservation schools learning the Lakota Language and other cultural ways, in addition to the standard courses taught in schools today.

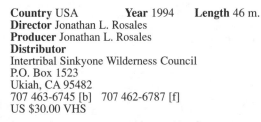

RUN TO SAVE SINKYONE, THE

Country USA   **Year** 1994   **Length** 46 m.   **Genre** DS
Director Jonathan L. Rosales
Producer Jonathan L. Rosales
Distributor
Intertribal Sinkyone Wilderness Council
P.O. Box 1523
Ukiah, CA 95482
707 463-6745 [b]   707 462-6787 [f]
US $30.00 VHS

This is the story of the struggle to repatriate Sinkyone Indian land and save California's dwindling rainforest. Located just 200 miles north of San Francisco, on the "Lost Coast" of northern Mendocino County, Sinkyone land was the home of Indian People since time immemorial. But in the mid-1800s, as Manifest Destiny made its barbaric sweep through Northern California, most Sinkyone Peoples were annihilated through massacres and other forms of genocide. After her people were killed, the Sinkyone land suffered massive destruction from the timber industry, which systematically clearcut old-growth redwood forests until a lawsuit in 1985 halted the logging.

The Run to Save Sinkyone is an award-winning 46 minute Native American-produced and directed documentary film chronicling the struggle of eleven Northern California Indian Tribes to save 3,900 acres of their sacred ancestral homeland from the timber industry's chainsaws by returning it to traditional land stewardship and uses.

RUNNING AWAY ARTIST: LORRIE CHURCH

Country Canada   **Year** 1999   **Length** 4 m.   **Genre** MV
Producer Eaglehill Music / George Atcheynum
Distributor
Eaglehill Music
Box 145
Gallivan, Sask.
S0M 0X0 Canada
360 937-7796 [b]
www.lorriechurch.com   1 877 256-7743 [b]
US $13.95 VHS, CAD $19.95 VHS

Lorrie Church is a singer/songwriter from the Sweetgrass First Nation
Indian Reserve in the province of Saskatchewan. She shares a heritage of
both Métis and Cree elements. Although her music is mainstream country
she draws a lot of strength from her rich cultural background, hence her
Cree name which means Grey Feathers.

"Running Away" is the first single off of her 1999 album I Never Gave Up
Hope.

RUNNING BRAVE

Country USA   **Year** 1986   **Length** 105 m.   **Genre** FF
Director D.S. Everett
Producer Ira Englander
Distributor
Available at Amzon.com
www.amazon.com
US $17.99 VHS

Of all the runners entered in the 10,000 meter competition at the 1964
Tokyo Olympic Games, the one rated least likely to succeed was Billy
Mills, a 26-year-old American Indian running for the U.S. Marines. No
American had ever won the Olympic 10,000 meter, and only two people
believed that Mills had a chance – Mills and his wife, Pat. Mills' Gold
Medal winning triumph in that sensational race is now the focus of
Running Brave. Actor Robby Benson plays Mills in this uniquely uplifting
film.

SACRED BUFFALO PEOPLE

Country USA   **Year** 1992   **Length** 58 m.   **Genre** DF
Director Deb Wallwork
Producer Deb Wallwork
Distributor
Center for International Education
P.O. Box 65343
St. Paul, MN 55165
651 227-2240 [t] and [f]
thecie@pobox.com
US $85.00 VHS

Also available at Shenandoah Films, Arcata, CA. 707 822-1030 [b].

In a rich tapestry of interwoven stories, Native American people from all
walks of life revere the buffalo as an animate spirit, cultural icon, and as a
living symbol of Native American survival. Engaging, heartbreaking, and
inspiring, this extraordinary documentary teaches us about our dependence
on nature and nature's dependence on us.

SACRED GROUND

Country USA   **Year** 1977   **Length** 52 m.   **Genre** DF
Director Geroge McCowan
Producer Bob Elliot and James Margellos
Distributor
Facets Multi-Media, Inc.
1517 W. Fullerton Avenue
Chicago, IL. 60614
773 281-9075 [b]   773 929-5437 [f]
www.facets.org   sales@facets.org
Currently out of print, but for possible rental call 1 800 532-2387 [b].

Sacred Ground is the story of North American Indians' intimate involvement with and reverence for places throughout our land that hold a special religious and traditional significance for them. *Sacred Ground* takes a detailed look at the specific geographic sites all over America that are and always were sacred to the American Indian.

SACRED GROUND

Country USA   **Year** 1983   **Length** 100 m.   **Genre** FF
Director Charles B. Peirce
Producer Arthur R. Dubs
Distributor
Pacific International Enterprises
Contact Donna Garney at 541 779-0990 [b]
pie@internet.cds.com

Also available through:
www.familyfilmentertainment.com
www.amazon.com

In 1861, mountain man Matt Colter makes the treacherous journey across the Rocky Mountains with his pregnant Apache wife to set up new traplines in the Oregon backcountry. Nearing the end of his travels, Colter almost loses everything when the bear he is hunting for dinner almost makes a meal of his wife and pack animals. He must face even greater danger at his destination when he unknowingly builds his cabin on a sacred burial ground.

A band of Paiutes arrive and perform a threatening ritual to drive the intruders from their sacred burial ground. In terror, Colter's woman goes into labor. Colter is given no chance to explain the situation as outraged warriors on horseback pull the cabin from its foundation back down to the bottom of the hill. The mountain man pulls his injured wife from the wreckage and helps her as she gives birth, with her last breath, to an infant son, while at the same time, the Paiute woman Wanetta is placing her dead infant on the burial scaffold. The first cry of the newborn seems almost supernatural and the Natives move away slowly, awestruck by the birth on their sacred ground.

SACRIFICE AREA

Country The Netherlands   **Year** 1983   **Length** 60 m. **Genre** DF
Director Otto Schuurman, Ernie Damen
Producer Otto Schuurman, Rolf Orthel
Distributor
Icaros Productions
Verversstraat 27
1011 HZ   Amsterdam
The Netherlands
31 20 625 6288 [b] and [f]
icaros@xs4all.nl
US $75.00 VHS

This film documents the relationship between traditional Native Americans and the escalating environmental pressure on the lands on which these people live. Resource exploitation in the Black Hills of South Dakota and in the Four Corners Area are examined, and the testimony of many Native Americans is recorded, including that of Russell Means, Winona La Duke, Roberta Blackgoat, Pauline Whitesinger, and Simon Ortiz. The threat posed to the ways of these people by coal and uranium exploitation is vividly described by people presently living in the Black Hills and at Big Mountain, Arizona.

SALT WATER PEOPLE

Country USA   **Year** 1993   **Length** 122 m.   **Genre** DF
Director Maurice Bulbulian
Producer Dennis Murphy, Jacques Vall`ee
Distributor
National Film Board of Canada Library
22-D Hollywood Avenue
Ho-Ho-Kus, NJ 07423
1 800 542-2164 [b] 201 652-1973 [f]
US $300.00 VHS, call for rental information and prices.
For purchase within Canada visit the NFB website at: www.nfb.ca
1 800 267-7710 toll free within Canada

Once the rivers and oceans of Canada's Pacific West Coast were teeming with life and the beaches offered up food in abundance. Now this fragile ecosystem is threatened by pollution, logging, and the endless demands of a consumer society. In *Salt Water People*, the aboriginal tribes of the West Coast bear witness to the destruction and describe the battle they wage to protect their land and rights. Filmed deep within the ocean and along the spectacular mountain coastline of British Columbia, *Salt Water People* follows the cycle of the seasons as it examines the past, present and future of the West Coast fisheries and the Native tribes who depend on them for survival. By giving voice to the values and traditions of the West Coast First Nations people, the film asks viewers to examine their own attitudes toward the natural world and the exploitation of its resources.

SCHOOL IN THE BUSH

Country Canada   **Year** 1987   **Length** 15 m.   **Genre** DS
Director Ian Rankin
Producer Dennis Sawyer, Andy Thomson (exec)
Distributor
National Film Board of Canada Library
22-D Hollywood Avenue
Ho-Ho-Kus, NJ 07423
1 800 542-2164 [b] 201 652-1973 [f]
US $145.00 VHS, call for rental information and prices.
For purchase within Canada visit the NFB website at: www.nfb.ca
1 800 267-7710 toll free within Canada

School in the Bush vividly communicates Cree values and culture, and the Cree reverence for the land. A young Cree woman reflects on a unique experience: a school year spent not in a formal white school, but with her family during a traditional Cree winter in the bush. The film shows this hunting culture's way of life, from the building of the winter camp and the divisions of labor to the celebratory feasts and rituals following a successful hunt. For the Cree, life and education are the same: children learn by working with their parents; schooling in the bush never stops. The film also touches on the jarring dichotomies experienced by Native children in city schools. An excellent discussion-starter on different cultures, different value systems and optimal learning experiences.

SEA IS OUR LIFE, THE

Country USA   **Year** 1980   **Length** 16 m.   **Genre** DS
Director Bo Boudart
Producer Bo Boudart
Distributor
Currently unavailable.

For eight Eskimo villages on the Alaskan Arctic coast, hunting the Bowhead whales along with migratory birds, seal, fish and walrus, still play an important part in the diet and culture of these people. They call themselves the Inupiat (Inoopee-yat), or "real people" of this region.

In the past few years an intense campaign has been waged by conservative groups to halt all whaling. The Inupiat Eskimos felt the impact of these efforts in 1978 when the federal government imposed a limited quota of whales to be taken by them. The majority of Eskimos felt this action to be unfair since they know their subsistence whaling does not endanger the survival of the Bowhead whales. In 1979, under the Alaska Eskimo Whaling Commission, Eskimo whalers decided not to comply with any outside regulations except their own.

On December 11, 1979, the department of Interior and the State of Alaska held a major offshore lease sale in the Beaufort Sea. This sea is the breeding and feeding waters of the Bowhead whales. Inupiat Eskimos have unanimously opposed this lease sale, as it will interfere with the whales' migration. Eskimos clearly see that their government has chosen to support oil development over their dependence on this sea for their food. In anticipation of the lease sale, several Eskimo village organizations wanted to protest this offshore oil lease sale or any sale of their seas. This film was produced with their support and participation. Additional funding has come from The Film Fund and National Endowment for Humanities.

SEASON OF GRANDMOTHERS, A

Country USA   **Year** 1977   **Length** 30 m.   **Genre** DS
Producer George Burdeau
Distributor
Lucerne Media
37 Ground Pine Road
Morris Plains, NJ 07950
1 800 341-2293 [b] 973 538-0855 [f]
www.lucernemedia.com   LM@lucernemedia.com
US $99.00 VHS educational

Also available through Lane Education Service 541 461-8200 [b]

This is the first television series made by and about American Indians, highlighting various aspects of past and present Indian life. This segment emphasizes the revival of traditional Indian education, reverence for elders, and a yearning for the old ways by looking at the traditional teachers - the Grandmothers. Part of The Real People series from NAPT. Produced by George Burdeau.

SEASONS OF A NAVAJO

Country USA   **Year** 1984   **Length** 57 m.   **Genre** DF
Director John Borden
Producer Peace River Films Inc.
Distributor
PBS Home Video
1 800 424-7963 [b]
US $19.98 VHS purchase

The film is about a Navajo family living in the Canyon de Chelly area of Northeastern Arizona. Filmed over a period of nearly a year, *Seasons of a Navajo* follows the family's elders—a married couple in their seventies—and their many children, grandchildren and great-grandchildren from the late winter through the fall as they plant their crops, care for their livestock and make traditional seasonal migrations between their three homes. Narrated with the voice-over dialogue of the people themselves, we are given a unique view of an American Indian family, how they see themselves and their own lives.

SELF DETERMINATION
FROM STORYTELLERS OF THE PACIFIC

Country USA   **Year** 1995   **Length** 58 m.   **Genre** DF
Director Phil Lucas, Lurline McGregor, Maria Yatar, Heather Guigni
Producer Frank Blythe, Lurline McGregor
Distributor
Lucerne Media
37 Ground Pine Road
Morris Plains, NJ 07950
1 800 341-2293 [b] 973 538-0855 [f]
www.lucernemedia.com   LM@lucernemedia.com
US $99.00 VHS educational - part of *Storytellers of the Pacific* series

These short documentaries are part of the series *Storytellers of the Pacific*.

"Contract with America," set in Washington State with Bill Frank Jr. representing the Nisqually people and Indians of the Pacific Northwest, documents the ongoing struggle to preserve the "Rights" guaranteed in the Indian people's first "contract with America."

"In Our Own Worlds" is set in Hawaii with Kauanoe Kamana representing the Native Hawaiian people. She tells of the struggle to regain the Native Hawaiian language that had been banned and outlawed by the U.S. government.

SEVENTH GENERATION, THE

Country Canada   **Year** 2000   **Length** 28 m.   **Genre** DS
Director Laura Milliken
Producer Laura Milliken, Jennifer Podemski
Distributor
Big Soul Productions
30 Duncan Street, #702
Toronto, ON
M5V 2C3 Canada
416 598-7762 [b] 416 598-5392 [f]   bigsoul@on.aibn.com
US $250.00 VHS for series, US $20.00 VHS per episode,
US $50.00 VHS rental of series

The Seventh Generation is a unique documentary /magazine television series. It is designed to act as a vehicle for young Aboriginal achievers to showcase their excellence in various fields, including arts, entertainment, music, business, politics, sports, medicine, science and technology.

The series profiles future leaders within the Native community. It casts a positive light on Aboriginal youth everywhere and takes a pro-active role in the breaking down of stereotypes. There has been a recognized absence of Aboriginal youth in the media. This void can be filled through positive programming that reflects this demographic and appeals to both Aboriginal and non-Aboriginal audiences.

The Seventh Generation is produced, directed, researched, written and hosted by an entirely Aboriginal production staff. The team also includes two production internship positions. The program is hosted by acclaimed film and television star Jennifer Podemski.

SHINGEBISS

Country USA　　　**Year** 1986　　**Length** 2 m.　　　**Genre** ANS
Director Sharon A. Altman
Producer Sharon A. Altman
Distributor
Please e-mail Shandrine Cassidy for availablility:
cassidy@cinema.usc.edu　or call
USC, School of Cinema at 213 740-4432 [b]

Shingebiss is an animated short subject film based on an Ojibway story about a duck-Shingebiss-who refuses to fly south for the winter and raises the ire of Kabibonokka, the North Wind, in doing so. A battle of wits ensues between Shingebiss and the North Wind. Kabibonokka tries to blow Shingebiss away with his cold breath, but the duck builds a fire that gets stronger the more Kabibonokka blows. The flames threaten Kabibonokka and force him to retreat. However, he wins his revenge by freezing the pond where Shingebiss' love, a fish, lives. In the end the forces of the natural world reign.

The artwork uses two-dimensional hinged puppets made out of paper treated with crayon and watercolour and directly manipulated under the camera.

SILENCING THE GUNS

Country Canada　　　**Year** 1996　　**Length** 86 m.　　　**Genre** FF
Director Rock Demers
Producer Arthur Lamothe
Distributor
Distribution La Fete
387 St. Paul West
Montreal, Quebec
H2Y 2A7 Canada
514 848-0417 [b]　514 848-0064 [f]　info@lafete.com
US $14.95 or CAD $19.95 VHS purchase
US $300.00 per screening day rental (35mm)

Silencing the Guns slowly unfolds the mystery surrounding the death of two Native salmon fisherman. The film follows Montreal biologist Jean-Pierre Lafond's (Jacques Perrin) hesitant-to-passionate search for the truth of the Native mens' death. The path leads him into a romance with the sister of one of the victims, Roxanne (Michele Audette); exposes him to the brutal racism of the neighboring white community; and bonds him to a brotherhood with the Natives.

Also featuring Gabriel Gascon, Louisette Dussault, Marco Bacon and Réginald Vollant.

SILENT ENEMY, THE (1930)

Country USA   **Year** 1995   **Length** 84 m.   **Genre** FF
Director H.P. Carver
Producer W. Douglas Burden, William C. Chanler
Distributor
Milestone Film and Video
P.O. Box 128
Harrington Park, NJ 07640-0128
1 800 603 1104 [b] 201 767-3035 [f]
milefilms@aol.com
US $39.00 VHS & DVD, US $200.00 for public performance rental.
Please call for more information.

Sixty years before *Black Robe* and *Dances With Wolves*, there was *The Silent Enemy*. An exciting and magical reconstruction of Ojibway Indian life in the time before the white man had settled the Hudson Bay region, *The Silent Enemy* is based on a 72-volume history of New France written by Jesuit missionaries. The "enemy" is hunger that threatens the tribe as it desperately tracks and hunts the caribou herds. The thunderous caribou stampede provides an absolutely thrilling finale.

Magnificently filmed on location, *The Silent Enemy* boasts an all-Indian cast with a compelling sound prologue by one of the stars, Chief Yellow Robe: "this is the story of my people… When you look at this picture, therefore, look not upon us as actors. We are Indians living once more our old life. Soon we will be gone. Your civilization will destroy us. But by your magic we will live forever." Critics proclaimed the film a masterpiece on its original release, and it remains so today. Milestone Film and Video restored the original 35mm nitrate material for this release, preserving the magnificent tints of the 1930 film.

Starring Chief Chauncey Yellow Robe, Chief Buffalo Child Long Lance, Chief Akawanush, Molly Spotted Elk and George McDougall.

SILENT TEARS

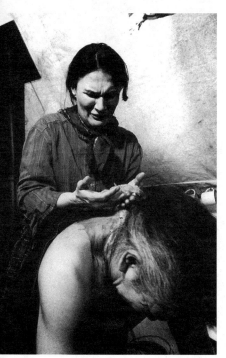

Country Canada   **Year** 1997   **Length** 28 m.   **Genre** LS
Director Shirley Cheechoo
Producer Shirley Cheechoo, Jerry Krepakevich
Distributor
National Film Board of Canada Library
22-D Hollywood Avenue
Ho-Ho-Kus, NJ 07423
1 800 542-2164 [b] 201 652-1973 [f]
US $195.00 VHS, call for rental information and prices.
For purchase within Canada visit the NFB website at: www.nfb.ca
1 800 267-7710 toll free within Canada

Based on a Cree family's true story, *Silent Tears* is a gripping drama that chronicles a very tough northern winter for nine-year-old Anne, her parents and siblings. Hunger sets in when her father, Roger, becomes sick and can no longer tend the trapline. When a horrendous tumor begins growing on the back of his neck, Anne's mother, Sarah, has to operate to remove it and save his life. While Sarah cares for Roger and the younger children, Anne takes on more responsibility, checking the traps herself. Eventually Roger is cured and he burns the tumor so that its terrible effects will never again be visited on the family. As Anne watches the fire consume the source of her father's pain, she discovers an appreciation for the mystery of the natural world and recognizes the rebirth symbolized by the ritual fire.

SILENT TONGUE

Country USA   **Year** 1993   **Length** 96 m.   **Genre** FF
Director Sam Shepard
Producer Carolyn Pfeiffer, Ludi Boeken
Distributor
Available on Amazon.com
www.amazon.com
US $13.99 VHS
Also check www.cdnow.com

When Talbot Roe's (River Phoenix) half-Indian wife Awbonnie (Shiela Tousey) dies in childbirth, he becomes crazed with grief and sits in lonely vigil in the middle of a desolate prairie, guarding her body in a burial tree. In order to save his son from going completely mad, Prescott Roe (Richard Harris) gallops across the vast prairie in search of Eamon MacCree (Alan Bates), who runs the Kickapoo Indian Medicine Show, and who had traded him Awbonnie for horses. Prescott intends to buy Eamon's second daughter, Velada (Jeri Arredondo), who is the medicine show's trick rider. He believes that only she can save Talbot from his terrible grief.

Eamon is willing to consider the deal, until his son Reeves (Dermot Mulroney) violently objects, forcing a delay in the trade. Unable to wait, Prescott kidnaps Velada and heads back across the plains to the burial tree.

Back at the tree, Awbonnie's ghost—a powerful and terrible presence—rises from the body and demands that Talbot let the animals devour her body and free her to enter the spirit world. Talbot refuses, throwing the ghost into a rage.

SINGING OUR STORIES

Country Canada   **Year** 1998   **Length** 49 m.   **Genre** DS
Director Annie Fraziér Henry
Producer Joy Barrett, Lodi Butler, Michael Chechik, Sara Diamond, Annie Fraziér Henry, George Johnson, Graydon McCrea
Distributor
Video Out Distribution
1965 Main Street
Vancouver, BC
V5T 3C1 Canada
604 872-8449 [b] 604 876-1185 [f]
videoout@telus.net
Call for pricing (purchase and rental available)

Three Cherokee women sit around the kitchen table singing, their voices blending effortlessly, rising into the leafy canyon. Rita Coolidge, her sister Priscilla Coolidge and niece Laura Satterfield are among the featured performers in *Singing Our Stories*, which profiles some of the First Ladies of North American indigenous music. The Monk-Sanders Singers, four generations of Tuscarora women, give a joyous impromptu concert on the porch of an old North Carolina plantation house. Blackfoot composer Olivia Tailfeathers teaches traditional songs to teenagers from Alberta's Blood Nation. The Zuni Olla Maidens perform their ancient pottery dance against the spectacular backdrop of New Mexico's Dowa Yallane Mountain. The film celebrates a rich musical heritage in a journey that takes viewers from the Smokey Mountains of North Carolina to Vancouver Island, from the plains of Alberta to the mesas of New Mexico.

SLA-HAL: THE BONE GAME

Country USA   **Year** 1982   **Length** 26 m.   **Genre** DS
Director P.J. Chvany
Producer P.J. Chvany
Distributor
Currently unavailable.

Filmed and recorded at the Makah Indian Days celebration in Washington State, the film offers a brief explanation of "SLA-HAL," the bone game, in its many forms in Native American cultures. Through interviews with Makah players, first-hand observations about the game as a means of socializing, learning language, and maintaining contact with tradition and culture are parlayed.

SLEEPING CHILDREN AWAKE

Country Canada   **Year** 1993   **Length** 50 m.   **Genre** DS
Director Rhonda Kara Hanah
Producer Rhonda Kara Hanah
Distributor
Currently unavailable.

Sleeping Children Awake combines clips from Shirley Cheechoo's one-woman play *Path with No Moccasins* with interviews with former school residents and their families, many of whom are still struggling with the effects of the resident boarding school experience. They speak of the loss of their language, their culture, and their families.

SMOKE SIGNALS

Country USA   **Year** 1998   **Length** 89 m.   **Genre** FF
Director Chris Eyre
Producer Larry Estes, Scott Rosenfelt
Distributor
Miramax Films
Available at www.cdnow.com
US $15.99 VHS
US $23.99 DVD

The first full-length feature film written, directed and co-produced by Native Americans, *Smoke Signals* is one of the most entertaining and rewarding films in recent years. Filled with the rich aesthetics and beautiful mood of American Indian culture, Chris Eyre's debut (from a story by Sherman Alexie) marks the first time that the struggles of contemporary Native Americans with issues of assimilation and identity have been communicated so tenderly, truthfully and humorously on film. The drama follows a young stoic (Adam Beach) who reluctantly pairs up with a gregarious storyteller (Evan Adams) from his Idaho reservation for a road trip to claim the remains of the father who abandoned him long ago. As he listens to his companion's long-winded yet mesmerizing tales, his stubbornness gives way to a richer understanding of his forefathers, his father, and ultimately, himself. Also featuring Tantoo Cardinal, Gary Farmer, and Irene Bedard.

SOMEDAY, I'LL BE AN ELDER

Country USA   **Year** 1987   **Length** 25 m.   **Genre** DS
Director Vern Korb, Richard Johnson
Producer Vern Korb and Project Renewal - Karuk Tribal Council
Distributor
Shenandoah Film Productions
538 "G" Street
Arcata, CA 95521
707 822-1030 [b] 707 822-1035 [f]
US $200.00 VHS, US $45.00 rental

Even our playful young people are often affected by alcohol and drug abuse, either directly or indirectly. This film is about a pilot substance prevention program - "Project Renewal" - featuring Karuk tribal members as they conduct the 3 week summer camp program, which emphasizes the renewal of traditional ways and values.

Narrated by Will Sampson.

SOMEPLACE YOU DON'T WANT TO GO

Country USA   **Year** 1992   **Length** 22 m.   **Genre** DS
Director Matt Tortes
Producer Shenandoah Film Productions
Distributor
Shenandoah Film Productions
538 "G" Street
Arcata, CA 95521
707 822-1030 [b] 707 822-1035 [f]
US $200.00 VHS, US $45.00 VHS rental

This film portrays vivid scenes of the hardcore "stark reality" of what a
life of drug and alcohol abuse lead to. Indian youth and adults illustrate
their own stories with openness and honesty. This is contrasted with the
traditional beliefs and values of our elders.

SOMETHING LEFT TO DO

Country Canada   **Year** 1995   **Length** 23 m.   **Genre** DS
Director Cordell Wynne
Producer Cordell Wynne
Distributor
BC Learning Connection
#3 8755 Ash Street
Vancouver, BC
V6P 6T3   Canada
604 324-7752 [b] 604 324-1844 [f]   1 800 884-2366 toll free
www.bclc.bc.ca   videos@bclc.bc.ca
CAD $26.00 VHS

Three Sto:Lo elders reflect on life and death, and demonstrate through
dance, prayer and preserving ancient sites how they fulfill their obligations
as Indian elders to maintain the culture and link the generations.

SONG OF HIAWATHA

Country Canada   **Year** 1996   **Length** 114 m.   **Genre** FF
Director John Danylkiw
Producer Jeffrey Shore
Distributor
Available on Amazon.com
www.amazon.com
US $9.98 VHS

This adaptation of Henry Wadsworth Longfellow's epic poem *The Song of
Hiawatha* celebrates the heroic deeds of the legendary Ojibway chief sent
by the Great Spirit to lead his people. The story of Hiawatha's (Litefoot)
feats and tragedies is told to fur trader Jean Betrand (Michael Rooker),
French priest Father Marcel (Davis Strathairn), and Indian interpreter
O'Kagh (Graham Greene) by his grandmother Nokomis (Sheila Tousey)
and tribal elder Iagoo (Gordon Tootoosis). Hiawatha's many adventures
include falling in love with the beautiful and unattainable Dakota maiden
Minnehaha (Irene Bedard) and marrying her. Eventually the immortal
Hiawatha must leave his people and join his father (Russell Means) in the
Kingdom of the West Wind.

Also starring Adam Beach.

SONGKEEPERS

Country USA   **Year** 1999   **Length** 48 m.   **Genre** DS
Director Bob Jackson, Bob Hercules
Producer Dan King
Distributor
America's Flutes
P.O. Box 189
Lake Forest, IL 60045
847 615-9200 [b] 847 615-9246 [f]
amerflutes@aol.com
Call for pricing (home video, educational, and broadcast)

The sound of the Native American Flute has echoed across the Americas for thousands of years. Today, this beautiful sound inspires millions of people around the world. This documentary explores the sound of the flute, its mysterious origins, honored legends, spiritual values, and the traditional as well as contemporary songs of five culturally diverse flute artists. Each artist, R. Carlos Nakai (Navajo/Ute), Kevin Locke (Lakota), Hawk Littlejohn (Cherokee), Sonny Nevaquaya (Commanche), and Tom Mauchaty-Ware (Kiowa) articulates their own personal experience and journeys; and honor those songkeepers who have influenced them personally and culturally. In this presentation the viewer is immersed in beauty, fashioned by culturally diverse human beings expressing themselves through their articulate human voice and heart felt flute voice, augmented by a backdrop of the landscape scenery of their ancestral land.

SOOP ON WHEELS

Country Canada   **Year** 1999   **Length** 52 m.   **Genre** DF
Director Sandy Greer
Producer Sandy Greer
Distributor
Filmakers Library, Inc.
124 East 40th Street
New York, NY 10016
212 808-4980 [b] 212 808-4983 [f]
info@filmakers.com   www.filmakers.com
US $295.00 VHS, US $75.00 VHS rental
Small non-profit organizations shound call for pricing info.

Soop on Wheels is a story of the tenacity of the human spirit. It is a story of hope and healing, in relating the life and contributions of Everett Soop, a Blackfoot political cartoonist and humorist whose survival skills have been an irreverent sense of humor, artistic gifts and the spiritual values taught to him by his grandparents. He has produced a remarkable body of published work, despite the affliction of muscular dystrophy. Everett is the only Aboriginal artist represented in the National Archives—yet he is ostracized in his own community because of his political outspokenness, as well as people's fear of a disability they do not understand. This film is a tribute to Everett Soop's courage to make peace with himself before he leaves this world. His story communicates a universal message in demonstrating the need to appreciate a physically challenged person as a whole person as well as interrogating the tendency in all human communities to marginalize the truth tellers.

SOUNDS OF FAITH

Country USA   **Year** 1997   **Length** 14 m.   **Genre** DS
Director Malinda M. Maynor
Producer Malinda M. Maynor
Distributor
Malinda Maynor
800 Pritchard Avenue, Ext. #F5
Chapel Hill, NC 27516
919 969-9680 [b] and [f]
US $15.00 VHS, CD-ROM study guide also available.

Sounds of Faith takes a personal look at the vibrant tradition of gospel music among the Lumbee Indians of North Carolina. The filmmaker gives the audience a unique view of the issues confronting an Indian community trying to pass its musical and spiritual traditions to younger generations.

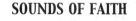

SOVERIGNTY TOUR

Country USA   **Year** 1998   **Length** 10 m.   **Genre** DS
Director Monique Sonoquie
Producer Monique Sonoquie
Distributor
Not in distribution.

Sovereignty Tour follows the organization and realization of a California bus tour spearheaded by the combined efforts of Reverend Jesse Jackson and the Rainbow Coalition, Priscilla Hunter of the Coyote Valley Pomo Tribe, and Henry Duro of the San Manuel Band of Mission Indians. The documentary follows the tour, with its stops at rallies, universities and community meetings along the way, from San Diego to Sacramento. The tour culminates with a four mile march and rally attended by over 15,000 Indians. Filmed by Monterey State graduate student Monique Sonoquie, *Sovereignty Tour* demonstrates the power of people working together.

SPIDER'S WEB – A WASHOE HISTORY, LEGEND AND MODERN STORY FOR YOUTH

Country USA   **Year** 1995   **Length** 30 m.   **Genre** DS
Director Jane Van Camp, Bill Thorpe
Producer Michon R. Eben
Distributor
Bill Thorpe
3421 Angel Lane
Placerville, CA 95667
530 622-9318 [b]
tva@inforum.net
US $29.00 VHS

Spider's Web—A Washoe History, Legend and Modern Story for Youth is a video production which began as an anti-tobacco awareness project for youth in the Washoe Tribe of Nevada and California. The first part of the presentation is a brief history of the Wa-she-shu people, their land, and their culture. The second part is an animated version of the old Washoe legend of Pawetsile, the weasel, and Damollale, the squirrel and their encounter with the bad ways of the spider. Animation by Bruce Morgan.

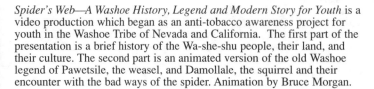

SPIRIT LIVES, THE

Country USA   **Year** 1985   **Length** 42 m.   **Genre** DS
Director Terri Li
Producer Terri Li
Distributor
Currently unavailable.

The Spirit Lives documents the dance and song of the Pomo Indians of Northern California.

The Spirit Lives was five years in the making, three years of which were research and gaining the friendship and trust needed for filming spiritual ceremonies inside the roundhouse (Indian Spiritual Community House). The film shows dance, both social and spiritual, and song as the foundation of Indian spirituality. Interwoven throughout the film are the elders and song leaders from various Northern California tribes, dancing and chanting, and talking about the old ways versus the new, and the importance of preserving their culture.

SPIRIT OF CRAZY HORSE, THE

Country USA　　　　**Year** 1991　　**Length** 55 m.　　　**Genre** DF
Director James Locker
Producer Michel Dubois, Kevin McKiernan
Distributor
Not in distribution.

"The heart of everything that is." These are the words which the Sioux Indians use to describe their ancestral homeland, the Black Hills of South Dakota. Those million acres form the spiritual core of the Sioux culture, and it's a land they have struggled to reclaim for a century. *The Spirit of Crazy Horse* is an eye opening vision of their quest, which has shaped the lives and destiny of the Sioux for six generations.

It is a tale recounted by Milo Yellow Hair, a fullblood Oglala Sioux, whose great-great-grandfather fought General Custer at the Little Big Horn. While the story echoes with famous names like Wounded Knee—the last major Indian massacre a century ago—this is more than a tale of long lost wars. *The Spirit of Crazy Horse* reveals the modern Sioux struggle to regain their heritage, and how places like Wounded Knee became sites for a fight that continues still.

SPIRIT OF THE DAWN

Country USA　　　　**Year** 1994　　**Length** 29 m.　　　**Genre** DS
Director Heidi Schmidt Emberling
Producer Heidi Schmidt Emberling
Distributor
New Day Films
22-D Hollywood Avenue
Ho-Ho-Kus, NJ 07423
888 367-9154 [b] 201 652-1973 [f]
www.newday.com　　orders@newday.com
US $150.00 VHS, US $89.00 VHS rental

The history of Native American peoples in the United States has been a struggle for autonomy in the face of powerful government opposition. Beginning in the late 1800s and continuing as late as the 1960s, Native American children were wrenched from their homes and sent to boarding schools to be "assimilated" into the dominant society. The consequences of that history is clearly seen in the widespread destruction of many Native cultures.

Today, Native Americans are fighting the legacy of the past. On reservations throughout the U.S., Indians are taking back control of their schools. Indian culture is now an integral part of classroom learning. Native legends are taught alongside Greek and Roman ones, giving Native American cultures a place among traditional academic subjects.

This documentary takes place on the Crow Reservation in southeastern Montana, where we meet two sixth graders, Heywood Big Day III and Bruce Big Hail. We see them at home with their families, traditional Crows who want their children to learn about both Native and mainstream American ways. After a decade of struggle by teachers, parents and community leaders, we see how this dream is coming true. Students are finally able to learn their own cultural history alongside general academic subjects.

SPIRIT OF THE HUNT

Country USA   **Year** 1982   **Length** 28 m.   **Genre** DS
Director Deborah Peaker
Producer Deborah Peaker
Distributor
Clearvue/eva, Inc.
6465 N. Avondale Avenue
Chicago, IL 60631
773 775-9433 [b]   773 775-9855 [f]
1 800 444-9855 toll free
www.clearvue.com   custserv@clearvue.com
US $50.00 VHS

This film highlights a modern version of an age old rite, possibly the last organized buffalo hunt in the world, and certainly the only one ever to be recorded on film. *Spirit of the Hunt* is not a mindless slaughter, but rather Indian hunters of today recapturing the footsteps of their ancestors.

Spirit of the Hunt was filmed entirely on location, from the foothills of the Rocky Mountains to the tundra of the Northwest Territories. Combined with rare archival material, the film brings to audiences of all ages the thundering echoes of North American's past, the visionary dreams of one man's future and the *Spirit of the Hunt*.

SPIRIT OF THE LAND: ALASKA: THE YUP'IK ESKIMOS

Country USA   **Year** 1985   **Length** 28 m.   **Genre** DS
Director Gail K. Evenari
Producer Chevron USA
Distributor
Chevron Electronic Classrooms
Free to downlink via satellite twice a year.
www.chevron.com
Select community and then electronic classroom.
For more information call 707 996-1996 [b].

This film documents the Yup'ik Eskimos of Western Alaska. These people, who have inhabited the Yukon-Kuckokwim Delta for about 3,000 years, have a special relationship with their natural environment, which is reflected in their subsistence lifestyle and their spiritual and cultural values.

Instead of perceiving the frozen tundra as a harsh enemy, Yup'iks see the land, rivers and sea as having bountiful resources which fulfill all their needs. Respect for the land and its inhabitants is fundamental and pervades every aspect of Yup'ik life. It is manifested through the generous sharing of food, clothing and gifts among families and friends; and the honor bestowed upon animals and plants, evident through their special customs and methods of hunting, fishing, gathering and preparing food.

Today, the Yup'ik people are faced with the challenge of maintaining their traditional values and lifestyle while keeping in step with the modern world.

Through interviews conducted in the Yup'ik language and observation of daily life in the villages, the film provides viewers a close look at today's Yup'ik people. Elders and teenagers alike voice their hopes and concerns—and they describe what it means to them to be Yup'ik.

SPIRIT OF THE WIND

Country USA   **Year** 1980   **Length** 98 m.   **Genre** FF
Director Ralph Liddle
Producer Raven Pictures
Distributor
Not in distribution.

Spirit of the Wind, the true story of world champion dog-sledder George Attla, is filmed in the panoramic background of the Alaskan wilderness. The film opens in the remote interior village of Huslia in the year 1947 where the Attla's, an Athabascan Indian family, live out a pattern of life largely unchanged from its traditional form. George is twelve years old, at the age where he must learn to survive in the beautiful but harsh land where he was born. In an effort not to disappoint his father, George attempts to hide a deteriorating condition in his right knee which is later diagnosed as tuberculosis of the bone. He is sent to a pediatric center in Sitka, Alaska, some 1,000 miles from his home, and does not return until eight years later when he is cured, but permanently crippled.

From this point on, we see the boy as he attempts to readjust to his home and culture after his long absence, and to overcome the handicaps imposed by his lame condition. Dog racing becomes his passion. He finds a lead dog, Jarvi, who was rejected by his former owner as "lacking heart," and together, after much failure and frustration, they are finally ready to compete in the world champion dog-sledding race. There is a dramatic build up as George competes in the increasingly difficult three day race. The climatic photo-finish brings the film to an unforgettable finale. Win or lose, George Attla challenged the champions and contributed to one of the greatest dog-sledding races in history.

Starring Pius Savage, Chief Dan George, Slim Pickens and George Clutesi.

SPIRIT OF TURTLE ISLAND, THE

Country Canada   **Year** 1989   **Length** 53 m.   **Genre** DF
Director Lenore Keeshig Tobias, Alan Collins
Producer Alan Collins
Distributor
Alfa Nova Productions
139 Booth Avenue
Toronto, Ontario
M4M 3M5 Canada
416 778-4307 [b]   carabas@visinet.ca
CAD $40.00 VHS

Turtle Island is a Native creation myth which explains how woman was the first being to inhabit the earth; the rest of human life grows from her.

The Spirit of Turtle Island Festival, a celebration of the strength and power of Native women, was held in Toronto in August of 1985. It was a demonstration that Native women of today are reclaiming their traditional roles, examining their present position, and instigating positive change for the future. *The Spirit of Turtle Island* concerns the search for contemporary manifestations of women's power and influence.

SPIRIT RIDER

Country Canada   **Year** 1993   **Length** 120 m.   **Genre** FF
Director Michael Scott
Producer Wayne Aaron, Derek Mazur
Distributor
Available on Amazon.com
www.amazon.com
US $13.99 VHS

Spirit Rider is the story of Jesse Threebears (Herbie Barnes), a 16 year-old Ojibway. For fourteen years Jesse has been shunted from one foster home to another. Now he is unwillingly returned to his reserve by the band council as part of a repatriation program. After many years away, Jesse has lost touch with his roots. He is critical of everything on the reserve—especially his grandfather, Joe Moon (Gordon Tootoosis).

The community offers friendship, but Jesse is distrustful. Even Vern (Graham Greene), the local radio deejay and Albert (Tom Jackson) who gives Jesse a job, can't break though his wall of anger and frustration. Add the hostility of Paul (Adam Beach), a teenager who views him as an outsider and a threat, Jesse's life seems miserable.

When Jesse and his grandfather capture a wild horse, the boy's outlook begins to change. Camilla (Michelle St. John), a girl who helps Jesse adjust to his new life, sparks feelings he has never experienced. She teaches him to ride so he can enter a high-stakes race.

SPIRIT WITHIN, THE

Country Canada   **Year** 1991   **Length** 51 m.   **Genre** DF
Director Wil Cambell, Gil Cardinal
Producer Jerry Krepakevich, Graydon McCrea
Distributor
National Film Board of Canada Library
22-D Hollywood Avenue
Ho-Ho-Kus, NJ 07423
1 800 542-2163 [b] 201 652-1973 [f]
US $195.00 VHS, call for rental information and prices.
For purchase within Canada visit the NFB website at: www.nfb.ca
1 800 267-7710 toll free within Canada

The Spirit Within looks at Native spirituality programs which have been set up in western Canadian federal penal institutions and in some provincial institutions. The programs, which are led by Native elders and assisted by liaison officers, include workshops and ceremonies which help to put the Native prison inmate back in touch with himself, his culture and his spirituality. The film deals with the impact of the programs, in particular that of the sweat lodge. *The Spirit Within* also serves as an introduction to the kind of life faced by Native inmates.

SPUDWRENCH - KAHNAWAKE MAN

Country Canada   **Year** 1998   **Length** 58 m.   **Genre** DF
Director Alanis Obomsawin
Producer Don Haig, Alanis Obomsawin
Distributor
National Film Board of Canada Library
22-D Hollywood Avenue
Ho-Ho-Kus, NJ 07423
1 800 542-2164 [b] 201 652-1973 [f]
US $250.00 VHS, call for rental information and prices.
For purchase within Canada visit the NFB website at:www.nfb.ca
1 800 267-7710 toll free within Canada

Meet Randy Horne, high steel worker from the Mohawk community of Kahnawake, near Montreal. As a defender of his people's culture and traditions, he was known as "Spudwrench" during the 1990 Oka crisis. Horne was behind the barricades, resisting the efforts of the municipality of Oka to expand a golf course onto sacred Mohawk land. Horne is one of many Mohawk high steel workers who have travelled the continent, working on some of the world's tallest buildings—but have never lost touch with their roots. *Spudwrench - Kahnawake Man* is both a portrait of Horne and the generations of daring Mohawk construction workers that have preceded him, and a unique look behind the barricades at one man's impassioned defense of sacred territory. This is the third film in Alanis Obomsawin's series on the events of 1990 at Oka.

STAND AND BE COUNTED

Country USA   **Year** 1994   **Length** 10 m.   **Genre** PS
Producer AIFI and Urban Rural Systems Associate Institute
Distributor
Not in distribution.

This film is a public service docu-drama concerning the health effects of tobacco misuse, which was developed and produced by students participating in the Native American Youth Media Mentor Program sponsored by the American Indian Film Institute and Urban Rural Systems Associate Institute.

STARING AT A FEARFUL OCEAN

Country Canada   **Year** 2000   **Length** 6 m.   **Genre** LS
Director Norm Fassbender
Producer Kate Holowach
Distributor
Atom Films / Megan O'Neil
401 Broadway, Suite 1012
New York, NY 10013
212 431-0407 [b] 212 431-0425 [f]
moneil@atomfilms.com
Please call for pricing information.

Izzy, a frightened inner city Métis (half Indian/half white) teen, confronts her violent past, her drug use and her warring spiritual beliefs (Christian and Native) in this thought provoking short subject.

STEWART INDIAN SCHOOL: UNCOMMON GROUND

Country USA   **Year** 1996   **Length** 30 m.   **Genre** DS
Director Creel Snider
Producer Phil Kowalski
Distributor
Currently unavailable.
Truckee Meadows Community College
7000 Dandini Blvd. - M09
Reno, NV 89512
775 673-7000 [b]

Stewart Indian School: Uncommon Ground visits an old Native American boarding school turned museum in Nevada. The film traces the history of the school, from its inception in the 19th century as a means of harshly assimilating Indians to Western society, to its status as the only ticket to allowing Natives into the White economic structure. The film examines both the tragic and the hope filled past of the school.

STORIES FROM THE SEVENTH FIRE

Country Canada   **Year** 1999   **Length** 24 m.   **Genre** ANS
Director Gregory Coyes, Tantoo Cardinal
Producer Gregory Coyes, Gerri Cooke, Ava Karvonen
Distributor
Filmoption International
3401 St-Antonie
Westmount, Quebec
H3Z 1X1 Canada
514 931-6180 [b]   514 939-2034 [f]
www.filmoption.com

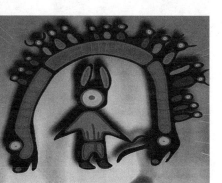

Storytelling is a gift from the Creator. To Native people with strong oral traditions, the art of storytelling holds great importance. In this way, all knowledge and history of the people has been passed on. *Stories From the Seventh Fire* is a unique package of traditional First Nations stories told through stunning animation and award winning, live action footage. The storyteller melds these components into an entertaining package for children and families. The animated segments focus on comedic Cree trickster, Wesakechak. Narrated and co-directed by Tantoo Cardinal.

STORY OF LIGHT

Country USA   **Year** 1996   **Length** 20 m.   **Genre** LS
Director Ivica Bilich
Producer Ivica Bilich
Distributor
Ivica Bilich
Unworld Productions
600 East 35 Street
Charlotte, NC 28205
704 342-9205 [b]
email: iviworld@aol.com
US $16.00 VHS

Shot on tribal lands of the Eastern Band of the Cherokee Nation, with per-formers cast out of the Cherokee Elementary School, *Story of Light* tells the ancient tale of how animals brought sunlight to the dark side of the earth. The Opossum and the Buzzard, both failing in their attempts to steal a spark from the sun, turn to the tiny Grandmother Spider. She succeeds by making a small clay pot and carrying the spark back to the land of the Cherokee.

STORY OF THE COAST SALISH KNITTERS, THE

Country Canada   **Year** 2000   **Length** 52 m.   **Genre** DF
Director Christine Welsh
Producer Christine Welsh, Gillian Darling Kovanic, Colleen Craig
Distributor
National Film Board of Canada Library
22-D Hollywood Avenue
Ho-Ho-Kus, NJ 07423
1 800 542-2164 [b] 201 652-1973 [f]
US $250.00 VHS, call for rental information and prices.
For purchase within Canada visit the NFB website at: www.nfb.ca
1 800 267-7710 toll free within Canada

For almost a century, the Coast Salish knitters of southern Vancouver Island have produced distinctive sweaters from handspun wool that are known and loved around the world. Combining the ancient wool-working traditions of the Coast Salish people and knitting techniques of English and Scottish settlers, Cowichan sweaters became a symbol of Canada's West Coast - the clothing of choice for those who worked and played in the great outdoors. They were warm and waterproof and lasted forever, and each one was unique. They've been worn by presidents, royalty and Hollywood stars, but for most of us they're simply old friends - well worn treasures that have been part of our lives and part of out families for gener-ations. Every sweater has its story, but this is the story of the people who make them.

Combining rare archival footage with the voices of three generations of Coast Salish knitters, *The Story of the Coast Salish Knitters* is a beautifully woven story of courage and cultural transformation by Métis writer/direc-tor Christine Welsh. Like most Aboriginal women, Coast Salish knitters are unsung heroines - strong, courageous and resourceful women who knit to put food on the table and have kept their families and communities alive through times of enormous hardship and change. Theirs is an inspiring story - a celebration of the threads that connect the past to the future, and of Aboriginal people's extraordinary ability to adapt and survive.

STORYTELLER

Country USA   **Year** 1999   **Length** 12 m.   **Genre** LS
Director Richard S. Dargan
Producer Laurie A. Volkin, Richard S. Dargan
Distributor
Dango Productions
10308 Delicado Pl. NE
Albuquerque, NM 87111
505 323-2732 [b]   darrol@aol.com
US $14.95 VHS, US $9.95 VHS rental

A bartender's tales of adventure may not be all that they seem when he meets a patron with a connection to the real story.

It's another day at the Golden West Bar, a dive on old Route 66 in Albuquerque, New Mexico. Nick, the bartender, regales the patrons with tales of travel and adventure, and steals moments with his waitress/girl-friend, Joline. But when a patron interrupts him with a story of his own, a story that involves a recent heist at a tribal casino, Nick is forced to make a decision about his future, one that may put him in conflict with Joline. *Storyteller* is a drama about facing your identity by coming to terms with the past.

STRAND IN THE WEB, A

Country USA   **Year** 1989   **Length** 28 m.   **Genre** DS
Director Madeline Muir
Producer Madeline Muir
Distributor
Currently unavailable.

A Strand in the Web is a video documentary focusing on the Navajo/Dineh Indians' successful fight against a toxic waste dump and incinerator proposed for their land in Dilcon, Arizona. It examines the history of exploitation on Indian lands by uranium and coal companies, and the recent trend for toxic waste companies to target Indian Land. The Navajo's struggle to keep out dangerous toxic disposal facilities is juxtaposed with efforts in communities throughout the Western States to stop proposed toxic waste facilities. By working together, individual citizens and community groups have been persuading industry to reduce toxic pollution at its source, the only real solution.

STRANGE CASE OF BUNNY WEEQUOD, THE

Country USA   **Year** 1999   **Length** 24 m.   **Genre** LS
Director Steve Van Denzen
Producer Dave Deleary, Brian Dennis, Gerry Flahive, John Roy
Distributor
National Film Board of Canada Library
22-D Hollywood Avenue
Ho-Ho-Kus, NJ 07423
1 800 542-2164 [b]   201 652-1973 [f]
US $175.00 VHS, call for rental information and prices.
For purchase within Canada visit the NFB website at: www.nfb.ca
1 800 267-7710 toll free within Canada

There's something funny going on in the lakes—and Bunny Weequod is, quite literally, going to get to the bottom of it. Bunny is puzzled by the number of fish dying in his lake. While out fishing one night he capsizes and is presumed dead, only to wash up the next morning a completely different man. Bunny's wife, Jasmine, worries about her husband's increasingly bizarre behavior, until an elder realizes the trouble: Bunny has been changed by the legendary little people of Ojibway lore, and now he must pay his respects to them in order to restore harmony to the lakes. *The Strange Case of Bunny Weequod* is a drama in Ojibway, with English sub-titles, that blends folklore and humor with a contemporary environmental theme. Created by a team of Aboriginal filmmakers, this work is a gift to both Native elders and the younger generation: it keeps alive sacred stories while ensuring that the Ojibway language flourishes well into the new millennium. Produced in collaboration with an expert on the language, this video is also ideal for Ojibway learners.

STUMBLINGBEAR: THE VIDEO

Country USA   **Year** 1994   **Length** 3 m.   **Genre** ANS
Director Dan Bigbee, Jr.
Producer Dan Bigbee, Jr.
Distributor
Not in distribution.

A fancy dancer of world renown, Stumblingbear is the creation of Buddy Big Mountain (Mohawk, Comanche, Apache). Stumblingbear's video debut has been screened at several film festivals around the country and purchased for the collection of the National Museum of the American Indian.

Stumblingbear's dancing ability is phenomenal. He can start and stop on a dime, and never misses a beat, no matter what happens. This is his video debut, and his final performance. Stumblingbear has since retired.

SUBSISTENCE: A WAY OF LIFE

Country USA   **Year** 1997   **Length** 16 m.   **Genre** DS
Director Vern Korb
Producer Shenandoah Film Productions
Distributor
Not in distribution.
Shenandoah Film Productions
538 "G" Street
Arcata, CA 95221
707 822-1030 [b]   707 822-1035 [b]

This documentary is a journey into the lives of the Inuits along the western coastal region of Seward Peninsula in Alaska. *Subsistence: A Way of Life* takes a look at how subsistence plays a major role in Inuit traditional and cultural values and how the government is setting regulations that are often impractical and contrary to Inuit beliefs.

SUMMER LEGEND

Country Canada   **Year** 1987   **Length** 8 m.   **Genre** ANS
Director Francoise Hartmann
Producer Eunice Macaulay, Douglas MacDonald
Distributor
National Film Board of Canada Library
22-D Hollywood Avenue
Ho-Ho-Kus, NJ 07423
1 800 542-2164 [b]   201 652-1973 [f]
US $80.00 VHS, call for rental information and prices.
For purchase within Canada visit the NFB website at: www.nfb.ca
1 800 267-7710 toll free within Canada

Silas Rand and Charles Leland first wrote down the legends of the great spirit Glooscap before the turn of the century. Since then, *Summer Legend* has been retold many times, but never more beautifully than in this colorful animated interpretation. It tells of the Micmac people in the cold white dawning of their world, and of how Glooscap battled with the giant Winter in order to bring Summer to the North.

SUMMER OF THE LOUCHEUX: PORTRAIT OF A NORTHERN INDIAN

Country Canada **Year** 1983 **Length** 28 m. **Genre** DS
Director Graydon McCrea
Producer Graydon McCrea, Linda Rasmussen
Distributor
Contact Graydon McCrea at 780 495-3015 [b].

This is the personal story of a young North American Native woman's struggle to reconcile a traditional lifestyle with the present. Each summer she joins four generations of her Loucheux (Kutchin) family at their summer camp on the Mackenzie River, Northwest Territories, to prepare dry fish. Mastering the skills of camp life, teaching her niece and listening to her 93-year-old grandmother's stories all contribute to her understanding of her American Indian culture and herself. This is a film about values, self-esteem and the critical importance of traditions.

SUN, MOON, & FEATHER

Country USA **Year** 1989 **Length** 30 m. **Genre** DS
Director Jane Zipp, Bob Rosen
Producer Jane Zipp, Bob Rosen
Distributor
The Cinema Guild
130 Madison Avenue, 2nd Floor
New York, NY 10016
212 685-6242 [b] 212 685-4717 [f]
thecinemaguild@aol.com
US $250.00 VHS, US $55.00 VHS rental

This prize-winning comedy/documentary is about three Native American sisters growing up in Brooklyn during the 1930s and 40s. It features Lisa, Gloria and Muriel Miguel, who have been performing their family stories together professionally for more than a decade as the Spiderwoman Theater, in a presentational style rich in humor and with an elemental power that recalls the spirit of American Indian myths. This film blends documentary (including excerpts from home movies shot over a thirty-year period, with scenes of family pow-wows and traveling medicine shows for white tourists), musical theater (song and dance reenactments of family and tribal stories), and personal memoirs (including scenes filmed in the Brooklyn home where the sisters grew up among a large extended family).

SUPER CHIEF

Country USA **Year** 1999 **Length** 75 m. **Genre** DF
Director Nick Kurzon
Producer Nick Kurzon
Distributor
IO Productions, Inc.
132 E. 17th Street #51
New York, NY 10003
212 533-1335 [b] kurzon@iname.com
US $150.00 VHS

The millions of dollars that come through the new casino on the White Earth Reservation stop at the tribal chairman's desk. And the man behind that desk—the self-proclaimed *Super Chief*—is getting richer by the day.

He's not getting away easy, though: there's a U.S. Prosecutor trying to haul him into court and a reservation schoolteacher determined to uncover his notoriously corrupt schemes. In the midst of it all, the Chairman is running for re-election. This year, he's facing fierce competition for his job from a retired welder with nothing to lose and a grocery store owner with a knack for politics and a winning handshake.

As the campaign season mounts, emotional debates flare on the reservation. Soon the filmmaker finds himself witness to a tangled struggle for power, money and justice: a struggle that builds, day by day, to a thrilling, unexpected conclusion.

SURVIVING COLUMBUS

Country USA   **Year** 1992   **Length** 120 m.   **Genre** DF
Director Diane Reyna
Producer IAIA, KNNE TV Albuquerque
Distributor
P.B.S. Home Video
1320 Braddock Place
Alexandria, VA 22314
1 800 645-4727 tele
US $19.98 VHS home video
US $49.95 VHS educational
US $59.95 VHS indexed version

Surviving Columbus uses interviews with Pueblo elders, scholars and leaders to tell the story of the Pueblo People, and archival photographs and historical reenactment to show that survival of Pueblo Indians was the result of a long struggle to control their own lives. *Surviving Columbus* is the story of the Pueblo Indians told in their voices and seen through their eyes. The film offers a different perspective of the Columbus Quincentenary — a perspective on American history that has been omitted from school texts and the public consciousness far too long.

SWEAT

Country USA   **Year** 1996   **Length** 27 m.   **Genre** LS
Director Valentina Lopez-Firewalks
Producer Dave Aron
Distributor
Currently unavailable

Sweat illustrates the dilemma of Natives trying to practice their religion and participate in sweat lodges in state penitentiaries. The movie focuses on Travis Shue, a prison guard and father, caught between a warden's oppresive orders and his own morality. He obeys the warden and participates in a sabotage of Indian inmates' religious practices. The sabotage leads to the death of inmate/sweat leader, Midthunder. Ultimately, the prison guard regrets his involvement and teaches his son the values of tolerance and understanding.

SXWEXWXIY'AM: THE STORY OF SIWASH ROCK

Country Canada   **Year** 1999   **Length** 24 m.   **Genre** LS
Director Annie Fraziér Henry
Producer Michael Chechik, Svend-Erik Erikson, Annie Fraziér Henry, George Johnson
Distributor
Video Out Distribution
1965 Main Street
Vancouver, BC
V5T 3C1 Canada
604 872-8449 [b] 604 876-1185 [f]
videoout@telus.net
Call for pricing (purchase and rental available).

"It is said the proud Siwash Rock resembles a certain young warrior of long, long ago... a brave young chief who pledged his honour to the love of a beautiful young girl from the north."--Chief Simon Baker. So begins *Sxwexwxwiy'am: The Story of Siwash Rock*, a contemporary dramatization of an ancient Coast Salish myth about the famous Vancouver landmark that symbolizes the most sacred of a man's vows, cleanliness of fatherhood. As Chief Simon Baker narrates in Squamish, the tale unfolds in Vancouver's inner city. We meet Andrew, a young Native man struggling to overcome the disillusionment of his people. Unemployed and faced with the unplanned and difficult pregnancy of his girlfriend Kelsey, Andrew must prove himself worthy of fatherhood by following the traditional path of his ancestors. *Sxwexwxwiy'am* is a gripping and life-affirming drama, featuring powerful performances by the film's young actors.

T'LINA: THE RENDERING OF WEALTH

Country Canada   **Year** 1999   **Length** 50 m.   **Genre** DS
Director Barb Cranmer
Producer Barb Cranmer, Cari Green, Selwyn Jacob
Distributor
National Film Board of Canada Library
22-D Hollywood Avenue
Ho-Ho-Kus, NJ 07423
1 800 542-2164 [b] 201 652-1973 [f]
US $200.00 VHS, call for rental information and prices.
For purchase within Canada visit the NFB website at: www.nfb.ca
1 800 267-7710 toll free within Canada

Every spring the people of the Kwakwaka'wakw Nation travel to Knight Inlet on the British Columbia coast for the annual harvest of eulachon, a small fish from which they extract t'lina, an oil which occupies a central place in their traditional culture and economy. Filmmaker Barb Cranmer's family has participated in this ritual for generations. T'lina was traded among the First Nations of the Pacific Northwest for centuries, valued as a food staple and an important ceremonial substance. In a celebratory gesture of thanksgiving, chiefs distribute it at festive potlatches, where dancers carry giant carved ladles of the oil. In recent years, the eulachon's numbers have been depleted through habitat destruction, by industrial logging, and overfishing by shrimp draggers. Combining footage of a contemporary harvest with archival images, Cranmer raises the alarm on the uncertain future facing this vital cultural practice and offers a lively history of a dynamic coastal First Nation.

TAOS PUEBLO, THE

Country USA   **Year** 1987   **Length** 9 m.   **Genre** DS
Director Paulle Clark
Producer Paulle Clark for OWL/TV
Distributor
Bullfrog Films
P.O. Box 149
Oley, PA 19547
610 779-8226 [b] 610 370-1978 [f]
www.bullfrogfilms.com   info@bullfrogfilms.com
US $49.00 VHS, US $20.00 VHS rental

A young girl visits a 1000-year old pueblo in Taos, New Mexico and learns how to build homes with adobe clay, traditional bread-making, and the making of Indian pottery in age old ways.

TEACHING ROCKS, THE

Country Canada   **Year** 1987   **Length** 19 m.   **Genre** DS
Director Lloyd Walton
Producer Lloyd Walton
Distributor
Currently unavailable.

In the Stony Lake area near Peterborough, Ontario there are outcroppings of soft rock.

Carved in the rocks are symbols which are similar to ones found in many parts of North and South America. The carvings are significant in the social and philosophical teachings of the Ojibway people... but the precise meanings of the many symbols are carefully shrouded in mystery.

The film *The Teaching Rocks* lifts the veil of mystery through the teachings of various Native elders. Fred Wheatley, an Ojibway elder, speaks of the teachings contained in this site, how it has been used in the past, and how it should be approached today. Other Native people share some of the teachings and feelings that this sacred area induces.

TEARS OF THE RAVEN

Country USA   **Year** 1993   **Length** 49 m.   **Genre** DS
Director Bill Baker
Producer Pamela Jennings
Distributor
Shenandoah Film Productions
538 "G" Street
Arcata, CA 95521
707 822-1030 [b] 707 822-1035 [f]
US $200.00 VHS, US $45.00 VHS rental

Suicide among Alaska's Natives is as much as twenty-six times the national average. This film examines the dissolution of Alaskan indigenous culture, the worst symptoms of which are alcoholism and suicide, and goes on to document the solutions that are springing up in far-flung communities throughout the nation's largest state.

The film then explores some of the things the Natives are doing to bring health and hope back to their communities. We watch as a 90 year-old Tlingit elder chooses a spruce tree for the making of a sea canoe. He calls to the spirit of the tree three times, saying, "We have come for you, at the foot of you, so that we may be able to use you for the canoe boat." The canoe carving project is one of the many cultural and spiritual events which the film documents.

TECUMSEH AND THE DREAM OF CONFEDERACY

Country USA   **Year** 1998   **Length** 43 m.   **Genre** DS
Director Gary Foreman
Producer Gary Foreman, Robert J. Nader (exec.)
Distributor
A&E Network / The History Channel
235 E. 45th Street
New York, NY 10017
1 800 423-1212 [b]
US $59.95 VHS
Part of "Legends of the Old Northwest Series," IV volumes

The lives and deaths of the legendary Shawnee warrior Tecumseh and his brother, the Prophet are recounted in this documentary. From the encroachment of Europeans, through the loss of their parents to their ultimately tragic ends, *Tecumseh and the Dream of Confederacy* looks at the conflicts with governor William Henry Harrison that culminated in the devastating battle at Tippecanoe. Through false promises and misalliances, we are shown the tragic losses suffered by the Shawnee at the dawning of the 19th century.

TEMAGAMI: A LIVING TITLE TO THE LAND

Country Canada   **Year** 1992   **Length** 30 m.   **Genre** DS
Director James Cullingham
Producer Gil Cardinal, Andy Thompson
Distributor
AIMS Multimedia
9710 De Sorto Avenue
Chatsworth, CA 91311-4409
818 773-430o [b] or 1 800 367-2467 toll free
www.aims-multimedia.com
US $47.45 VHS

The beautiful Temagami forest is the site of a decade-long conflict between the Ontario provincial government and the Teme-Augama Anishnabai, whose attachment to the land is rooted in 6,000 years of history. Reaching a just decision as to who owns the land and how it should be managed is a question of legal title versus a *living* title to the land.

TENACITY

Country USA **Year** 1995 **Length** 10 m. **Genre** LS
Director Chris Eyre
Producer Paul Mezey
Distributor
Third World Newsreel
545 8th Avenue
New York, NY 10018
212 947-9277 [b] 212 594-6417 [f]
twn@twn.org
US $175.00 VHS, US $50.00 VHS rental

Tenacity is the story of two Indian boys, Clint and Joseph, who encounter rednecks on a reservation road. Their confrontation, which takes place in a desolate and abandoned countryside, pits the quiet determination of a child against a corrupted and violent adult world where the hit-and-run nature of the Native experience is recreated in a brutal filmic text. Filmed in the Onondaga Territory near Nedrow, New York, this award winning short narrative is a story of friendship and the loss of innocence.

THAT WAS HAPPY LIFE

Country USA **Year** 1993 **Length** 28 m. **Genre** DS
Director Mark Gandolfo, JoAnne Penden
Producer JoAnne Penden
Distributor
JoAnne Peden
180 Leo Drive
Sparks, Nevada 89436
775 425-6365 [b]
US $24.95 VHS

This documentary is a portrait of Katie Frazier, a Northern Paiute woman born in 1892, just three generations after the white incursion into her people's homeland. Katie's childhood was a period of drastic and irreversible change. There was no longer only one world, seamless and comprehensible, stretching back as far as the people's oral traditions could retain. Strangers with incomprehensible ways consumed the good land, lakes and rivers upon which the Northern Paiutes had depended for plants, foods and game, and fish. The white world not only took away, it brought wholly different requirements for survival: a new language, different customs and technology, formal education in the white man's ways, and wage labor as the means of making a living rather than living off the land. These changes cast adrift the lifeways and customs of a people wisely adapted to the harsh environment of a high, cold desert.

THINGS WE DO ARTIST: INDIGENOUS

Country USA **Year** 1998 **Length** 5 m. **Genre** MV
Director Chris Eyre
Producer Chris Eyre, Anthony Vozza
Distributor
For information on the band visit their website at:
www.indigenousrocks.com

Indigenous, a family of musicians from the Yankton Indian Reservation in South Dakota present their first music video entitled "Things We Do," from their album of the same name, directed by Chris Eyre of *Smoke Signals* fame. Members of the Nakota Nation, brothers Mato Nanji, Pte, sister Wanbdi and their cousin Horse play with house shaking rythms that have attracted followers and fans from all over.

THIRD VERSE, 500 YEARS,
THE LAND OF THE CHILDREN

Country USA   **Year** 1993   **Length** 9 m.   **Genre** DS
Director Joanelle Romero
Producer Joanelle Romero
Distributor
Spirit World Productions
818 730-5084 [b] & [f]
Please call for pricing.

Best known for her leading roles in such films as *Pow Wow Highway* and
A Girl Called Hatter Fox, veteran Native American actress Joanelle
Romero's concern about American Indian children's desperate need for
role models helped provide the inspiration for forming her own production
company, and for producing *Third Verse, 500 Years, Land of the Children*,
the new company's first documentary short. Weaving the past with the present, including images of Edward Curtis' famous photographs of Indian
elders and children, Romero's film emphasizes continuity as a source of
strength.

THIS WORLD IS NOT OUR HOME

Country USA   **Year** 1994   **Length** 13 m.   **Genre** DS
Director Kim Johnson
Producer Kim Johnson
Distributor
UC Extension Center for Media and Independent Learning
2000 Center Street, Fourth Floor
Berkeley, CA 94704-1223
510 642-0460 [b]   510 643-9271 [f]
cmil@uclink.berkeley.edu
US $125.00 VHS purchase   US $40.00 VHS rental

This World Is Not Our Home tells the story and documents the experiences
of Elvina Brown, the oldest Pomo Indian woman living on the Sulphur
Bank Reservation in Northern California. Using Elvina's commentary, stories and songs, *This World Is Not Our Home* serves to both remind and
teach people important traditional Pomo ideas and cultural values from
which people of all cultures can learn.

THOUSAND YEARS OF CEREMONY, A

Country USA   **Year** 1997   **Length** 37 m.   **Genre** DS
Director Christopher McLeod
Producer Christopher McLeod
Distributor
Not in distribution.
Earth Image Films
P.O. Box C-151
La Honda, CA 94020
650 747-0685 [b]   eif@igc.org

This film was made for the Wintu people, for their own internal cultural
use. The footage was later incorporated into the film *In the Light of
Reverence*.

THREE WARRIORS

Country USA   **Year** 1977   **Length** 98 m.   **Genre** FF
Director Kieth Merrill
Producer Saul Zaentz, Sy Gomberg
Distributor
Check for availablity at local video stores.
For further information call:
Saul Zaentz Company
2600 Tenth Street
Berkeley, CA 94710
510 486-2140 [b] 510 486-2108 [f]

Three Warriors was filmed entirely on location in Oregon amidst the lush forests of Mt. Hood and in the village of Simnasho on the Warm Springs Indian Reservation.

The film's co-producer, Sy Gomberg, is also the author of the original screenplay which tells the story of a 13-year-old Indian boy, Michael, who returns to the reservation to see his aging grandfather. Having lived the past seven years in the tough ghetto areas of the city, the boy has lost a sense of his origins and has little use for the teaching of the old man. However, after several adventures in the wilderness with him, Michael learns to value his Indian culture, the "ways of the warrior," and grows to love his grandfather. Starring McKee "Kiko" Redwing, Charles White Eagle, Lois Red Elk, Christopher Lloyd and Randy Quaid.

THROUGH THE EYES OF A BASKETMAKER

Country USA   **Year** 1998   **Length** 26 m.   **Genre** DS
Director Kathy Wallace
Producer Vivien Hailstone
Distributor
California Indian Basketweavers Association (CIBA)
c/o Kathy Wallace
3433 Norwalk Place
Fairfield, CA 94533
707 428-6778 [b]
US $30.00 VHS, plus US $5.00 shipping.
Make checks to CIBA

Through the Eyes of a Basketmaker is a documentary that tells the story of a people through their art - basketry. Poetry, music and pictures are used to convey the rich heritage of the Indians of Northern California. Throughout the film, the beautiful landscape of the North Coast makes a backdrop against which the baskets are displayed. *Through the Eyes of a Basketmaker* was produced, directed and written by three Indian women who felt this was a story that needed to be told. Basketweaver Vivien Hailstone shows us basketry materials and techniques that are used by the Hupa, Yurok and Karuk people. More importantly, however, she examines the evolution of a people and the changes basketry has undergone from her Great Grandmother's time. The film weaves a tale about life and history in Northern California as seen through the eyes of a Basketweaver.

THUNDER AND LIGHTNING

Country USA **Year** 1989 **Length** 12 m. **Genre** ANS
Director Jonathon Nordlicht
Producer Jonathon Nordlicht
Distributor
Clearvue/eva, Inc.
6465 N. Avondale Avenue
Chicago, IL 60631
773 775-9433 [b] 773 775-9855 [f]
1 800 444-9855 toll free
www.clearvue.com custserv@clearvue.com
US $75.00 VHS, includes teachers guidee

In *Thunder and Lightning*, Hopi Indian Legend comes to life in clay animation! This 12 minute film is based upon the Hopi Indian Creation Myth. Hopi legend describes four different worlds.
The first is called TOKPELA, a world of infinite space.
The second is called SOTUKNAG, a world of endless darkness.
The third is called KOSKURZA, a world of chaos and upheaval.
And the fourth is called TUWAQUACHI, which is the world complete, and the one in which we live. In this world there are many choices and limitless opportunities, but each person should make one's way by following one's own cloud by day, and one's own star by night - thus to create one's own path of life. Kowitoma's adventure involves encounters with various animal symbols, each in its separate world; which is based on situations that appear repeatedly in Hopi legend, particularly Coyote, the Trickster.

THUNDER IN THEIR HEARTS

Country USA **Year** 1992 **Length** 24 m. **Genre** DS
Director Robert Yuhas
Producer Robert Yuhas
Distributor
Currently unavailable.

Thunder In Their Hearts is a documentary produced for Columbia TriStar International to coincide with the international release of the feature film *Thunderheart*. The film weaves together clips from *Thunderheart* and the feature length documentary *Incident at Oglala*, along with interviews with actors Val Kilmer, Graham Greene, Sheila Tousey, director Michael Apted, screenwriter John Fusco, and Indian activist John Trudell, to tell the story of injustices committed against Native Americans, particularly the Lakota Sioux, dating as far back as the late 1800s and continuing until present times.

THUNDERHEART

Country USA **Year** 1992 **Length** 127 m. **Genre** FF
Director Michael Apted
Producer Robert DeNiro, Micheal Nozik (exec.)
Distributor
Columbia TriStar
10202 W. Washington Blvd.
Culver City, CA 90232
310 244-4000 [b]
Also available on Amazon
www.amazon.com
US $9.95 VHS, US $16.99 DVD

Val Kilmer, Sam Shepard and Graham Greene star in this powerful murder mystery. Kilmer plays Ray Levoi, a hotshot FBI agent who's thrust into a strange new world when he is sent to solve a murder on an Indian reservation in the Badlands. Hand-picked because of his part Sioux ancestry, Levoi is teamed with a legendary older agent (Shepard) to capture a radical Indian activist. Levoi encounters the irreverent local sheriff (Greene), and the tribe's religious leader (Chief Ted Thin Elk), who knows secrets about Levoi's own lost heritage. As Levoi's awareness of the Native culture grows, so does his belief that the U.S. government has framed an innocent man. Also featuring Fred Ward, Sheila Tousey, John Trudell and Fred Dalton Thompson.

TIKINAGAN FROM AS LONG AS THE RIVERS FLOW

Country Canada   **Year** 1991   **Length** 57 m.   **Genre** DF
Director Gil Cardinal
Producer Douglas Cole, James Cullingham, Graydon McCrea, Dale Phillips, Peter Raymont
Distributor
National Film Board of Canada   1 800 267-7710 toll free within Canada
For purchase within Canada visit the NFB website at: www.nfb.ca
For US distribution information contact the NFB at:
212 629-8890 [b]

In 1987, the path towards self-government took an unexpected turn for the First Nations people of northwestern Ontario. To fill a sudden void in child welfare services and provide an alternative to the old, non-Native controlled system, the First Nations people formed Tikinagan Child and Family Services.

TIME IMMEMORIAL

Country Canada   **Year** 1991   **Length** 60 m.   **Genre** DF
Director Hugh Brody
Producer James Cullingham, Kent Martin, Peter Raymont
Distributor
National Film Board of Canada   1 800 267-7710 toll free within Canada
For purchase within Canada visit the NFB website at: www.nfb.ca
For US distribution information contact the NFB at:
212 629-8890 [b]

For over a century, the Nishga'a people of northwestern British Columbia have fought for title over their traditional lands. Their determined and persistent lobbying has propelled the issue of Native land claims into the mainstream political arena. Archival material and interviews recount the clash of cultures over four generations and retrace the steps that carried the Nishga'a's case to the Supreme Court of Canada.

TO BE CALLED A NATION

Country USA   **Year** 1992   **Length** 28 m.   **Genre** DS
Director Tom Zapiecki
Producer Tom Zapiecki and WNIT Television
Distributor
WNIT Public Television
2300 Charger Blvd.
Elkhart, IN 46514
219 675-9648 [b]
US $21.85 VHS

Although much attention has been given to American Indian tribes in the Western United States, there are surviving communities in the Midwest. The Potawatomi continue to live in Northern Indiana and Western Michigan.

To Be Called a Nation documents the history of the Pokagon band of Potawatomi and chronicles their efforts to gain official federal recognition as an Indian nation, an ironic goal considering it was the federal government's Indian Removal Policy which led to the Pokagon band's formation.

TO FIND OUR WAY and FIRST STEPS

Country USA   **Year** 1993   **Length** 31 m.   **Genre** DS
Director Tim Farrow
Producer Sacred Heart Center
Distributor
AIMS Multimedia
9710 DeSoto Avenue
Chatsworth, CA 91311
1 800 367-2467 [b] 818 341-6700 [f]
US $149.00 VHS

Two compelling programs examine domestic violence in the American Indian community.

To Find Our Way. Bill is a young Native American man whose repeated episodes of alcoholism and wife battering leave intense physical and emotional scars on his wife and two children. For Bill, a jail sentence is the outcome.

First Steps. Now out of jail, Bill is in his second marriage and the cycle of violence is uncahanged. Ordered by the court to attend weekly counseling sessions, Bill must now take his first steps toward a life without violence.

TO RETURN: THE JOHN WALKUS STORY

Country Canada   **Year** 2000   **Length** 45 m.   **Genre** DS
Director Annie Fraziér Henry
Producer Annie Fraziér Henry
Distributor
Video Out Distribution
1965 Main Street
Vancouver, BC
V5T 3C1 Canada
604 872-8449 [b] 604 876-1185 [f]
videoout@telus.net
Call for pricing (purchase and rental available)

Also available through Shenandoah Films, Arcata, CA. 707 822-1030 [b]

This powerful documentary witnesses and celebrates young Kwakwaka'wakw artist John Walkus Green's journey home to the village he was forcefully adopted out of as a child. This story is also an investigation into the British Columbia Provincial Government's Adoption policies that had tragic consequences for the children it was meant to protect.

John Walkus was raised in and around Tsulquate, a Native village near Port Hardy. As a young child he was "adopted out" to a non-Native family. The traumatic experience of being stripped of his culture and cut off from his birth family emotionally scarred John. He passed through six long years of delinquency before starting out on the difficult journey home.

John finally went back to his village but he was rejected for being "white" and had to face the bitter truth: it is difficult for 'adoptees' to return to the world they were taken away from. With the loss of family, heritage, language, and ceremony, many adoptees grow up feeling different. Torn between two cultures yet discriminated against by both, they often struggle between two worlds. While many non-Native foster and adoptive parents did their best to nurture, heal and raise the First Nations children entrusted to their care, the consequences were often disastrous.

Through the commitment and strength of this young man's struggle to belong, combined with the voices of other young adoptees and the advocates who fight for them, John's story becomes a remarkable journey - as he 'carves' his way home.

TOBACCO: KEEP IT SACRED

Country USA   **Year** 1995   **Length** 10 m.   **Genre** PS
Director Don Thompson
Producer Marni Bragg
Distributor
Please email for availability:
ttrpit96@aol.com

A live stage presentation tells the stories of the spiritual significance of tobacco in the tradition from tribal elders in the Fresno area of California. It then tells of a modern family and their use of tobacco in a non-traditional way. Finally, it urges a respect for tradition in general and more specifically, a respect for traditional use of tobacco.

TODAY IS A GOOD DAY:
REMEMBERING CHIEF DAN GEORGE

Country USA   **Year** 1998   **Length** 44 m.   **Genre** DS
Director Loretta Todd
Producer Loretta Todd
Distributor
Not in distribution.
Eagle Eye Films
301-1645 Comox Street
Vancouver, BC
V6G 1P4 Canada

This remarkable film, which is visually evocative and emotionally up-lifting, goes to the very soul of Chief Dan George. It tells the story of an unassuming Native Indian man who became an actor in his sixties, yet would change forever the very image of Aboriginal people in cinema. Using a deft combination of family stories, film clips and poignant re-creations, *Today is a Good Day* takes the viewer inside the life of Chief Dan George. Interviews with Dustin Hoffman and Arthur Penn (both of *Little Big Man* fame) underscore how important Dan was to the profound shift in the portrayal of Native Americans in film. The narrative examines the whole man, from his deep and abiding love for his wife, Amy, to his determination to provide for his family no matter what, and his sense of humor that saw him through bad times. Through it all, Chief Dan George was a man who was proud of who he was as an Aboriginal person. He was an ordinary man with an uncommon passion to restore truth and dignity to a culture trampled by centuries of colonial oppression.

TOKA

Country USA   **Year** 1994   **Length** 24 m.   **Genre** DS
Director Dave & Cyndee Wing
Producer Cyndee Wing
Distributor
Currently unavailable.

Toka is a centuries old game that is played exclusively by the Tohono O'odham women. The Tohono O'odham Nation is located in the Desert Southwest. In this documentary film, Ina Lopez shares with younger generations of O'odham women what the tradtion of Toka has meant to their people. Young girls are being taught the game, but Ina explains that these young women will never be able to know how important the game was to women in the past.

Harry Moristo gathers the mesquite branches that are made into the implements for the game. Camillus Lopez shares a legend about a mother obsessed with the game of Toka. Games played by the women of Big Fields and Santa Rosa demonstrate the technique and excitement of the game.

TONKA

Country USA   **Year** 1975   **Length** 97 m.   **Genre** ANS
Director Lewis R. Foster
Producer Walt Disney
Distributor
Not in distribution.

A young Sioux named White Bull (Sal Mineo) comes across a beautiful wild stallion, tames him, and names him Tonka Wakan (The Great One). The boy gives Tonka to his older cousin who mistreats the horse and sells him to the captain of the U.S. Cavalry. White Bull, distraught at being separated from Tonka, sneaks into the fort to be with the horse but is apprehended. The captain, however, understands the boy's love for his horse, as he too cares for Tonka. The captain rides Tonka into the battle of Little Big Horn, but a happy ending still prevails in this Walt Disney-produced family adventure film.

Original Release Date - 1958.

TOTEM TALK

Country Canada   **Year** 1997   **Length** 22 m.   **Genre** ANS/LS
Director Annie Fraziér Henry
Producer George Johnson
Distributor
Video Out Distribution
1965 Main Street
Vancouver, BC
V5T 3C1 Canada
604 872-8449 [b] 604 876-1185 [f]
videoout@telus.net
Call for pricing (purchase and rental available)

Traditional Northwestern Native spiritual images combine with cutting-edge computer animation in this surreal story about the power of tradition. Three urban Native teens are whisked away to an imaginary land by a magical raven. Here, the young people meet a totem pole whose characters (a raven, a frog and a bear) come to life, becoming their teachers, guides and friends—demonstrating their significance to Northwest Native cultures and allowing the teens to understand the strength of their own traditions. *Totem Talk* features a special interview segment with J. Bradley Hunt, the celebrated Northwest Coast Native artist on whose work the computer-animated characters are based.

TRACKS IN THE SNOW

Country Canada   **Year** 2000   **Length** 28 m.   **Genre** DS
Director Shirley Cheechoo
Producer Shirley Cheechoo
Distributor
Shirley Cheechoo
Box 59
West Bay, Ontario
P0P 1G0 Canada

Tracks in the Snow is about a Native community called Whapmoogstui, located on the shoreline of Hudson's Bay in Quebec. This video documents a 62 mile traditional journey into the bush during which 10 Cree students (aged 10-12), three elders and some adults walked and camped for four days and four nights, teaching their children the traditional way of life. It is an educational video that can be used for lectures and conferences, but also helps protect the Cree way of life and brings self-esteem back to Aboriginal children.

TRADITIONAL KIND OF WOMAN, A: TOO MUCH, NOT 'NUFF

Country USA   **Year** 1997   **Length** 45 m.   **Genre** DS
Director Lance Richmond
Producer Lance Richmond
Distributor
AICH Productions
708 Broadway, 8th Floor
New York, NY 10010
212 598-0100 [b] 212 598-4909 [f]
akwesasne@aol.com
Please call for pricing and rental information.

A Traditional Kind of Woman: Too Much, Not 'Nuff is a collection of stories gathered from around Native America addressing health issues that face Native women. Adapted from an hour-long stage play created by two Chichimec sisters, Hortensia and Elvira Colorado, the film tackles themes including bad habits, cultural identity, AIDS and incest.

TRADITIONAL USE OF PEYOTE

Country USA   **Year** 1993   **Length** 17 m.   **Genre** DS
Director Gary Rhine, Fidel Moreno
Producer Gary Rhine
Distributor
Not in distribution.
Kifaru Productions
23852 Pacific Coast Hwy. #766
Malibu, CA 90265
1 800 400-8433 [b] 310 457-2688 [f]
www.kifaru.com kifaru1@aol.com

The Traditional Use of Peyote is a brief summary of the religious freedom crisis confronting members of the Native American Church. The U.S. Supreme Court "Smith Decision" denied protection of first amendment religious liberty to the sacramental use of Peyote by Indian people, one of the oldest forms of worship in North America. This decision sent shock waves through religious communities around the country, initiating two legislative efforts to reinstate religious freedom.

TRANSITIONS: DESTRUCTION OF A MOTHER TONGUE

Country USA   **Year** 1992   **Length** 28 m.   **Genre** DS
Director Darrell Kipp, Joe Fisher
Producer Daniel Hart
Distributor
Native Voices
Padelford 514C - Box 345305
University of Washington
Seattle, WA 98195
206 616-7498 [b] 206 616-3122 [f]
US $39.95 VHS home use, US $99.95 VHS educational use
US $39.95 VHS rental
Teachers study guide available for US $4.00

This film by Blackfeet producers explores the relationship between language, thought and culture, and the impact of language disappearance in Native communities.

TRAUMA OF YOUTH SUICIDE: VOICES OF HOPE

Country Canada   **Year** 1998   **Length** 19 m.   **Genre** DS
Director Sue Hutch
Producer Sue Hutch
Distributor
Not in distribution.
Tomali Pictures Ltd.
AF 44 4321 Quesnay Wood Drive, SW
Calgary, Alberta
T3E 7K5 Canada
403 262-8422 [b]   403 262-8421 [f]

Youth suicide is a serious problem among a growing number of Native communities. Many of these communities feel helpless to prevent further suicides and live in grief and fear from having no idea how to handle their children. This short documentary is directed towards the leaders of the communities, encouraging them to become involved, take control, and be part of the solution to the problem. The video presents the voices of elders, spiritual leaders, and education specialists as they encourage the viewers to take active roles and join them as voices of hope for the future of the children.

TRAVELING THE DISTANCE – THE SHINNECOCK 50TH ANNIVERSARY POW-WOW AND ITS PEOPLE

Country USA   **Year** 1997   **Length** 54 m.   **Genre** DF
Director Ziggy Attis, Ofer Cohen
Producer Ziggy Attis
Distributor
Ziggy Films
35 Roosevelt Avenue
East Northport, NY 11731
631 754-8455 [b]   zigattias@aol.com
US $99.00 VHS, US $40.00 VHS rental

Filmmakers Ofer Cohen and Ziggy Attias go on a quest to find whether Native Americans still exist on Long Island, NY. The result of their search is the documentary, *Traveling the Distance*, a filming of the Shinnecock Tribe's 50th anniversary powwow. Along the way, through conversations with members of different tribes from the United States and Canada, participants describe what a powwow is and what it used to be, as well as the Shinnecock tribe's past before and during the colonization of America. At its heart, *Traveling the Distance* is an important look into the significance of the powwow ceremony.

TRIAL OF BILLY JACK

Country USA   **Year** 1975   **Length** 171 m.   **Genre** FF
Director TC Frank
Producer Mary Rose Solti
Distributor
Taylor - Laughlin Distribution & Warner Bros.
P.O. Box 840
Moorpark, CA 93021
877 253-4567 [b]
US $14.95 VHS & DVD
Check local video stores for rental information.

The third film in the Billy Jack series, *The Trial of Billy Jack* finds the hero facing a murder trial. Meanwhile, at the Indian Reservation's "Freedom School," the student television station has been exposing political cover-ups and the reporters come under attack by forces wishing to silence them. Tom Laughlin wrote, directed and starred as Billy Jack.

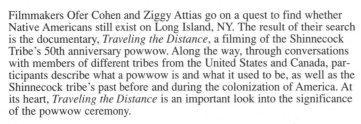

TRIAL OF STANDING BEAR, THE

Country USA   **Year** 1988   **Length** 117 m.   **Genre** DD
Director Marshall Jamison
Producer Eugene Bunge, Nebraska Educational Telecommunications
Distributor
Great Plains National
P.O. Box 80669
Lincoln, Nebraska 68501
1 800 228-4630 [b]   1 800 306-2330 [f]
US $24.95 VHS including shipping and handling

The Trial of Standing Bear is a two-hour drama produced by the Nebraska
ETV Network for national broadcast on the Public Broadcast Service
(PBS). The production is based on the landmark 1879 legal case involving
Ponca Chief Standing Bear, which established for the first time that Native
Americans were recognized as having protection under the U.S.
Constitution. In the words of presiding judge Elmer Dundy in the Omaha,
Nebraska, Federal District Court decree: "An Indian is a 'person' in the
eyes of the law."

TRIBAL BUSINESS IN THE GLOBAL MARKETPLACE

Country USA   **Year** 1992   **Length** 11 m.   **Genre** IND
Director Thomas Hudson
Producer Carol Rand
Distributor
Currently unavailable.

Over the last generation, the Montana tribes of the Chippewa, Cree,
Assiniboine, Sioux, Blackfeet, Cheyenne and Crow developed manufactur-
ing companies to provide jobs on the reservations. The companies originally came into existence with federal assistance and subcontracts.

Today, seven of these tribally-owned firms comprise a new foundation
called the Montana Indian Manufacturer's Network. The Network was
formed in their transition from federal contracts to serving the private sector. They hope to create even more jobs in economically depressed areas
after substantial outward migration from the state.

TRIBAL TOBACCO POLICIES – PROTECTING COMMUNITIES

Country USA   **Year** 1998   **Length** 15 m.   **Genre** PS
Director Carole Nee-Takey Marie
Producer Carole Nee-Takey Marie, Cloud Rider Productions
Distributor
American Indian Tobacco Education Network
California Rural Indian Health Board, Inc.
1451 River Park Drive
Sacramento, CA 95815
916 929-9761 [b]
Please call for pricing information.

Tribal Tobacco Policies juxtaposes the story of sacred and traditional uses
of tobacco from an American Indian elder's perspective with the tragic
epidemic health effects of second hand smoke, and commercial tobacco
abuse, which has inundated rural California Indian communities. Tribal
leaders speak to these issues by shaping tribal tobacco policies to protect
their members.

Included in the footage are images of rarely seen California Indian tobacco
baskets containing sacred tobacco to be used for traditional ceremonies.
Also shown on screen is a California tribal roundhouse where many of the
ancient ceremonies take place.

TROUBLE IN PARADISE:
CRISIS ON THE CHEMEHUEVI RESERVATION

Country USA   **Year** 1995   **Length** 58 m.   **Genre** DF
Director Larry Cano, Rusty Two Crows Sandate (assoc.)
Producer Larry Cano, Rusty Two Crows Sandate (assoc.)
Distributor
Not in distribution.

In 1992, Larry Cano was approached by members of the Chemehuevi tribe in Lake Havasu, California and was asked to help them with a difficult situation. The tribe was embroiled in turmoil and a powder keg was about to erupt. Christine Walker, Tribal chairwoman, had led the tribe for a number of years and presided over what most tribal members felt was a dictatorship. Walker was at war with the non-Indians who leased trailer park spaces and homes on the reservation as well.

The video documents how tribal members were finally able to regain control of their council in a peaceful and democratic fashion.

TRUE WHISPERS

Country USA   **Year** 2000   **Length** 15 m.   **Genre** DS
Director Valerie Red-Horse
Producer Valhalla Motion Pictures in assoc. with Red-Horse Pro.
Distributor
Not in distribution.
Red-Horse Productions
6028 Calvin Avenue
Tarzana, CA 91356
818 705-2588 [b] 818 705-4969 [f]
redhorse88@aol.com

True Whispers is the personal story of the Navajo Codetalkers. These brave young Native American men, many in their early teens, were recruited from harsh reservation/government boarding schools into the Marines from 1942 to 1945. Their mission was to devise a code in their Native language for the purpose of stumping the Japanese, who America was battling in the World War II arena of the South Pacific.

At the outset, the entire Navajo code talker project was highly classified and there is no indication that any message traffic in the Navajo language — while undoubtedly intercepted — was ever deciphered.

In recognition of their dedicated service to America during World War II, the Navajo code talkers were awarded a Certificate of Appreciation from the President of the United States in December 1981. Their unique achievements constitute a proud chapter in the history of the United States Marine Corps. Their patriotism, resourcefulness, and courage also have earned them the gratitude of all Americans.

TULALIP TRIBES & ADMINISTRATION FOR NATIVE AMERICANS:
PARTNERSHIP PROJECTS FOR FUTURE PROSPERITY

Country USA   **Year** 1990   **Length** 20 m.   **Genre** IND
Director Bev Hauptli
Producer Bev Hauptli
Distributor
Tulalip Tribes - Communications Department
6729 Totem Beach Road
Marysville, WA 98271-9714
360 651-3332 [b] 360 651-4334 [f]
seeyahtsub@aol.com
Replacement videos available - please call for information.

Tulalip Tribes and Administration for Native Americans is a video record of successful projects completed by the Tulalip Administration for Native Americans. Seven Tribal members and four government officals explain how Tulalip Tribes have advanced economically with ANA funding.

TULALIP TRIBES: YESTERDAY AND TODAY

Country USA   **Year** 1991   **Length** 11 m.   **Genre** IND
Director Bev Hauptli
Producer Bev Hauptli
Distributor
Tulalip Tribes - Communications Department
6729 Totem Beach Road
Marysville, WA 98271-9714
360 651-3332 [b] 360 651-3334 [f]
seeyahtsub@aol.com
Replacement tapes available, call for pricing.

This 11 minute video shows how one small tribe in the Pacific Northwest is diversifying its economic base to better serve its people. Descendents of fishermen and loggers, the 2,000 members of Tulalip Tribes are aggressively pursuing businesses (land-leasing, logging, liquor sales, bingo, business park) to bring jobs and services to its members. The Tribes fund programs in education, including a pre-school and an alternative school, drug and alcohol treatment, family counseling, a health clinic, and housing for its elders.

TUSHKA

Country USA   **Year** 1998   **Length** 90 m.   **Genre** FF
Director Ian Skorodin
Producer Ian Skorodin
Distributor
Not in distribution.
For more information contact:
Ian Skorodin
1801 N. Kingsley Drive, #102
Los Angeles, CA 90027
323 466-7400 [b]   www.barcid.com

Most people are not aware of the many atrocities committed against the Native Americans nor are they aware that they still go on today. In 1972, a Native American activist, involved in the popular American Indian Movement, led a rally to the steps of the FBI headquarters in Washington, D.C. Two days later, his house was firebombed, killing his parents, his wife, their two girls and an infant.

Tushka is a ninety-minute, color 16-mm, fiction piece that was produced, directed and written by Ian Skorodin, a young Choctaw filmmaker. *Tushka* details the events that led to these murders. The story interprets actual events into a narrative about the FBI's actions against Tushka, a fictional Native American organization. The film follows the story of Jack Raines, a FBI agent, who is assigned to "neutralize" Marcuz Bearns, leader of Tushka.

Starring Bobby Eades, Orvel Baldridge and Tim Johnson.

TWO DECADES OF INUPIAT SELF-DETERMINATION

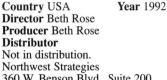

Country USA   **Year** 1992   **Length** 40 m.   **Genre** IND
Director Beth Rose
Producer Beth Rose
Distributor
Not in distribution.
Northwest Strategies
360 W. Benson Blvd., Suite 200
Anchorage, AK 99503
907 563-4881 [b]   907 562-2570 [f]

The 1950s and 1960s represented a tumultuous time for Alaska Natives. Although Natives had lived in the north for thousands of years, western education, religion, and businesses began to threaten the traditional way of life. This was especially true in Alaska's North Slope, where great oil fields were discovered.

When Prudhoe Bay was discovered, the traditional hunting and fishing ground of the Inupiat Eskimos was immediately placed in jeopardy by oil companies, the state of Alaska and the federal government. Each of these entities sought to develop these fields without regard to the people who held aboriginal rights to the land.

In 1966, the Inupiat Eskimos, through the Arctic Slope Native Association, laid legal claim to all the land in the North Slope. This action touched off a fierce land claim battle that involved Alaska Natives throughout the state.

Two Decades of Inupiat Self-Determination tells the story of how the Inupiat people fought for, and won, the battle over rights to their land. It records how the Inupiat people were instrumental in getting the 1972 Alaska Native Claims Settlement Act passed, which established Native regional corporations throughout the state and entitled Alaska Natives to land and a cash settlement. Finally, it tells how Arctic Slope Regional Corporation (ARSC), the Native corporation established for the 6,500 Inupiat Eskimos of Alaska's North Slope, was able to grow from a fledgling business to one of Alaska's largest and most profitable companies.

TWO TRIBES, ONE LAND

Country USA   **Year** 1994   **Length** 25 m.   **Genre** DS
Director Mary Fitzpatrick
Producer Mary Fitzpatrick
Distributor
Currently unavailable.

This documentary explores the effects of a construction freeze on 1.7 million acres of land on the Navajo Reservation in Arizona. The freeze, established by the Bureau of Indian Affairs in 1966, was later enacted into law by Congress in 1980. The intention was to prevent the overdevelopment of the land while the Navajo Nation and the Hopi Tribe were in suit against each other for the rights to this area of land. This "prevention of development" hindered over 1,000 Navajo families from installing utilities, adding and repairing homes, paving roads, and building community facilities without permission from the Hopi Tribe or the Secretary of the Interior of the U.S. Government. This law remained in effect for over 26 years. This film is about the freeze and how it affected the land and the people.

UNBOWED

Country USA   **Year** 1999   **Length** 120 m.   **Genre** FF
Director Nancy Rosov
Producer Nancy Rosov and Lisa Karadian
Distributor
Currently unavailable.
Filmanthropic
834 A Westmount Drive
West Hollywood, CA 90069
323 464-9119 [b]

This provocative story of forbidden love between a spirited Black student, Cleola, and Waka Mani, a defiant Indian Warrior, is set against the rigid society of the American South in the late 1890s, a generation after the Civil War. Based on historic events, *UnBowed* brings the story of Indians forced into Negro schools to the screen for the first time.

Cleola, passing as a weathly orphan, is engaged to Richard, the most afflu-ent student at Beckwourth College. Three Lakota prisoners-of-war are dragged to the elite Negro College, forced to cut their hair and don 'white man's' clothes.

Waka Mani awakens a passion in Cleola that is absent with Richard. When her mother dies, she can tell only Waka Mani the truth – her mother was born a slave and worked at the local laundry to send Cleola to school so she could "marry a man like Richard." For the first time, the proud Waka Mani shares his pain of being the only surviving member of his family. He knows "the fighting is over" and his people have lost. When Jenius, a bright Negro student who served in the Calvary and hated "savages," threatens to expose their passion, they must flee to an uncertain future or live apart forever.

More than a passionate love story, *UnBowed* confronts racism through the eyes of African and Native Americans. There are only two Caucasian char-acters, but the dramatic impact of white dominance and forced assimilation is pervasive.

Starring Jay Tavare, Tembi Locke, Mark Abbott, Vincent McLean, Ron Glass, Hattie Winston and Orson Bean.

UNCLE SAM'S MEN

Country USA   **Year** 1997   **Length** 26 m.   **Genre** DS
Director Mike Martz
Producer Mike Martz
Distributor
Lucerne Media
37 Ground Pine Road
Morris Plains, NJ 07950
1 800 341-2293 [b] 973 538-0855 [f]
www.lucernemedia.com LM@lucernemedia.com
US $99.00 VHS educational

This program tells the story of the men and women who served in the Tundra Army of Alaska's Territorial Guard during World War II. Of the 6,000 Alaskans who volunteered for the Territorial Guard, over half were Alaskan Natives. The role these citizen soldiers played in defending Alaska's western and Arctic coasts from the threat of Japanese invasion is told through the recollections of Tundra Army veterans, rare film footage, and photographs of the Tundra Army in action.

UNDERSTANDING THE AMERICAN INDIAN RELIGIOUS FREEDOM ACT

Country USA   **Year** 1993   **Length** 15 m.   **Genre** DS
Director Gary Rhine
Producer Gary Rhine
Distributor
Not in distribution.
Kifaru Productions
23852 Pacific Coast Hwy. #766
Malibu, CA 90265
1 800 400-8433 [b] 310 457-2688 [f]
www.kifaru.com   kifaru1@aol.com

Understanding the American Indian Religious Freedom Act is a 15 minute summary of the issues involved in the 1993 amendment to the American Indian Religious Freedom Act, including use of sacred Eagle feathers, Indigenous prisoners' rights, the sacramental use of peyote by members of the Native American Church, and protection of sacred sites. Entitled the Native American Free Exercise Of Religion Act, this bill was introduced into the U.S. Senate Select Committee On Indian Affairs. This program, designed to inform legislators, educators and the public, features testimony by Vine Deloria, professor of law, religion and Indian Studies at The University of Colorado; Walter Echo Hawk, staff attorney for the Native American Rights Fund; and Senator Daniel Inouye, chairman of The Senate Select Committee On Indian Affairs.

UNSETTLED

Country USA   **Year** 1993   **Length** 43 m.   **Genre** DS
Director Charlotte Hill
Producer Charlotte Hill
Distributor
Not in distribution.

Unsettled is about the cultural and social impact the 1980 land claim settlement of the Penobscot and Passamaquoddy tribes has had on the Passamaquoddy reservations at Indian Township and Pleasant Point, Maine. Some of the other issues the documentary focuses on are loss of language and traditional culture; i.e. T.V. replacing the rich oral tradition, the divide between those who stayed on the reservations and those who left for the cities in search of work and then came back as a consequence of the land claims, the conflict between the "haves" and the "have nots" and the struggle to balance traditional culture with economic pursuit.

URANIUM

Country Canada   **Year** 1991   **Length** 48 m.   **Genre** DS
Director Magnus Isacsson
Producer Graydon McCrea, Dale Phillips
Distributor
Bullfrog Films
P.O. Box 149
Oley, PA 19547
1 800 543-3764 [b] 610 370-1978 [f]
www.bullfrogfilms.com   info@bullfrogfilms.com
US $49.00 VHS, US $25.00 VHS

Also distributed by - National Film Board of Canada   www.nfb.ca
212 629-8890 [b] within US   1 800 267-7710 toll free within Canada

Uranium explores the consequences of uranium mining in Canada. Because of toxic and radioactive waste, there are profound, long-term environmental hazards associated with uranium mining. For miners who work at the sites, there is the substantially increased risk of getting cancer. Also, because most of the mining to date has been on land historically used by Canada's Native populations, uranium mining violates the traditional economic and spiritual lives of many aboriginal people. Given our limited knowledge of the risks associated with uranium mining, this film questions the validity of its continuation.

URBAN ELDER

Country USA   **Year** 1998   **Length** 29 m.   **Genre** DS
Director Robert S. Adams
Producer Robert S. Adams, Louise Lore, Cornelia Principa, Peter Starr
Distributor
National Film Board of Canada Library
22-D Hollywood Avenue
Ho-Ho-Kus, NJ 07423
1 800 542-2164 [b] 201 652-1973 [f]
US $129.00 VHS, call for rental information and prices.
For purchase within Canada visit the NFB website at: www.nfb.ca
1 800 267-7710 toll free within Canada

In the last forty years, Canada has seen a major population shift of Aboriginal peoples to the cities. Toronto has become home to the largest urban Native population in the country, with an estimated 65,000 Aboriginal people living there now. Today's urban Indians (both those with a direct connection to land-based reservation life, and those who have always lived in cities) are developing an urban Native culture. They are discovering ways to integrate important expressions of traditional Native culture into city life, including the tradition of the Elder: a person of great wisdom who dispenses advice, settles disputes, and acts as a model and arbitrator of acceptable behavior in accordance with Native customs.

Meet Vern Harper, Urban Elder, who walks the "Red Road" in a fast-paced, urban landscape. The camera follows Vern as he leads a sweat lodge purification ceremony, watches his 11-year-old daughter Cody at a classical ballet rehearsal, conducts a private healing ceremony, participates in a political march of 150,000 people, and counsels Native prisoners at Warkworth Federal Prison. In his own voice, Vern Harper tells the *Urban Elder* story of how he reaches into the past for his people's traditions, blending those old ways into the present so that the future can be a time of personal growth and spiritual strength.

URBAN FRONTIER

Country USA   **Year** 1983   **Length** 29 m.   **Genre** IND
Director Gray Warriner
Producer Gray Warriner
Distributor
Camera One
8523 15th Ave. NE
Seattle, WA 98115
206 523-3456 [b] 206 523-3668 [f]
email: cameraone@prodigy.net
US $14.95 VHS

Urban Frontier is an award-winning documentary film which explores the alarming problems that now confront the first Americans. For example, in Seattle and the Puget Sound area of Washington, the average Indian life expectancy is only 47 years.

The film asks the question why? Why in this land of opportunity are so many Indians disadvantaged? *Urban Frontier* gives an insight into the historical problems that have confronted Indian culture, and that have set the stage for the difficulties of adaptation in today's fast-paced society. But more importantly, *Urban Frontier* is a story which is told by Indians themselves. It is a film which illustrates how Indians have banded together in cities to form urban Indian centers; how they are putting their traditional values to work to help solve their problems.

For Indians in the 20th Century, urban life is the new frontier. *Urban Frontier* is a success story about how Indians are meeting the new challenges - challenges every bit as formidable as those posed by the wilderness frontier of years past.

UTE MOUNTAIN TRIBAL PARK

Country USA   **Year** 1990   **Length** 15 m.   **Genre** IND
Director Doug Bowman
Producer Doug Bowman
Distributor
Not in distribution.

Ute Mountain Tribal Park is part of the Ute Mountain Ute Reserve and encompasses approximately 125,000 acres. The Park has been set aside by the Tribe to preserve the prehistoric culture of the Anasazi.

VIDEO BOOK

Country USA   **Year** 1996   **Length** 10   **Genre** LS
Director Beverly R. Singer
Producer Beverly R. Singer
Distributor
Third World Newsreel
545 8th Avenue
New York, NY 10018
212 947-9277 [b] 212 594-6417 [f]
twn@twn.org
US $225.00 VHS, US $50.00 VHS rental

Video Book is a personal and introspective look into the interior life of a woman. Musing on regrets, as well as the beauty in her life, the video-maker layers imagery, voice-over narration, and audio in a moving tapestry about her life.

VISION OF SEEKS-TO-HUNT-GREAT, THE

Country USA   **Year** 1990   **Length** 25 m.   **Genre** LS
Director John Reynolds
Producer Deborah Walley
Distributor
Swiftwind Productions
P.O. Box 1226
Sedona, AZ 86339
520 204-1719 [b]   520 204-1358 [f]
dwswiftwind@hotmail.com
US $19.95 VHS

A grandfather teaches a young boy a lesson in perspectives by telling him the story of Seeks-To-Hunt-Great. Seeks-To-Hunt-Great, a young Indian of long ago, risks his life in a quest for balance by following his vision to embrace a fierce mountain lion. He must track the cat, learn from it and eventually gain its trust. For many months and changes of season, he must survive the hardships and dangers of living in the wild. His quest is full of excitement, surprises, suspense and much humor.
Starring Michael Horse.

VISIONS: A POETRY FILM

Country Canada   **Year** 1995   **Length** 9 m.   **Genre** LS
Director Annie Fraziér Henry
Producer Annie Fraziér Henry
Distributor
Video Out Distribution
1965 Main Street
Vancouver, BC
V5T 3C1 Canada
604 872-8449 [b] 604 876-1185 [f]
videoout@telus.net
Call for pricing (purchase and rental available)

A poetry film based on oral tradition, *Visions* is a stunning visionary jour-ney of spiritual reclamation. Surrounded in a multi-textured audio land-scape of music, voice, and sound, this film translates into a powerful sequence of visual images, both of illusion and reality, the historic struggle of aboriginal people and their transcendence from oppression onto a road of new beginnings. Only through the eyes of the child, who magically receives the truth, are the spirits of wisdom, strength, and beauty re-awak-ened for all to share.

VOICES FROM THE TALKING STICK

Country Canada   **Year** 1996   **Length** 20 m.   **Genre** DS
Director Todd Tyarm
Producer Carol Wallace
Distributor
Shenandoah Film Productions
538 "G" Street
Arcata, CA 95521
707 822-1030 [b]   707 822-1035 [f]
US $100.00 VHS, US $45.00 VHS rental

Voices From the Talking Stick is a positive and revealing story of the past, present, and future told by the Haida people. Maintaining the oral tradition of their culture, the narrators Robert Davidson, John Yeltarzie, and Woodrow Morrision, embark on a journey in four vignettes. The film discusses how art, culture, the environment and family are part of the Haida identity. The mesmerizing voices of the narrators and engaging cinematography echo the artistic tradition so important to the Haida and serve to heighten the viewer's awareness of a culture similar to others, yet so often overlooked.

VOICES IN THE WIND

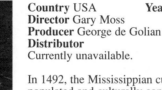

Country USA   **Year** 1990   **Length** 57 m.   **Genre** DD
Director Gary Moss
Producer George de Golian
Distributor
Currently unavailable.

In 1492, the Mississippian cultures of the Southeast were among the most populated and culturally complex in North America. Mississippian Indians lived in towns of up to 10,000 people, mined and worked metals, created elaborate ceremonial objects and magnificent works of art. Some maintained a level of direct democracy unmatched by any political system today. The descendants of these cultures today include the Choctaw, Chickasaw, Creek, Seminole, and Cherokee people.

Voices In The Wind is a 57 minute dramatic film based on Cherokee Indian sacred myths and legends that blends some of the finest Southeastern Native American scholarship, art, and myth to create an authentic and provocative portrait of early Southeastern Indian life.

Voices In The Wind shows how it might have looked and felt to be a Cherokee in 1692 and corrects many common misconceptions about Southeastern Indians. They were a settled, agriculturalist society – not nomadic gatherers and hunters. Cherokee women enjoyed extensive property and personal rights, and held positions of leadership. Politically, Cherokee society was stable and non-coercive, having no army, police force, judiciary, or penal system, and leaders led by example and argument – not compulsion.

VOYAGE OF REDISCOVERY

Country USA   **Year** 1992   **Length** 47 m.   **Genre** DS
Director Phil Lucas
Producer Phil Lucas
Distributor
Not in distribution.
Phil Lucas Productions
1075 N.W. Glenwood Court
Issaquah, WA 98027

This video documents the story of Frank Brown, who as a young Heiltsuk Native boy of Bella Bella, B.C., Canada found himself in trouble with the law. In an agreement between his family and the judge, traditional Heiltsuk law was applied and he was exiled from his village to a remote island for eight months. As a result, his life was transformed.

WABANAKI: A NEW DAWN

Country USA   **Year** 1995   **Length** 28 m.   **Genre** DS
Director Dennis Kostyk, David Westphal
Producer Acadia FilmVideo
Distributor
Maine Indian Tribal-State Commission
P.O. Box 87
Hallowell, ME 04347-0087
207 622-4815 [b] 207 622-2310 [f]
US $24.95 VHS

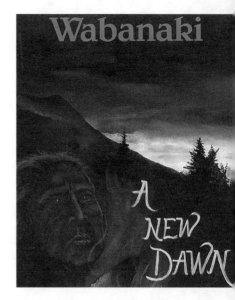

The Wabanaki, the People of the Dawn Land, have lived in what is now
Maine and Maritime Canada for more than 11,000 years. It was not until
the early 1600s that Europeans came to live in the territory inhabited by an
estimated 32,000 Wabanaki. The contact was disastrous. From 1616 to
1619, ninety percent of the Wabanaki died. *Wabanaki: A New Dawn* shows
the quest for cultural survival by today's Wabanaki - the Maliseet,
Micmac, Passamaquoddy, and Penobscot People.

WAKE, THE

Country Canada   **Year** 1987   **Length** 58 m.   **Genre** FF
Director Norma Bailey
Producer Norma Bailey, Ches Yetman
Distributor
National Film Board of Canada Library
22-D Hollywood Avenue
Ho-Ho-Kus, NJ 07423
1 800 542-2164 [b] 201 652-1973 [f]
US $150.00 VHS, call for rental information and prices.
For purchase within Canada visit the NFB website at: www.nfb.ca
1 800 267-7710 toll free within Canada

The year is 1985 and a hundred years have passed since the Riel
Rebellion. In twentieth century Alberta, the Métis still live on the edge of
town, their land a small reserve of clapboard houses. There is a strong
sense of community but there is also a sense of isolation, a separateness
that is defined by racial origin and economics. When the local high school
sponsors its annual Mardi Gras Queen contest there is more than populari-
ty at stake. The real issue is color, Métis versus white.

When the sick and troubled Cora has her children brutally taken from her,
the injustice is a shocking revelation to a young constable. He attempts to
befriend the family and soon falls in love with a young Métis woman.
Their love, overshadowed as it is by mistrust, anger and frustration, offers
a new sense of hope and the possibility of new beginnings.

Then one dark winter night on a frozen lake something happens that will
change their lives forever.

Starring Victoria Snow, Dianne Debassige and Timothy Webber.

WALKING IN PAIN: WARRIORS OF THE PLAINS

Country Canada   **Year** 1989   **Length** 50 m.   **Genre** DS
Director Harvey Crossland
Producer Ric Beairsto
Distributor
Kinetic Inc.
511 Bloor Street, West
Toronto, Ontario
M5S 1Y4 Canada
416 538-6613 [b]   416 538-9984 [f]
Silence is a state that often hides pain, and denies the existence of prob-
lems. But it is a cover that is lifted when alcoholics enter the Round Lake
Treatment Centre, near Vernon, B.C. "I'm not going to hide anymore,"
vows a client in *Walking in Pain,* which documents Round Lake's success-
ful approach to healing, put into action by respected counselor Marge
Mackie-Orr. Individually and in circle counseling sessions, the clients find
their voices, and the strength to overcome their fears and problems.

WAR AGAINST THE INDIANS, THE

Country Canada   **Year** 1992   **Length** 145 m.   **Genre** DF
Director Harry Rasky
Producer Harry Rasky, Canadian Broadcasting Corporation
Distributor
Canadian Broadcasting Corporation, Non-Broadcast Sales
P.O. Box 500, Station A
Toronto, Ontario
M5W 1E6 Canada
416 205-6384 [b] 416 205-3482 [f]
edsales@toronto.cbc.ca
US $225.00 VHS (educational), call for home video pricing.
Also available on www.cdnow.com for home use.

This documentary feature from award winning director/producer Harry
Rasky combines moving images and historical and archival material. The
film explores the impact of the so-called "discovery" of the New World on
the First Nations people of North America. As North Americans re-exam-
ine the significance of Christopher Columbus' voyage 500 years ago, *The
War Against the Indians* provides an important historical perspective.

In a voyage of discovery that has taken three years and 25,000 miles of
travel, *The War Against the Indians* pieces together in conversations, magnificent scenery, historic paintings, drama and music, the story of the
"Great Island" that is North America.

The story begins 40,000 years ago and continues to the present. It covers
the Columbus "invasion," the Spanish massacres, the destruction of the
Huron Nation, the near extinction of the buffalo, the victory over Custer,
the Massacre at Wounded Knee, the life of young students at forced bording schools and the stand-off at Oka, Quebec. It also encorporates the
beautiful art and music of the First Nations people.

WAR PARTY

Country USA   **Year** 1989   **Length** 97 m.   **Genre** FF
Director Franc Roddam
Producer John Daly, Derek Gibson, Bernard Williams
Distributor
Check for availablity on Amazon.com
www.amazon.com

Milk River, Montana. One hundred years ago, the U.S. Cavalry massacred
a tribe of Blackfeet Indians. Now many of the townspeople see the centennial as a tourist opportunity, and stage a re-enactment of their famous battle using rubber tomahawks and blank ammunition. But for Sonny
Crowkiller (Billy Wirth), Skitty Harris (Kevin Dillon) and Warren Cutfoot
(Tim Sampson) the day becomes much more that a re-creation of the past.
Resentment and racial tension explode when a vindictive "cavalryman"
fires live rounds and murders one of the young Indians during the re-enactment. Sonny, Skitty and Warren take swift revenge, re-igniting a battle that
never really ended, and Milk River runs red with blood once more. They
find themsleves leading a War Party - stalked by renegades and bounty
hunters, risking their lives in honor of their ancestors and the memory they
cannot let die.

Also featuring M. Emmet Walsh, Tantoo Cardinal, Dennis Banks, Jackie
Old Coyote, Dianne Debassige and Rodney A. Grant.

WARRIOR CHIEFS IN A NEW AGE

Country USA   **Year** 1992   **Length** 28 m.   **Genre** DS
Director Dean Curtis Bear Claw
Producer Daniel Hart
Distributor
Native Voices
Padelford 514C - Box 345305
University of Washington
Seattle, WA 98195
206 616-7498 [b]   206 616-3122 [f]
US $39.95 VHS home use, US $99.95 VHS educational use
US $39.95 VHS rental
Teachers study guide available for US $4.00

Warrior Chiefs in a New Age chronicles the lives of Native chiefs whose
personal dreams and visions foretold both tragedy and Native people's
power to heal and restore themselves. In many ways, the film works as a
primer on trends in Native spirituality, past and present. Footage of the
"Old West" goes hand in hand with sequences of present-day drum groups
and the on-camera reminiscing of elders. The relationship of grandparent-
to-grandchild is perceived as especially important — the passing of the
old, traditional knowledge into the hearts and minds of the young. The life
of Chief Plenty Coup, the last of the traditional Crow chiefs, is examined,
and his message has become a guidepost to this present generation. He
stressed education in order to be the "white man's equal, not victim."

WARRIOR IN TWO WORLDS

Country USA   **Year** 2000   **Length** 56 m.   **Genre** DF
Director Ann Spurling
Producer Ann Spurling and Kallen Martin
Distributor
Chip Taylor Communications
2 Eastview Drive
Derry, NH 03038
1 800 876-2447 [b]   603 432-2723 [f]
www.chiptaylor.com   sales@chiptaylor.com
US $24.00 VHS

Warrior in Two Worlds explores the life and legacy of Ely S. Parker, a 19th
Century American Indian who struggled to succeed in two very different
worlds. As a Six Nations Chief, Parker negotiated with Governors,
Congressmen and U.S. Presidents to save Seneca lands from a fraudulent
treaty. Then he became a renowned federal engineer, Civil War Secretary
to Ulysses S. Grant, and the first Native American to serve as U.S.
Commissioner of Indian Affairs.

At first glance, Parker's story appears to be one of success and triumph.
Yet he died in relative obscurity, estranged from his people and dismissed
by political leaders he once considered friends. Today, he is a footnote in
American History and the subject of controversy within the Seneca Nation
- was Ely Parker a hero or traitor? *Warrior in Two Worlds* examines the
social and political currents that forced Parker to choose between his traditional culture and life amidst the 19th Century white mainstream. It is a
story for all ages and nations - perhaps most relevant in today's increasingly globalized world society. Hosted by acclaimed actor Wes Studi with
original soundtrack by award-winning singer/songwriter Joanne
Shenandoah.

WARRIOR: THE LIFE OF LEONARD PELTIER

Country USA   **Year** 1991   **Length** 84 m.   **Genre** DF
Director Suzie Baer
Producer Suzie Baer
Distributor
Cinnamon Productions
19 Wild Rose Road
Westport, CT
203 221-0613 [b] 203 227-0840 [f]
www.nativevideos.com Nativevideos@aol.com
US $149.00 VHS institutional use
US $49.00 VHS home use
Also available through Shenandoah Films, Arcata, CA 707 822-1030 [b].

On June 26, 1975, a shoot-out erupted on the Pine Ridge Reservation in South Dakota. By the time the firing stopped, two agents and one Indian man lay dead. Within hours, the FBI initiated the biggest manhunt in its history. Four men would be indicted for the killing of the two agents: two of them were tried and acquitted on the grounds that they fired in self-defense, charges against the third were dropped. The fourth man - Leonard Peltier, an American Indian Movement activist - was tried and convicted, and is currently serving two terms of life imprisonment at Leavenworth Penitentiary. Peltier's conviction is shrouded in controversy. The FBI has refused to release 6,000 documents pertaining to Peltier's case, claiming that "national security" is at stake.

Warrior, The Life of Leonard Peltier is the story of one man's odyssey through the criminal justice system. But it also the story of the larger issues facing the Native American community, issues to which this story can serve as a dramatic introduction.

WARRIORS – HONORING NATIVE AMERICAN VETERANS OF THE VIETNAM WAR

Country USA   **Year** 1988   **Length** 60 m.   **Genre** DF
Director Deb Wallwork
Producer Deb Wallwork
Distributor
Center for International Education
P.O. Box 65343
St. Paul, MN 55165
651 227-2240 [b]
thecie@pobox.com
US $85.00 VHS

Also available through Shenandoah Films, Arcata, CA 707 822-1030 [b].

In Vietnam, every combat squad seemed to have at least one Indian, a quiet loner, usually referred to as "Chief." He was expected to have the instincts of his ancestors, an acute sense of danger, and the ability to disappear into the jungle without a trace. When the patrol moved out, inevitably it was the Indian who was sent to lead it—a particularly dangerous position known as "walking point." What was Vietnam really like for American Indians? *Warriors*, an hour-long documentary about Native American Vietnam Veterans, looks at the traditional beliefs and contemporary dilemmas of the Indian Vet.

Since World War I, Native Americans have served in the United States Armed Forces. During the Vietnam War, close to 90% of the 86,000 who enlisted volunteered, giving Native Americans the highest record of service per-capita of any ethnic group. Over half served in combat. Why were so many Native Americans willing to go and fight in America's most controversial war? What is their view of Vietnam twenty years later?

Hear Indian veterans discuss their personal experiences in Vietnam and the difficulties they still face. *Warriors* is a moving video, honest, humorous, sincere, and unflinching. It is a portrait of contemporary Indian people caught in a cross current of American history, finding their traditional ways is the key to understanding and moving forward.

WARRIORS SONG

Country USA   **Year** 1996   **Length** 40 m.   **Genre** DS
Director Vladan Mijailovic
Producer George Amiotte
Distributor
Heaven Fire Productions, Inc. / Exclusive Pictures
15951 Arminta Street
Van Nuys, CA 91406
818 901-1392 [b] 818 904-9004 [f]
www.ExclusivePictures.com   sales@ExclusivePictures.com
US $19.95 VHS

Warrior's Song explores the legacy of post traumatic stress disorder, as four individuals share their personal stories of trauma and the methods they incorporated into their healing process. While the film focuses on the healing challenges facing veterans of war, it also shows the common ground shared by individuals who have experienced other forms of trauma.

WASHING OF TEARS, THE

Country Canada   **Year** 1994   **Length** 55 m.   **Genre** DF
Director Hugh Brody
Producer Barb Cranmer, Gillian Darling, Cari Green, George Johnson
Distributor
National Film Board of Canada Library
22-D Hollywood Avenue
Ho-Ho-Kus, NJ 07423
1 800 542-2164 [b] 201 652-1973 [f]
US $250.00 VHS, call for rental information and prices.
For purchase within Canada visit the NFB website at: www.nfb.ca
1 800 267-7710 toll free within Canada

In 1903, a unique and magnificent Whaler's shrine was shipped from Friendly Cove, on the far northwest coast of Canada, to the Museum of Natural History, New York. The shrine had lain at the cultural heart of the Mowachaht, whale hunters and fishermen who had lived at Friendly Cove for thousands of years. In the 1960s and 70s, all but one family left their ancient village - they moved to Vancouver Island, to a new site under the walls of a pulp mill. They suffered extremes of pollution, violence and alcohol. Then, in the 1990s, in defiance of the agony of their history and to overcome the grief of the present, the Mowachaht and their neighbors, the Muchalaht, revived their songs and dances, revisited their shrine and rediscovered their pride.

WAYS OF THE GLADES ARTIST: CHIEF JIM BILLIE

Country USA   **Year** 1998   **Length** 4 m.   **Genre** MV
Director Leslie M. Gaines
Producer John Mc Euen
Distributor
Seminole Broadcasting, Seminole Tribe of Florida
6300 Stirling Road
Hollywood, FL 33024
954 967-3417 [b] 954 967-3485 [f]
Please call for pricing

Music video by Chief Jim Billie of the Seminole Tribe of Florida. "Ways of the Glades" is the first single from his 1998 album *Alligator Tales*.

WE ARE THESE PEOPLE

Country USA   **Year** 1982   **Length** 15 m.   **Genre** LS
Director Carol and Vern Korb
Producer Carol and Vern Korb, Shenandoah Film Productions
Distributor
Shenandoah Film Productions
538 "G" Street
Arcata, CA 95521
707 822-1030 [b] 707 822-1035 [f]
US $200.00 VHS, US $45.00 VHS rental

We Are These People (a 15-minute film featuring Will Sampson) is designed to foster an appreciation for the Native American cultures and promote social support by reinforcing traditional values. Teaches friendship, sharing and respect for all people.

WE BELONG TO THE LAND

Country USA   **Year** 1978   **Length** 30 m.   **Genre** DS
Director Shenandoah Film Productions
Producer Shenandoah Film Productions
Distributor
Shenandoah Film Productions
538 "G" Street
Arcata, CA 95521
707 822-1030 [b] 707 822-1035 [f]
US $200.00 VHS, US $45.00 rental

Utterly bored with conventional school classes, an Indian youth finds the opportunity to spend some time with Joe Giron, an Apache and professional range manager. The visit re-affirms the relationship between the land and the Indian, as has existed throughout generations. Through the scenery, a cattle drive, an evening campfire, and other outdoor experiences, our young adventurer grows in awareness of the world around him. The possibilities of a life and career in natural resources is brought out as a "natural" for a people that "come from the land, care for the land, and belong to the land."

WE HAVE NO WORDS FOR THIS

Country Canada   **Year** 1992   **Length** 60 m.   **Genre** DF
Producer Jim Hyder
Distributor
Currently unavailable.
TV Ontario
2180 Young Street
Box 200, Station Q
Toronto, Ontario
M4T 2T1 Canada
416 484-2665 [b] customer service

We Have No Words For This portrays a diverse group of people each expressing their own sense of what it is to be Tlingit in today's world. For some, this is best done through the arts – dancing, carving and weaving. For others, meaning comes from teaching children to speak Tlingit or to respect nature. For still others, this is done by harvesting and preparing food in traditional ways or restoring community cemeteries.

WE HAVE SUCH THINGS AT HOME

Country Canada   **Year** 1997   **Length** 53 m.   **Genre** DF
Director James Cullingham
Producer James Cullingham
Distributor
Currently unavailable.

We Have Such Things at Home investigates the parallels and differences
between the plight of Native peoples in Canada and conditions faced by
black South Africans. At the dawn of the post-apartheid era, the camera
follows a delegation of Canadian Natives led by Phil Fontaine (newly
elected National Chief of The Assembly of First Nations) on a voyage of
discovery to South Africa. The delegation visits former townships, homelands and meets dignitaries such as Archbishop Desmond Tutu. The film
also documents the return visit of South African land claims officials to
reserves in Manitoba. *We Have Such Things at Home* reveals evidence –
unearthed after more than ten years of research – linking Canada and
Africa and explores the new vision of hope and political change.

WE HOLD THE ROCK – THE AMERICAN INDIAN OCCUPATION OF ALCATRAZ 1969–1971

Country USA   **Year** 1997   **Length** 23 m.   **Genre** DS
Director Jon Plutte
Producer Jon Plutte
Distributor
Not in distribution.
Jon Plutte / Golden Gate National Parks Assoc.
201 Fort Mason
San Francisco, CA 94123
415 561-3037 ext. 3721 [b]

For the first time, the Native reclamation of Alcatraz is told on film. *We
Hold the Rock* is about the occupation of Alcatraz Island by American
Indians in 1969. Lasting nineteen months, this occupation was one of the
first incidents in which Natives took back land from the federal government. Among those interviewed are student leaders and members of the
more established Indian organizations of the time, as well as many occu-
piers, participants and government representatives, in this informative look
at an important incident in modern Indian History.

WE PRAY WITH TOBACCO

Country USA   **Year** 1998   **Length** 60 m.   **Genre** DF
Director John and Ismana Carney
Producer Ismana Carney
Distributor
Shenandoah Film Productions
538 "G" Street
Arcata, CA 95521
707 822-1030 [b] 707 822-1035 [f]
US $200.00 VHS, US $45.00 VHS rental

Through interviews, storytelling, traditional singing, drumming and reenactments, the story of tobacco and its sacred significance to Native
American communities is told. These cultural traditions have existed from
the beginning of tribal memory and are still practiced in many traditional
communities and Native American circles today. Demonstrated in *We Pray
With Tobacco* are the wide range of cultural uses, and tobacco's specific
powers when combined with other herbs as well as alone.

WE REMEMBER

Country Canada   **Year** 1980   **Length** 60 m.   **Genre** DF
Director Raymond Yakalaya
Producer Raymond Yakalaya
Distributor
Currently unavailable.

Through a series of interviews with tribal elders of the North West Territory, a sense of community evolution into today's world is retold. Canada's North has been called the Last Frontier – but to the Indian peoples, it has always been home and a way of life. The North, because of its isolated distance and harsh climate, became the last place where the white man intruded with their life styles, culture and values. The elders in this film lived and experienced all these changes and tell their own personal stories of how and why things changed in the evolution of the North.

WE'RE THE BOYZ ARTIST: ROBBY BEE AND THE BOYZ

Country USA   **Year** 1994   **Length** 4 m.   **Genre** MV
Director Magnet Films, Edward Nachieb
Producer Robby Bee
Distributor
SOAR Corporation
5200 Constitution NE Avenue
Albuquerque, NM 87110
505 286-6110 [b]
US $19.95 mail order VHS
US $14.95 wholesale VHS

On the album *Reservation of Education*, Robby Bee and the Boyz from the Rez have created a dynamic new musical genre: powwow hiphop or tribal rap. "We're the Boyz" is the self-introducing first song on the album. Filmed in the hills of northern New Mexico, it is a whirling dervish of a video, replete with hundreds of images.

WEAVE OF TIME, A

Country USA   **Year** 1987   **Length** 60 m.   **Genre** DF
Director Deborah Gordon
Producer Susan Franshel
Distributor
Shenandoah Film Productions
538 "G" Street
Arcata, CA 95521
707 822-1030 [b] 707 822-1035 [f]
US $100.00 VHS, US $45.00 rental

In 1938, at the age of 24, noted anthropologist John Adair travelled to the Navajo Reservation with a 16mm, hand-wound motion picture camera. Close to 50 years later, director Susan Fanshel returned with Adair and co-producer Deborah Gordon to make this unique documentary film. *A Weave of Time* combines Adair's previously unseen historic footage with present-day scenes to create a complex portrait of a Navajo family through four generations. In this film, we meet the Burnsides – a family struggling to bridge the gap between traditional values and the demands of modernization. Through provocative juxtapositions of past and present, *A Weave of Time* raises important questions that challenge facile notions of identity and ethnicity.

WELCOME HOME HERO

Country Canada   **Year** 1991   **Length** 22 m.   **Genre** LS
Director Nancy Trites Botkin
Producer Nancy Trites Botkin
Distributor
Currently unavailable.

This is the story of two Native brothers who have been separated through twenty years of misunderstanding. Upon returning home for the funeral of the father, a war hero, Billy, the older brother, is confronted by his younger brother Walt's anger and resentment. There had been a shooting accident one night twenty years earlier. Walt was left lame, and Billy, his hero, split. Now, on the back roads to the reserve burial site, the brothers get stuck in the hearse in the middle of a prairie storm. They must face each other, their dysfunctional past, and the residue of living with an alcoholic father.

WELCOME TO HEAD START

Country USA   **Year** 1997   **Length** 10 m.   **Genre** DS
Director David W. Stamps
Producer David W. Stamps
Distributor
American Indian Institute
555 Constitution Street, Suite 237
Norman, OK 73072
405 325-6962 [b] 405 325-7757 [f]
US $25.00 VHS

Welcome to Head Start is an orientation video for three and four year olds starring Native children of the same age who are involved in the Native American Head Start Student program. The students demonstrate table manners, playground etiquette, medical checkups, bus safety, brushing teeth, and friendships that are part of Head Start programs.

WEMAWE: FETISH CARVING OF THE ZUNI PUEBLO

Country USA   **Year** 1998   **Length** 26 m.   **Genre** DS
Director Anistacia Barrak, Michelle Nunez
Producer Anistacia Barrak, Michelle Nunez/Road Runner Productions
Distributor
Shenandoah Film Productions
538 "G" Street
Arcata, CA 95521
707 822-1030 [b] 707 822-1035 [f]
US $175.00 VHS, US $45.00 VHS rental

Wewame: Fetish Carving of the Zuni Pueblo is a documentary describing fetish carvers of the Zuni Pueblo in New Mexico. Entirely in the words of Zuni individuals, it tells of the history of Zuni fetishes from the creation story to the "realistic style" of the carving of today. Personal stories and beliefs regarding the spiritual uses of some fetishes, such as healing and protection, are shared. Differences between traditional vs. realistic carving styles are explained, as are the identification of authentic Zuni carvings and forgeries. Narrator Ken Seowtewa weaves together the statements of the carvers with his own words of inspiration and good-will for all people. Hundreds of photographic stills of fetishes are melded together with an enchanting soundtrack by Fernando Cellicion, the renowned Zuni flutist. The movie shares a heartfelt view of what carving means to the artists interviewed, shining a spotlight on Zuni creativity. *Wewame* is an appreciation of the magnificent artwork that comes from Zuni-land, and is a celebration of their life philosophy.

WHEN MY SHIP COMES IN ARTIST: TUDJAAT

Country Canada   **Year** 1997   **Length** 4 m.   **Genre** MV
Director Larry Carey
Producer Randall Prescott
Distributor
Sony Music Canada
1121 Leslie Street
Toronto, ON
M3C 2J9 Canada
416 391-1960 [b]
Note: This music video is currently sold out. However, once there is a sufficient demand more will be produced.

"When My Ship Comes In" is a music video that tells the story of 85 Inuits who were relocated to an unlivable island high in the Arctic Circle. Canadian singing duo Tudjaat's grandmother, one of the survivors of the experiment, plays a featured role in the video.

WHEN THE FIRE DIMS

Country USA   **Year** 1998   **Length** 17 m.   **Genre** LS
Director Daniel Golding
Producer Daniel Golding
Distributor
New Day Films
22-D Hollywood Avenue
Ho-Ho-Kus, NJ 07423
888 367-9154 [b] 201 652-1973 [f]
www.newday.com   orders@newday.com
US $125.00 VHS educational use,
US $99.00 VHS community organizations
US $50.00 VHS rental

Jimmy, a Pomo Indian, has left the reservation for promises of a better life in the urban environment of San Francisco. The hopeless realities of loneliness eventually move him to escape through the use of alcohol. Images of the family he left behind and the culture he once lived in come back to life before him and provide him with temporary relief.

However, Jimmy eventually falls victim to this unforgiving cycle of alcoholism, causing the fire that is his spirit to slowly dim. Each day Jimmy must decide the path he will take. *When the Fire Dims* examines the complex relationship colonization, cultural alienation and alcoholism play in one man's life as he struggles to survive in an unfamiliar world.

WHERE THE RED ROAD MEETS THE INFORMATION SUPERHIGHWAY

Country USA   **Year** 1994   **Length** 14 m. **Genre** PS/IND
Director Gary Robinson
Producer Gary Robinson / Joanelle Romero
Distributor
Contact Spirit World Productions for current information on this film:
818 703-5084 [b] and [f]

This video introduces tribal communities to the latest in digital telecommunications technologies and shows how these technologies are already being used in some Indian communities to benefit Indian people. The program features Indian people using Long Distance Interactive Instructional TV, Telemedicine, Geographic Information systems, and the Internet. The program also makes a case for Indian people to become involved in the creation of the Information Highway.

WHERE THE RIVERS FLOW NORTH

Country USA   **Year** 1993   **Length** 111 m.   **Genre** FF
Director Jay Craven
Producer Jay Craven
Distributor
Kingdom Country Productions
949 Somers Road
Barnet, VT 05821
802 592-3190 [b]
US $19.95 VHS home use
Please call for educational use prices.

Where the Rivers Flow North tells the story of Noel Lord (Rip Torn), an indomitable old Yankee logdriver who finds his way of life condemned to extinction by changes in Vermont's "Kingdom Country."

It is the fall of 1927, the year of Vermont's most devastating flood. Lord and his irrepressible Indian housekeeper, Bangor (Tantoo Cardinal), are living marginally at their dilapidated logging camp when they learn that their home and livelihood are threatened by the region's first big hydro-electric dam, which will flood their land, leaving only a stand of virgin pines on the ridge.

Lord woodenly refuses to move from his doomed camp, heightening tensions with the Power Company and exacerbating his already-charged relationship with Bangor. Will he accept the company's final guy-out offer, she wants to know, or will he spitefully permit them to resort to eviction, destroying all they have and driving them into the poorhouse?

WHERE THE SPIRIT LIVES

Country Canada   **Year** 1989   **Length** 108 m.   **Genre** FF
Director Bruce Pittman
Producer Paul Stephens (exec), Heather Goldin, Eric Jordan, Mary Young Leckie
Distributor
Shenandoah Film Productions
538 "G" Street
Arcata, CA 95521
707 822-1030 [b] 707 822-1035 [f]
US $175.00 VHS

It is 1937. Ashtoh-Komi (Michelle St. John), a twelve year old Blackfoot girl, lives in a remote village in the Rocky Mountains. A floatplane lands and the children run to see the wonderful machine. The smiling white Indian agent, Taggart, lures them on board with candy. He then locks the hatch and reads a government decree to their parents, which states by law their children must have an education. The plane flies away with the children, and Ashtoh-Komi's terrible adventure begins.

Few incidents in the history of Canada's Native policies are as heinous as the one in which *Where the Spirit Lives* is based: determined to instill Native children with a sense of white, Christian values, the government empowered agents to virtually abduct children from communities that disregarded orders to send their young to English schools. Their ties to family and tradition cut, their language forbidden, Native children found themselves in remote schools where they were force-fed the bitter medicine of a Christian missionary education. While this is the lot of Ashtoh-Komi, renamed Amelia, she proves a poor subject for cultural modification. Irrepressibly rebellious, Amelia clings to her language and customs, yielding only when she's told her family on the reserve has been wiped out by illness. Even then, however, Amelia's "Anglicization" proceeds only shakily. Befriended by a naïve, conscience-striken young teacher (Anne-Marie McDonald), Amelia proves a far better teacher than she is a student. A person of uncontainable cultural integrity, Amelia is a symbol of liberation for the students in an insurrection against the school administration. If there is a prize to be won from the ensuing struggle, it is the spirit of Amelia, rather Ashtoh-Komi, herself.

WHISPERS: THE CHUMASH

Country USA   **Year** 1991   **Length** 29 m.   **Genre** DS
Director George Angelo, Jr.
Producer George Angelo, Jr.
Distributor
Lucerne Media
37 Ground Pine Road
Morris Plains, NJ 07950
1 800 341-2293 [b] 973 538-0855 [f]
www.lucernemedia.com   LM@lucernemedia.com
US $99.00 VHS educational

Whispers: The Chumash is juxtaposed through interviews, archival footage and the filming of indigenous dance and folklore. Whispers reflects many impulses to refute stereotypes, to address an information gap in non-Native society, and to reach inward to Native American oral and visual traditions.

WHITE DAWN, THE

Country USA   **Year** 1975   **Length** 110 m.   **Genre** FF
Director Philip Kaufman
Producer Martin Ransohoff Production
Distributor
Available on Amazon.com
www.amazon.com
US $17.99 VHS

Based on James Houston's true story of an Arctic adventure, *The White Dawn* relates the story of three sailors who are separated from their ship during an Arctic hunt for polar bear and walrus. Eskimos who live on Baffin Island, just south of the North Pole, save their lives, but one angry sailor brings fear and violence to all. Magnificent location footage and realistic hunting scenes bring a striking flavor to the intense and passionate conflict.

Starring Warren Oates, Lou Gossett Jr., Timothy Bottoms, Simonie Kopapik and Joanasie Salamonie.

Original Release Date - 1974.

WHITE SHAMANS AND PLASTIC MEDICINE MEN

Country USA   **Year** 1995   **Length** 26 m.   **Genre** DS
Director Terry Macy, Daniel Hart
Producer Native Voices
Distributor
Native Voices
Padelford 514C - Box 345305
University of Washington
Seattle, WA 98195
206 616-7498 [b]   206 616-3122 [f]
US $39.95 VHS home use, US $99.95 VHS educational use
US $39.95 VHS rental
Teachers study guide available for US $4.00

With humor, anger and thoughtful insight, this documentary explores the appropriation and commercialization of Native American spiritual and religious practices by non-Indians. This practice has been termed "… a new growth industry known as Native American Spiritual Shucksterism." Important questions are asked of those seeking to exploit ritual and sacred ceremony as well as those vested with safeguarding their ancient ways.

"Yeah, they say 'I was an Indian in a former life' … well, you're white now!"

- Charlie Hill,
American Indian comic

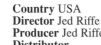

WHO OWNS THE PAST?

Country USA   **Year** 1999   **Length** 56 m.   **Genre** DF
Director Jed Riffe
Producer Jed Riffe
Distributor
UC Extension Center for Media and Independent Learning
2000 Center Street, 4th Floor
Berkeley, CA 94704
510 642-0460 [b] 510 643-9271 [f]
cmil@uclink.berkeley.edu
US $225.00 VHS, US $90.00 VHS rental

The final decades of the twentieth century have brought unprecedented changes for American Indians, especially in the areas of Indian rights and tribal sovereignty. In 1990, after a long struggle between Indian rights groups and the scientific establishment, the Native American Graves Repatriation and Protection Act (NAGPRA) returned to Indian people the right to control the remains of their ancestors. For American Indians, this was perhaps the most important piece of civil and human rights legislation of this century. Skeletons and grave goods that had been gathering dust in museums around the country could come home again, and Indian graves would be protected from further desecration. Indian people were not only being heard; their moral claims on their past were being turned into law. Now a new case is testing these claims.

The discovery of a 9000-year-old skeleton on the banks of the Columbia River near Kennewick, Washington has reignited the conflict between anthropologists and Indian people over the control of human remains found on ancestral Indian lands. Anthropologists insist that these remains hold the key to America's past and must be studied for the benefit of mankind, while many Indian people believe that exhuming and studying them is a desecration of their ancestors. In *Who Owns the Past?*, producer and director Jed Riffe *(Ishi the Last Yahi, Rosebud to Dallas)*, and Blackfeet co-producer and co-director George Burdeau *(Surviving Columbus, The Native Americans)* use the Kennewick Man case as a frame to explore the roots of this conflict, roots that reach back down to the very beginnings of American History.

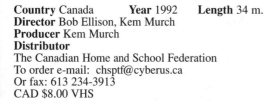

WHO WE ARE: A CELEBRATION OF NATIVE YOUTH

Country Canada   **Year** 1992   **Length** 34 m.   **Genre** PS
Director Bob Ellison, Kem Murch
Producer Kem Murch
Distributor
The Canadian Home and School Federation
To order e-mail: chsptf@cyberus.ca
Or fax: 613 234-3913
CAD $8.00 VHS

This video/guide features candid, action oriented profiles of young Native people, their elders and other inspiring Native role models across Canada. It provides positive messages to Native youth about continuing their education, valuing their culture and making their own unique contributions to their communities – both urban and rural. From a Haida potlatch in B.C., to an Inuit elder's igloo, to a Native rock concert in Quebec – Native youth are invited to share in a spirit of pride and celebrate who they are.

WHOSE LAND IS THIS?

Country Canada   **Year** 1997   **Length** 60 m.   **Genre** DF
Director Renae Morriseau
Producer Richard Hersley
Distributor
Motion Visual
Suite 503 - 130 W. Keith Road
N. Vancouver, BC
V7M 1L5 Canada
604 990-9337 [b]   coyote@uniserve.com
US $149.00 VHS, US $49.00 VHS rental

Whose Land is This? is a one hour made-for-television documentary that
seeks to go to the heart of the Native land question in British Columbia.
By examining Native and non-Native land ownership matters, it uncovers
deep-seated emotions and attitudes on the historical rights of Native land
claims within this province. Created by award-winning producer/writer
Renae Morriseau and Richard Hersley, *Whose Land is This?* is packed
with a wealth of knowledge on British Columbia First Nations and land
territories.

WIIGWAASIJIIMAAN (The Birchbark Canoe)

Country USA   **Year** 1979   **Length** 25 m.   **Genre** DS
Director Yvonne Hogg (project coordinator)
Producer Bemidji State University and the Saginaw Chippewa Indian
Tribe
Distributor
Saginaw Chippewa Indian Tribe
2250 Enterprise Drive
Mt. Pleasant, MI 48858
517 775-5218 gift shop or 517 775-4121 for Patrick Collins / Pat Wilson
US $14.00 VHS

The Ojibwe canoe builders were among the most skilled of the various
tribes that used the birch canoes. Styles varied from band to band, with the
Michigan Ojibwe using a straight or slight back angle lean to the ends,
whereas the Ojibwe bands in the Minnesota –Ontario region built a round-
ed end sometimes called the "long nose" canoe.

Today, the traditional method of birchbark canoe making is still known
among the Ojibwe and is carried on by a few. The film, *Wiigwaasijimaan*,
allows you to visit this fascinating cultural aspect of the Ojibwe. The 25
minute, 16mm color sound movie narrated in Ojibwe with English subtitles describes how materials are gathered, prepared and formed into a
birchbark canoe.

WINDWALKER

Country USA   **Year** 1980   **Length** 105 m.   **Genre** FF
Director Kieth Merrill
Producer Arthur R. Dubs & Thomas E. Ballard
Distributor
Available at Amazon.
www.amazon.com
US $9.20 VHS

Windwalker, based on the best selling novel by Blaine M. Yorgason, is an
epic story chronicling four generations of a Cheyenne family before the
coming of the white man. *Windwalker* portrays the Cheyenne and Crow
Indians as proud peoples with emphasis on their love of family, culture and
language.

Windwalker stars the famed British actor Trevor Howard, who portrays an
old Cheyenne warrior who learns from the Great Spirit the meaning of life
after he has been left for dead atop a burial scaffold. Also featuring Nick
Ramus, James Remar and Serene Hedin.

WIPING THE TEARS OF SEVEN GENERATIONS

Country USA **Year** 1991 **Length** 52 m. **Genre** DF
Director Fidel Moreno, Gary Rhine
Producer Gary Rhine
Distributor
Kifaru Productions
23852 Pacific Coast Hwy #766
Malibu, CA 90265
1 800 400-8433 [b] 310 457-2688 [f]
www.kifaru.com   kifaru1@aol.com
US $85.00 VHS institutional, US $29.95 VHS home video
US $250.00 16mm rental

For 100 years the Lakota Nation, known to the non-Indian culture as the Sioux, mourned the lives lost at the Wounded Knee Massacre. They also mourned the loss of some of their people's sacred knowledge which passed away with the elders who died that day. Then, in the mid 1980s, inspired by dreams and visions, a group of Lakota decided to bring their people out of mourning through a traditional Lakota ceremony which they call Washigila, "Wiping the Tears."

Each December from 1986 through 1990 they rode horseback, retracing the route traveled 100 years earlier by Chief Bigfoot's band, the victims of the massacre. They called it Si Tanka Wokiksuya, "The Bigfoot Memorial Ride." At first a small group, but eventually 300 horseback riders with support crews of hundreds more, rode for 2 weeks through bitter, sub-zero winter weather, reverently praying and mourning. It was a sacrifice, a prayer and a healing, signifying the end of mourning over the massacre and the celebration of the resurgence of Lakota culture and spirituality.

The documentary begins with a short history of the Lakota people, which includes photographs of life shot before the turn of the century. Historical photos and paintings interlaced with interviews help the viewer understand the events leading up to the Wounded Knee Massacre. Descendants of the survivors of the massacre retell their ancestor's eyewitness accounts, and The Bigfoot Riders discuss their commitments and their hopes for the future. Some of the interviews are in English, while some are in the Lakota language with English subtitles.

WISDOM OF TWO WORLDS

Country USA **Year** 1981 **Length** 46 m. **Genre** DS
Director James Mulryan
Producer James Mulryan
Distributor
Currently unavailable.

This film shows how a 14 year old Hopi boy maintains traditional values while living in Los Angeles. We see Frank Poolheco, Jr. learning these values from his parents, his grandparents, and other relatives. We also see him learning western values from school and church teachers and peers.

WITH CLEAN HANDS AND STRAIGHT EYES

Country USA   **Year** 1987   **Length** 7 m.   **Genre** DS
Director Nicole Paradis Grindle
Producer Nicole Paradis Grindle
Distributor
Currently unavailable.

With Clean Hands and Straight Eyes is a documentary short about Leon Chief Elk, a Blackfoot/Assiniboine man, and his personal history with alcohol. The film was produced for Four Winds Lodge, a San Jose shelter for Native American men with drinking problems.

Leon tells the story of his childhood introduction to drinking in Montana. He discusses the attitudes and beliefs which shaped his drinking habits and his cultural identity. He recounts how he was finally forced to re-evaluate his habits when his younger brother died in an automobile accident while driving drunk. As a result of this experience, Leon stopped drinking and has since found continual support from the community at Four Winds Lodge. At the same time, he has developed a new sense of cultural identity, and has high hopes for his own son's sense of cultural pride and individual freedom.

WITH HAND AND HEART

Country USA   **Year** 1988   **Length** 28 m.   **Genre** DS
Director Bill Synder
Producer New Dimension Media, Inc.
Distributor
Shenandoah Film Productions
538 "G" Street
Arcata, CA 95521
707 822-1030 [b] 707 822-1035 [f]
US $125.00 VHS, US $45.00 rental
For home use try CD Now at: www.cdnow.com

With Hand and Heart bridges the gap between nomadic Indians who peopled our land nearly two thousand years ago and those who today continue an art cultivated by the land and its forces. A compelling documentary on the history of Southwestern Native American art as seen through a selected group of contemporary practicioners and storytellers, *With Hand and Heart* integrates landscape, art and ceremony to provide a contemporary view of the Southwest Native American cultures.

WITHIN ALL WOMEN

Country USA   **Year** 1991   **Length** 28 m.   **Genre** DS
Director Randy Croce
Producer Randy Croce
Distributor
Minnesota Indian Women's Resource Center
2300 15th Avenue, South
Minneapolis, MN 55404
612 728-2000 [b] 612 728-2039 [f]
US $40.00 VHS

Counselors and graduates of the Minnesota Indian Women's Resource Center show the importance of recognizing and affirming their culture on the path to recovery from chemical dependency.

The center successfully counsels women failed by a state social service system that misunderstands cultural practices and takes Indian children away from their homes to place them in foster care. Staff help women keep sober by building on their strengths: the connections to their families and community.

WITHOUT RESERVATIONS: NOTES ON RACISM IN MONTANA

Country USA   **Year** 1995   **Length** 27 m.   **Genre** DS
Director Shane Ross, Paula Mozen, Dave Wheelock,Lance Dream, Sonia Whittier, Chris Burnside, Sam Olbecks
Producer Native Voices
Distributor
Native Voices
Padelford 514C - Box 345305
University of Washington
Seattle, WA 98195
206 616-7498 [b]   206 616-3122 [f]
US $39.95 VHS home use, US $99.95 VHS educational use
US $39.95 VHS rental
Teachers study guide available for US $4.00

Without Reservations – Notes on Racism in Montana is a documentary in three parts. The first segment features the story of a public schools administrator on the Flathead Reservation, and her struggle to introduce indigenous subject matter into the curriculum. The second segment tells the story of a mixed-race marriage between a Native American and his Estonian wife, exploring questions of perspective as experienced by each partner. The final story chronicles the legal battle of a Native American's lawsuit against the Hill County Sheriff's Department for employment discrimination.

WOMEN AND MEN ARE GOOD DANCERS

Country USA   **Year** 1996   **Length** 6 m.   **Genre** LS
Director Arlene Bowman
Producer Arlene Bowman
Distributor
Third World Newsreel
545 8th Avenue
New York, NY 10018
212 947-9277 [b]   212 594-64117 [f]
twn@twn.org
US $125.00 VHS, US $50.00 VHS rental

Women and Men Are Good Dancers is a translation from the Cree language of an intertribal Pow Wow song. Arlene Bowman was inspired to create this tape by the "Nizhoni" (Dine) or "it is beautiful" of the Plains song and dance, in particular the Grass Dance. Working with dancers from several different traditions, she uses a combination of video art effects, studio performance and a playful end credit sequence to create a video document that simultaneously acknowledges and exceeds the boundaries of both ethnography and conventional dance performance documentation.

WOMEN IN THE SHADOWS

Country Canada   **Year** 1992   **Length** 56 m.   **Genre** DF
Director Norman Bailey
Producer Christine Welsh, Signe Johansson, Tony Snowsill, Ginny Stikeman
Distributor
National Film Board of Canada Library
22-D Hollywood Avenue
Ho-Ho-Kus, NJ 07423
1 800 542-2164 [b]   201 652-1973 [f]
US $250.00 VHS, call for rental information and prices.
For purchase within Canada visit the NFB website at: www.nfb.ca
1 800 267-7710 toll free within Canada

This intensely personal documentary follows First Nations writer and filmmaker Christine Welsh as she embarks on an extraordinary physical and spiritual journey in search of her Métis foremothers. It is the story of one Métis woman's reconciliation with her past and her people — a coming to terms with loss and with the price that has been paid for assimilation, and a celebration of survival.

WOODLANDS-THE STORY OF THE MILLE LACS OJIBWE

Country USA   **Year** 1995   **Length** 55 m.   **Genre** DF
Director Tom Jenz
Producer Tom Jenz and the Millie Lacs Band of Ojibwe
Distributor
Mille Lacs Band of Ojibwe
c/o Geff and Howard
255 E. Kellogg Blvd. #102
St. Paul, Minnesota 55101
651 292-8062 [b] 651 292-8091 [f]
$US 9.95 VHS

Narrated by Native actor Graham Greene, *The Woodlands – the Story of the Mille Lacs Ojibwe* traces 300 years of Mille Lacs Band history, from their arrival in Minnesota up to the present day. The film combines interviews featuring tribal elders and noted historians with historical photos and documents, plus archival and modern location footage and traditional Ojibwe music.

WOPILA TATANKA

Country USA   **Year** 1992   **Length** 19 m.   **Genre** IND
Director Fidel Moreno
Producer Fidel Moreno, James Swan
Distributor
Native Visions
320 Central South West
Albuquerque, NM 87102
505 242-2300 [b] 505 242-4880 [f]
US $29.95 VHS

"We can't go back to the past, but we can accept the sacred gift of the Creator and bring the buffalo back into our communities… there's healing in our roots, and there's healing in the buffalo."

Today there are some 120,000 buffalo alive, and it is possible to restore buffalo herds on reservation lands, not only restoring the natural ecology of America, but healing a tragic wound in cultural history.

WORDS OF WISDOM

Country Canada   **Year** 1993   **Length** 15 m.   **Genre** LS
Director Annie Fraziér Henry
Producer Annie Fraziér Henry
Distributor
Video Out Distribution
1965 Main Street
Vancouver, BC
V5T 3C1 Canada
604 872-8449 [b] 604 876-1185 [f]
videoout@telus.net
Call for pricing (purchase and rental available)

A poetic and haunting vision of the process of healing – both within the Native community, and between the Native and non-Native communities. In telling her story through movement, poetry, imagery, and narrative, Annie Fraziér-Henry asks: How can this be accomplished? Who should help us heal? And who will heal the healers?

In Native tradition, the elders carried the sacred and essential knowledge of healing to individuals, families, and communities. This knowledge has been kept alive in spite of over a century of oppression in the form of residential schools, the legislated banning of First Nations cultural practices, and both blatant and subtle racism.

Each image of the film, from the despair of Native youth caught in a void of rootless urban culture, to the dignity of an elder's face and the symbolic freedom and purity of an eagle circling in the sky, reiterates the strength of a cultural healing power that was long oppressed, but never destroyed, through the elders' voices.

WORKING TOGETHER:
CALIFORNIA INDIANS AND BASKETRY TRADITION

Country USA   **Year** 1993   **Length** 9 m.   **Genre** DS
Director Rick Brazeau, Vern Korb
Producer Rick Brazeau, Vern Korb, Sonia Tamez (ex)
Distributor
Audience Planners
5341 Derry Avenue, Suite Q
Laguna Hills, CA 91301
1 800 683-8366 toll free
www.r5.fs.fed.us/video.com
Free rental and lone, call for more information.
Call for purchase possibilities.

This documentary short represents a breakthrough in cooperative relations
between the Forest Service and Indian tribes in California to sustain an
important contemporary pratice: the weaving of baskets. The video reflects
the significance of the basketry tradition for Indian communities today, and
the need for agencies like the Forest Service to modify their land management policies to maintain the availability of basketry plants.

In the program, the weavers discuss their concerns over the management
of basketry material and other resources in national forests. The video provides information about the types of plants used in weaving and Indian
perspectives on caring for the land.

YAKOANA

Country USA/Brazil   **Year** 1997   **Length** 60 m.   **Genre** DF
Director Ahn Crutcher
Producer Ahn Crutcher
Distributor
Shenandoah Film Productions
538 "G" Street
Arcata, CA 95521
707 822-1030 [b] 707 822-1035 [f]
US $100.00 VHS, US $45.00 rental

Yakoana is the indigenous peoples' story of earth. Culled from interviews
with leaders, ceremonies, and music of indigenous peoples from around
the world, *Yakoana* weaves a picture of ancient culture and the modern
fight for sustainable survival. Shot in Brazil at the First World Conference
of Indigenous Peoples, this is an educational and spiritual journey, a warrior's insight and a politically potent message.

By special AIFI invitation.

YEHA NOAH ARTIST: SACRED SPIRITS

Country USA   **Year** 1995   **Length** 4 m.   **Genre** MV
Director Hitesh Teli
Producer Klaus Zundel
Distributor
SOAR Corporation (for CD information)
5200 Constitution NE Avenue
Albuquerque, NM 87110
505 268-6110 [b]

Featuring the vocals of Navajo singer Kee Chee Jake, this video was
filmed in Gallup, New Mexico and surrounding areas of the Navajo reservation. The result is an exciting Dineh flavored view of contemporary
Native America, from rodeo cowboys to traditional dancers and singers, in
a uplifting celebration of life.

YELLOW WOODEN RING

Country USA   **Year** 1998   **Length** 39 m.   **Genre** LS
Director Barrett Tripp
Producer Barrett Tripp
Distributor
Barrett Tripp
310 315-9363 [b]
barretttripp@earthlink.net
US $30.00 VHS

Yellow Wooden Ring tells the coming-of-age story of Valma Jaeger, a half American Indian girl. Although always alienated in the white world in which she was raised, she feels dread and apprehension surround her when she moves to the reservation. Faced head-on with a culture and heritage she has denied as her own, Valma is once again the outsider who must overcome her fears and prejudices in order to gain acceptance. Along the way, she uncovers the secrets of her mother's past, and begins to see her "new" culture as more of a blessing then a curse.

YOUR HUMBLE SERPENT:
THE WISDOM OF REUBEN SNAKE

Country USA   **Year** 1996   **Length** 60 m.   **Genre** DF
Director Gary Rhine
Producer Gary Rhine
Distributor
Kifaru Productions
23852 Pacific Coast Hwy. #766
Malibu, CA 90265
1 800 400-8433 [b]   310 457-2688 [f]
www.kifaru.com   kifaru1@aol.com
US $85.00 VHS institutional
US $29.95 VHS home video

In this portrait of a contemporary American Indian leader, the late Reuban Snake discusses ecology, sacredness, intuitive thinking, and "the rebrowning of America." As Reuban grew up, his elders taught him that a leader is a servant to the people. As a leader, Reuban Snake created the Native American Religious Freedom Project, which led to the passage of the 1994 Amendment to the American Indian Religious Freedom Act. Combining Reuban Snake's storytelling with interviews of friends and relatives, *Your Humble Serpent* provides an enlightening and inspiring look at a modern day American Indian leader and role model.

YUXWELUPTUN: MAN OF MASKS

Country Canada   **Year** 1999   **Length** 22 m.   **Genre** DS
Director Dana Claxton
Producer Selwyn Jacob, Graydon McCrea
Distributor
National Film Board of Canada Library
22-D Hollywood Avenue
Ho-Ho-Kus, NJ 07423
1 800 542-2164 [b] 201 652-1973 [f]
US $150.00 VHS, call for rental information and prices.
For purchase within Canada visit the NFB website at: www.nfb.ca
1 800 267-7710 toll free within Canada

In 1868 the Canadian government passed the Indian Act to subdue Native peoples by confining them to reserves, outlawing their languages, destroying land rights and denying them a vote. *Yuxweluptun: Man of Masks* opens at the Bisley Rifle Range in Surrey, England, where Lawrence Paul Yuxweluptun is shooting the "Indian Act," a performance piece to protest the ongoing effects of the legislation on Aboriginal people. Back in Canada, "An Indian shooting the Indian Act" opens at Vancouver's Grunt Gallery where framed copies, riddled with bullet holes, are on display. Yuxweluptun is a modernist whose artistic influences come from his home in Vancouver, British Columbia. His surrealist canvases deal with ozone depletion, land claims, Aboriginal rights, clear-cut logging and racism. One of Canada's most important painters, this Salish artist has exhibited in Paris, Zurich, Barcelona and Switzerland. Interviews with Yuxweluptun, striking images of his paintings and a visit to his virtual reality longhouse provide a glimpse into contemporary First Nations art making and the politics of the artist.

25 Years of the American Indian Film Festival

1. Rodney A. Grant in *Hawkeye* 2. Wes Studi in *Geronimo* 3. Charlie Hill in *Harold of Orange* 4. Tantoo Cardinal 5. Will Sampson and Greg Masten 6. Graham Greene in *Clearcut* 7. Adam Beach in *Squanto* 8. Chief Dan George 9. Tina Keeper 10. Michael Greyeyes in *Crazy Horse* 11. Kimberley Norris-Guerrero, Valerie Red-Horse and Irene Bedard 12. Evan Adams 13. AIFI's Director Michael Smith and Bernie Whitebear 14. Sandra and Michael Horse 15. Joseph Ashton in *The Education of Little Tree* 16. Michael Greyeyes, Adam Beach and Ryan Black in *Dance Me Outside* 17. Sheila Tousey

25 Years of the American Indian Film Festival

1. Kateri Walker 2. Jack Nicholson and Will Sampson in *One Flew Over the Cuckoo's Nest* 3. Henry Kingi 4. Gail Maurice and Jorge Manzano 5. Jennifer Podemski 6. Saginaw Grant 7. Randy 'L Teton 8. Michael Smith, Director of AIFI 9. Irene Bedard, Alexis Cruz and A Martinez in *Grand Avenue* 10. Valentina Lopez-Firewalks 11. Will Sampson and Clint Eastwood in *The Outlaw Josey Wales* 12. Adam Beach and AIFI's Mytia Rose Smith 13. Pure-Fé, Soni and Jennifer of Ulali 14. Benjamin Bratt 15. Will Sampson and Heather O'Rourke in *Poltergeist II* 16. John Trudell 17. Diane Debassige in *Places Not Our Own*

25 Years of the American Indian Film Festival

1. Tim Sampson, Lawrence Bayne and Michael Horse in *Lakota Woman* 2. Wes Studi and Al Pacino in *Heat* 3. Drew LaCapa 4. Jay Tavare 5. Litefoot in *Indian in the Cupboard* 6. Floyd Westerman and Wes Studi in *The Broken Chain* 7. Gary Farmer 8. Tim Sampson 9. Tom Jackson 10. Annie Fraziér-Henry 11. Chief Dan George and family 12. Sheila Tousey in *Silent Tongue* 13. Jackie Old Coyote 14. Nataniel Arcand in *Forgotten Warriors* 15. Steve Reevis 16. Val Kilmer and Graham Greene in *Thunderheart*

25 Years of the American Indian Film Festival

1. August Schellenburg in *Black Robe* 2. Pierce Brosnan and Annie Gallipeau in *Grey Owl*
3. Tom and Robby Bee 4. Joseph Ashton, James Cromwell and Tantoo Cardinal in *The Education of Little Tree* 5. Ian Skorodin 6. Pow Wow Princess Shawna Tom 7. *Dances With Wolves* 8. Floyd Red Crow Westerman 9. Irene Bedard and Adam Beach in *Smoke Signals* 10. Kevin Dillon, Billy Wirth and Tim Sampson in *War Party* 11. James Luna 12. Wes Studi 13. A Martinez and Gary Farmer in *Pow Wow Highway* 14. Ryan Black in *Dance Me Outside* 15. Kimberley Norris-Guerrero 16. Michael Dorris

25 Years of the American Indian Film Festival

1. Chief Dan George and Michael Smith 2. Gary Farmer and Johnny Depp in *Dead Man* 3. Max Gail and Charlie Hill in *Indian Time* 4. AIFI's "Breath of Life" performers 5. Walela 6. Kiyoshi Miyata 7. Saginaw Grant and Raymond E. Spiess 8. Kateri Walker and Steve van Denzen 9. Michael Horse and AIFI's Jennifer Shinall 10. Irene Bedard and Evan Adams 11. Indigenous 12. Ryan Black

25 Years of the American Indian Film Festival

1. Loretta Todd 2. Karina Lombard 3.Jack Nicholson and Will Sampson in *One Flew Over the Cuckoo's Nest* 4. Michael Greyeyes in *Stolen Women, Captured Hearts* 5. Greg Sarris, Lucinda Spencer and A Martinez 6. Renae Morriseau and Shirley Cheechoo 7. Jay Tavare and Vincent McLean 8. Kevin Red Star and Raymond Chavez 9. Rodney A. Grant, Floyd Red Crow Westerman and Jim Wilson 10. Tantoo Cardinal and Wes Studi 11. John Balloue 12. Robert Redford, Michael Smith and Susan Masten 13. Dawn Jackson and Mark Abbott

25 Years of the American Indian Film Festival

1. Yvonne Russo 2. Lois Red Elk 3. Selina Jayne 4. Alanis Obomsawin 5. Chris Eyre 6. Saginaw Grant 7. Chief Dan George, Susan Masten and Michael Smith 8. Michelle St. John 9. Millie Ketcheshawno 10. Ray Tracey 11. Mayor Willie Brown and AIFI's Michael Smith 12. Floyd Red Crow Westerman and Chief Jim Billie 13. Randy Redroad 14. Rance Hood 15. Sarah Brave and Sheila Tousey in *Thunderheart* 16. Larry Sellers 17. Charlie Hill

25 Years of the American Indian Film Festival

1. Lorrie Church 2. Eric Schweig 3. Victor Aaron 4. Jade Herrera 5. James Duval 6. Long Lance
7. Michelle Thrush 8. Susan Masten, Michael Smith and Lucinda Spencer 9. Bettina 10. Elaine Miles
11. Steve Reevis and Selina Jayne 12. Joanne Shenandoah 13. Jennifer Podemski
14. Apensanahkwat 15. Sam Vlahos 16. Adam Beach and Evan Adams in *Smoke Signals*
17 Jeri Arrendondo

25 Years of the American Indian Film Festival

1. Russell Means 2. Wayquay 3. Hattie Kauffmann 4. Joanelle Romero 5. Denise Lanceley
6. Sherman Alexie 7. Michael Smith and Michael Horse 8. Don Burnstick 9. Bill Miller 10. Phil Lucas
11. Tudjaat 12. Kashtin 13. Jim Boyd 14. Frank Howell 15. Kateri Walker and AIFI's Gunter Lange
16. Jan-Marie Martel 17. Chief Dan George and AIFI's Michael Smith

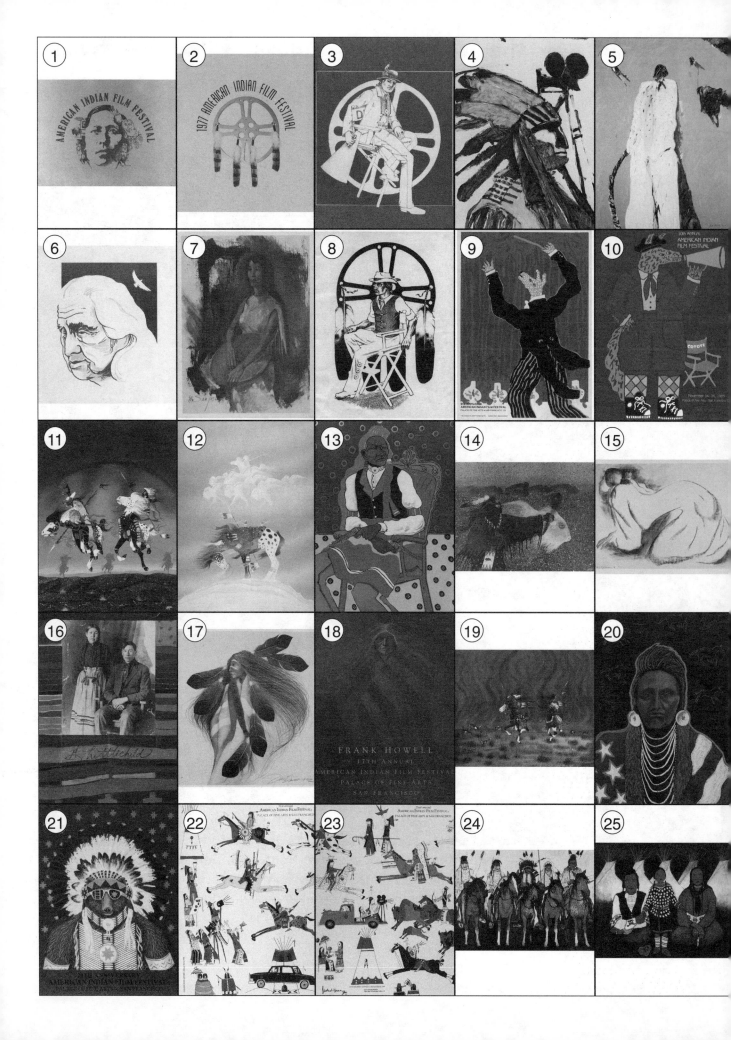

American Indian Film Festival

POSTERS

2000

Please pick out the posters you'd like to purchase with the form below

NEW! 2001

No.	Year	Artist	Price	Qty	No.	Year	Artist	Price	Qty
1.	1975	Roger Fernandes	N/A	✕	14.	1989	Rance Hood	$25	
2.	1977	John Garlow	N/A	✕	15.	1990	R.C. Gorman	$25	
3.	1978	WBLE/Rampton	N/A	✕	16.	1991	George Littlechild	$25	
4.	1979	Fritz Scholder	N/A	✕	17.	1992a	Frank Howell	$25	
5.	1980	Fritz Scholder	N/A	✕	18.	1992b	Frank Howell	$25	
6.	1981	Roger Fernande	N/A	✕	19.	1993	Rance Hood	$25	
7.	1982	Will Sampson	$25		20.	1994	Ron Jackson	$25	
7a.	1982a	Will Sampson (signed)	$50		21.	1995	John Balloue	$35	
8.	1983	Michael Dixon	N/A	✕	22.	1996	Michael Horse	$50	
9.	1984	Harry Fonseca	N/A	✕	23.	1997	Michael Horse	$50	
10.	1985	Harry Fonseca	N/A	✕	24.	1998	Kevin Red Star	$25	
11.	1986	Rance Hood	N/A	✕	25.	1999	Kevin Red Star	$25	
12.	1987	Rance Hood	$35		26.	2000	Noah Billie	$25	
13.	1988	T.C. Cannon	$25		27.	2001	Brian Larney	$25	
							Total		

Please add $5.00 for shipping & handling

Please send check or money order to:

American Indian Film Institute
333 Valencia St., Suite 322
San Francisco, CA 94103

Name _____
Address _____
City _____
State, Zip _____

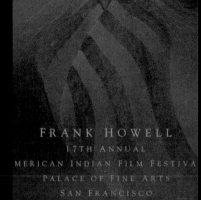

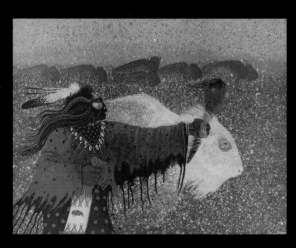

ISBN 0-9713794-0-8

AMERICAN INDIAN FILM INSTITUTE
SAN FRANCISCO, CA. $39.95 U.S.